UWorld
YOUR WORLD OF LEARNING
ROGER CPA Review

FAR

Financial Accounting and Reporting

Written By:

Roger Philipp, CPA, CGMA

UWorld
9111 Cypress Waters Blvd
Suite 300
Dallas, TX 75019
accounting.uworld.com/cpa-review

Permissions

Printed in English, in the United States of America.

ABOUT THE AUTHOR

Roger S. Philipp, CPA, CGMA
Founder and Instructor, UWorld Roger CPA Review

Roger Philipp, CPA, CGMA, is one of the most celebrated motivators and instructors in the accounting profession. Roger believes you should enjoy what you do—in life, business, and learning. Guided by this philosophy, he strives to create dynamic and engaging instruction that makes learning concepts enjoyable. This focus has helped aspiring accountants across the globe reach career success for almost 30 years.

Roger launched Roger CPA Review in 2001 with the goal to create a CPA review course that would alter the landscape of accounting education. With the program now part of UWorld, Roger continues to act as a key inspiration and spark for company innovation. The success of the program is fueled by his unique approach to teaching, in which he breaks down and simplifies complex topics, with support from memory aids and mnemonic devices, to help students understand and retain information.

Roger's early career began in public accounting at Deloitte & Touche, where he earned his CPA designation, before transitioning to educational instruction. He was a lead instructor at Mark Dauberman CPA Review, before starting Roger CPA Review. Roger attributes his entrepreneurial success to the many doors his CPA license opened, as well as his passion for making professional education engaging and relevant for optimum effectiveness. In recent years, Roger was featured as one of Accounting Today's Top 100 Most Influential People in Public Accounting.

Today, Roger is a member of the AICPA, CalCPA, and has served on the Board of Directors for the American Professional Accounting Certification Providers Association (APACPA). He resides in San Francisco with his wife and co-founder of the company, Louisa, and their three children. He enjoys traveling with his family, enjoying the arts, and volunteering at his local food bank.

Acknowledgements

Keeping the course materials updated and accurate would not be possible without the contribution of our content expert **Jae Johnson**, CPA. Jae has been the driving force behind the updates and improvements for this year's textbooks.

FAR

Table of Contents

UWorld
YOUR WORLD OF LEARNING
ROGER
CPA Review

Introduction

Introduction

Table of Contents

Lecture 0.01 – Course Introduction

Lecture 0.02 – FAR Introduction

Welcome to your UWorld Roger CPA Review Course!

Greetings Student,

It is an honor to be your partner on your CPA Exam journey. Your success is our success, which is why we are 100% dedicated to providing you with a learning experience that inspires, delights and delivers results with optimum efficiency. With the power or our new alignment with UWorld, enhanced question explanations, the strength of our SmartPath Predictive Technology™ and the profession's leading video lectures, you'll be on your way to the CPA in no time.

This course is structured for a variety of student types. Each topic is broken down from the beginning and taught as if the student has little to no prior knowledge of the particular topic at hand. Therefore, whether you are a first-time review student who has never attempted an exam part, or a seasoned professional returning to the exam after an earlier attempt, you will be prepared.

As you work through the material, you will be able to gauge your competency on each topic using SmartPath Predictive Technology™, a tool that provides targets based on the performance of previous students who have passed the CPA Exam. We recommend that you achieve each target in order to be fully prepared to take the exam.

Ultimately, you control your destiny. As your instructor Roger Philipp, CPA, CGMA always says, "The CPA Exam is not an IQ test. It is a test of discipline. If you study, you will pass!" You will find on the next page our **"Guide to Using Your Course."** This will provide you with our recommended approach to preparing with this course and its support features.

We wish you all the best on this journey and are here to guide you along the way.

Sincerely,

The UWorld Roger CPA Review Team
#TaketheSmartPath

Follow us on social media for CPA Exam tips and tricks at @RogerCPAReview.

Subscribe to our blog to get the most up-to-date CPA Exam information, as well as plenty of advice on careers, education and the CPA Exam at accounting.uworld.com/blog/cpa-review.

Guide to Using Your Course

Plan

Before you start studying, log into your course and navigate to the Study Planners (located under "Study Resources"). Choose between a 3, 6, 9 or 12 month planner, and customize to meet your needs. It is important to follow your planner steadily so that you can work through all of the material before your exam date. If you miss a day, make it up!

Learn

In this program, you will build your foundation in core CPA Exam concepts as you work through practice questions and simulations that match the actual exam.

Tip:
Download the app! This gives you access to everything your course offers while on-the go.

When you first log into your course you will be presented with the QBank. This is where you will setup custom practice sessions to work through problems. When you are still learning the material, we recommend turning on *Tutor Mode*. This will provide you with clear and concise expert-written answer explanations directly after answering each question. Pay attention to these because this is where much of the learning happens! You should have a grasp on *why* you have answered each question correctly or incorrectly. This *learn by doing* method is called *active learning* and is proven to help students obtain and retain information.

Improve

As you work through your course, keep track of your performance and progress using SmartPath Predictive Technology™. SmartPath is a data-driven platform that provides recommended targets based on previous successful students. This is an important tool to help you gauge whether you are *exam-ready.* Your ultimate goal is to hit both targets per course chapter: (1) number of question attempts and (2) score.

Tip:
Don't over-study! SmartPath™ helps determine when you can move on to the next topic.

If you are having trouble with some of the concepts and/or falling short of reaching your targets, there are tools to help you improve:

- Video Lectures – You have access to the profession's most motivating and effective lectures from Roger Philipp, CPA, CGMA. Lectures break down difficult topics into simplified concepts and provide helpful memory aids. These are especially recommended for visual and audio learners.
- Textbooks – The text is a companion to the video lectures. Some students find benefit in following along and taking notes in the textbooks while watching the lectures. You can also use these as a reference if you need further explanation of a related question.
- Digital Flash Cards – Create your own flash cards within the courseware and flip through them whenever you need a quick drill (this is a great option with the mobile app!). To create a flash card from your practice question content, simply highlight the relevant text and the option to

create a flash card will appear. Depending on your program package, your course may also be pre-loaded with an "Expert Deck" of flash cards covering the most heavily tested topics.

Review

As you get ready for exam day, review your SmartPath data to ensure you have hit all targets. Revisit any areas marked "Needs Improvement." If it is included in your program package, use the Cram Course to do a final review of the most heavily tested topics.

Finally, we recommend taking at least one full practice exam before exam day (go to QBank > Create Test, and then choose the "Exam Sim" tab.) This allows you to hone your test-taking skills in an environment that follows the same 5-testlet, 4-hour structure of the exam.

Plan Your Time!

Ensure success on the exam by following our recommendations for time allocation:

FAR Exam	
Testlet 1 *33 MCQ*	**45 min**
Testlet 2 *33 MCQ*	**45 min**
Testlet 3 *2 TBS*	**30 min**
Testlet 4 *3 TBS*	**60 min**
Testlet 5 *3 TBS*	**60 min**
Total Time:	4 hours

Things to consider:

- FAR includes calculations
- Allocate 80 seconds per multiple choice question as a benchmark
- Allocate 15-20 minutes per task-based simulation, depending on complexity
- Plan to use no more than 10 minutes per research question
- Take the standard 15-minute break after the 3rd testlet – it doesn't count against your time

CPA Exam Blueprints

This course is based on the CPA Exam Blueprints, which are created by the American Institute of Certified Public Accountants (AICPA) to help candidates know what skills and content topics will be tested on the CPA Exam.

Not only are the CPA Exam Blueprints intended to assist candidates in preparing for the exam, but they also take into account the minimum level of knowledge and skills necessary for initial licensure once candidates become CPAs.

We have already used the blueprints to guide our course materials, so you are already on the right path. However, if you'd like to reference the blueprints to better understand what's required on the exam, we've provided a helpful guide below.

Overview of the CPA Exam

The blueprints provide an overview of how much time candidates have for each section and how many questions by question type each section contains. Question types include Multiple Choice Questions (MCQ), Task-based Simulations (TBS), and Written Communication (WC).

Section	Section Time	MCQs	TBSs	WC
AUD	4 hrs	72	8	-
BEC	4 hrs	62	4	3
FAR	4 hrs	66	8	-
REG	4 hrs	76	8	-

Scoring Weight for All Question Types

Here candidates can see how the question types for each section are weighted and account for their overall score.

Section	MCQs	TBSs	WC
AUD	50%	50%	-
BEC	50%	35%	15%
FAR	50%	50%	-
REG	50%	50%	-

Skill Allocations

Each exam section has a Skill Allocation framework based on the revised Bloom's Taxonomy of Educational Objectives. These are the skills that CPA candidates need to learn and successfully demonstrate on the CPA Exam.

Evaluation	**The examination or assessment of problems and use of judgment to draw conclusions.**
Analysis	The examination and study of the interrelationships of separate areas in order to identify causes and find evidence to support inferences.
Application	The use or demonstration of knowledge, concepts, or techniques.
Remembering & Understanding	The perception and comprehension of the significance of an area utilizing knowledge gained.

Skill Levels to be Assessed on Each Section of the Exam

To break it down even further, here are how each of the skills above will be assessed on every section of the exam.

Section	Remembering & Understanding	Application	Analysis	Evaluation
AUD	30-40%	30-40%	15-25%	5-15%
BEC	15-25%	50-60%	20-30%	-
FAR	10-20%	50-60%	25-35%	-
REG	25-35%	35-45%	25-35%	-

Summary Blueprint Snapshot

Below is an overview of the content and skill allocation for each section of the exam.

AUD Content Area Allocation	Weight
I. Ethics, Professional Responsibilities and General Principles	15-25%
II. Assessing Risk and Developing a Planned Response	20-30%
III. Performing Further Procedures and Obtaining Evidence	30-40%
IV. Forming Conclusions and Reporting	15-25%

AUD Skill Allocation	Weight
Evaluation	5-15%
Analysis	15-25%
Application	30-40%
Remembering and Understanding	30-40%

BEC Content Area Allocation	Weight
I. Corporate Governance	17-27%
II. Economic Concepts and Analysis	17-27%
III. Financial Management	11-21%
IV. Information Technology	15-25%
V. Operations Management	15-25%

BEC Skill Allocation	Weight
Evaluation	-
Analysis	20-30%
Application	50-60%
Remembering and Understanding	15-25%

FAR Content Area Allocation	Weight
I. Conceptual Framework, Standard-Setting, & Financial Reporting	25-35%
II. Select Financial Statement Accounts	30-40%
III. Select Transactions	20-30%
IV. State and Local Governments	5-15%

FAR Skill Allocation	Weight
Evaluation	-
Analysis	25-35%
Application	50-60%
Remembering and Understanding	10-20%

REG Content Area Allocation	Weight
I. Ethics, Professional Responsibilities & Federal Tax Procedures	10-20%
II. Business Law	10-20%
III. Federal Taxation of Property Transactions	12-22%
IV. Federal Taxation of Individuals	15-25%
V. Federal Taxation of Entities	28-38%

REG Skill Allocation	Weight
Evaluation	-
Analysis	25-35%
Application	35-45%
Remembering and Understanding	25-35%

How Skills are Applied to Exam Tasks (A Sample)

Each blueprint area is broken down further by content topic, skill, and representative task. This helps candidates identify the topics and subtopics they will be tested on in each section and which skill they will be required to demonstrate as they answer questions regarding those topics. Lastly, the representative task gives detailed, specific information on what they will be expected to perform on the exam related to those topics. (As the AICPA points out, the representative tasks are not an all-inclusive list of items that will appear on the exam.)

To see how the content topic, skill, and representative tasks are presented in the blueprints, here is an excerpt from the AUD section:

Content group/topic	Skill: Remembering and Understanding	Application	Analysis	Evaluation	Representative task
A. Nature and scope					
1. Nature and scope: audit engagements	✓				Identify the nature, scope and objectives of the different types of audit engagements, including issuer and nonissuer audits.
2. Nature and scope: engagements conducted under Government Accountability Office Government Auditing Standards	✓				Identify the nature, scope and objectives of engagements performed in accordance with Government Accountability Office Government Auditing Standards.
3. Nature and scope: non-audit engagements	✓				Identify the nature, scope and objectives of the different types of non-audit engagements, including engagements conducted in accordance with the attestation standards and the accounting and review services standards.
B. Ethics, independence and professional conduct					
1. AICPA Code of Professional Conduct	✓				Understand the principles, rules and interpretations included in the AICPA Code of Professional Conduct.
	✓				Recognize situations that present threats to compliance with the AICPA Code of Professional Conduct, including threats to independence.
		✓			Apply the principles, rules and interpretations included in the AICPA Code of Professional Conduct to given situations.
		✓			Apply the Conceptual Framework for Members in Public Practice included in the AICPA Code of Professional Conduct to situations that could present threats to compliance with the rules included in the Code.
		✓			Apply the Conceptual Framework for Members in Business included in the AICPA Code of Professional Conduct to situations that could present threats to compliance with the rules included in the Code.
		✓			Apply the Conceptual Framework for Independence included in the AICPA Code of Professional Conduct to situations that could present threats to compliance with the rules included in the Code.

Conclusion

We hope you found this guide on how to read and understand the blueprints helpful. As we mentioned before, the UWorld Roger CPA Review course curriculum is directly mapped to and guided by these blueprints, so there is no need for you to spend considerable time studying the blueprints, as your course will guide you through the material. Rest assured that the practice questions in this course are designed to challenge critical thinking skills, ensuring you are thoroughly prepared to pass the CPA Exam.

To see the full AICPA Blueprints, visit **https://www.aicpa.org/becomeacpa/cpaexam/examinationcontent**.

UWorld
YOUR WORLD OF LEARNING

ROGER
CPA Review

FAR 1 – Basic Concepts & Financial Statements

FAR 1 – Basic Concepts & Financial Statements

Table of Contents

Basic Concepts & Financial Statements

Lecture 1.01 – FASB Standards & Frameworks

Financial Reporting Frameworks

Financial reporting frameworks (FRFs) may be general purpose frameworks or special purpose frameworks.

- Publicly held entities are required to submit their F/S to the SEC prepared in accordance with a general purpose framework, either GAAP or IFRS.
- Nonpublic entities, however, have a greater number of choices and select a framework that fairly balances the needs of their F/S users and the cost of providing information. Like public entities, nonpublic entities may prepare their F/S under either GAAP or IFRS; however, they also may use a special purpose framework.

A financial reporting framework (FRF) includes:

- **Recognition criteria** that determine what will appear on financial statements (F/S) and when it will appear.
- **Measurement criteria** that determine the amount at which it will be reported.
- **Presentation criteria** that determine where it will appear on the F/S.
- **Disclosure criteria** that determine what information and how much information must be provided to F/S users.

General Purpose Frameworks

There are currently two general purpose frameworks:

- U.S. Generally Accepted Accounting Principles (GAAP)
- International Financial Reporting Standards (IFRS)

The Financial Accounting and Reporting (FAR) exam tests the CPA candidate's knowledge of how transactions, events, and circumstances are accounted for and how they are reported upon. Most FAR questions are based on U.S. GAAP.

Special Purpose Frameworks

A special purpose framework is an FRF other than GAAP or IFRS. Statements prepared under a special purpose framework must have modified titles showing the basis of accounting—for example, "Consolidated Statements of Assets, Liabilities and Equity (FRF for SMEs Basis)." There are numerous special purpose frameworks:

- **Cash Basis**
  - Revenues are recognized when they are received, regardless of when they are earned.
  - Expenses are recognized when they are paid, regardless of when they are incurred.
  - Fixed assets are expensed and not capitalized.
  - **Modified cash basis** is considered a sort of *hybrid* approach between cash and accrual, where assets could be capitalized and taxes and inventory could be accrued.

- **Tax Basis**
  - Revenues and expenses are recognized for financial reporting purposes in the same periods and in the same amount as they are recognized when the entity is preparing its income tax return.
  - The tax basis could be cash-basis or accrual-basis.
- **Contractual Basis**
  - May be required to be used by a party to a contract.
  - Generally designed to assist users in determining whether or not terms of the contract, and other requirements related to it, are being adhered to.
- **Regulatory Basis**
  - May be imposed by a governmental regulatory agency to which the entity is required to report.
- **FRF for SMEs (**Financial Reporting Framework for Small- and Medium-Sized Entities)

With the exception of the cash basis of accounting and in some cases the tax basis, both general purpose frameworks and most special purpose frameworks apply the **accrual basis** of accounting. Under the accrual basis, revenues are recognized in the periods in which they are earned, regardless of when they are received; and expenses are recognized in the periods in which they are incurred, regardless of when they are paid.

☛ The CPA exam periodically includes questions that require the candidate to determine the amount of revenue or expenses that should be recognized on the accrual basis when given the amount of cash received or paid and the opening and closing balances of various accrual accounts, or changes in them. This will be covered in detail later in the course.

A closely related topic is the statement of cash flows. In order to prepare the statement, the amounts of revenue and expense items determined under the accrual basis are generally known and the amounts of cash received and paid must be determined, a common area of testing on the CPA exam. The process to be applied, discussed later, is basically the reverse of the procedure used to convert from cash to accrual.

Alternative Accounting Approaches for Nonpublic Entities

In order to reduce the cost of financial reporting for **nonpublic entities**, and to bring the cost more in line with the benefits derived by users of F/S, the FASB created the **Private Company Council** (**PCC**). The PCC is charged with evaluating existing GAAP to determine if there are:

- Requirements, including disclosures, from which nonpublic entities should be exempt; or
- Simplified accounting approaches that may be applied to transactions or F/S elements that will reduce the cost of reporting without diminishing the relative value of the information provided.

The PCC has developed alternative accounting approaches for goodwill; certain interest rate swaps (a common form of derivative); for the recognition of identifiable intangible assets acquired in a business combination; and for potential variable interest entities (VIEs). These alternative accounting approaches may only be applied by a nonpublic entity. To do so, the entity will elect the alternative accounting treatment by including information in its *Summary of Significant Accounting Policies*.

- In the period of adoption, the entity will indicate that it is adopting the alternative treatment and the primary differences between it and the previous requirements.

- It will also be disclosed in subsequent periods, since it represents a choice among acceptable alternative accounting treatments.

An entity electing to adopt the alternative accounting approaches is still preparing its F/S in accordance with GAAP since the pronouncements of the PCC are incorporated into the ASC. As indicated, they apply to nonpublic entities, which are all entities that are not considered public entities. FASB defines *public entities* as those that:

- Submit F/S to the SEC, either as a result of a requirement to do so or do so voluntarily
- Are regulated under the 1934 Securities Exchange Act
- Issue securities that are traded or have securities that are listed on an exchange
- Are required to apply GAAP and have securities that are not restricted as to transfer

FASB Accounting Standards Codification (ASC)

GAAP is developed by the Financial Accounting Standards Board (FASB), who is authorized to establish accounting standards by the Securities and Exchange Commission (SEC). The FASB Accounting Standards Codification (ASC) is the single source of authoritative GAAP for nongovernmental entities. The Codification reorganized thousands of GAAP pronouncements into approximately 90 accounting topics (see Research Appendix for more specifics).

Topic Groups	Numbered
Presentation	200-299
Assets	300-399
Liabilities	400-499
Equity	500-599
Revenues	600-699
Expenses	700-799
Broad Transactions	800-899
Industry	900-999

GAAP hierarchy now consists of two levels:

- Authoritative (in ASC) — updated with Accounting Standards Updates (ASUs), but which are not in themselves authoritative
- Nonauthoritative (not in ASC)

Emerging Issues Task Force (EITF) was created in 1984 by the FASB to reach a consensus on how to account for new and unusual financial transactions that have the potential for creating differing financial reporting practices. The FASB works on long-term problems, while the EITF deals with short-term emerging issues.

FASB Conceptual Framework for Accounting

The FASB periodically issues **Statements on Financial Accounting Concepts (SFACs).** SFACs are not applications of GAAP to specific situations, but instead represent the conceptual framework that guides the development of financial accounting and reporting standards. The conceptual framework defines the objectives and concepts that underlie financial reporting (per SFAC 8).

The **Objectives** of financial reporting (which focus on the **USERS** of F/S) are:

1. **Primary Objective** - To provide information that is useful to existing and potential **investors, lenders, and other creditors** (ie, users) in making decisions about providing resources to the entity.
2. Information about a reporting entity's **economic resources** and claims against the entity (ie, financial position) – *Balance Sheet (B/S).*
3. **Changes** in economic resources and claims.
4. Financial performance reflected by **accrual accounting** – provides a better basis for assessing the entity's past and future performance than does cash basis – *Income Statement (I/S).*
5. Financial performance reflected by past **cash flow** – *Statement of Cash Flows*
6. Changes in economic resources and claims **NOT** resulting from financial performance (eg, issuing additional stock) – *Statement of Changes in Owners' Equity*.

We can achieve our objectives if F/S have certain **Primary Qualitative Characteristics** that makes information **useful.** In order to be useful, information must have *both* relevance and faithful representation.

- **Relevance** – Information is capable of making a difference in a user's decision-making process if it has one or both of the following components:

  Roger is **PC.**

  - *<u>P</u>redictive value* – Helps decision makers predict or forecast future results.
  - *<u>C</u>onfirmatory value* (Feedback value) – Confirms or corrects prior predictions.
- **Faithful Representation** – The information depicts what it purports to represent. The 3 components are:

  Roger is never on the ***FENC***e.

  - *Free from <u>E</u>rror* – No errors or omissions in the information.
  - *<u>N</u>eutrality* (w/o bias) – The information is free from bias.
  - *<u>C</u>ompleteness* – Adequate or full disclosure of all necessary information.

Enhancing Qualitative Characteristics that relate to both relevance and faithful representation:

Roger is ***CUT*** like a ***V***.

- *<u>C</u>omparability* – Same *principles* being used with business enterprises in similar Industry.
  - Consistency – Same accounting *methods* in different periods.
- *<u>U</u>nderstandability* – Classifying, characterizing and presenting information clearly and concisely.
- *<u>T</u>imeliness* – Information is available to a decision maker when it is useful to make the decision.
- *<u>V</u>erifiability* – Different sources agree on an amount through either direct or indirect verification.

Constraints that override the usefulness of information:

- **Cost/benefit** – Cost of obtaining and presenting the information shouldn't exceed the benefit.
- **Materiality** – Capable of making a difference in the *user's* decision-making process if omitted or misstated (auditor's judgment). Considered an entity-specific aspect similar to *Relevance* that applies at the individual entity level.

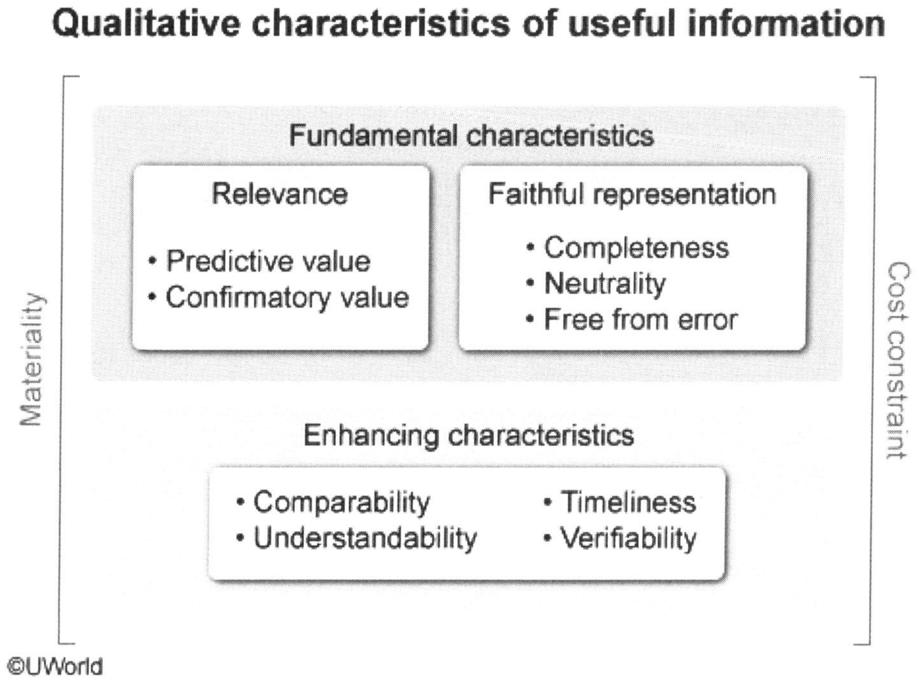

Lecture 1.02 – Elements of Financial Statements

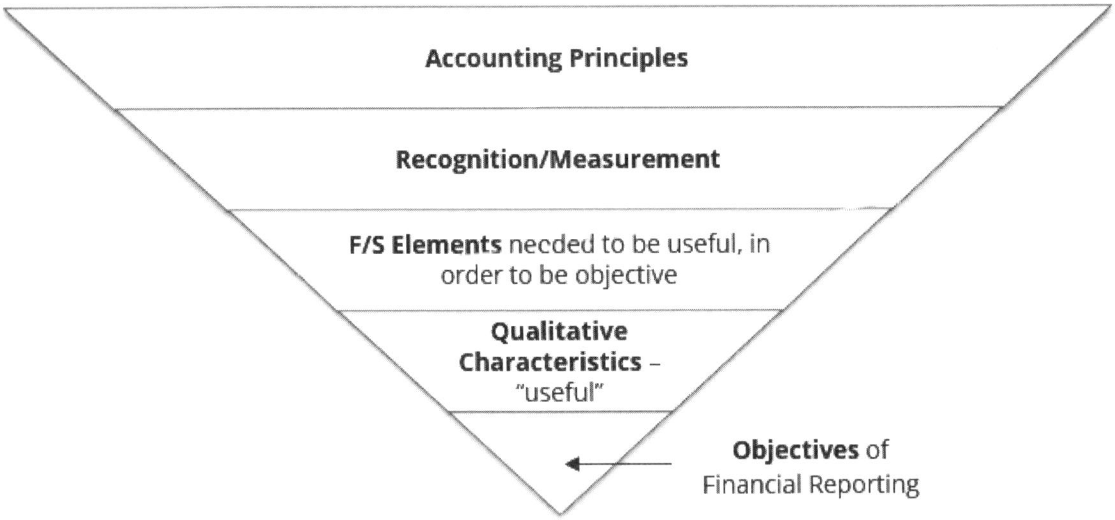

Full set of Financial Statements

- Statement of Position (Balance sheet)
- Statement of Earnings Financial & Comprehensive Income (Income statement)
- Statement of Cash Flows
- Statement of Changes in Owners' Equity (Statement of Investments by and Distributions to Owners)

10 Key Elements (SFAC 6)

The F/S elements need to be **useful**. There are 10 key elements that make up all the F/S. The first 3 are the basic elements:

- **Assets** – An economic resource that has a probable future benefit, one can obtain the benefit, and the transaction creating the benefit has already occurred.
- **Liabilities** – An economic obligation in which one needs to use or transfer an asset, it can't be avoided and the transaction has already occurred.
- **Equity or Net Assets** – Assets left over after deducting liabilities. **Equity** consists of 3 elements:
  - Investments by owners (ie, contributions)
  - Distributions to owners (ie, dividends)
  - **Comprehensive Income –** All changes in equity other than "owner" sources. Comprehensive income has 4 elements:
    - **Revenues** – Inflows from an entity's primary operations
    - **Expenses** – Outflows due to an entity's primary operations
    - **Gains** – Increases in equity from incidental transactions
    - **Losses** – Decreases in equity from incidental transactions

Note, however, that comprehensive income is separated into the following two categories on the income statement (discussed further later):

- Net income
- Other Comprehensive Income (DENT[1]):
  - **D**erivative cash flow hedges
  - **E**xcess adjustment of Pension PBO and FV of plan assets at year end
  - **N**et unrealized gains or losses on "available-for-sale" securities
  - **T**ranslation adjustments for foreign currency

When deciding what will be included in income (comprehensive or net income), the capital maintenance concept being used needs to be known.

- **Physical capital maintenance concept** – Only recognize an event when an asset is sold or a liability is settled (measures the effects of price changes in nominal or constant dollars).
- **Financial capital maintenance concept** – Recognize an event as a change in the value of an asset or liability occurs (recognize holding gains and losses – current GAAP).

Current accounting methods emphasize the physical capital approach with fixed assets (not adjusted to market value) but emphasize the financial capital approach with most marketable securities (generally reported at market value). Part of the reason relates to the enhancing qualitative characteristic of verifiability:

- Market values of fixed assets are *difficult to verify* and adjustments based on management estimates are subject to biases.
- The active market for investment securities provides numbers that are *verifiable* and not subject to management bias.

General Accounting Rules & Concepts

Accounting rules and concepts that go along with the key elements:

- **Consistency** – Same principle each year
- **Conservatism** – Considering all risks inherent in the business (accruing a contingent loss)
- **Cost/Benefit** – Costs don't exceed benefits to be derived
- **Matching** – Recognizing a cost as an expense in the same period as the benefit (usually a revenue) is recognized
- **Allocation** – Spreading a cost over more than one period
- **Full Disclosure** – Providing all useful info in the F/S
- **Recognition** – Booking an item in the F/S
- **Realization** – Converting noncash resources into cash or a claim to cash

[1] Most commonly tested items.

Lecture 1.03 – Recognition & Measurement

When to Recognize Financial Statement Elements (SFAC 5)

- Meets definition – The item meets the definition of an element (asset, liability, etc.).
- Measurable – Element is capable of being measured in monetary terms.
- Relevant – The item is capable of making a difference in user decisions.
- Reliable – The information is faithfully represented and verifiable (ie, useful).

Measurement in Monetary Terms

- Historical cost – Amount paid (eg, PP&E)
- Replacement (current) cost – Cost to replace an item (eg, inventory)
- Fair Value (FV) – The price that would be received to sell an asset or paid to transfer a liability in an orderly transaction between market participants at the measurement date (ASC 820)—aka, Fair Market Value (FMV)
- Net realizable value (NRV) – Amount expected to be converted into (eg, A/R)
- Present Value (PV) – Discounted cash flows due to the time value of money (used for notes receivable, bonds payable, leases)

Revenue & Expense Recognition

Under the accrual basis of accounting, revenues are recognized in the period earned, regardless of when they are collected and expenses are recognized in the period incurred, regardless of when they are paid.

- *Revenue is* recognized when they are:
  - Earned – Earnings process is complete (goods delivered), and
  - Realizable (realized) – Collect cash or a claim to cash.
- *Expenses or losses* are recognized as incurred or when a loss of future economic benefits is discovered.
  - Economic benefit is used up (**consumed**) or assets lose future benefit (ie, it is evident that the future economic benefits of an asset have been reduced or eliminated).
    - Cause and effect – Expenses that produce revenue at identifiable points in time can be matched directly to revenues (eg, cost of goods sold).
    - Systematic and rational allocation – Expenses that produce revenue over long periods of time are matched to those periods using a reasonable means of allocation (eg, depreciation).
    - **Immediate recognition** – Some expenses cannot be directly related to specific benefits and are expensed as incurred (eg, monthly salaries of selling, general & administrative employees).

Using Cash Flow Info & PV in Accounting Measurements (SFAC 7)

When assets or services are exchanged for future cash, the most appropriate means of measuring the transaction may be the present value of future cash flows. For this reason, SFAC 7 introduces the expected cash flow approach, which:

- Provides a framework for using future cash flows as the basis for accounting measurements at initial recognition or fresh-start measurements and for the interest method of amortization.

- Differs from the traditional approach by focusing on explicit assumptions about the range of possible estimated cash flows and their respective probabilities.

Note that SFAC 7 is limited to measurement issues (how to measure); it does not address recognition questions (when to measure).

The factors that must be considered are:

- Risk – The probability that the cash will actually be paid or received.
- Timing – The periods in which the payments are expected to be received.
- Interest – The interest rates that would be appropriate, taking into consideration market rates and the credit standing of the parties involved.
- Amount of cash flows
    - Traditional approach – Use most likely cash flow amounts.
    - Expected approach – Use weighted average of different possibilities.

Cash flow has a 10% chance of being $100, 60% chance of $200, 30% chance of $300.

- **Traditional** – $200 (since it is most likely)
- **Expected** – $220 (10% × $100 + 60% × $200 + 30% × $300)

    - When measuring a liability, one must look at the credit standing of the entity who owes the money.

Lecture 1.04 – Fair Value Measurement

Overview

ASC 820 defines the term *fair value (FV)* for financial reporting purposes, describes the various methods by which fair value can be measured for an asset and for a liability, and indicates the disclosures that are required to be provided when items are reported at fair value on the F/S. This section of the ASC does not allow, nor require, assets or liabilities to be reported at fair value unless there is another requirement to do so.

Items Required to be Reported at Fair Value

An entity is required to recognize various items at fair value, including the following:

- Investments in **marketable debt securities** that are classified as either **trading** securities or **available-for-sale (AFS)** securities are reported at fair value (ie, *marked to market*) as of each balance sheet date.
- Investments in **equity securities,** except those accounted for under the equity method; those required to be consolidated; and, when an appropriate election is made, those for which the market value is not readily determinable.
- With very few exceptions, **assets acquired** and **liabilities assumed** in a **business combination** are initially recognized at fair value, but are not adjusted to fair value in subsequent periods for presentation on the balance sheet unless that asset/liability is being reported at fair value for some other reason.
- **Impairment losses** result in the reduction of an asset's carrying value to its fair value in the period of the impairment.
- All **derivatives** are reported at fair value, *except* for interest rate swaps that are hedges when the alternative accounting approach available to nonpublic entities is elected.

Fair Value Definition

ASC 820 defines fair value as "the price that would be received to sell an asset or paid to transfer a liability in an orderly transaction between market participants at the measurement date." For a transaction to be orderly, it cannot be a forced transaction. Instead, the asset or liability is assumed to be exposed to the market for a time period that is customary for that type of asset or liability. **Market participants** are parties that are:

- Independent of the entity
- Reasonably knowledgeable about the asset or liability
- In a position to acquire the asset or assume the liability
- Voluntarily willing to acquire the asset or assume the liability

Note that the definition of fair value focuses on the price that would be received to sell the asset or paid to transfer the liability (ie, the ***exit price****), not the price that would be paid to acquire the asset or received to assume the liability (ie, the* ***entry price****).*

Determining Fair Value

Fair value measurements are not intended to be an application of conservatism. Assets, other than financial assets, are measured on the basis of their "highest and best use." Some assets are more valuable **in exchange** and are measured at what would be received upon their sale. Others are more valuable **in use** and are measured at the value represented in the form of some combination of potential revenues earned and cost savings that result from their use.

- It is assumed that a transaction will occur in the **principal market** in which the asset or liability would most frequently be traded.
- When there is no principal market, values are based on the assumption that a transaction would occur in the **most advantageous** market.

This is intended as a measure of an asset's or liability's fair value without assuming that the asset will actually be disposed of or the liability transferred. As a result, the value is determined without taking into consideration costs of the transaction, such as costs to transfer the asset or liability. If an asset (eg, a commodity) needs to be transported to its principal market, however, the cost of doing so is considered when measuring the asset's fair value.

Three Valuation Techniques (MIC)

- The **market approach** involves using information generated by market transactions that involve identical or comparable assets or liabilities.
- The **income approach** involves analyzing future amounts in the form of revenues, cost savings, earnings, or some other item.
- The **cost approach** involves measuring the cost that would be incurred to replace the benefit derived from an asset.

Three Levels of Inputs

- **Level I**, the most reliable, involves the use of observable data from actual market transactions, occurring in an active market, for identical assets or liabilities.
- **Level II** also involves the use of observable data from actual market transactions but *either*:
  - The transactions did not occur in an active market**,** *or*
  - The transactions relate to similar, but not identical, assets or liabilities.
- **Level III** involves the use of unobservable data and are largely based on management's judgment.

Practical Expedient for Certain Equity Interests

In some cases, an entity will have an equity interest in an entity that reports its net asset value per share. As a practical expedient, such an investment may be reported at the published net asset value per share.

- Since the fair value is not determined using a technique designated by standards for doing so, the fair value measurement does not fit into the hierarchy.
- As a result, an entity applying the practical expedient is not required to disclose the level of inputs that were used to determine fair value.

Steps to Fair Value Measurement

Fair value measurement may be applied using the following approach:

1. Identify the asset or liability to be measured.
2. Determine the principal or most advantageous market (*highest and best use*).
3. Determine the valuation premise (*in-use or in-exchange*).
4. Determine the appropriate valuation technique (*market, income, or cost approach*).
5. Obtain inputs for valuation (*Level 1, Level 2, or Level 3*).

   - Fair value hierarchy must be used to prioritize the inputs to valuation techniques.
6. Calculate the fair value of the asset.

Disclosures

Disclosures about the use of fair value to measure assets and liabilities should provide F/S users with better information about:

- The valuation techniques and inputs that the entity uses to arrive at its measures of fair value, including judgments and assumptions made
- The uncertainty in the fair value measurements as of the reporting date
- The effect of changes in fair value measurements on entity performance (ie, earnings or changes in net assets) and cash flows

In developing ASC 820, the Board considered the need for increased **consistency** and **comparability** in fair value measurements and for expanded disclosures about fair value measurements. Some of the required disclosures include:

- Identification of which items are reported at fair value and where they can be found in the F/S
- The level of inputs (I, II, or III) that were applied in measuring fair value
- The valuation technique applied (market, income, or cost)
- The disposition of changes in fair value (income or comprehensive income)

Fair Value Option

In addition to those items that are required to be measured at fair value, ASC 825 allows an entity to **elect** to report some or all of its financial instruments (aka, financial assets and liabilities) at their fair values. A **financial instrument** is defined as *cash*, evidence of an *ownership interest* in an entity, or a *contract* that *both*:

- Imposes on one entity a contractual **obligation** either:
   - To deliver cash or another financial instrument to a second entity
   - To exchange other financial instruments on potentially unfavorable terms with the second entity
- Conveys to that second entity a contractual **right** either:
   - To receive cash or another financial instrument from the first entity
   - To exchange other financial instruments on potentially favorable terms with the first entity

Examples of financial assets and liabilities that would qualify for the fair value option include:

- Most investments that do not already require FV measurement, such as investments accounted for under the equity method.
- Firm commitments involving financial instruments, such as forward exchange contracts to purchase or sell a foreign currency.

Certain items have their own established accounting principles, which are required to be followed. These items may involve measurements at fair value, but they **do not qualify** for the "fair value option" election:

- Pension plan, post-retirement, and other post-employment benefits (ASC 712 and 715)
- Leases (ASC 842)
- Financial instruments that are components of equity (ASC 505)

- Share-based payments and stock options (ASC 718)

If an entity decides to elect the fair value option, it may apply it to any qualifying financial instrument, without being required to apply it to others, including those that are similar. An election may be made only when a financial asset or liability is acquired, or in other limited circumstances, referred to as election dates. Likewise, once elected, the fair value option is permanent and may only be discontinued on a subsequent election date.

When the fair value option is elected, **unrealized gains and losses are reported in income.**

Lecture 1.05 – Credit Losses

Overview

ASC 326 specifies the reporting for declines in the value (ie, credit losses) of financial assets, such as accounts receivable and loans receivable, that result from the expected inability of the debtor to make all of the payments called for in the instrument. There are two types of assets that are subject to the recognition of credit losses under ASC 326 (referred to as the *current expected credit loss* or CECL method):

- Assets measured at amortized cost* (discussed here)
- Available-for-sale (AFS) debt securities (differences in accounting are discussed in a later section)

**Amortized cost* is the amount at which a financial asset originates or is acquired, adjusted for accrued interest, accretion, amortization, collections, writeoffs, and other accounting adjustments.

Assets Reported at Fair Value

Financial assets reported at fair value generally are not subject to the recognition of credit losses. This is because fair value is determined on the basis of market transactions, which assumes that the risk of credit loss is taken into account when the buyer and seller determine the exchange price.

While AFS debt securities are reported at fair value, if the fair value is lower than the present value of expected future cash flows, the instrument generally will be held and the cash flows will be realized. If, however, the fair value is higher, it generally will be sold at its fair value rather than being held for the cash flows. As a result, the allowance for credit losses would never be greater than the amount by which the amortized cost exceeds the fair value.

Assets Measured at Amortized Cost (and Other Assets)

The following assets measured at amortized cost are subject to the recognition of credit losses:

- Accounts receivable resulting from recognizing revenue (under ASC 605, 606 and 610)
- Financing receivables
  - Defined as a contractual right to receive money on demand or on fixed or determinable dates, and which is recognized in the balance sheet.
  - Examples include loans, trade accounts receivable, notes receivable, credit cards, and certain lease receivables.
- Held-to-maturity debt securities
- Financial assets addressed in ASC 860, which concerns transfers and servicing of financial assets (eg, mortgages transferred to Fannie Mae but serviced by Wells Fargo)

Credit losses also may be incurred in relation to other assets, including[2]:

- A lessor's net investments in leases (ie, sales-type and direct financing leases)
- Off-balance-sheet credit exposures that are not accounted for as insurance, such as:
  - Off-balance-sheet loan commitments
  - Standby letters of credit

[2] This list also includes reinsurance recoverables resulting from insurance transactions under ASC 944. Since these transactions are industry specific, and thus generally not tested, we have excluded them.

- Financial guarantees
- Similar instruments other than derivatives that are subject to the provisions of ASC 815, *Derivatives and Hedging*

Exclusions

There are some financial assets that are **not subject to credit losses**:

- *Financial assets measured at fair value* with changes reported in net income (eg, equity securities and trading debt securities).
- Loans by defined contribution employee benefit plans made to participants.
  - Since these loans are generally limited by a participant's interest in the plan, the participant absorbs the loss, not the plan.
- *Loans of an insurance entity made to the policy owners*, which are also generally limited to the owner's net investment in the policy's surrender value.
- *Promises to give recognized by a nonprofit entity*, such as pledges receivable, since pledges are not made in exchange for goods and services and are often not legally binding commitments.
- *Loans and receivables between entities under common control* since these represent the principals of both companies essentially making a loan to themselves.
- *Operating lease receivables*, which are accounted for under ASC 842.

Recognizing Expected Credit Losses

Allowance for Credit Losses

Rather than reduce the recorded balance of a financial asset, credit losses are accumulated in a contra-asset account (ie, valuation account)—**Allowance for Credit Losses**. The carrying value is measured at amortized cost, using the effective interest rate at the inception of the instrument, and is reduced by the allowance for credit losses. On each reporting date, the allowance is adjusted so that the net amount equals what management expects to be collected.

- Increases in the allowance are reported in a **Credit Loss Expense** account.
- Decreases in the allowance are reported in a **Reversal of Credit Loss Expense** account.

Pooling Assets

Financial assets that have similar risk characteristics are considered a pool and are evaluated for credit losses on a collective basis. While it is difficult to determine if a specific instrument is collectible without a significant investigation, averages can be applied to groups of similar assets. Financial assets that do not have similar risk characteristics are evaluated individually. No financial assets should be evaluated both separately and on a collective basis.

Measuring the Amount

In performing the evaluation of credit losses, a variety of methods may be applied, such as the following:

- *Discounted cash flow method* – Losses are estimated by determining the present value of the expected future cash flows.
  - Although the discounted cash flows method is widely used, it is not required. Also, when another technique is applied, there is no requirement to evaluate the results by comparing them to the results derived under the discounted cash flows method.
- *Loss-rate method* – Losses are estimated as a percentage of total exposure.

- *Roll-rate method* – Losses are estimated on the basis of the time required for the conversion cycle, the period required for instruments to be realized.
- *Probability-of-default method* – Losses are estimated by multiplying a likelihood that an instrument will be defaulted upon by the balance of the instrument.
- *Aging method* – The instruments are stratified, often on the basis of when they will mature, and different percentages are applied to each stratum.

When credit losses are estimated by applying a **discounted cash flow method**, expected future cash receipts are required to be discounted using the **effective interest rate** of the financial instrument being evaluated. The valuation allowance under this method will equal the difference between the amortized cost and the present value of the future payments expected to be collected.

When financial assets have a contractual rate that varies based on an index, the effective interest rate will take into account the changes that have occurred over the life of the instrument. The effective rate may *not*, however, take into account *projected changes*. Other factors that should *not* affect the effective interest rate include the following:

- *Expected credit losses* - The effective rate is the rate at inception that will result in the present value of expected future cash inflows that will equal the issue price of the instrument. If it is determined that less will be received, the effective rate is not adjusted to cause the present value of expected collections to equal the carrying value, which will result in recognizing lower amounts of interest income without recognizing the effects of credit losses.
- *Effects of expectations of extensions, renewals, or modifications of the instruments*, unless a troubled debt restructuring with the debtor is reasonably expected to occur as of the reporting date.

Prepayments may be taken into account in measuring credit losses. This is also true of estimated future prepayments and future interest cash flows when inclusion is consistent with the method being applied. All available relevant information should be considered, including internal and external information. Reliance should not be placed exclusively on historical loss information and both qualitative and quantitative information should be considered.

Off-Balance-Sheet Risk

An entity may have a risk of credit loss that is not associated with a financial asset or any other item(s) that are reported on the balance sheet. This results in an off-balance-sheet risk of credit exposure.

A common example is an entity's guarantee of another entity's obligations. If the other party is not able to satisfy its financial obligation, the guarantor entity will be required to do so. Unless the obligation is *unconditionally cancellable*, it will result in a credit loss that is required to be reported on the entity's F/S.

Credit Enhancements

Some entities will reduce exposure to credit losses through the use of credit enhancements, such as requiring a guarantor. Factors that include the guarantor's financial position, its apparent willingness to pay its obligation if necessary, or the existence of subordinate obligations all affect the estimate of credit losses. Assets or other instruments obtained or entered into for the purpose of mitigating these losses may not, however, be used to reduce amounts reported.

For example, an entity may acquire a credit default swap to protect it against potential credit losses in relation to a mortgage note receivable. If the potential for default requires the recognition of a credit loss and an allowance for credit losses, the positive value of the credit default swap may not be offset against the loss.

Purchased Financial Assets with Credit Deterioration (PCD Assets)

If an entity acquires a financial asset with credit deterioration (ie, more than an insignificant amount), it will likely be purchased at a larger discount because of the potential for credit loss. As a result, the discount is based **on** both market risk due to a potential difference between the instrument's stated rate and a comparable market rate, and credit risk due to the potential of noncollection. This discount must be appropriately allocated:

- The portion associated with market risk, may be a discount, premium, or neither, depending on whether the stated rate is higher, lower, or equal to the market rate, respectively. Such a discount or premium is recognized as an *adjustment to the carrying value of the instrument and is amortized under the effective interest method*, affecting interest income.
- The remainder, which is associated with credit risk, is not recognized and amortized in relation to interest expense. The initial amount is instead added to the cost of the investment and accounted for in the same manner as other credit losses.

After the initial acquisition and recognition of a financial asset, a current estimate of expected losses is measured each reporting period, using the same measurement technique as was used originally. The allowance is adjusted to the appropriate amount and the related increase or decrease in the allowance is recognized as an additional credit loss expense or a reversal. The same is true for off-balance-sheet credit exposures.

- As discussed previously, financial assets with similar characteristics will be evaluated as a pool.
- Those that do not have characteristics that are similar to others will be evaluated separately.

Collateral

Many financial assets are secured by collateral to provide the holder another means of recovering the investment it made. Regardless of the initial measurement method of expected credit losses, when it becomes **probable** that the financial asset will be settled through exercise of lien rights and foreclosing upon the collateral, the entity will report the financial asset at the fair value of the collateral (less costs to sell the collateral, if applicable).

Changes in the value of collateral may require continual adjustments to the allowance for credit losses; thus, in these circumstances, there is a practical expedient that allows the entity to measure the allowance by simply comparing the amortized cost of the financial asset to the fair value of the collateral on the reporting date.

- In some arrangements, the debtor is required to replenish collateral when values decline to make certain that the value of the collateral always exceeds the amortized cost basis of the financial asset, eliminating the need for an allowance.
- Many entities borrow using merchandise inventory for collateral with terms requiring the borrower to maintain inventory according to some ratio. When a secured line of credit cannot be drawn down to an amount exceeding 80% of the outstanding balance of the loan, for example, as inventory is sold, the debtor is required to either replenish inventory or pay down the loan to maintain that ratio.

Writing Off Financial Assets

Financial assets are required to be written off (partially or in full) in the period in which it is determined that they are **uncollectible**. The asset is reduced to zero and the allowance for credit losses is decreased by the same amount. Recoveries of amounts written-off should be credited back to the allowance for credit losses.

Change in Classification of Loans

When a decision has been made to sell a loan that is not currently classified as held for sale, the loan is transferred to the held-for-sale classification; however, any uncollectible portion of the amortized cost basis will need to be written off before the loan is transferred to the held-for-sale classification.

Measuring Interest Income on PCD Assets

ASC 326 does not provide guidance on the recognition of interest income by the holder of the instrument. Some entities apply a method, such as the cost-recovery method or a cash-basis approach, under which the amount expected to be collected exceeds the amortized cost. When a financial asset is purchased with credit deterioration:

- The discount associated with the deteriorated credit of the debtor is accounted for (separately from other discounts or premiums) using an allowance for credit losses, with adjustments increasing or decreasing the amount of losses recognized.
- The other discounts or premiums are generally the means by which the instrument's effective rate is adjusted to approximate the existing market rate, and amortization is a component of interest income.

Income from PCD assets can only be determined if amounts to be collected can be reasonably estimated. Once the PCD asset is initially recognized, the entity may place it on nonaccrual status so that income that is not likely to be received will not be reported.

Such a financial asset may be acquired, however, to provide the entity with the benefits to be derived from operation of the underlying collateral. When this is the case, interest income may be recognized, but it is limited to the extent that its recognition would increase the net investment reported to an amount greater than the actual payoff amount.

Financial Statement Presentation

Balance Sheet

- When presenting financial assets measured at amortized cost on the balance sheet, the allowance for credit losses is to be reported separately from the amortized cost of the financial asset.
- Off-balance-sheet credit risk exposures are to be reported as expected credit losses in the liability section.
  - The liability is reduced or eliminated, as appropriate, when the instrument expires, results in the recognition of a financial asset, or is otherwise settled.
  - Estimates of expected credit losses related to off-balance-sheet credit risk are to be reported separately from the allowance for expected losses related to recognized financial assets.

Income Statement

- Changes in the present value of a financial asset from one reporting period to the next may result from the passage of time as well as from changes in estimates of the timing or the amounts of future cash flows to be received. When credit losses are measured using the discounted cash flow approach, the entity may either:
  - Report the *entire change* in fair value as *credit loss expense*, or
  - Recognize the portion of the change attributable to the passage of time as *interest expense* and the remainder as *credit loss expense*.
- Changes in the fair value of collateral securing a financial asset that is collateral-dependent are reported as:
  - Credit loss expense for decreases.
  - Reversal of credit loss expense for increases.

Credit Loss Disclosures

Disclosures related to credit losses associated with financing receivables, which also apply to the net investment in leases, may be provided for each portfolio segment or for each class of financing receivable. Disclosures related to investments in debt securities are to be provided for each major security type. The level of detail required is to be determined by considering the surrounding facts and circumstances.

The required disclosures are designed to provide a user of the F/S with an understanding of the following:

- The credit risk associated with an investment portfolio and how it is being monitored by management
- An estimate of credit losses
- Changes in the estimate

Disclosures regarding **credit quality** should enable F/S users to understand how management monitors credit quality and assesses the risks resulting from the credit quality of its financial assets. It is required to include both qualitative and quantitative aspects. Disclosure, by class of financing receivables and major security type, will include:

- Information about credit quality indicators used to evaluate it, except for receivables measured at the lower of the amortized cost basis or market value, or trade receivables due within one year.
- The amortized cost basis of financial assets, organized by the credit quality indicator applied.
- The date on which the information was updated, or range of dates, for each credit quality indicator.

These disclosures apply to financing receivables and a net investment in a lease. They are not required for off-balance-sheet credit exposures. Nor do they apply to reinsurance receivables or repurchase agreements and securities lending agreements.

- The amortized cost basis is presented for financing receivables and the net investment in leases, with few exceptions.
- Amounts are reported within each credit quality indicator by year of origination, using the initial date on which the instrument was issued, not the date on which it was acquired.

Disclosures related to the **estimation of credit losses** should enable F/S users to understand how the allowances for credit losses were developed; the information used in developing current estimates; and circumstances responsible for changes to the allowance, affecting the period's credit loss expense. The disclosures, required to be presented by portfolio segment and major security type, include:

- How expected loss elements are developed
- Accounting policies related to estimating the allowance for credit losses and the methodology applied, along with factors considered, such as past events, current conditions, and forecasts that are reasonable and supportable
- Risk characteristics of each portfolio segment
- Changes in factors influencing management's estimates
- Changes to relevant accounting policies and methods applied, including their rationale and quantitative effects
- Reasons for significant changes in write-offs, if any
- The reversion method applied for periods too distant to enable reasonable and supportable forecasts
- Significant purchases of financial assets that occurred during the period
- Amounts of significant sales or reclassifications of financial assets

Creditors choosing to report interest expense based on changes due to the passage of time and credit losses separately, as opposed to combining them and reporting the total as credit loss expense, are also required to disclose the amount of interest income representing changes in present value due exclusively to the passage of time.

F/S users should be able to understand activity causing changes in the allowance for credit losses for each period, and separately by portfolio and major security type. Disclosures related to the allowance for credit losses are to include:

- The beginning balance
- The current period's provision for expected credit losses
- The amount initially recognized in the allowance for PCD assets, if any
- Writeoffs charged to the allowance during the period
- Recoveries of amounts previously written off
- The ending balance

An aged analysis of the amortized cost basis for financial assets past due as of the reporting date is to be provided by class of financing receivable and by major security type, indicating when a financial asset is considered to be past due. The disclosures related to the instruments' past due status is *not* required for:

- Receivables measured at the lower of amortized cost basis or fair value
- Trade receivables due in one year or less, unless they are credit card receivables resulting from transactions that provide revenue

When financial assets are placed on **nonaccrual basis**, users should be able to understand the credit risk, and the interest income recognized, by class of financing receivable and major security type. The disclosures will provide:

- Their amortized cost basis at the beginning and end of the reporting period
- Interest income recognized

- The amortized cost basis of financial assets not on nonaccrual status on the reporting date, despite being past due for 90 days or more
- The amortized cost basis of financial assets that are on nonaccrual status but do not have an allowance for credit losses

In an entity's summary of significant policies for financial assets, excluding receivables measured at the lower of amortized cost basis or fair value, or trade receivables, other than credit card receivables incurred in transactions falling under the guidelines of revenue recognition (ASC 605) or revenues from contracts with customers (ASC 606), the following should be included:

- Nonaccrual policies, including those related to discontinuing and renewing the accrual of interest, as appropriate
- Policies for determining when a financial asset is past due or delinquent
- Policies for recognizing writeoffs

If financial assets with credit deterioration were purchased during the current period, the following should be disclosed:

- The difference between their par values and their purchase prices should be reconciled, showing the purchase price
- The acquiring entity's assessment supporting the allowance for credit losses at acquisition
- Any discount or premium attributable to factors other than the credit deterioration
- The par value

Disclosures also will provide information about financial assets that are collateral-dependent and off-balance-sheet exposures.

Lecture 1.06 – Financial Statement Disclosures

Notes to Financial Statements

The notes to the F/S are used to ensure that all disclosures that are required under GAAP are made (ASC 235).

- Summary of significant accounting policies – This is usually either the first or second footnote and describes the selection of significant accounting principles and methods used in the F/S (eg, inventory costing method). Specific items it will include are:
    - The basis for consolidation
    - Depreciation methods
    - Amortization of intangibles
    - Recognition of revenue from contracts with customers
    - Recognition of revenue from leasing contracts
- Summary of significant assumptions – For **prospective** F/S (those that present forecasted or projected future results), this describes the assumptions used to estimate future amounts (eg, anticipated rate of inflation).
- Other notes to the financial statements – The other footnotes contain all the other relevant information that investors and creditors may find useful, such as information regarding:
    - Contingent liabilities
    - Contractual obligations
    - Amount coming due for bonds and leases in the next 5 years and the aggregate beyond 5 years
    - Significant changes in account balances

Inflation Accounting

Accounting for the **effects of changing prices** is **optional** (ASC 255). When the client elects to present such data as supplementary information accompanying the basic financial statements, it may present two different types of information:

- Current cost information
- Price-level adjusted data

To understand the effects of changing prices, it is important to distinguish monetary assets and liabilities from nonmonetary items.

- A **monetary** item is an asset or liability whose value is *fixed in money terms*. Examples include:
    - Cash
    - Accounts and notes receivable
    - Bond investments that will be held to maturity
    - Prepaid expenses
    - Accounts, notes, and bonds payable
- A **nonmonetary** item is one that does not guarantee a fixed amount of money being received or paid. Examples include:
    - Inventories

- Plant and equipment
- Intangibles
- Marketable securities (including bonds that may be sold prior to maturity)

Current cost accounting reports assets on the balance sheet at replacement cost. In determining the replacement cost of fixed assets, the estimated cost of a used asset must be utilized. If this isn't available, the cost of a new asset may be adjusted for estimated depreciation.

Assume the client acquired a machine with a 10-year life and no expected salvage value on 1/1/X1 for $100, and that it was being depreciated on a straight-line basis. At 12/31/X3, accumulated depreciation was $30 and book value was $70.

In determining the current cost of the machine, the client is unable to identify a price for a 3-year-old machine, but the replacement cost for an identical new machine on 12/31/X3 was $120.

By applying the same depreciation approach, accumulated depreciation is estimated at $120 × 3 / 10 = $36, and the current cost of the machine is reported at $120 – $36 = $84.

On the income statement, cost of sales is reported at the average current cost of goods sold.

Assume the following historical information is available for FIFO calculation of cost of sales in 20X1:

	Units	**Dollars**
Beginning inventory	10	100
Purchases	40	440
Ending inventory	(20)	(280)
Cost of sales	30	260

The current cost of the inventory was $10 per unit at 1/1/X1 and $14 per unit at 12/31/X1, so the average current cost per unit was $12. The average current cost of goods sold was 30 units × $12 per unit = $360.

Price-level adjusted numbers continue to carry assets at historical cost, but nonmonetary items are adjusted to reflect changes in the consumer price index.

For example, if land was acquired in 20X1 at $500 when the price index was 1.00, and the price index at 12/31/X3 is 1.10, the land is carried on a price-level adjusted 12/31/X3 balance sheet at $500 × 1.10 / 1.00 = $550.

Monetary assets and liabilities are not adjusted for inflation, since they do not increase in value from it. The failure of these items to increase results in a purchasing power loss when monetary assets are held and a purchasing power gain when monetary liabilities are held (since the failure of assets to rise in value is unfavorable but the failure of liabilities to increase is favorable).

To measure purchasing power gains and losses, a calculation is made of the change in value that would have occurred on net monetary items if they had been nonmonetary, and this is compared to their actual value. Since the calculation is being made of the gain or loss over the course of the year, all amounts are adjusted to reflect the average price level for the year.

If inflation:	
Monetary ASSET	Purchasing power LOSS
Monetary LIABILITY	Purchasing power GAIN

Assume a client began the year with net monetary assets of $400 and ended the year with net monetary assets of $600. The price index at the beginning of the year was 1.00 and at the end of the year 1.20, with an average of 1.10. Expressed in nominal dollars, the change during the year can be summarized as:

Beginning	$400
Increase	$200
Ending	$600

If all of the figures are adjusted to a common price level of 1.10 (the average for the year), then beginning net monetary assets are $400 × 1.10 / 1.00 = $440, the increase (which occurred over the course of the year) is $200 × 1.10 / 1.10 = $200, and the ending net monetary assets are $600 × 1.10 / 1.20 = $550. The amounts do not reconcile, though, and the discrepancy is the purchasing power loss:

Beginning	$440
Increase	$200
Subtotal	$640
Ending	$550
Discrepancy	$90

The discrepancy is a purchasing power loss to the company, because it represents the difference between what the assets would have been worth if they had benefited from inflation ($640) and what they were actually worth ($550).

Risks and Uncertainties

ASC 275 requires disclosure in the F/S of risks and uncertainties existing as of the date of those statements. The **four areas of disclosure** are:

- Nature of operations
- Use of estimates
- Certain significant estimates
- Current vulnerability associated with certain concentrations

Disclosure of the **nature of operations** will include a description of how the entity generates revenue, such as major products and services and principal markets served.

- Entities providing multiple products and services will include an indication of their relative importance.
- Not-for-profit entities will include a description of the principal services provided and the entity's revenue sources.

Disclosures related to the **use of estimates** should indicate that the preparation of F/S in accordance with GAAP, as well as other applicable financial reporting frameworks, require the use of estimates. Users are also cautioned that actual results may differ from those estimates.

Certain significant estimates include those for which it is at least reasonably possible that a material change in the estimate will occur in the near term. For these items, the entity will disclose the nature of the uncertainty and that a change in the estimate is at least reasonably possible. When the estimate relates to a contingent liability, disclosure will include:

- An estimate of a possible loss (the possible range of loss when a specific amount cannot be reasonably estimated), or
- The fact that an estimate cannot be made, if appropriate.

Current vulnerability due to certain concentrations occur when an entity does not diversify. This may result from doing large amounts of business with a limited number of customers; relying on a limited number of products or services; providing goods or services to customers in limited geographical areas or with limited demographics; or relying on few suppliers for materials, labor, or services. An entity will disclose information about such concentrations that exist at the balance sheet date if:

- The entity is vulnerable to a possible severe impact in the near term; and
- Events that would cause the severe impact are at least reasonably possible in the near term.

Lecture 1.07 – Balance Sheet

Overview

The balance sheet, also called the Statement of Financial Position, reports the effect of transactions at a point in time. It consists of assets, liabilities, and stockholders' equity. (ASC 210)

Assets = Liabilities + Shareholders' Equity

Assets and liabilities are broken down into *current* and *noncurrent*:

- **Current assets** are assets that will be used up or converted into cash within one year or the operating cycle, whichever is longer. Examples include cash, temporary trading securities, accounts receivable, notes receivable, inventories and prepaid expenses.
- **Current liabilities** are liabilities that will be settled within one year or the operating cycle, whichever is longer. Examples include accounts payable, accrued expenses, dividends payable, income taxes payable, current portion of long-term debt.

Cash and Cash Equivalents

Cash is the most liquid asset of an enterprise; thus, it is usually the first item presented in the current assets section of the balance sheet.

A **cash equivalent** is a financial instrument (investment) that meets the following criteria:

- It is easily convertible into a known amount of cash (**highly liquid**).
- It has an **original maturity of three months or less** from the date of purchase.

For example, a 5-year U.S. Treasury Note will be considered a cash equivalent if the investor acquires the investment on the open market when its remaining time to maturity is under three months. Such an investment so close to maturity presents very little risk of change in value due to changes in interest rates.

An investment that has been excluded from cash equivalents because of a term exceeding three months will not be reclassified to cash equivalents as it approaches the maturity date. This is because there is no transaction or event occurring three months before maturity that would justify the preparation of a journal entry.

Other examples of cash and cash equivalents include:

- Coin and currency on hand (petty cash)
- Money market accounts
- Unmailed checks
- Savings accounts
- CDs with an original maturity of three months or less
- Negotiable paper (bank checks, travelers' checks, money orders)

Items **excluded** from cash:

- **Compensating balances** – These are *legally restricted* deposits that are either a current or noncurrent asset, but are not considered part of cash. If funds are *not* legally restricted, they are presented along with cash.
- **Postdated checks or NSF** (NonSufficient Funds) are receivables.
- **Overdraft protection**
  - If there is more than one account in the same bank, net them. If positive, show it as cash. If negative, show it as a current liability.
  - Cash accounts in different banks cannot be netted. Show the positive account as an asset, and the negative account as a current liability.
- **Restricted cash**
  - **Balance sheet**
    - **Current** – Cash that is restricted for use on a current asset/liability within one year is considered current. However, it is segregated from cash because it is not available for use in current operations.
    - **Noncurrent** – Cash that is restricted for use on a noncurrent asset/liability (eg, bond sinking funds) is considered noncurrent. It is presented in the either other assets or investments.
- **Postage stamps** are considered supplies (prepaid expense).

Bank Reconciliation

Bank reconciliations are used to reconcile differences between cash balances per bank and per book to arrive at a corrected balance between the two. Several factors can cause a difference between bank and book cash balances, such as deposits in transit, outstanding checks, errors, or bank service charges. A simple bank reconciliation looks something like this:

Balance on bank statement

+	Deposits in transit
-	Outstanding checks
±	Errors made by bank
=	Corrected balance

Checkbook balance

+	Amounts collected by bank
-	Unrecorded bank charges
±	Errors made in recording transactions
=	Corrected balance

Roger Company
GAAP BALANCE SHEET/Statement of Financial Position
December 31, 20X7

Assets

Current Assets

- Cash and cash equivalents
- Restricted cash (current)
- Temporary term investments (trading securities)
- Receivables (NRV)
  - Tax and other refunds
  - Receivables from affiliates and employees and overpayments to creditors
  - Accounts receivable, net of allowance for credit losses
  - Current portions of installments receivable and notes receivable
- Inventories (LCNRV)
  - Raw materials
  - Work-in-process
  - Finished goods
- Prepaid expenses (eg, insurance and rent)

Total Current Assets

Noncurrent Investments

- Nonmarketable securities (eg, equity method securities)
- Long-term investments in marketable debt securities
  - Available for sale
  - Held to maturity

Property, Plant, and Equipment (Fixed Assets)

- Land, buildings, and improvements
- Machinery and equipment, leased assets
- Less accumulated depreciation

Intangible Assets (net of amortization)

- Goodwill
- Other identifiable intangibles (such as patents, trademarks, and copyrights)

Other Assets

- Deposits
- Restricted cash (noncurrent)
- Noncurrent receivables (including noncurrent portions of installments receivable and notes receivable)
- Noncurrent deferred tax asset
- Equipment to be disposed of

Total Noncurrent Assets

Total Assets

Liabilities & Stockholders' Equity

Current Liabilities

- Short-term notes payable
- Accounts payable
  - Accrued expenses (eg, salaries and wages, interest, and utilities)
  - Estimated current liabilities (eg, warranty expense)
  - Taxes payable (eg, income taxes, collected sales taxes, and withheld payroll taxes)
  - Unearned revenues (including rents or fees collected in advance)
- Dividends payable
  - Current portion of long-term debt (eg, noncurrent portions of finance lease obligations and notes and loans payable)

Total Current Liabilities

Noncurrent Liabilities

- Notes payable (net of current portion)
- Bonds payable
- Noncurrent deferred tax liability
  - Other noncurrent liabilities (eg, noncurrent portions of finance lease obligations and warranty obligations)
  - Deferred liabilities (eg, liabilities under pension plans, post-employment plans, and post- retirement plans)

Total Noncurrent Liabilities

Stockholders' Equity

- Contributed capital (APIC)
  - Preferred stock
  - Common stock (net of T/S at par)
  - Additional paid-in capital (APIC)
- Noncontrolling interest
- Earned capital
  - Retained earnings (appropriated and unappropriated)
  - Accumulated other comprehensive income (**OCI**) - (**DENT**)

Subtract

- Treasury stock at cost

Total Shareholders' Equity

Total Liabilities & Equity

Lecture 1.08 – GAAP Income Statement

ON-TIDe-N-OC

Roger Company
Statement of Earnings and Comprehensive Income
(Statement of Profit and Loss)
For the Year Ended December 31, 20X7

Sales		$2,000,000
Cost of sales		600,000
Gross profit		1,400,000
Less:		
Selling expenses	$340,000	
General & administrative expenses	260,000	
Depreciation Expense (impairment loss – public co)	100,000	700,000
Operating income (O)		700,000
Other income and (expense): (**Nonoperating**)		
Interest/Dividend income	10,000	
Interest expense/unusual and/or infrequent items	(20,000)	
Loss due to earthquake	(72,000)	
Gain on sale of equipment/Investments (imp loss–nonpublic)	30,000	(52000)
Income before income tax		648,000
Provision for income Tax (T):		
Current	150,000	
Deferred	40,000	190,000
Income from continuing operations **(I)**		$ 458,000
Gain (loss) from operations of **Discontinued component unit, (ASC 205)** *net of tax* of $30,000 **(De)**		45,000
Net income (N)		$503,000
Other Comprehensive income **(OCI) (DENT) (net of tax) (O)**		
Derivative cash flow hedge gain/loss		xxx
Excess adjustment of pension PBO and FV of plan assets at year-end		(xxx)
Net unrealized holding gains (AFS) arising during period		xxx
Translation adjustment of Foreign currency		xxx
Other comprehensive income		xxx
Comprehensive Income (C)		**$xxx,xxx**
Earnings per share:		
Income from continuing operations		$2.29
Income from Discontinued operations		.23
Net Income per share		$2.52

Lecture 1.09 – Financial Statement Analysis

Key Ratios

When users of financial statements examine them, they often compute certain key ratios to evaluate the company's performance. There are hundreds of different ratios that can be computed from a set of financial statements, and it isn't realistic to attempt to learn more than a handful. However, there are six that are tested regularly that we will discuss.

A couple of extremely common ratios used to determine the **ability of the company to cover its upcoming bills** are:

- Current ratio
- Quick (acid test) ratio

The current ratio is simply *current assets divided by current liabilities* at the balance sheet date. The quick ratio is *quick assets divided by current liabilities*. Quick assets are those that can be converted into cash rapidly, and normally include:

- Cash
- Marketable securities
- Accounts receivable

Other current assets, such as inventory and prepaid expenses, are not considered quick assets because they are difficult to convert to cash without substantial effort.

For example, assume a client had the following assets and liabilities at the balance sheet date:

Cash	100
Accounts receivable	50
Inventories	500
Trading securities	150
Machinery & equipment	180
Total assets	980
Accounts payable	60
Current portion of note payable	140
Long-term portion of note payable	400
Total liabilities	600

- Current assets = 100 + 50 + 500 + 150 = 800
- Quick assets = 100 + 50 + 150 = 300
- Current liabilities = 60 + 140 = 200
- Current ratio = 800 / 200 = 4 to 1
- Quick ratio = 300 / 200 = 1.5 to 1

Two ratios are used to measure the **efficient use of inventory:**

- Inventory turnover ratio
- Number of days' sales in average inventory

Inventory turnover ratio measures the number *of times the average inventory is sold. The formula is cost of* sales divided by average inventory. **Number of days' sales in average inventory** is a different way to measure the same thing. The formula is *average inventory divided by daily cost of sales.*

To complicate the question, the exam often doesn't provide cost of sales, and it must be computed using the standard formula:

Cost of sales = Beginning inventory + Purchases – Ending inventory

Also, it may not provide average inventory, which is computed as follows:

(Beginning Inventory + Ending Inventory) / 2

For example, assume the following facts are available:

Inventory, 1/1/X1	200
Inventory, 12/31/X1	300
Sales in 20X1	900
Purchases in 20X1	600
Working days in 20X1	250

- Cost of sales = 200 + 600 – 300 = 500
- Daily cost of sales = Cost of sales / Working days per year = 500 / 250 = 2
- Average inventory = (200 + 300) / 2 = 250
- Inventory turnover ratio = 500 / 250 = 2 times
- Number of days' sales in average inventory = 250 / 2 = 125 days

The final set of regularly-tested ratios measures the **efficiency of receivables**:

- Receivables turnover ratio
- Number of days' sales in average receivables

The **receivables turnover ratio** is *credit sales divided by average receivables*, and the **number of days' sales in average receivables** is *average receivables divided by daily credit sales*. The questions are usually straightforward.

For example, assume the following facts apply:

Accounts receivable, 1/1/X1	100
Accounts receivable, 12/31/X1	200
Cash sales in 20X1	400
Credit sales in 20X1	750
Working days in 20X1	250

- Average receivables = (Beginning A/R + Ending A/R) / 2 = (100 + 200) / 2 = 150
- Daily credit sales = Credit sales / Working days per year = 750 / 250 = 3
- Receivables turnover ratio = 750 / 150 = 5 times
- Number of days' sales in average receivables = 150 / 3 = 50 days

It is important to understand the ratios and their Purpose or Use.

Ratio	Formula	Purpose or Use
Liquidity – Measures of the company's short-term ability to pay its maturing obligations.		
Working Capital	Current assets – Current liabilities	Measures ability to meet current expenses
Current ratio	Current assets / Current liabilities	Measures short-term debt-paying ability
Quick or acid-test ratio	Cash, marketable securities, & receivables (net) / Current liabilities	Measures immediate short-term liquidity
Current cash debt coverage ratio	Net cash provided by operating activities / Average current liabilities	Measures a company's ability to pay off its current liabilities in a given year from its operations
Defensive interval ratio	Cash, marketable securities, & receivables (net) / Average daily expenditures	Measures the length of time a company can continue to pay its bills with its existing liquid assets.
Activity – Measures how effectively the company uses its assets		
Receivables turnover	Net credit sales / Average trade receivables (net)	Measures liquidity of receivables
# days' sales in average receivables	365* / Receivables Turnover	Measures number of days required to collect receivables
Inventory turnover	Cost of goods sold / Average inventory	Measures liquidity of inventory
# days' supply in average inventory	= 365* / Inventory Turnover **or** = Average (ending) inventory / Average daily cost of goods sold	Measures number of days required to sell inventory
Asset turnover	Net sales / Average total assets	Measures how efficiently assets are used to generate sales
Length of Operating Cycle	# days' sales in average receivables + # days' supply in average inventory	Measures operating efficiency
Cash conversion cycle	Days sales in A/R + Days in Inventory – Days of payables outstanding	Measures operating efficiency
Days of payables outstanding	Ending accounts payable / Cost of goods sold / 365*	Measures how efficiently payables are paid

**Candidates should use 365 days unless told to assume 360 days.*

Ratio	Formula	Purpose or Use
Profitability – Measures of the degree of success or failure of a given company or division for a given period of time.		
Profit margin on sales	Net income / Net sales	Measures net income generated by each dollar of sales
Rate of return on assets	Net income / Average total assets	Measures overall profitability of assets
Return on total assets	Net income + Interest Expense, net of tax / Average total assets	Measures overall profitability before interest and taxes
Rate of return on common stock equity (Return on equity)	(Net income – preferred dividends) / Average common stockholders' equity	Measures profitability of owners' investment
Earnings per share	(Net income – preferred dividends) / Weighted shares outstanding	Measures net income earned on each share of common stock
Price-earnings ratio	Market price of stock / Earnings per share	Measures the ratio of the market price per share to earnings per share
Dividend payout ratio	Cash dividends / Net income	Measures % of earnings distributed in the form of cash dividends
Coverage – Measures of the degree of protection for long-term creditors and investors.		
Debt to equity	Total debt / Stockholders' equity	Shows creditors the corporation's ability to sustain losses
Debt to total assets	Total debt / Total assets	Measures the percentage of total assets provided by creditors
Times interest earned	Income before interest expense & taxes / Interest expense	Measures ability to meet interest payments as they come due
Cash debt coverage ratio	Net cash provided by operating activities / Average total liabilities	Measures a company's ability to repay its total liabilities in a given year from its operations
Book value per share	Common stockholders' equity / Outstanding shares	Measures the amount each share would receive if the company were liquidated at the amounts reported on the balance sheet

Lecture 1.10 – Financial Statements for Pension Plans

Overview

Types of Pension Plans

A pension plan is an agreement between an employer and employee (the participant) to give the employee benefits once they retire. There are two main types of plans:

- **Defined Contribution Plan** – The employer and employee contribute specific amounts during the time of service, and the retired employee receives whatever sum these contributions and earnings produce (eg, 401k plan). Accounting for this type of plan is straightforward:
  - The company accrues the required contributions at the time services are rendered by employees, and reports pension expense.
  - Contributions are normally required by law to be paid before the due date of the tax return for the contribution to be deductible, so companies generally fund liabilities quickly.
- **Defined Benefit Plan** – The employer guarantees certain benefits to be paid to retired employees, and is responsible for setting aside sufficient amounts to fulfill these promises. This type of plan is far less common than a defined contribution plan these days, and accounting for them is much more complicated due to the following:
  - **Matching** – Pension expense must be recognized at the time of employee service, not when benefits are paid to retired employees.
  - **Estimation** – Costs are difficult to determine as they depend on the lifespan of employees, changes in wage rates, and the rates of return earned on investments. To compute pension expense, an *actuary* must first compute the present value (aka, actuarial present value) of the pension obligation three ways (ie, based on vested benefits, current wage rates, and future wage rates). Each computation represents the amount needed in a plan today to pay benefits to employees for service to date.

Note that the CPA Exam is no longer testing the calculation of pension cost/expense or the funded status of pension plans, so we won't be reviewing the accounting for these types of plans further. They are, however, still testing pension plan financial statements.

Required Financial Statements

There are two required financial statements (F/S) for defined contribution and defined benefit retirement plans. The purpose of these F/S is to provide information to users about the plan's ability to pay benefits.

- A statement of net assets available for benefits (as of fiscal year end)
- A statement of *changes* in net assets available for benefits (for the fiscal year)

In addition to the above F/S, a defined benefit pension plan will also provide statements or notes to the F/S regarding information about:

- The actuarial present value (APV) of accumulated plan benefits (ie, benefits expected to be paid)
- Changes in the APV of accumulated plan benefits

As with any set of F/S, **additional information** is required including:

- A statement of a plan's obligations
- A statement of changes in a plan's obligations
- Notes to the F/S

Statement of Net Assets Available for Benefits

To have funds to satisfy future retirement obligations, a pension plan must have sufficient plan assets (eg, securities, real estate). A statement of net assets available for benefits reports the net assets actually available to be used in the future to satisfy pension plan obligations. It can be thought of as the equivalent of the **balance sheet**.

The statement has two sections:

- **Plan assets** (includes any receivables related to plan assets)
  - The plan assets are generally reported at **fair value**.
  - Any investments considered to be **fully benefit-responsive**, however, are measured at **contract value**. "Fully benefit-responsive" means that the investment guarantees a certain value (ie, the contract value) to be paid to plan participants.
- **Plan liabilities** (excluding future obligations to employees)
  - Examples of liabilities include refunds for excess contributions or accrued amounts owed related to the assets.

The net assets available for benefits, when compared with the benefit obligations, indicates the financial funding status of the plan (ie, over/under-funded).

ABC Company 401(k) Plan
Statement of Net Assets Available for Benefits
Year Ended December 31, 20X1

Assets:	
Investments:	
Investments at fair value	$4,424,500
Investments at contract value	1,300,000
Total investments	5,724,500
Receivables:	
Receivable for employer contribution	10,000
Receivables for participant contribution	43,000
Notes receivable from participants	250,000
Total receivables	303,000
Total assets	6,027,500
Liabilities:	
Accrued expenses	7,500
Excess contributions payable	17,500
Total liabilities	25,000
Net assets available for benefits	$6,002,500

Statement of Changes in Net Assets Available for Benefits

A statement of *changes* in net assets available for benefits reconciles the beginning balance of the plan assets to the ending balance of the plan assets. The ending balance equals the net asset available for benefits reported on the statement of net assets available for benefits. This statement can be thought of as the equivalent to an **income statement**.

ABC Company 401(k) Plan **Statement of Changes In Net Assets Available for Benefits** *Year Ended December 31, 20X1*	
Additions:	
Investment income:	
Interest	$ 100,000
Dividends	50,000
Net appreciation in fair value*	200,000
	350,000
Interest income on notes receivable from participants	10,000
Contributions from:	
Employer	300,000
Participants	600,000
Rollovers	100,000
	1,000,000
Total additions	1,360,000
Deductions:	
Benefits paid	350,000
Administrative expenses	7,500
Total deductions	357,500
Net increase (decrease) in assets	1,002,500
Net assets available for benefits:	
Beginning of year	5,000,000
End of year	$6,002,500

*Note that changes in market value include:

- **Unrealized gains/losses** on investments acquired during the period or held for the entire period
- **Realized gains/losses** on sales of investments, net of unrealized gains/losses previously recognized

UWorld
YOUR WORLD OF LEARNING
ROGER
CPA Review

FAR 2 - Revenue Recognition

FAR 2 – Revenue Recognition

Table of Contents

Revenue Recognition

Lecture 2.01 – Revenue Recognition Overview & Step 1

Background

Until recently, U.S. GAAP recognized numerous revenue recognition principles. Some differed due to the industry, nature of the transactions, and a variety of other reasons. The FASB and the IASB developed a joint standard that replaces almost all of the individual revenue recognition standards that currently exist.

ASC 606, *Revenues from Contracts with Customers*, applies to all entities entering into **contracts with customers** unless the contracts are accounted for under another set of standards (eg, leases and insurance contracts).

Overview of Revenue Recognition Principles

The core revenue recognition principle consists of two components:

- Revenue is to be recognized upon the **transfer** of promised goods and services to customers; and
- The amount of revenue recognized represents the consideration the entity **expects to receive** in exchange for those goods and services.

Five-Step Process

Revenues are recognized by applying a *five-step process*:

1. Identify contracts with customers – Determine when:
   - An arrangement is considered a contract with customers.
   - Multiple contracts with the same customer should be combined and accounted for as a single contract.
2. Identify all separate performance obligations within each contract.
3. Determine the total consideration for the contract.
4. Allocate the total consideration among the separate performance obligations.
5. Recognize revenue, either:
   - *When* the entity has *satisfied* its performance obligations (eg, delivered products); or
   - *While* the entity is *satisfying* its performance obligations (eg, providing services).

1. Identify Contracts with Customers

There are two issues that must be addressed to determine if ASC 606 applies.

- For one, it must be determined that the counterparty to the transaction is a *customer*.
- Second, the arrangement must be a *legally binding contract*.

There is no requirement that the contract be in writing. It may be formal or informal, written or oral, and may even be implicit based on the normal manner in which the entities or individuals act (ie, in certain industries or specific circumstances).

A **customer** is defined as "a party that has contracted with an entity to obtain goods or services that are an output of the entity's ordinary activities in exchange for consideration."

A **contract** is an arrangement between two or more parties that creates legally enforceable rights and obligations. If either party can terminate the arrangement without penalty prior to either party's performance, it is not considered a contract. A contract will conform to four criteria:

- The parties have approved the provisions and have *committed to perform*.
- The *rights* in the contract and the *payment terms* can be identified.[1]
- The contract has commercial *substance*.
- *Collection is probable* (ie, customer has the ability and intent to pay).

If all of the criteria are met, the arrangement is a contract with a bona fide customer and will be accounted for using the 5-step process. The arrangement does not have to be reevaluated again unless there is a significant change in the facts and circumstances (eg, collection becomes unlikely) or the arrangement is modified.

Revenue Arrangements that are Not Contracts with Customers

An entity may enter into an arrangement that has some of the characteristics of a revenue-related contract in that it involves providing goods/services in exchange for compensation. It may not, however, meet all of the criteria. As long as the arrangement does not meet the criteria, all amounts received will be recognized as a *liability*.

Cash	XX	
Deferred revenue		XX

The arrangement will be reevaluated every reporting period to determine whether it has met the criteria, at which time the method of accounting will be changed to the 5-step process.

If the criteria are never met, the liability is *derecognized* and treated as *revenue* when *consideration* received from the customer is *nonrefundable and one of the following* scenarios applies:

Deferred revenue	XX	
Revenue		XX

Scenario 1	Scenario 2	Scenario 3
• The entity has *no remaining obligations*, and • All, or substantially *all*, of the *consideration* has been *received*.	• The arrangement has been *terminated*.	• Consideration received relates to *goods/services*, the control of which, has been *transferred*; and • The entity has stopped transferring goods/services, and neither has an obligation to, nor intends to, provide any additional goods/services.

Combining Contracts

In general, each contract is considered a separate accounting unit; thus, each contract is evaluated and accounted for separately. There are circumstances in which an arrangement with a customer appears to be numerous contracts but in substance they are equivalent to a single contract. This

[1] FASB separates rights and payment terms into two separate criteria. Since rights and obligations go hand-in-hand, we combined them to reduce the number of criteria to remember.

may be done for a variety of reasons, but most provide the seller with the opportunity to accelerate or delay the recognition of revenue.

Contracts should be **combined** if one or more of the following criteria are met:

- Contracts are negotiated as a **single package** with a single commercial objective.
- **Price** to be paid in one contract **depends on** the price or performance of **other contracts** (multiple deliverables).
- Goods/services promised in the contracts are a **single performance obligation**.

Package with Single Objective

In some cases, two or more *contracts are negotiated as a package with a single objective*. These contracts will be combined and accounted for as if they were a single contract.

For example, a manufacturer may purchase several pieces of equipment from a single supplier, each on a separate contract, with all the equipment intended to be part of an assembly line. Assume none of the equipment will be used for any other purpose and that the assembly line requires the use of all the equipment. Since the buyer doesn't have resources that can be readily put to use until they receive all of the equipment, the contracts should be combined.

Price Depends on Other Contracts

When multiple deliverables are involved, a seller could accelerate the recognition of revenue by placing all items to be delivered in the current period into one contract at inflated prices, and all items to be delivered in a subsequent period into a separate contract at discounted prices. Thus, when the consideration agreed upon for one contract is affected by the consideration agreed upon for another contract, the contracts should be combined and accounted for as a single contract.

For example, an entity may be selling two identical machines using separate contracts, each of which has a normal sales price of $100,000. One may be scheduled for delivery in the current fiscal period and the other scheduled for delivery in the next fiscal period.

The seller may attempt to accelerate revenue recognition by establishing a contract price of $150,000 for the machine to be delivered in the current period and only $50,000 for the one to be delivered in the next period.

The seller would not likely sell the second machine for $50,000 if the first one was not sold to the same customer for $150,000. Thus, the prices are interdependent, the contracts would be combined, and the two machines will be accounted for as two identical performance obligations that are part of a single contract. The total consideration of $200,000 will be allocated $100,000 to each machine.

Single Performance Obligation

Contracts will also be combined when *the goods/services called for in two or more contracts constitute a single performance obligation*. This would be the case if the customer is unable to benefit from the goods/services received in one contract without the goods/services in the other.

For example, assume an entity was to sell the shell of a piece of equipment to a customer in one contract and the working parts of that equipment in another. This arrangement will be evaluated to determine if the customer can benefit from one without the other.

If the equipment is not unique, the customer may be able to acquire all of the working parts for the equipment from another supplier and could benefit from receiving just the shell. Since the customer could benefit from one without the other, they represent distinct performance obligations, with revenue recognized as each performance obligation is satisfied.

If, however, the working parts were not readily available to the customer from another supplier, they would be considered a single performance obligation and the contracts would be combined.

In some cases, contracts having similar characteristics may be combined into a **portfolio** and treated as a single contract. This would be done to reduce the cost and burden associated with doing a lot of contracts, especially if they are not individually material.

Contract Modifications

When a contract is modified, the nature of the modification will dictate the accounting treatment to be applied.

- Some contract modifications are treated as *new, separate contracts*.
- Others are considered effective *terminations* of the existing contract, *replacing* it with a *new contract*.
- The remaining modifications are treated as an *adjustment to an existing contract*.
- Some modifications represent some *combination* of these alternatives.

A modification may be in the form of an amendment, a change order, or a variation. It may be written, oral, or implicit from the behavior of the parties. When a modification involves a change in the consideration in an unknown amount, the change will be estimated using the same approaches that are used to estimate variable consideration (discussed later).

In addition, the estimate of the change in price is subject to the constraint on estimates of variable consideration. It requires that it be probable that, when the uncertainty is resolved, there will be no significant reversal of the cumulative amount of revenue that has already been recognized. In applying the constraint, the likelihood and magnitude of a potential reversal are considered.

New, Separate Contract

A contract modification is considered a new, separate contract when the modification calls for an *increase* in *both* the *scope* and *price* (ie, for additional distinct goods/services). A modification of this sort is accounted for by applying the 5-step process.

Cancellation with New Contract

A contract modification is treated as a cancellation of the existing contract accompanied by a new contract *when the performance obligations that remain unsatisfied are distinct* from those that have been satisfied up through the date of the modification. Total consideration for the new contract will be equal to:

- The remainder of the consideration from the original contract that has not yet been recognized, plus
- Any additional consideration resulting from the modification.

The total consideration for the new contract will be allocated among all remaining performance obligations, including those from the original contract and any new ones added. The entity will use the same 5-step process for recognizing revenue on the new contract.

Adjustment to Existing Contract

When remaining goods/services that are yet to be delivered do not represent distinct performance obligations, they are combined into a single performance obligation that is considered partially satisfied. Total consideration will consist of the original amount combined with any adjustments resulting from the modification. This will be applied to the single performance obligation, including the changes that result from the modification.

- If the contract qualifies for revenue recognition while the performance obligation is being met, revenue is recognized in the current year on a catch-up basis. The amount of revenue that would have been earned if the contract had originally been analyzed with the modification included is reduced by revenues recognized to date, with the difference recognized in the current period.
- If the contract does not qualify for revenue recognition while the performance obligation is being satisfied, balance sheet accounts will be adjusted for additional amounts received and costs incurred; however, no revenue will be recognized until the single performance obligation has been satisfied.

Lecture 2.02 – Revenue Recognition Step 2

2. Identify Separate Performance Obligations

A contract will have at least one, and often more than one, **performance obligation**, which is an enforceable promise to transfer goods/services to a customer. The goods/services may be either:

- A single good/service or a bundle of goods/services; or
- A series of distinct goods/services that are substantially the same with the same pattern of transfer (eg, monthly cleaning service).

Performance obligations are identified at the inception of the contract. They may be explicitly stated in the contract or may be implicit due to the entity's business practices. For example, the customer expects a car wash with her oil change because the dealership customarily provides such service along with oil changes.

Performance obligations are identified at the inception of the contract. Examples include:

- Selling goods produced or purchased by the entity
- Reselling rights to goods/services that were purchased by the entity
- Performing a task that is agreed upon
- Being prepared to provide a good/service or making goods/services available to the customer with transfer at the customer's discretion
- Arranging for another party to provide goods/services to a customer
- Providing the rights to future goods/services to a customer who may, in turn, resell or otherwise provide them to their customers
- Creating an asset on behalf of a customer
- Granting licenses
- Granting options to purchase additional goods/services

An activity that does not result in the transfer of goods/services to a customer is **not** a performance obligation.

Individual performance obligations are either identified as distinct performance obligations or are combined with other performance obligations until such combination constitutes a distinct performance obligation. **Distinct performance obligations** are those that meet *two criteria:*

- The customer must be able to **benefit from the good or service on its own** or together using other resources that are readily available to the customer; and
- The promise to transfer the good or service is **separately identified from other promises** in the contract.

A good or service can be *used on its own* if it can be consumed, sold for more than scrap, or used for economic benefit. Resources are readily available if they are sold separately, by the same seller or others, or if the customer has previously acquired them. For example:

- If a furniture dealer was selling a kitchen table and a living room sofa to a customer, the kitchen table could be used without the sofa and vice versa. Thus, they would each represent a distinct performance obligation.
- If the two items were a unique tabletop and a base that was designed exclusively for that tabletop, neither the tabletop nor the base could be used without the other. Thus, neither

would be a distinct performance obligation but, on a combined basis, they make up a single distinct performance obligation.

- If the tabletop was a standard size and the customer could acquire a base from a variety of vendors, the tabletop and the base would each be a distinct performance obligation.

Promises are *separately identifiable* in a contract if goods/services are promised separately as opposed to promising to deliver goods/services on a combined basis, with promised goods/services being used as inputs. For example:

- Promises may be made to deliver a computer and an operating system.
  - The intent may be to use the operating system in the computer.
  - Since an operating system could be acquired from a different vendor and installed into the computer, and the operating system could be installed in a computer purchased from a different vendor, the computer and the operating system are separately identifiable and would be distinct performance obligations.
- A promise may be made to deliver a computer with an operating system installed.
  - Since the contract combines the computer and the operating system into a single promise, the promises are not separately identifiable.
  - Even though the operating system could be used with another computer and the computer with another operating system, since they are not separately identifiable, they are not distinct performance obligations.

Other factors may indicate that promises are separately identifiable:

- The entity does not need to integrate the goods/services with others that are part of the contract.
- Other goods/services are not significantly modified by the good or service in the contract.
- Goods/services are neither highly dependent on, nor highly interrelated to, other goods/services in the contract.

When goods/services are not material, it is not necessary to determine if they constitute performance obligations. In addition, an entity may elect to consider shipping and handling costs that are incurred after the control of goods has been transferred as a cost of fulfilling a promise, rather than as a separate promise.

Warranties

Warranties can be accounted for in a variety of ways and the circumstances surrounding the warranty will determine which accounting approach is most appropriate.

Warranties may be *purchased separately*. This will often be true when the customer is purchasing an item that has no warranty, a limited warranty with significant gaps in coverage, a warranty that ends too quickly, or some combination.

- The price of the warranty is generally either established or negotiated separately.
- The warranty is a distinct performance obligation.

Some products *provide warranties* without requiring an additional or separate payment. The cost of the warranty is included in the purchase price of the goods to which the warranty relates. Some of these warranties are *assurance-type* warranties, while others are *service-type* warranties.

An **assurance-type warranty** protects the customer from obtaining a product that is not capable of performing at the level that the seller indicated that it would. These warranties are generally only available from the seller. To the seller, such a warranty is a contingent liability.

- A liability will be incurred if the product does not perform.
- Unless this is a unique product to the seller, the seller should be able to estimate:
  - The frequency with which these products will not perform at an acceptable level; and
  - The average cost incurred to repair or replace the product when it does not perform acceptably.
- It is very likely that there will be some units that will not perform acceptably.
  - Even entities with outstanding internal control experience some human error.
  - In addition, some units are bound to have parts fail or other problems.
- As a result, an assurance-type warranty represents a **contingent liability** that is **probable and estimable** and should be accrued in the period incurred, generally the period of sale.

A **service-type warranty** generally provides a customer with repairs in the form of parts and labor in addition to making certain that the product performs as promised. Service-type warranties may be required by law, may extend beyond the reasonable amount of time it should take to evaluate the product's performance, or may provide services that extend beyond making certain that the asset performs as expected.

- A service-type warranty is a separately identifiable promise in a contract; and
- It is a distinct performance obligation.

To illustrate an *assurance-type warranty*, assume a company sells drilling equipment at an average sales price of $40,000, which it acquires at a cost of $25,000. The seller provides a warranty to assure the buyer that the drill will perform to a certain standard and be suitable for drilling through certain types of materials.

- The company has been manufacturing these drills for several years and they are confident in their manufacturing process, the quality of the materials used, and the quality of its labor force.
- Despite that, human error, the occasional faulty material, or some other factor causes 1 out of every 100 units to fail and require replacement.
- At a cost of $25,000 per drill, a loss of 1 out of every 100 will cost the company $250 per drill on average.

The sale of a single drill will be recorded as follows:

Cash (or A/R)	40,000	
Sales Revenue		40,000
Cost of sales	25,000	
Inventory		25,000
Warranty expense	250	
Estimated warranty liability		250

To illustrate a *service-type warranty*, assume a company sells washing machines to the public. To stimulate sales, the company provides a three-year warranty that basically will repair the machine, regardless of the cause of the malfunction, for a period of three years.

- The washing machine has a sales price, including the warranty, of $1,200. Although the company does not sell their machines without the warranty, an appliance store within a mile of the company's store does sell the same washing machine for $950 on an "as-is" basis.
- The washing machine costs the company $600.
- The company does sell 3-year service contracts, comparable to the warranties, to owners of washing machines purchased from other dealers at a sales price of $250.
    - The company estimates that it costs approximately $175 to service the warranty.
    - Both the washing machine without the warranty and the warranty are distinct performance obligations.

Since both the washing machine and the service-type warranty are distinct performance obligations, the revenue of $1,200 will be allocated based on their relative standalone prices. The revenue allocated to the washing machine will be recognized upon satisfaction of the performance obligation (ie, the point of sale). The revenue allocated to the warranty will be recognized while the performance obligation is being satisfied over the three-year term.

Cash (or A/R)	1,200	
Sales		950
Deferred revenue – warranty		250
Cost of sales	600	
Inventory		600

Option to Purchase Additional Goods or Services

In some cases, a contract with a customer may include an option to purchase additional goods or services at a discount. That discount may be comparable to a discount that is available to a wide range of individuals, including customers and noncustomers alike. This would *not* be considered a distinct performance obligation since customers who receive the discount when making the purchase are not getting anything of value that is not available to others who make no purchase.

When a discount of this sort exceeds what is available to noncustomers, the customer is receiving something of value (ie, a material right); thus, both the goods sold and the discount represent *distinct performance obligations*. Therefore, the gross sales price will be allocated between the sale of the merchandise in the current period and the discount on future purchases.

- **The value of the merchandise** will be equal to what it would be sold for if there was no discount on future purchases or any other benefits.
- **The value of the future discounts** will be based on an estimate of the discounts expected to be applied. The estimate will be adjusted to its present value since at least a portion of the discounts will be applied in future periods.

Revenue allocated to the sale of goods will be recognized upon satisfaction of the performance obligation, at the point of sale. Revenue allocated to the future will be recognized while the performance obligation is being satisfied in the pattern in which the discounts are estimated to be taken, or when it expires if it's a discount voucher, for example.

As part of a contract for the sale of a Product for $100, the entity gives the customer a 40% discount voucher for future purchases up to $100 that is good for 30 days. The entity is also offering a 10% discount to all customers for the next 30 days. The 10% discount is not combinable with the 40% discount voucher. Since all customers will receive a 10% discount during the next 30 days, only the additional 30% discount constitutes a separate performance obligation.

The entity estimates that there is 80% chance that a customer will redeem the voucher and will, on average, purchase $50 of additional products. The standalone selling prices and the resulting allocation of the $100 transaction price are calculated as follows:

Performance Obligation	Standalone Selling Price	
Product	$100	
Discount voucher	12	($50 avg. × 30% disc. × 80% probability)
Total	$112	

Performance Obligation	Allocated Transaction Price	
Product	$89	Recognize when control transfers (100/112 × 100)
Discount voucher	11	Recognize when redeemed/expired (12/112 × 100)
Total	$100	

Cash	100	
Revenue		89
Deferred Revenue		11

(ASC 606, Example 49)

Nonrefundable Prepayments

Generally, when prepayments are received (eg, customer buys a gift card), the entity should record a contract liability for the customer's unexercised rights to goods/services. However, when those prepayments are nonrefundable, they may be taken into income to the extent the rights created by those payments are not expected to be redeemed by the customer (aka, breakage). Such payments are recognized:

- As revenue in proportion to the pattern of rights exercised by customers if **breakage is expected.**
- As revenue when the likelihood that the customer will exercise the rights becomes remote if **breakage is not expected**.
- **As a liability** when the amounts are required to be remitted to a third party (eg, a government agency due to unclaimed property laws).

Assume $1,000 of gift cards were sold in Year 1 and the entity expects only 80% ($800) to be redeemed. Since the entity expects 20% breakage, it will recognize revenue for the breakage as the gift cards are redeemed:

	Redeemed	**+ Breakage**	**= Revenue Recognized**
Year 1	$600	600/800 × 200 = 150	750
Year 2	<u>$200</u>	200/800 × 200 = 50	<u>250</u>
Total	$800	$200	1,000

If, however, the entity expected all the gift cards to be redeemed, they would wait to recognize the revenue on unredeemed gift cards until there is only a remote possibility of redemption.

Lecture 2.03 – Revenue Recognition Step 3

3. Determine the Transaction Price

The transaction price is the amount of consideration that the entity *expects* to be entitled to in exchange for transferring goods/services in a satisfactory manner, excluding amounts to be collected on behalf of others, such as sales taxes. There are many factors that will affect the amount of revenue that is recognized.

- Whether the reporting entity is a **principal or an agent** in the transaction will affect whether the gross or net amount of revenues is recognized.
- **Variable consideration** (eg, discounts, rebates, etc.) may be estimated and included or may be excluded and recognized in the period earned.
- **Time value of money** – Amounts may be reported at their present values when there are potentially lengthy periods between satisfaction of the performance obligations and the transfer of funds.
- There may be **nonmonetary consideration** (eg, shares of stock) requiring measurement.
- The seller may be **providing consideration to the customer**.

Principal Versus Agent Considerations

When more parties than a seller and a buyer are involved in revenue-related transactions involving contracts with customers, the roles of the parties must be understood to determine the amount of revenue to be recognized by each party.

- When the seller is a **principal** in the transaction, the entire amount of revenue will be recognized and amounts paid to third parties will be recognized as expenses or as a component of cost of sales.
- When the seller is an **agent**, only the net amount of revenue to be retained after paying the principal is recognized.
  - A principal has the obligation to provide goods/services.
  - An agent has the obligation to arrange for another party, the principal, to provide goods/services.

To distinguish between a principal and an agent, a significant factor to consider is **who has control** of the goods/services that are the subject of the contract before they are transferred to the customer.

- A principal controls goods/services before the transfer and may either satisfy the performance obligation or may engage another to do so.
- The fact that a party obtains control of the goods and immediately transfers them to a customer does not constitute control.
- A principal has control of:
  - Goods or assets obtained from another party and transferred to the customer
  - Rights to a service to be provided by another party at the direction of the principal
  - Goods/services obtained from other parties to combine with other goods/services to satisfy a performance obligation (eg, chocolate and wine combined to create a gift basket)
- Indications of who has control of goods/services prior to transfer to the customer include:
  - *Primary responsibility* for providing goods/services to the customer

- *Risk of loss* associated with inventory both before delivery to the customer and after delivery to a customer, such as when a customer returns goods
- *Authority to set prices* for the goods/services

Similar to the relationship between a principal and an agent, a seller may collect funds on behalf of a third party, such as when a sale is subject to state sales tax, which is collected by the seller and remitted to the taxing authority. These funds are not considered part of the consideration in a contract.

Variable Consideration

Variable consideration may result from discounts or rebates provided to buyers; credits, price concessions, or incentives; performance bonuses; or penalties. Variable consideration may also result from contingencies, such as the occurrence or nonoccurrence of a future event, or a performance bonus based on achieving a milestone.

Variable consideration is a factor when either:

- The customer has a valid expectation that the seller will accept less than the contract amount in the form of a discount, rebate, refund, credit, or other price concession; or
- Facts indicate that the seller intended, as of the inception of the contract, to make a price concession.

Variable consideration is estimated at the inception of a contract and is included in the total consideration to be earned through the satisfaction of all performance obligations. The amount will be estimated, applying one of two approaches:

- Under the **expected value approach**, different amounts that will be obtained based on various levels of performance will each be assigned a probability with the total of the probabilities equaling 100%. Each amount is multiplied by the probability of achieving it and the total is the expected amount of variable consideration.
- Under the **most likely amount approach**, different outcomes are each assigned a probability such that the total of the probabilities equals 100% and the outcome with the greatest probability of occurrence is assumed to be the amount that is to be recognized.

In a period in which cash receipts exceed the expected amount, the excess is reported as a refund liability.

The standard establishes a **constraint** on the amount of variable consideration that can be recognized. The constraint is designed to prevent an entity from recognizing revenues in one period only to be required to reverse it in a subsequent period. In applying the constraint, the entity should consider the likelihood and the magnitude of a potential reversal. Factors that increase the likelihood or the magnitude of a **potential reversal** include:

- Amounts that are susceptible to factors, such as market volatility, that are beyond the control of the entity.
- Uncertainties that are not likely resolved for long periods.
- Amounts due cannot be reliably anticipated due to a lack of experience or having experience that is not predictive.
- There has been the practice of making price concessions or changing terms and conditions.
- There is a wide range of possible consideration amounts.

Variable consideration is required to be reassessed each period such that the transaction price at the end of any given period reflects the circumstances at that time.

Time Value of Money

The time value of money is considered when measuring consideration if either the buyer or seller obtains a significant financing benefit. Such benefit may be due to a provision of the contract or because of a time lag (ie, generally more than one year) between performance and payment.

Financing is considered significant when there is a difference between the amount of consideration and the cash price for the goods/services. The effect will depend on the time lag between performance and payment and prevailing interest rates.

There is no financing component included in measuring consideration if:

- The customer paid in advance and the timing of performance is at the discretion of the buyer;
- Variable consideration is significant and is contingent on factors outside the control of the entity; or
- The difference between the amount of consideration and the cash price for the goods/services is due to factors other than financing and the amount is commensurate with some factor such as protection from nonperformance.

When the time between performance and payment is expected to be one year or less, no financing component is required.

When a financing component is included, it may be calculated using the discount rate that is applicable for separate financing transactions between the parties, or the rate at which the present value of the consideration is equal to its equivalent cash price.

- The financing component is recognized as interest income or expense, separate from revenues from customers; and
- Interest income or expense is only recognized to the extent that a contract asset or liability has been recognized.

Noncash Consideration

Noncash consideration (eg, shares of stock) is measured at *fair value.*

- When the fair value is not determinable, it will be measured by reference to the standalone selling price of goods/services exchanged.
- Resources contributed by the customer to assist the entity in satisfying a performance obligation is accounted for as noncash consideration if the entity obtains control.

Consideration Paid to a Customer

A seller may make a payment to a customer in cash, or in the form of a credit, coupon, or voucher.[2] It may also be paid to another party purchasing the entity's goods/services from the customer, such as in the form of a rebate.

When consideration paid to a customer is in exchange for distinct goods/services, it is accounted for as an asset or expense, as appropriate.

---

[2] Consideration payable to the customer may also include equity, which is accounted for under ASC 718 as share-based payments (discussed in a later section).

- If the amount paid exceeds the value of the distinct goods/services, the excess reduces the transaction price.
- If the value of the goods/services cannot be determined, the entire payment reduces the transaction price.

A reduction to the transaction price is recognized at the *later of*:

- The recognition of revenue resulting from the transaction, or
- The payment of the consideration to the customer or the promise to do so.

An entity enters a contract with Walmart to sell them $20 million of their products, but Walmart wants a $2 million payment upfront to reconfigure shelf space. The $2 million payment reduces the $20 million transaction price to $18 million since Walmart isn't providing a good or service in exchange for the $2 million. If the goods are to be transferred over 10 months, revenue of $1.8 million [($20M -$2M)/10] will be recognized for each delivery.

Nonrefundable Upfront Fees

Nonrefundable upfront fees are often intended as compensation to the seller for an activity performed near the inception of the contract. Since amounts received are only recognized in income when a performance obligation has been satisfied, upfront fees are generally considered part of the total consideration and are allocated among distinct performance obligations.

For example, a health club membership fee is charged to cover the administrative costs of setting up the contract. The customer does not obtain anything of value at this point. Since the value to customer is the use of the facility, the membership fee is recognized over the course of the contract.

Sale with Right of Return

Goods may be sold under terms that allow the customer to return the goods for a refund. In this case, the entity recognizes revenue in an amount equal to the portion that is expected to be retained by the entity.

- Estimated amount of returns are recognized as a *refund liability*.
- Right to recover goods from the customer is recognized as an *asset.*

Assume an entity sells the customer $100 of goods and they have 90 days to return the merchandise. If the seller expects that 20% will be returned, they will record:

Cash (or A/R)	80	
Right to recover goods	20	
Sales revenue		80
Refund liability		20

Lecture 2.04 – Revenue Recognition Step 4

4. Allocate Transaction Price to Performance Obligations in the Contract

The total consideration from a contract is allocated to all performance obligations in proportion to their standalone selling prices. The **standalone selling price** is the price the entity sells a good or service for separately in comparable transactions. If they sell it separately, we have an *observable price*, so we can use that price as the best evidence of the standalone price.

However, if they don't sell them separately, then we must estimate the standalone selling price (as of date of the *inception* of the contract) using one of the following *three approaches*:

- **Adjusted market assessment –** Evaluate the market, see what a customer might be willing to pay or also look at competitors.
- **Expected cost plus a margin –** Forecast expected costs and add an appropriate profit margin for that good or service.
- **Residual value method** – Use only if either:
  - Some goods/services are sold for different amounts to different customers; or
  - The good/service has not previously been sold as a standalone product or service and a price has not yet been set.

Discounts in General

Discounts, equal to difference between the total of standalone sales prices and total consideration, are generally allocated proportionately among performance obligations. However, discounts may be allocated to some but not all performance obligations when four criteria apply:

- Each distinct good or service in the contract is also sold as a standalone good or service on a regular basis;
- Some distinct goods and services are also sold as a bundle at a discount;
- The discount on the contract is comparable to the discount on the distinct goods and services sold in a bundle at a discount; and
- If allocated to some but not all performance obligations, the residual approach is not applied until after the discounts have been allocated.

An entity enters a contract to provide a software license, installation, and three years of tech support as a bundle for $70,000. They use the following information to determine standalone prices:

- The entity would normally sell the software license for $50,000.
- They don't normally sell the installation, but their competitors sell it for $10,000.
- They also don't have a price for the tech support. They estimate that it will cost them $32,000 and they would like to make a profit of 25% on top of that, so the standalone selling price for tech support is $40,000 ($32,000 × 1.25).

Thus, the total of the standalone selling prices is $100,000. Since the entity is selling the bundle for $70,000, this represents a $30,000 discount. Also, there is no observable evidence that indicates that the discount relates to any particular product; therefore, the discount will be allocated by allocating the total revenue to the different products based on their relative standalone selling prices.

Product	Method Used	Standalone Selling Price	Allocation Calculation	Price Allocation
Software license	Observable price	$50,000	50/100 × 70,000	$35,000
Installation	Adjusted market assessment	10,000	10/100 × 70,000	7,000
3 years tech support	Expected cost plus margin	40,000	40/100 × 70,000	28,000
Total		$100,000		$70,000

Now assume all the same facts as in the last example, except that there is no observable price nor another estimated price for the tech support. In this case, the price for the tech support will simply be the remaining amount of the transaction price after subtracting the two prices that are known/estimated.

Product	Method Used	Standalone Selling Price	Calculation	Price Allocation
Software license	Observable price	$50,000		$50,000
Installation	Adjusted market assessment	10,000		10,000
3 years tech support	Residual value	XX,XXX	70K – 50K – 10K	10,000
Total		$70,000		$70,000

Discounts in a Multiple Element Arrangement

In a *multiple element arrangement*, if a bundle of goods is sold at a discount and is also included in a bigger bundle with a discount that exceeds the one on the smaller bundle, the discounts are allocated on a **step basis**.

- **Step 1** – First, the discount that applies to the smaller bundle will be allocated among the items in that bundle.
- **Step 2** – Next, the remaining discount is allocated among all items using:
  - The standalone sales prices for those items that were not included in the smaller bundle, and
  - The *adjusted* standalone sales prices (ie, standalone sales price – first discount) of the items in the smaller bundle.

There is another store that sells **recreational vehicles**. There is a water package that consists of a jet ski with a normal standalone sales price of $2,900 and a motorized raft with a normal standalone sales price of $3,600. They can be purchased in a bundle for $5,525. In addition, they sell a small off-road motorcycle with a normal standalone sales price of $2,800 and a snowmobile that has a normal standalone sales price of $3,000; these items are being bundled as the off-road package for a total of $5,220. The store also sells a larger bundle, consisting of all four items in their sportsman's package at a total cost of $10,100.

To determine how the $10,100 will be allocated, the discounts will be allocated on a step basis. The water package includes the jet ski with a normal standalone sales price of $2,900, and a motorized raft with a normal standalone sales price of $3,600, for a total of $6,500. With a bundle price of $5,525, there is a discount associated with that bundle of $975, which is 15% of the total of the standalone sales prices. As a result, the discount on the jet ski will be 15% × $2,900, or $435, resulting in an adjusted standalone sales price of $2,465. The motorized raft will have a discount of 15% × $3,600, or $540, resulting in an adjusted sales price of $3,060 and a total for the water package of $2,465 + $3,060, or $5,525. Alternatively:

Water Package				
Product	**Standalone Selling Price**	**Allocation Calculation**	**Price Allocation (Step 1)**	**Discount**
Jet ski	$2,900	2,900/6,500 × 5,525	$2,465	$435
Motorized raft	3,600	3,600/6,500 × 5,525	3,060	$540
Total	$6,500		$5,525	$975

The off-road package consists of the motorcycle at $2,800 and the snowmobile at $3,000, for a total of $5,800. The bundle price is $5,220, there is a discount of $580, which is 10%. Thus, the discount allocated to the motorcycle will be 10% × $2,800, or $280, resulting in an adjusted price of $2,520. The discount allocated to the snowmobile will be 10% × $3,000, or $300, resulting in an adjusted standalone sales price of $2,700. The total for the off-road package is $2,520 + $2,700, or $5,220. Alternatively:

Off-road Package				
Product	**Standalone Selling Price**	**Allocation Calculation**	**Price Allocation (Step 1)**	**Discount**
Motorcycle	$2,800	2,800/5,800 × 5,220	$2,520	$280
Snowmobile	3,000	3,000/5,800 × 5,220	2,700	$300
Total	$5,800		$5,220	$580

The two packages combined would then be $5,525 + $5,220, or $10,745. Since the package can be purchased for $10,100, there is a discount of $645; this is 6% of $10,745. Thus, the additional discount to be allocated to the jet ski would be 6% × $2,465, or $148, adjusting the price to $2,317. The discount allocated to the motorized raft would be $6% × $3,060, or $184, resulting in an adjusted priced of $2,876. The discount allocated to the motorcycle would be 6% × $2,520, or $151, resulting in an adjusted price of $2,369. The discount allocated to the snowmobile would be 6% × $2,700, or $162, for an adjusted price of $2,538. Thus, the total consideration would be allocated as follows:

Sportsman's Package				
Product	**Adjusted Standalone SP**	**Allocation Calculation**	**Price Allocation (Step 2)**	**Discount**
Jet ski	$2,465	2,465/10,745 × 10,100	2,317	$148
Motorized raft	3,060	3,060/10,745 × 10,100	2,876	184
Motorcycle	2,520	2,520/10,745 × 10,100	2,369	151
Snowmobile	2,700	2,700/10,745 × 10,100	2,538	162
Total	$10,745		$10,100	$645

Allocation of Variable Consideration

Variable consideration may relate to the entire contract or only part of it, such as one or more performance obligations or, more specifically, one or more goods/services. For example, variable consideration:

- May relate to a single performance obligation, such as a bonus for timely performance.
- May be an increase in the cost to be incurred in satisfying a performance obligation.

Variable costs/revenues (ie, consideration) are generally required to be allocated to all performance obligations on the same basis as the allocation of other consideration. However, they may be allocated to specific performance obligations or specific goods/services if two criteria apply:

- The variable payment is associated with
  - The entity's *efforts* to satisfy a specific performance obligation or to deliver a distinct good/service, or
  - The *outcome* from satisfying such obligation.
- Allocation of the entire amount of variable consideration is **consistent** with the objectives of the standard with regard to the allocation of transaction price to performance obligations (ie, the amount allocated is the amount the entity expects to be entitled to for that performance obligation).

For example, it would be appropriate to not allocate the variable consideration to the entire contract when the contract calls for granting the use of:

- License A for $800 (fixed amount) and
- License B for 5% royalties based on the customer's sales related to the license (variable consideration). The royalties are expected to amount to $1,000.

Allocating the entire amount of variable consideration to only License B makes sense because it is (1) related to the use of the license (ie, the outcome) and (2) the amount represents the consideration the entity expects to receive for that particular performance obligation.

Price changes are dealt with similarly to variable consideration. The same criteria as applied to variable consideration applies for purposes of allocating a price change to a specific performance obligation or good/service, but not the entire contract. Otherwise, they are allocated to all distinct performance obligations on the same basis as total consideration using standalone selling prices.

- Changes to standalone selling prices are not considered.
- May result in allocation to performance obligations already satisfied. Portions allocated to performance obligations already satisfied are taken into income immediately.

Lecture 2.05 – Revenue Recognition Step 5 & Disclosures

5. Recognizing Revenue as Performance Obligations are Satisfied

Revenue is recognized when a performance obligation is satisfied or, in some circumstances, while it is being satisfied.

A performance obligation is considered satisfied when the entity has transferred the promised goods/services to the customer, which occurs **at a point in time** when the *customer has control* of those goods/services.

A **customer has control** over goods and services when the customer can:

- Direct the use of the goods/services,
- Prevent others from benefitting from them, and
- Obtain benefits from the goods/services in the form of cash flows (ie, inflows or savings).

When **control is uncertain**, other factors to consider include whether customer has:

- Legal title to goods
- Physical possession of the goods
- Significant risks and rights associated with ownership of the goods
- Accepted the goods

Revenue may be recognized while the performance obligation is being satisfied if the goods/services promised are transferred to the customer **over time**. This is determined at the inception of the contract based on the existence of one of three conditions:

- The customer consumes the goods/services as they are being delivered.
- The customer has control over the asset while it is being created or enhanced.
- The entity has no alternative use for the goods/services and is entitled to payment for performance completed to date.

Consuming Goods or Services Upon Delivery

Certain performance obligations, by their natures, are being consumed as they are being delivered. This is generally true of recurring services being provided to a customer, such as cleaning services.

Sometimes it is hard to determine whether goods/services are being consumed as they are being delivered. In such cases, one should ask: if another entity were engaged to complete the performance obligation, would they need to substantially reperform what the original entity completed? If yes, the customer has not been consuming the goods/services. If not, then the customer has been consuming the goods/services upon delivery.

Customer Control Over Asset

In determining whether the customer controls an asset while it is being created or enhanced, the same criteria that are used to determine whether control has been transferred to the customer should be applied.

Lack of Alternative Use and Entitlement to Payment

An asset is considered to not have an alternative use to the seller if the seller would be required to dispose of it at a substantial cost. For example:

- The entity would not be able to transfer the goods/services to another customer (perhaps due to unique design specifications), or they would incur a significant loss to do so.
- Significant costs would be incurred to rework the asset in order to apply it to another use.

Assuming the contract was terminated for a reason other than the entity's inability to complete performance, the entity must also be entitled to payment for work completed to date. The amount should reflect the approximate selling price of the goods/services transferred. That is, the entity should be entitled to recover its costs plus a reasonable profit; the profit, however, need not be equal to that which would have been earned upon completion.

Recognizing Revenue While Performance Obligation is Satisfied

In order to recognize revenues while the performance obligation is being satisfied, there must be some means for measuring progress toward completion of the obligation. The two acceptable methods for measuring progress are the output method and the input method.

Output Method

The focus of the output method is the *value the customer derives* from the goods/services that have been transferred to the customer up to that point. When using the output method, the entity should select a base to use for measuring progress that faithfully reflects the entity's performance toward completion. Alternatives may include:

- Surveys, such as engineering studies, of the work completed
- Appraisals of results achieved
- Milestones reached
- Time elapsed
- Units produced or delivered

In some cases, contracts call for consideration on the basis of some criteria, such as the number of hours a professional works on a project that is being billed on an hourly basis. When there is such a measurement guideline, it may also be used as a basis for measuring outputs.

The output method is not always the most practical or reliable way to measure progress and some situations require the use of the input method. This may be the case, for example, when progress is not necessarily observable or when the information necessary to apply the output approach is not readily available.

Input Method

The focus of the input method is the *effort put forth by the entity*. Measurement may be based on a wide variety of inputs, including:

- Resources consumed
- Labor hours expended
- Costs incurred
- Time elapsed
- Machine hours used

If an entity's inputs are expended or efforts are put forth somewhat uniformly over the period during which the performance obligation is being satisfied, it may be appropriate to recognize revenue on a straight-line basis over such period.

The input method may not be appropriate in all circumstances. This would be true, for example, for contracts where there is no direct relationship between the inputs used by the entity and the transfer of benefits to the customer.

Inputs that do not depict the entity's performance should be excluded when applying the input method. For example, when using costs incurred as the basis for measuring progress, adjustments may be required for:

- Cost incurred that do not contribute to the progress toward completion, such as amounts spent for an unanticipated high amount of waste
- Costs that are incurred disproportionately with progress toward completion

Licensing

When revenue is generated by granting a license to use intellectual property, the method used to recognize revenue will depend on the nature of the licensing arrangement—that is, whether it grants a *right to use* the intellectual property or a *right to access* intellectual property.

- When a license grants the customer the **right to use** intellectual property (eg, a photo), it is assumed that the property is functional as is and that the licensor does not have any obligation to maintain the property; thus, revenue will be recognized **at a point in time** (ie, when the property is made available for use).
- When a **right to access** intellectual property is granted to a customer, the customer will have access to the property for a period of time and the licensor will usually have an obligation to support or maintain the intellectual property during that time. Since the performance obligation largely consists of the duty to support and maintain the intellectual property over a period of time, revenue will be recognized **over the term of the license**.

Onerous Performance Obligations

If, at any time, the expected cost of satisfying a performance obligation (or contract) is greater than the amount of revenue allocated, it is referred to as an onerous performance obligation (or contract). The entity will **recognize the expected loss and a corresponding liability immediately**.

- Applies to construction-type and production-type contracts (ASC 605-35).

Accounting for Costs Incurred

Costs incurred in satisfying a performance obligation will be accumulated and reported on the income statement in the period in which the related revenues are recognized. Generally, costs of obtaining a contract will be recognized as expenses in the period in which they are incurred. Certain costs, however, should be capitalized.

- **Recoverable incremental costs of obtaining a contract** are capitalized until the related revenue is recognized on the income statement. For example, a land broker may pay to have land rezoned to increase the value of the property. These costs are incremental costs of obtaining the contract that should be capitalized because they will be recovered when the broker sells the property.

- **Certain costs are required by various standards** to be capitalized while others are required to be expensed.
- **Costs meeting all of the following criteria** are required by the revenue recognition standards to be capitalized**:**
  - The costs relate directly to a contract that is in existence or a specific contract that is currently being negotiated;
  - The costs generate or enhance resources that will be used to satisfy performance obligations in the future; and
  - The costs are expected to be recovered.

Recovery of costs may be through collections of revenues on the contract if they were anticipated when the contracts were negotiated, or they might have resulted from changes made to the performance obligation that are reimbursable by the customer.

Disclosures

The objective of the revenue recognition disclosure requirements is to disclose sufficient information to enable users of F/S to understand the *nature, amount, timing,* and *uncertainty* of *revenue* and *cash flows* arising from contracts with customers. To achieve this, an entity should provide qualitative and quantitative disclosures regarding:

- Contracts with customers
- Significant judgments (and any changes) made in applying the revenue recognition rules to those contracts
- Assets recognized from the costs to obtain or fulfill such contracts

The disclosures will generally be in the footnotes to the F/S. They may be in a separate footnote devoted exclusively to revenue recognition or may be included in a more general footnote, such as the summary of significant accounting principles.

Both public and nonpublic entities are required to provide information about disaggregated revenues, contracts balances, and performance obligations:

- If the entity elects not to provide information about disaggregated revenues that is required for public entities, it should disclose, as a minimum, revenues that are disaggregated according to the timing of the transfers of goods/services and qualitative information about how economic factors affect the nature, amount, timing, and uncertainty of revenue and cash flows
- Opening and closing balances of receivables, contract assets, and contract liabilities, unless otherwise provided on the F/S
- When the entity typically satisfies its performance obligations
- Significant payment terms
- The nature of the goods/services the entity has promised to deliver, emphasizing obligations to arrange for delivery by another entity when the reporting entity is acting as an agent
- Obligations related to returns, refunds, and similar items

Public entities are also required to provide the following disclosures:

- Information about disaggregated revenues in categories that show how the nature, amount, timing, and uncertainty are affected by economic conditions

- A reconciliation of the disaggregated revenues to the amount reported in various segments if the entity is reporting segment information
- Revenues recognized from contracts with customers, distinguished from revenues from other sources
- Impairment losses recognized on receivables or contract assets derived from transactions involving revenues from contracts with customers
- Information about the timing of the satisfaction of performance obligations and the its relationship to the timing of payments, along with their effects on contract assets and contract liabilities
- Qualitative and quantitative information explaining significant changes in contract assets and contract liabilities during the period including, as appropriate:
    - Changes due to business combinations
    - Cumulative catch-up adjustments due to changes to the measurement of progress toward completion; estimates of the contract price, including those related to variable revenues or the constraint on variable revenues; and contract modifications
    - Contract asset impairments
    - Changes affecting the time for a right to compensation becoming unconditional and being reclassified from a contract asset to a receivable
    - Changes to the time expected to be required for satisfaction of a performance obligation
    - Types of warranties and related obligations

While a nonpublic entity may elect not to disclose it, if a public entity has a performance obligation that is part of a contract that has an original expected duration of more than one year, and it does not have the right to consideration in an amount that exactly equals the value to the customer of the entity's performance to date, the entity will disclose:

- The aggregate amount of the transaction price allocated to performance obligations not satisfied as of yearend; and
- An indication as to when the entity expects to recognize that amount as revenue, either:
    - Qualitatively or
    - Quantitatively, using time bands most appropriate for the duration of the remaining performance obligations

Lecture 2.06 – Collectibility of Receivables is Uncertain

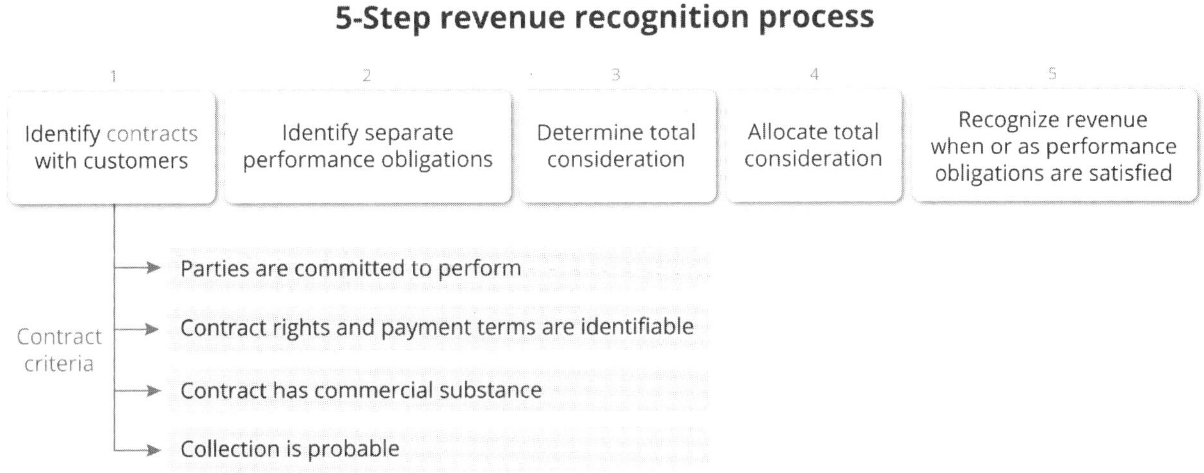

©UWorld

Collection Uncertainty

When a sale is made in exchange for a receivable, the entity must determine whether the receivable is likely to be collected.

Collection is Probable

If an entity determines that it is *probable* (ie, likely) that *substantially all* (generally about 90%) of a receivable will be collected, revenue will be recognized under the 5-step process. Keep in mind that even when collection is probable, an allowance for uncollectibility (ie, credit losses) will still be recorded.

Assume an entity has a contract to provide goods to a customer for $900. The goods cost $540. When the performance obligation was satisfied, $150 was received from the customer and a receivable was recorded for the remaining amount owed. However, the entity expects that 10% of the receivable will not be collected. The following journal entries would be made:

Accounts receivable (A/R)	750	
Cash	150	
Sales revenue		900
Cost of Goods Sold	540	
Inventory		540
Credit loss expense*	75	
Allowance for credit losses*		75

A/R less the allowance for credit losses is the amount expected to be collected, or Net Realizable Value (NRV).

*These accounts may also be referred to as bad debt expense and allowance for doubtful accounts, respectively.

Assessing Probability of Collection

To determine the likelihood of payment, an entity should consider whether the customer has the ability and intent to pay for goods/services *expected to be transferred*. This means the entire duration of a contract doesn't necessarily need to be considered collectible in order for revenue to be recognized. That is, only amounts the entity expects to be entitled to for the transfer of goods/services must be collectible in order for those amounts to be recognized as revenue.

In some circumstances, the magnitude of uncertainty regarding collectibility (ie, credit risk) can be significantly mitigated by the terms of the agreement.

- For example, if *payments are due prior to the provision of goods/services*, a contract would be considered collectible even if it is likely that the customer will default. This is because there is no risk that the entity will not be paid for goods/services provided.
- Credit risk would also be significantly diminished if the entity can *stop transferring goods/services* if the customer fails to pay amounts as they become due.

Note that an entity cannot consider the ability to repossess goods transferred as mitigation of credit risk.

Collection is Not Probable

There are numerous reasons an entity may sell to a customer when collection is not probable. For example:

- A sale could be at such a great margin that the initial payments plus the value of the merchandise that will be repossessed upon the customer's default still provides a profit to the seller.
- The seller may believe that a sale to a start-up business in a competitive environment could increase market share if the customer performs, making the risk worthwhile.

The *probability of collection*, however, is one of the four criteria that are required for the transaction to be considered a contract for revenue recognition purposes. So, if collection is highly uncertain and credit risk cannot be mitigated, revenue from the transaction would *not* be recognized under the 5-step process. The arrangement will be reevaluated every reporting period to determine whether it has met the criteria, at which time the 5-step process will apply.

Revenue Arrangements that are Not Contracts with Customers

As previously mentioned, when an entity enters into an arrangement that meets some of the contract criteria, but not all (eg, collection is not probable), revenue will be recognized in accordance with another approach, usually resulting in revenues being recognized later. Under this method:

- All receipts from the customer for the goods/services that are the subject of the arrangement are reported as a *liability*.
- The liability represents the entity's obligation to provide such goods/services or to refund the consideration received.

Assume the same facts as the last example, except the arrangement is not considered a contract for revenue recognition purposes (eg, because substantially all amounts due are not likely to be collected) and only a fourth of the goods, costing $135, have been provided. When the entity receives the $150, the following journal entries would be recorded:

Cash	150	
Unearned (deferred) revenue		150
Cost of goods sold	135	
Inventory		135

If the contract criteria are never met (eg, collection is never considered probable), the liability is *derecognized* and treated as *revenue* when *consideration* received from the customer is *nonrefundable and one of the following* scenarios applies:

Scenario 1	Scenario 2	Scenario 3
• The entity has *no remaining obligations*, and • All, or substantially *all*, of the *consideration* has been *received*.	• The arrangement has been *terminated*.	• Consideration received relates to *goods/services*, the control of which, has been *transferred*; and • The entity has stopped transferring goods/services, and neither has an obligation to, nor intends to, provide any additional goods/services.

In our example, let's say that the arrangement is terminated, all amounts paid are nonrefundable, and the entity will not be transferring the remaining goods (ie, Scenario 3). At this point, the revenue can be recognized since there are no remaining obligations:

Unearned revenue	150	
Revenue		150

Installment Sales Method (For TAX)

Prior to the introduction of the revenue recognition standard in ASC 606, when collectibility of a receivable was uncertain and the amount to be collected was not readily determinable, the installment sales method was applied. While this method is no longer allowed under GAAP, it is still used for tax purposes (discussed later).

- Gross profit = Sales – COGS
- Gross profit % = Gross profit / Sales price
- Gross profit recognized for tax purposes = Cash collected × Gross profit %

Lecture 2.07 – Long-Term Contracts

Overview

Many industries provide services that may require several accounting periods to complete. The construction industry is one example. Contractors may enter contracts with governmental units to construct infrastructure, including roads and highways, which may require several accounting periods. These circumstances call for the use of **long-term construction-type contracts** that, in some cases, will have a single distinct performance obligation.

In other industries, companies will enter long-term supply contracts because their customers want to be able to rely on a supply of a resource that is considered critical without the need to renegotiate every purchase. Thus, suppliers will use **long-term production-type contracts**, which may:

- Commit the customer to purchase all output produced by the supplier, usually with limitations
- Commit the supplier to produce all of the resources needed by the customer
- Commit the supplier to produce and the customer to purchase a certain amount or quantity of the resource over an extended period of time

Recognizing revenue over the course of these contracts makes sense because the work that generates the revenue is performed over the term of the contract. ASC 606 indicates that certain conditions must be met for the entity to recognize revenue while the performance obligation is being satisfied. Otherwise, revenues are recognized upon satisfaction of the performance obligation.

Long-term construction contracts often allow the contractor to bill the customer at intervals, as it reaches various milestones in the project. These billings do not represent the amounts that should be recognized as revenue and are generally for amounts that are lower than what a payment would be for a proportionate amount of work completed on the contract. They are generally designed to:

- Make certain that the customer has enough of an investment in the project to assure the contractor that the customer will meet its obligation to accept and pay the contractor
- Provide the contractor with working capital to enable the contractor to pay sub-contractors and for materials, providing assurance to the customer that the project can be completed
- Make certain that the contractor has something to gain (ie, the remaining unpaid balance on the contract) by completing the contract on a timely basis

Costs of Obtaining & Fulfilling a Contract

Costs incurred in satisfying a performance obligation will be accumulated and reported on the income statement (I/S) in the period in which the related revenues are recognized.

- When recognizing revenues while the performance obligation is being satisfied (aka, the percentage-of-completion method*), costs are charged against income in proportion to the revenues being recognized.

- When revenues are recognized upon satisfaction of the performance obligation (aka, the completed-contract method*), costs are recognized upon the completion of the contract in the same period in which revenues are recognized.

*Note that the revenue recognition standards and the CPA exam no longer use the specific terms "percentage-of-completion method" and "completed-contract method," but the accounting under the new standards is so similar that this terminology is still used in practice.

Costs incurred are inventoried as they occur in a *construction-in-progress (CIP) account*, while billings are accumulated in a current liability account called *billings on uncompleted contracts*. Notice that both accounts are current, not long-term. This is because the income from such contracts is realized in only *one operating cycle* of the company; when the cycle is longer than a year, items that normally would seem to be long term are classified as current.

Some costs of obtaining and fulfilling a contract are expensed in the period in which they are incurred (eg, general and administrative costs). Other costs, however, should be **capitalized** in accordance with the principles found in ASC 340, *Other Assets and Deferred Costs*:

- **Recoverable incremental costs of obtaining the contract** – If the entity expects to recover the costs of obtaining a contract, they should be capitalized. These are costs that either:
    - Wouldn't have been incurred if the contract had not been obtained (eg, commissions), or
    - Are chargeable to the customer even if the contract is not obtained.

  For example, a land broker has land zoned for agricultural use and a customer is seeking land zoned for multi-family residential units. Costs incurred to re-zone the property for the customer would be recoverable because the zoning change will increase the value, and the selling price, of the property.
- **Costs to fulfill a contract required to be capitalized by other standards** – Various ASC topics specify that some costs must be capitalized (eg, inventory) while others must be expensed.
- **Costs to fulfill a contract that meet all of the following criteria**:
    - The costs relate directly to a contract that is in existence or a specific contract that is being negotiated.
    - The costs generate or enhance resources that will be used to satisfy performance obligations in the future.
    - The costs are expected to be recovered.

The last category of costs includes those that are normally incurred and accumulated in construction in progress (CIP). Recovery of costs may be through collections of revenues on the contract:

- If they were anticipated when the contracts were negotiated, or
- They might have resulted from changes made to the performance obligation that are reimbursable by the customer.

Percentage of Completion versus Completed Contract Method

	Percentage-of-Completion Method	Completed Contract Method
Revenue recognition	*Over time* – as construction is completed	*At a point in time* – when construction is complete
	Appropriate portion of total revenue expected from the contract is recorded at end of each period (I/S)	No profit/revenue entries are made until completion (I/S)
	Billings and collections are recorded in B/S accounts	
Costs incurred	Charged against income in proportion to revenues recognized during period	Held in CIP account (B/S) until completion
	Anticipated losses recognized immediately (I/S)	
Conditions for use*	1. Customer consumes benefits of asset(s) as they are delivered 2. Customer has *control* over asset(s) during creation or enhancement 3. Entity lacks alternative use for asset(s) and is entitled to payment for completion to date	Customer has *control* over asset(s)
Measuring progress*	*Output method* – % complete with respect to output (eg, milestones reached, units completed, etc.) *Input method* – % complete with respect to effort put in (eg, costs incurred, labor hours, etc.)	

**Previously discussed.*

Percentage of Completion: Cost-to-Cost Approach

The cost-to-cost approach is an *input method*. Under this method, the costs incurred to date are compared to the total estimated costs of completing the performance obligations; the resulting ratio is considered the percentage complete.

The profit recognized in each period is determined on the accrual basis, taking into account:

- The estimated profit on the contract,
- The portion of the contract that is completed (% complete), and
- Any profit that has been previously recognized.

Accounting During Year

- Billings are added to *billings on uncompleted contracts* (ie, a contra account to CIP).

- As cash is collected, the receivable is reduced.
- As **costs that qualify for capitalization** are incurred, they are added to **CIP**.

> All the accounting for percentage of completion and the completed contract method is the same up to this point.

- **Gross profit** is added to **CIP**. Gross profit for the current period is calculated as follows:
  1. Total contract price – Total construction costs = Total estimated profit
  2. Costs incurred to date / Total construction costs = % complete
  3. Total estimated profit × % complete = Gross profit (GP) to date
  4. GP to date – GP to date at end of last period = GP in current period
- At year end, **Billings and CIP are netted** on the B/S to report either:
  - *Current contract asset:* CIP in excess of billings
  - *Current contract liability:* Billings in excess of CIP
- The I/S will report:
  - **Revenue** earned to date = (Total contract price × % complete) – Revenue previously recognized
  - **Cost of sales** equal to costs (not profit) added to CIP during the current period

Roger Builders has agreed to construct a building for CPA Inc. at a total contract price of $4,000,000. The estimated construction costs at inception are $3,000,000 and the actual costs for both years 1 and 2 are below. The construction was completed after year 2.

Total contract price	$4,000,000
– Estimated costs	$3,000,000
= Estimated Profit	$1,000,000

	Cumulative	
	Year 1	**Year 2**
Costs incurred to date	700,000	1,650,000
Estimated costs to complete	2,800,000	1,650,000
Billings	850,000	1,800,000
Cash collections	800,000	1,500,000

		Year 1		**Year 2**	
% complete	Costs **incurred** to date / **Total** construction costs (ie, Actual + Estimated to complete)	700 / 700 + 2,800	20%	1,650 / 1,650 + 1,650	50%
× Total Profit *	Total contract price –Total construction costs	4,000 –3,500	500	4,000 – 3,300	700
= Profit recognized to date			100		350
– Profit previously recognized			(0)		(100)
= Profit to recognize this year			100		250

**Total Profit will always change, so use new profit amount.*

	Percentage-of-Completion Method			Completed Contract Method		
Billings	Construction receivable	850		Construction receivable	X	
	Billings*		850	Billings		X
Collections	Cash	800		Cash	X	
	Construction receivable		800	Construction receivable		X
Costs	CIP*	700		CIP	X	
	Cash		700	Cash		X
Recognize profit Year 1	CIP*	100		No income until done		
	Gross profit on CIP (I/S)		100			
	CIP	100				
	Construction expense (3,500 × 20%)	700				
	Construction revenue (4,000 × 20%)		800			
**Net Billings (850) and CIP (800) on B/S at end of year = $50 contract liability (ie, Billings in excess of CIP)*						
Recognize Profit Year 2	CIP	250		No income until done		
	Construction expense [(3,300 × 50%) – 700)]	950				
	Construction revenue [(4,000 × 50%) – 800]		1,200			

UWorld
YOUR WORLD OF LEARNING
ROGER
CPA Review

FAR 3 – Investments in Debt & Equity Securities

FAR 3 – Investments in Debt & Equity Securities

Table of Contents

Investments in Debt & Equity Securities

Lecture 3.01 – Investments in Debt Securities – Trading

Securities Overview

There is a wide variety of investments an entity may decide to make, including the securities of other entities. Securities fall into two basic categories:

- Debt securities (eg, bonds are most common)
- Equity securities (ie, shares of stock and derivative instruments associated with stock)

The FASB Accounting Standards Codification (ASC) provides principles and guidance for accounting for securities under several different ASC topics:

- ASC 320 relates to investments in **debt securities**. Note that ASC 320 does *not* apply to:
    - Brokers and dealers (ASC 940)
    - Defined benefit pension and other postretirement or postemployment plans (ASC 960, 962, and 965)
    - Investment companies (ASC 946)
- ASC 321 relates to investments in **equity securities**.
- ASC 323 relates to the **equity method of accounting** for certain equity securities and joint ventures.
- ASC 325 relates to other investments, such as investments in insurance contracts and beneficial interests in securitized financial assets (not likely to be tested).

Debt Securities in General

Generally, if an entity acquires the debt securities of other entities, depending on the nature of the securities, it is essentially becoming a creditor with a receivable from the other entity. While holding the receivable, it will generally be receiving periodic interest payments and, depending on the terms of the instrument, also may be receiving periodic payments to reduce the principal. In other cases, the principal may be paid as a single lump sum at the end of the receivable's term.

The value of a receivable is equal to the present value of the payments to be received, applying an appropriate interest rate. The rate used may be the investor's cost of capital, the return on other investments, or some target based on whatever criteria the investing entity determines is applicable. The rate, and ultimate valuation, is adjusted to consider both market risk and credit risk.

- **Market risk** is the risk that a receivable will diminish in value due to:
    - A rise in market interest rates, making the lower rate less desirable, or
    - Other investments will become available that offer a greater return.
- **Credit risk** is the risk that the debtor will not perform, which could mean that some or all payments will be missed or late.

Some investments in debt securities are made for reasons other than the generation of regular cash flows (some do not provide interest and principal payments). Such investments may be made to:

- Benefit from gains on trades and other transactions

    - The value of securities is affected by a wide variety of factors, such as market interest rates, the issuing entity's credit rating, the availability of investment alternatives, or economic conditions. An investor may speculate that changes in one or more of these factors will lead to an increase in value.
- Balance out an investment portfolio
- Establish or enhance a fund for obtaining assets or retiring debt
- Enhance a relationship with the issuer of the security

The ASC defines a **debt security** as "any security representing a creditor relationship with an entity." The term "debt security" also includes:

- Preferred stock that by its terms either must be redeemed or is redeemable at the option of the investor
- A collateralized mortgage obligation (or other instrument) that is issued in equity form but is required to be accounted for as a nonequity instrument regardless of how that instrument is classified (whether equity or debt) in the issuer's statement of financial position
- U.S. Treasury securities
- U.S. government agency securities
- Municipal securities
- Corporate bonds
- Convertible debt
- Commercial paper
- All securitized debt instruments, such as collateralized mortgage obligations and real estate mortgage investment conduits
- Interest-only and principal-only strips

The term "debt security" **excludes**:

- Option contracts
- Financial futures contracts
- Forward contracts
- Lease contracts
- Receivables that do not meet the definition of a security, such as:
    - Trade accounts receivable arising from sales on credit by industrial or commercial entities
    - Loans receivable arising from consumer, commercial, and real estate lending activities of lending institutions

Investments in debt securities are reported on an investor's balance sheet (B/S) in one of three categories:

- **Trading Securities (HFT – Held For Trading)** – Investments in debt instruments (eg, bonds), which the investor has acquired in an attempt to make profits by buying and selling within a short period of time.
    - Normally classified as current assets.
- **Available-For-Sale (AFS) Securities** – Investments in marketable debt instruments that do not fit the definitions of HTM or trading securities.

- These may be classified as current or noncurrent assets, depending on the expected date of sale. If the holding period of the securities is indefinite, they should be classified as noncurrent assets.

- **Held-To-Maturity (HTM) Securities** – Investments in bonds and other debt instruments that the investor has the *ability and intent* to hold until the due date for repayment.
  - Classified as noncurrent assets until the maturity date is less than one year from the B/S date.
  - When principal is paid in installments, whether annually at the end of the term, or in some other pattern, the principal that will be paid within the next year is classified as a current asset.
  - If an entity has an operating cycle that exceeds a year, the current amount will be the principal amount to be paid within the next operating cycle.

Debt Securities Overview			
	Trading (HFT)	**Available for sale (AFS)**	**Held to maturity (HTM)**
Balance Sheet	Usually current Fair Value	Current/noncurrent Fair Value Amortized cost & allowance for credit losses (parenthetically) **Unrealized gains/losses** (other than credit losses) in OCI (Statement of Comprehensive Income) & accumulated OCI in Stockholders' Equity (separately)	Noncurrent/current Amortized cost Allowance for credit losses (separately)
Income Statement	**Unrealized gains/losses** Realized gain/loss Interest income	Credit loss expense/reversal Realized gain/loss Interest income	Credit loss expense/reversal Realized gain/loss Interest income
Statement of Cash Flows	Usually operating activity (purchase or sale)	Investing activity	Investing activity

Accounting for Trading Securities

Balance Sheet

Trading securities are initially **recorded at cost**, but they are **carried at fair value** (ASC 320). That is, carrying values of the securities are adjusted to their current market prices every period, including interim periods if interim F/S are prepared in addition to the annual F/S.

Income Statement

- Due to the marketable nature of these securities, and the intention to sell them in the near future, **unrealized gains and losses** (temporary) resulting from fluctuations in market price are reported in net income.
- Any **realized gain or loss** (permanent) from the sale or other disposal of these securities is also reported in net income.
- **Interest income** is also reported.

Statement of Cash Flows

- Since trading securities are generally purchased for the purpose of generating *profits from resale in the short term*, they are a *part of the entity's working capital*, and transactions are **normally** reported in the **operating** activities section of the statement of cash flows.
- Cash flows related to the acquisition (outflows) or disposal (inflows) of trading securities may be classified as **operating or investing** activities on the statement of cash flows, however, depending on the nature and purpose for which they were acquired:
  - When trading securities are acquired for **short-term appreciation**, they are reported as **current** assets and the cash flows are classified as **operating** activities on the statement of cash flows. This is the more common classification.
  - When trading securities are acquired for **long-term appreciation**, they are reported as **noncurrent** assets and the cash flows are classified as **investing** activities.

An entity acquires bonds of another entity with a cost and face value of $100. They are being held in anticipation of an increase in value due to an expected decrease in market interest rates. The following information relates to cost and market values.

Purchase price, 1/1/X1	$100
Fair value, 12/31/X1	$140
Fair value, 12/31/X2	$ 90

To purchase:

Investment in trading securities	100	
Cash		100

At 12/X1, the fair value is now $140, resulting in a **gain of $40**. Since the security must be reported at fair value, the increase is recorded in the investment account, or set up as a valuation allowance.

Market Adjustment - Trading Security (B/S)	40	
Unrealized gain **(I/S)**		40

The market adjustment account is on the balance sheet and increases the carrying value of the trading security in the current asset section. The unrealized gain is on the income statement as part of income from continuing operations.

At 12/X2, the fair value is now $90, resulting in a **loss of $50** ($140 – $90).

Unrealized Loss **(I/S)**	50	
Market Adjustment – Trading Security (B/S)		50

The income statement effect in 20X1 is $40, and in 20X2 is ($50). These amounts represent the current year effects only since they are both income statement items. The valuation allowance will have a credit balance of $10, resulting from a debit of $40 in 20X1 and a credit of $50 in 20X2.

Lecture 3.02 – Investments in Debt Securities – Available for Sale

Accounting for Available-For-Sale Securities

Available-for-sale (AFS) debt securities are those that do not fall into either the trading or held-to-maturity categories. AFS securities are similar to trading securities in that they are likely to be sold prior to maturity.

Balance Sheet

AFS securities are initially recorded at cost but are carried at fair value (ASC 320), with the amortized cost basis and the allowance for credit losses reported parenthetically.

- Changes in market price (ie, fair value) and credit losses are reflected whenever the entity prepares the F/S.

AFS securities may be classified as **current or noncurrent**, depending on the expected holding period.

- Generally considered noncurrent if the holding period is indefinite.
- AFS securities are not purchased primarily to gain short-term profits from resale and are not reported as current assets until management has decided to dispose of them, or otherwise believes they will be disposed of, within one year.

Unrealized gains/losses resulting from fluctuations in fair value must be evaluated to determine whether any portion is due to credit losses (reported in income). Any remaining increases/decreases in the fair values of AFS securities are not reported in income until the securities are disposed of. Instead, they are included in **other comprehensive income (OCI)** on the statement of comprehensive income and accumulated in the equity section of the B/S as **accumulated OCI** (AOCI).

- Unrealized losses in excess of credit losses are reported as a reduction to the investment in a contra-asset account—we'll call it *AFS securities – unrealized losses*. Similarly, unrealized gains are recognized as an increase to the investment account in a valuation account, *AFS securities – unrealized gains*.
    - If FV is lower than the original cost, the difference, net of credit losses, is credited to AFS securities – unrealized losses.
    - If FV is higher than the original cost, the difference is debited to an AFS securities – unrealized gains.
    - If FV is lower in one period and higher in a subsequent period, the AFS securities – unrealized losses account is eliminated, and the excess is recognized in AFS securities – unrealized gains.
    - If FV is higher in one period and lower in a subsequent period, the AFS securities – unrealized gains account is eliminated, and the excess is recognized in AFS securities – unrealized losses.

Income Statement

The increase/decrease in the allowance for **credit losses** will be reported on the income statement (I/S) in the period of the change as credit loss expense or reversal of credit loss expense, respectively. **Realized gains and losses** also appear on the I/S as does **interest income**.

Statement of Cash Flows

Cash flows related to the acquisition (outflows) and disposal (inflows) of AFS investments are reported as **investing activities** on the statement of cash flows.

Same example as above, except for the treatment of the unrealized gain and loss (not due to credit losses).

To purchase:

Investment in AFS security	100	
Cash		100

At 12/X1, the fair value is now $140. Since the security is required to be reported at fair value, the increase is recorded in the investment account, or set up as a valuation allowance.

Market Adjustment - AFS Security (B/S)	40	
Unrealized gain **(Stmt of comp inc)**		40

The market adjustment account is on the B/S and increases the carrying value of the AFS security in the asset section. The unrealized gain is reported on the statement of comprehensive income as a component of OCI and accumulated in the stockholders' equity section of the balance sheet in Accumulated OCI.

At 12/X2, the fair value is now $90, resulting in a loss of $50 ($140 – $90).

Unrealized Loss **(Stmt of comp inc)**	50	
Market Adjustment – AFS Security **(B/S)**		50

Note: The unrealized gain in 20X1 of $40, and the unrealized loss in 20X2 of ($50), are reported in OCI in each period's statement of comprehensive income. The amount is accumulated in a stockholders' equity account (Accumulated OCI) on the B/S. The amount, which is the same as the balance in the valuation account, is a negative equity amount (debit balance) of $10.

GAAP Statement of Comprehensive Income (ON-TIDe-N-OC)	**20X1**	**20X2**	
Operating Income			
Nonoperating	40	(50)	If Trading, goes here
Taxes			
Income continuing operations			
Discontinued Operations			
Net Income	100	200	300 to RE
Other Comprehensive Income (OCI)	**40**	**(50)**	**(10) Accumulated OCI**
Comprehensive Income	140	150	290 net effect on B/S

When an entity has items to be reported in OCI, they are reported separately from items that are recognized in earnings. The above items may be presented in a single statement of comprehensive income, as shown, or in two separate statements, as follows:

- **Income statement** (aka, statement of earnings or statement of operations) – Includes all elements leading to net income or "earnings."
- **Statement of comprehensive income** – Immediately follows the income statement when both statements are presented. It combines net income with other comprehensive income items to determine comprehensive income.

Lecture 3.03 – Credit Losses & Sales of AFS Debt Securities

Overview

As previously mentioned, ASC 326 specifies the reporting for declines in the value (ie, credit losses) of financial assets that result from the expected inability of the debtor to make all of the payments called for in the instrument. The two types of assets that are subject to the recognition of credit losses under ASC 326 include:

- Assets measured at amortized cost (previously discussed)
- Available-for-sale (AFS) debt securities (discussed here)

Remember, financial assets reported at fair value generally are not subject to the recognition of credit losses. This is because fair value is determined on the basis of market transactions, which assumes credit risk is considered when the the exchange price is determined.

While AFS debt securities are reported at fair value (ie, carrying value), if the fair value is lower than the present value of expected future cash flows, the instrument generally will be held and the cash flows will be realized (Scenario 1). If, however, the fair value is higher, it generally will be sold at its fair value rather than being held for the cash flows (Scenario 2). As a result, the allowance for credit losses would never be greater than the amount by which the amortized cost exceeds the fair value.

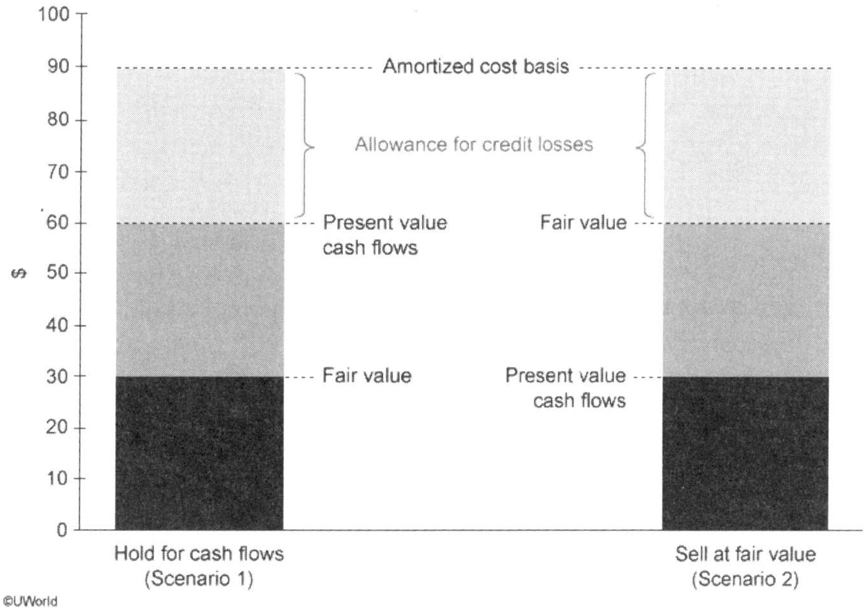

Initial Measurement

Purchased financial securities are generally measured at the purchase price plus any costs incurred at acquisition that are appropriate for capitalization.

Purchased Financial Asset with Credit Deterioration (PCD Assets)

Sometimes an AFS debt security is purchased with credit deterioration (PCD asset). This status is determined based on credit loss indicators and other criteria. When an AFS debt security is a PCD asset, the *initial allowance for credit losses is added to the purchase price* of the security (instead of being expensed) to get the *initial amortized cost basis*. Subsequent changes in the allowance will be recorded as credit loss expense.

Credit Loss Indicators

Examples of credit loss indicators include:

- The difference between the security's amortized cost basis and its lower fair value
- Adverse conditions affecting the security, the industry of the issuer, or a relevant geographic area, which may result from:
  - Changes in technology
  - Discontinuation of a business segment that could adversely affect the issuer's future earnings or those of underlying loan obligors
  - Changes in credit quality
- The payment structure, along with the issuer's ability to make payments that increase in later periods
- Failure to make scheduled payments
- Changes in the issuer's security rating determined by a rating agency

Impairments

Once the security has been recognized, an evaluation is to be performed each subsequent financial reporting date to determine if the AFS debt security has been impaired. If the **fair value** is **lower** than its **amortized cost** basis on the financial statement date, the asset is **impaired**. One must determine if the impairment is due to credit losses or other factors.

Declines in the values of financial assets had previously all been recognized as impairment losses. Although they are not determined or measured in the same manner, credit losses are essentially the same as those impairment losses that result from the inability to pay, rather than those resulting from changes in market conditions.

Determining Whether a Credit Loss Exists

When the present value of the cash flows expected to be received in settlement of the financial asset exceeds the amortized cost of the asset, there is no credit loss. If, however, the present value of future cash flows expected to be received is lower than the amortized cost basis of the asset, a contra-asset (valuation) account, **allowance for credit losses**, and a credit loss expense is recognized. The allowance cannot reduce the carrying value of the asset below fair value though.

Credit losses are evaluated on investments individually or in groups, depending on how the entity aggregates them to recognize realized and unrealized gains/losses for financial reporting purposes. See the credit loss indicators above for considerations in determining whether a credit loss exists.

Estimating Expected Credit Losses

All applicable available information should be used in making the determination of amounts and timing of cash flows expected to be collected. The information should include past and current events and conditions, and forecasts that are reasonable and supportable. Information considered should include:

- The remaining payment terms
- Prepayment speeds
- The issuer's financial condition
- Expected defaults
- The value of collateral, if any

Other sources of information that may relate to the evaluation include:

- Reports and forecasts of industry analysts
- Credit ratings
- Other relevant market data

Changes in Credit Loss Allowance

It is possible for the timing of payments to be accelerated or delayed; the amount that is likely to be collected may increase/decrease; and a change in the market rate may cause the fair value of the instrument to increase/decrease. Depending on how these factors affect the fair value of the instrument, the valuation allowance may require an adjustment.

- Adjustments **increasing** the **allowance** create **credit loss expenses** in the period.
- Adjustments **decreasing** the **allowance** create a recovery of previously recognized credit losses, causing an **increase** in **income**.

Decisions to Sell

In some cases, the entity may intend to sell the security, or it may be forced to do so due to working capital or other needs. Any **allowance for credit losses** associated with these securities is to be **eliminated**, and the security is to be **written down** to its **fair value**. The difference, an incremental impairment, is recognized in the period's earnings. If the entity does not intend to sell the security, it should still determine if it is more likely than not that it will be required to do so.

- After a security has been written down as a result of an intent to sell, the *difference between* the *new amortized cost basis* and *cash flows expected* to be collected is recognized as an *adjustment to interest income*.
- Subsequent increases in expected cash flows are recognized as prospective adjustments to the instrument's yield.
- Subsequent *increases in fair value* are recognized in *OCI*.

Accrued Interest

If an entity reports accrued interest separately from the fair value and amortized cost basis of an AFS debt security, in the event that the cash flows are impaired, the entity may elect to write off the accrued interest receivables by reversing interest income or recognizing credit loss expense, or some combination of both.

Financial Statement Presentation

An entity presents AFS debt securities on its balance sheet at its fair value, reporting the amortized cost basis and the allowance for credit losses parenthetically. Components of accumulated OCI related to AFS debt securities are reported separately in the balance sheet.

No guidance is provided as to where credit losses are to be reported on the income statement. That may be determined on the basis of management's judgment, the component(s) of the entity the transaction was intended to benefit, or the component that generated the resources that were invested.

Credit Loss Disclosures

Disclosures related to credit risk and the measurement of credit losses should provide information about:

- AFS debt securities with unrealized losses and no allowance for credit losses
- The allowance for credit losses
- Purchased financial assets with credit deterioration

The disclosures should enable financial statement users to understand:

- The credit risk that is inherent in AFS debt securities
- Management's estimate of credit losses
- Changes in estimated credit losses that occurred during the period

Sales of AFS Debt Securities

When the investment in **AFS is sold**, the difference between the cost and the proceeds is treated as a **realized gain/loss**. Ignore the allowance account and adjust to the new target balance without the security that was just sold, unless it is the last investment, then the allowance and the unrealized gain/loss must both be eliminated.

Reclassifications

Reclassifications may occur due to changes in management's intentions (ASC 320). Securities may be reclassified from one of the categories to another, and the accounting approaches vary depending on the old and new classifications. The approach is to treat the securities as if they are being sold from the portfolio they are leaving, then repurchased at the current market price into the portfolio they are entering. In other words, current market price is used to determine the transfer.

<table>
<tr><th>Type of transfer</th><th>Revalue at</th><th>Treatment of difference
(ie, unrealized holding gains/losses)</th></tr>
<tr><td>To trading*</td><td rowspan="4">Fair value</td><td>Recognize in earnings (I/S)</td></tr>
<tr><td>From trading</td><td>N/A (amounts already recognized in I/S are not reversed)</td></tr>
<tr><td>From AFS to HTM</td><td>Amortize amounts in AOCI (B/S) over remaining life of security**</td></tr>
<tr><td>From HTM to AFS</td><td>Recognize in OCI and transfer to AOCI (B/S)</td></tr>
</table>

**Eliminate any related valuation allowance accounts.*

***Since AFS securities are carried at fair value, unrealized holding gains/losses should already be recognized in OCI and transferred to AOCI.*

Exam testing has historically focused more heavily on reclassifications between trading securities and AFS securities.

Lecture 3.04 – HTM Debt Securities & Equity Securities

Accounting for Held-to-Maturity Securities

HTM Securities are investments in the debt securities of other entities that the entity has both the intent and the ability to hold until maturity. Securities are considered held to maturity if sale occurs after at least **85% of principal** has been collected.

In the rare case that these securities are not held to maturity, an *ordinary gain/loss* results on disposal. This would be true, for example, when the issuer of the debt security exercises a call provision, compelling the investor to redeem them early. If the future exercise of a call provision on a purchased callable debt security is considered likely, any premium is required to be amortized over the period from purchase through the expected exercise date.

Balance Sheet

HTM securities are initially **recorded at cost** and then **carried at amortized cost** (ie, face amount, net of unamortized discount or premium).

- The difference between the cost and the face/maturity value is amortized over the life of the security, using the effective rate method (discussed later in the bonds section); however, the straight-line method may be used if it doesn't materially differ.
- Since HTM securities are not going to be sold, fluctuations in market price are disclosed but not recorded.

HTM securities are generally considered **noncurrent** assets unless the maturity date is less than one year from the balance sheet date.

Any **allowance for credit losses** is **reported separately** from the amortized cost of the financial asset on the balance sheet.

There are no unrealized gains/losses with respect to HTM securities.

Income Statement

- The increase/decrease in the allowance for **credit losses** will be reported on the I/S in the period of the change as credit loss expense or reversal of credit loss expense, respectively.
- **Realized gains/losses** should not happen but could.
- Report **interest income** net of amortization on the income statement.

Statement of Cash Flows

The cash effects of purchases (outflows) and sales or redemptions (inflows) of HTM securities are classified as **investing** activities on the statement of cash flows.

In addition to the three methods of accounting for and reporting investments in debt securities, the investor may elect to apply the fair value option. Under the fair value option, the securities will be reported at FMV (B/S) and both realized and unrealized gains/losses will be reported as a component of income from continuing operations (I/S).

Investments in Equity Securities of Other Entities

ASC 321 applies to most investments in equity securities of another entity and to other ownership interests, such as investments in partnerships, unincorporated joint ventures, and limited liability entities as if those interests were equity securities. It does *not* apply to:

- Investments accounted for under the "adjusted cost method" or the equity method (discussed later)
- Investments in consolidated subsidiaries
- A membership in an exchange representing an ownership interest in the exchange
- Federal Home Loan Bank and Federal Reserve Bank Stock

Balance Sheet

Investments in equity securities are originally **recorded at cost** but are adjusted to **fair value** each balance sheet date (ie, the **fair value approach**). If the fair value is not readily determinable, then we use the "adjusted cost method" (discussed later), which is cost minus any impairment losses.

On the balance sheet, the classification of these investments will be determined by the measurement category they fall into, either **current or noncurrent** assets, as specified in ASC 825, *Financial Instruments*.

Income Statement

Unrealized gains/losses (temporary) are reported as a component of income from continuing operations. This is the same as the accounting for investments in debt securities classified as trading securities.

Realized gains/losses are always on the income statement along with interest and dividend income.

Statement of Cash Flows

On the statement of cash flows, the classifications of cash flows related to the acquisition (outflows) or disposal (inflows) related to these investments will be based on the nature and purpose for which they are acquired, either **operating or investing**.

Fair Value Option

As previously mentioned, ASC 825 allows an entity to value various **eligible items** at **fair value** at certain dates, referred to as **election dates**. Once the fair value option is elected, it is **irrevocable** until a subsequent election date. **Eligible items** include:

- Most recognized financial instruments
    - Includes both financial assets and financial liabilities
    - Does *not* include certain instruments:
        - Subsidiaries or VIEs required to be consolidated
        - Deferred compensation arrangements, including pension or other postretirement or post-employment obligations and stock option or stock purchase plans
        - Assets or liabilities recognized under leases
        - Deposit liabilities of depository institutions
        - Financial instruments classified as a component of stockholders' equity
- Firm commitments involving only financial instruments that would not be recognized at inception

- Written loan commitments
- Rights and obligations under insurance contracts or warranties when certain requirements are met:
  - The insurance contract or warranty is not a financial instrument.
  - The insurer or warrantor is allowed by the terms to pay a third party to provide goods or services to settle the obligation.

Election dates include:

- When the entity first recognizes an eligible item on its F/S
- The date on which the entity enters into a firm commitment
- When an item that was reported at fair value due to specialized accounting principles, with unrealized gains or losses reported in earnings, no longer qualifies for the specialized accounting treatment
- When an investment becomes subject to the equity method
- A circumstance requiring the item to be reported at fair value at a point in time but not at each reporting date, other than an impairment

An election date also occurs when *an event* requires an eligible item to be reported at fair value or to be recognized initially, such as:

- Business combinations
- Consolidation or deconsolidation of a VIE
- Significant debt modifications

The fair value option can be elected on an instrument-by-instrument basis. Electing the fair value option for a particular instrument does not require election for a similar instrument held by the same entity. This includes a circumstance where the investor holds bonds, for example, with a total face value of $100,000, allowing the investor to elect the fair value option for one portion and account for the remainder as held to maturity securities.

Some of the specific applications of the fair value option include the following:

- An investment which otherwise qualifies for the **equity method** would be reported at fair value on each balance sheet date, increases or decreases will be recognized as unrealized gains or losses on the income statement, and dividends received will be recognized as income. In other words, the fair value option overrides the equity method.
- **HTM securities** continue to be accounted for at amortized cost, recognizing interest income under the effective interest method. In addition, the carrying value is adjusted to fair value on each balance sheet date with the increase/decrease recognized as a component of net income.
- **AFS debt securities** will be reported at fair value on each balance sheet date, as already required. Unrealized gains or losses are reported as a component of net income, however, instead of OCI.

Note that trading debt securities are not affected.

Disclosures under Fair Value Option

When an entity elects the fair value option, certain disclosures are required as of each balance sheet date.

- Management's reasons for electing the fair value option for each item for which the election was made
- If elected for some, but not all, items within a group of similar items, a description of the similar items, the reasons for a partial election, and how the similar items affect line items on the statement of financial position
- The differences between fair value amounts and principal balances of receivables or payables with contractual principal amounts
- Disclosures required when applying the fair value option for investments that would have been accounted for under the equity method if the fair value election had not been made

Disclosures are also required for each period for which an income statement is presented:

- Amounts of each gain or loss recognized in earnings as a result of changes in fair values
- An indication as to where interest and dividends are reported on the income statement and how they are measured
- For receivables held as assets, the gains or losses resulting from changes in the instrument's credit risk, including how it is measured
- For liabilities affected by changes in the instrument's credit risk during the period, the gains or losses resulting from changes in the instruments credit risk, reasons for the change, and how the gains or losses are measured

Lecture 3.05 – Investments in the Stock of Other Entities

Overview

An investor may acquire equity securities (common or preferred stock), debt securities (bonds), and derivatives (eg, stock rights) of other companies. When a company acquires equity securities of another entity, they are generally reported on the balance sheet at their *fair market values* as of the balance sheet date, with both realized and unrealized gains/losses being reported in *income*.

As indicated previously, however, there are three circumstances that either require or allow a different accounting treatment.

0 – 20% **Adjusted cost method***	**20 – 50%** **Equity method** (one-line consolidation)	**50% +** **Consolidation** (another section)
▪ Investor cannot exercise significant influence over investee. ▪ Used when fair value is not readily determinable. ▪ Requires election.	▪ Investor can exercise significant influence over the entity. ▪ Investor does not have a controlling financial interest.	▪ Investor has a controlling financial interest in the investee (Acquiree). ▪ May result from equity ownership or other factors, such as representation on the BOD, making the investor the primary beneficiary of a VIE.

**There is no longer an official term for the accounting for these types of investments. "Adjusted cost method" is used for the sake of convenience.*

Equity Method

The equity method is used when the investor can exercise **significant influence** over the operating and financial policies of the investee. This method is more consistent with accrual accounting in that the investor recognizes its share of the investee's income in the period earned, regardless of if or when the income is distributed to equity holders. (ASC 323)

It is generally assumed that the investor has such ability when it holds 20% or more of the voting equity stock, but that is not required. When ownership is less than 20%, the degree of influence held by the investor is a matter of professional judgment and considers various **factors**:

- Significant intercompany transactions, or technological dependency.
- Officers of the investor serving as officers or board members of the investee.
- The investor is a major customer or supplier of the investee
- The investor owns at least 20% of the voting stock of the investee provided:
  - No other investor holds a larger voting block, or
  - A small group of investors own a majority of the equity and exercises total control.
- The investor has definite plans to acquire additional stock in the future to bring their interest up to at least 20%.

When applying the equity method:

- The investment is originally recorded at Cost
- As the investee reports earnings, it is reported on the investor's income statement as "**equity in earnings,**" equal to the investor's percentage owned multiplied by the investee's earnings, as a component of continuing operations.
  - Similar to consolidated financial statements, the effects of intercompany transactions are eliminated.
  - The investor increases the investment by the same amount.
- If the investee reports losses, the entity will recognize its share of the losses in earnings as "equity in losses," reducing the investment by the same amount.
  - In general, losses cannot be recognized that reduce the carrying value of the investment below zero, unless the investor has guaranteed investee obligations or is committed to provide additional financial support.
  - If the investee subsequently becomes profitable again, unrecognized equity method losses will be offset against the investor's share of profits until they have been absorbed.
- Dividends received are considered a reduction of the investment account and do NOT appear on the income statement. The assumption is that the investor already recorded its share of the investee's income prior to its being distributed in the form of dividends.
- When the purchase price is not equal to the investor's percentage owned multiplied by the investee's book value, adjustments to equity in earnings will result in order to reflect the investor's true share of the investee's income.
  - Those differences are considered:
    - Fair value write up of assets (Fair value increment)
      - **PP&E** – depreciated
      - **Inventory** – written off when sold
      - **Land** – not depreciated but written off when sold
      - **Goodwill** – not amortized but impairment losses recognized

Ownership of **preferred stock** cannot, by itself, give an investor significant influence. However, the investor may have such influence due to other causes and, thus, may use the equity method of accounting for the preferred stock investment.

Preferred stock income under the equity method is equal to the dividends allocated to it.

- For noncumulative preferred stock, this will equal declared dividends only.
- For cumulative preferred stock, this will equal the annual dividend preference regardless of payments in that year.

To illustrate the accounting under the equity method, assume an investor paid $300 on 1/1/X1 to acquire 30% of the stock of an investee, at a time when the investee's net assets (equity) equaled $1,000. As a result, the original investment equaled the investor's 30% share of equity.

In 20X1, the investee reported net income of $400 and paid dividends totaling $100 to stockholders of record on 12/31/X1 with a payment date of 1/7/X2. The investment entry is:

1/1/X1	Investment	300	
	Cash		300

The entry to report the investor's share of income is:

12/31/X1	Investment	120	
	Equity in Investee Income		120

The entry to record the dividend:

12/31/X1	Dividends receivable	30	
	Investment		30

There is also an entry on 1/7/X2 for the collection of the receivable. Notice that the investor's investment account changes as the equity of the investee changes.

	S/E of Investee	Investment (30%)
Purchase Date, 1/1/X1	$1,000	$300
Net Income	400	120
Dividends	(100)	(30)
Balance, 12/31/X1	1,300	390

In the example, the $300 purchase price equaled 30% of the equity of the investee. When the purchase price exceeds the investor's share of equity, the excess needs to be identified, and accounted for in an appropriate manner. First, any assets with fair values differing from carrying values are identified, and the investor determines their percentage share of that excess (or deficiency). Any remaining excess is assumed to represent goodwill on the purchase.

The excess of the cost of the investment over book value is not reported separately on the financial statement; it is included in the investment. Nevertheless, it will have an impact on the subsequent reporting of income by the investor that depends on the nature of the asset causing the difference:

- **Depreciable and amortizable assets** – Differences will be amortized against the reported equity in investee income based on the appropriate life of the asset.
- **Goodwill** – Amount initially recorded will later reduce reported income in periods in which impairment losses are recognized. If the alternative accounting approach for nonpublic entities is elected, it is amortized.
- **All assets** – Outstanding differences will be written off against reported income at the time the asset is sold or otherwise disposed of.

These adjustments are necessary for reporting the investor's true share of the investee's earnings.

For example, an equity method investee may have a building that had a book value of $50,000 when the investor acquired its shares. However, if the fair value of the building was greater, say $1,000,000 on that date, the value, and therefore the purchase price of the shares, would include the $1,000,000 amount, not the $50,000.

When the investee is depreciating the building, its depreciation expense will be based on the book value of $50,000. The investor, on the other hand, is paid the equivalent of its share of $1,000,000 and has to depreciate the difference.

Assume the investor's 30% investment in the previous example cost $380 instead of $300; that $10 of the excess was attributable to inventory, which was sold during 20X1; $30 was attributable to land, which was still owned by the investee at the end of 20X1; and the remaining $40 represented a building, with an estimated useful life of 40 years.

The inventory excess should be written off in 20X1, the land excess should remain, and building depreciation of $40 / 40 = $1 should be recorded in 20X1. As a result, the equity in investee income reported by the investor is $109, computed as follows:

Net income of investee	400
Percentage	30%
Investor share	120
Inventory	(10)
Land	(0)
Building	(1)
Equity in investee income	109

Examine the changes in the investment account in 20X1, in comparison to the changes in the investor's share of the investee's equity:

	S/E of Investee	Investment (30%)	Equity (30%)	Excess
Purchase Date, 1/1/X1	$1,000	$380	$300	$80
Net Income	400	109	120	(11)
Dividends	(100)	(30)	(30)	-----
Balance, 12/31/X1	1,300	459	390	69

By including the adjustments for the sale of inventory and depreciation on the building in income, the excess of cost over book value in the initial investment is gradually being written off. After the land is sold by the investee and building is completely depreciated, the investment will equal equity, and further reported income will simply be the investor's ownership percentage multiplied by the investee's reported income.

On 1/1/X1, we acquire 30% of a company for $1,000. The fair value (FV) of the investee is $3,000 and the book value (BV) is $2,500. The difference is from PP&E with an FV $500 higher than its BV. During the year, the investee reports income of $120 and pays dividends of $40. PP&E is depreciated over 10 years, and 10% of initial goodwill (GW) is impaired that year.

A significant amount of research was performed, and experts were consulted, to assist in the measurement of the FV of the entity to enable a reasonable purchase price. Generally, however, the FV of this investment is not readily determinable and there were no observable market transactions involving the security during the period X1.

In addition, reviewing all relevant information, there were no indications that the investment was impaired or that the investee would have a substantial doubt as to its ability to continue as a going concern.

Investee's balances at 1/1/X1	FV	$3,000 / Investee's income is $120 / GW impaired by 10%
	BV	$2,500 / Dividend paid is $40

Purchase price	$1,000	$100 Goodwill—impaired by $10	
FV of investor's share of investee	$900 (3,000 × 30%)		
		$150 FV PP&E / 10 yrs =	$15 yr
BV of investor's share of investee	$750 (2,500 × 30%)		
			$25

The journal entries under the **Equity method** would be:

1. **Record acquisition of investment at cost**

Investment	$1,000		($750 BV + $150 PP&E + $100 GW)
Cash		$1,000	

2. **Record % of earnings** ($120 annual income × 30% = $36)

Investment	$36	
Equity in earnings (I/S)		$36

3. **Record % of Cash dividend** ($40 dividend received × 30% = $12)

Cash	$12	
Investment		$12

4. **Record amortization/depreciation/impairment of excess** between purchase price and BV

Equity in earnings (I/S)	$25		($10 GW + $15 PP&E)
Investment		$25	

Investment T-account

1,000	
36	
	12
	25
999	

Note: The investment account changes as the investee's equity account changes (better accrual accounting).

Lecture 3.06 – Adjusted Cost Method

No Significant Influence – Measurement

Initial Measurement

When an investor has neither a controlling financial interest (consolidated) nor the ability to exercise significant influence over the activities of the investee (equity method), the investor will initially record the investment at cost.

Fair Value Method

In most cases, it will then be adjusted to its fair value (Fair Value Method) on each balance sheet date with both realized and unrealized gains/losses recognized in income. Realized gains/losses, of course, will be adjusted for any portion that may have been reported in a prior period as an unrealized gain/loss. This is similar to the trading securities approach previously discussed.

When **market value** is **not readily determinable,** the entity will determine if it is eligible to measure fair value using a practical expedient. It involves using the published fair value of net assets per share, or equivalent amount, multiplied by the number of shares/units held. This approach can be used only when the fair value per share is calculated in accordance with ASC 946, *Financial Services—Investment Companies*.

Adjusted Cost Method

If the investment also does not qualify to be measured by applying the practical expedient, the entity may **elect** to report it at an amount equal to its **cost minus any impairment losses** (we call this the "**Adjusted Cost Method"**) that have been recognized and adjusted for any changes resulting from observable price changes.

- The entity is required to make a qualitative assessment every reporting period, evaluating impairment indicators to determine if the investment is impaired. Examples of impairment indicators are provided in the Impairments discussion below.
- An observable price change occurs when there is an orderly transaction involving an identical security or a similar security of the same issuer.
- Once elected, the investment continues to be accounted for in that manner until it no longer qualifies to use it.
    - This will occur when either the market value becomes readily determinable or when it becomes eligible for the practical expedient. Additionally, the investor may gain the ability to exercise significant influence over the investee, at which point the equity method would be appropriate, applied on a *prospective basis*.
    - As long as this approach is in use, the entity is required to reassess whether the investment continues to qualify to use this measurement every reporting period.

Impairments

Each reporting period, the entity is required to perform a qualitative analysis to determine if there is an indication that the investment has been impaired. The qualitative evaluation will look for circumstances that might adversely affect the investee, such as:

- A deterioration in earnings, financial position, credit rating, asset quality, or business prospects
- Changes in the regulatory, economic, or technological environment

- Changes in the market conditions relevant to the entity's geographical area or industry
- A bona fide offer to purchase the entity, or a completed auction process, for less than the carrying amount of the net investment
- Factors affecting the investee's ability to continue as a going concern

When there is such an indication, the entity will determine if an estimate of the fair value is lower than the carrying value, in which case an impairment loss is recognized. The impairment loss reduces the carrying value of the investment and is reported in the *current period's income*. The impairment loss may be recovered as more information is obtained and the securities are adjusted back upward to fair value.

As is true for all investments in equity securities that are not required to be accounted for via consolidation or the equity method, dividend income from investments in equity securities is reported in income.

- The original investment is recorded at cost
- When the investee earns money, no journal entry is recorded
- When a dividend is received it is recorded as **Dividend Income** on the income statement (not a reduction of the Investment)
  - In rare cases, if the dividend received is greater than the investor's proportionate share of the investee's income since acquisition, then it is recorded as a **reduction** of the investment (these usually are distributions of an investee's earnings that occurred BEFORE the investor made their purchase of the investee).

Cash	X	
Investment		X

- No difference between BV and purchase price is taken into consideration (no excess amortization or depreciation as in the equity method).

Disclosures

Disclosures for equity investments accounted for under this approach when the fair value is not readily determinable will include:

- The carrying amount of the investments
- Impairment losses, if any, both for the current period and on a cumulative basis
- Upward adjustments to the investment, both for the current period and on a cumulative basis
- Considerations applied in determining the carrying amounts of the investments, upward or downward adjustments, and additional information the entity considers necessary to enable users to understand the qualitative disclosures

Notice that while the investor's share of the investee net income is \$120 × 30% = \$36, only the dividend received of \$40 × 30% = \$12 is recorded in income. The reason for the difference in the handling of income and dividends is the difference in the relationship between investor and investee under each circumstance.

- Since the equity method is used when the investor has the ability to exercise significant influence over the activities of the investee, it is assumed that the investor could convince the investee to distribute more, or even all, of its income in the form of dividends. This is considered an application of the accrual method.

- When the investor *does not* have the ability to exercise such influence, it has no assurance that it will receive any dividends beyond those which have been declared. Although this is not consistent with the accrual method, it is not considered a departure since accrual of a receivable that is not necessarily probable would be considered inappropriate.

In general, dividends from investments in equity securities are reported as income. This would not be true, of course, if the investee is a consolidated subsidiary, in which case dividends from the subsidiary to the parent are eliminated. Nor would it be the case under the equity method, where the investor reports its entire share of investee income as an increase in the investment, and distributions of dividends reduce the investment.

When dividends are received from investments that are either reported at fair value or via the adjusted cost method, however, they are generally reported as income.

Dividends received, however, are not always distributions of income to the investor. If the investee declares dividends that exceed the cumulative income it has earned since the date of the investment, the excess distribution is a **return of capital** to the investor, and is accounted for as a reduction in the carrying value of the investment.

For example, if the investee declares a dividend of $450, and the income earned since the investment date is only $400, the entry on the dividend record date by a 10% investor would have been:

Dividends receivable	45	
Dividend income		40
Investment		5

If an investee declares a **stock dividend or issues stock rights** or other classes of stock to existing shareholders, no income is reported. Instead, the carrying value of the investment is simply allocated over the increased quantity of securities.

- If the securities are all of the same class, no entry is needed, and the number of shares is disclosed in the notes to the financial statements, if material.
- If the new securities are in a different class, an entry is made to transfer part of the carrying value, using the relative fair value approach.

For example, assume a client purchased 100 shares of stock at a price of $22 per share, or a total cost of $2,200:

Investment in stock	2,200	
Cash		2,200

If the investee declares a **10% stock dividend**, then the number of shares held by the investor will increase to 110, but no entry is made. Instead, the $2,200 is allocated over 110 shares, so that the cost basis of each share becomes $20.

If, instead, the investee issues a **stock right** for each existing share, and the fair value of the stock and the stock rights on the record date are $24 per share and $6 per right, respectively, then the rights will be allocated 6 / (24+6) = 20% of the carrying value of the securities:

Investment in rights	440	
Investment in stock		440

No income is reported on dividends in arrears on cumulative preferred stock under the cost method, since this represents dividends that have not been declared. Only once they are declared and the date of record is reached can they be reported in the investor's records as dividend income.

The purchase of **life insurance** on an officer can be a form of investment when it builds up a cash value (**cash surrender value**). The portion of the premium that increases the cash value is accumulated as an asset (noncurrent asset) on the balance sheet, and the rest of the premium is recognized as life insurance expense. If the officer dies, the proceeds from the policy are recognized as income only to the extent they exceed the cash value.

Dividends on life insurance are treated as reductions of the net premium cost and are not reported as dividend income.

Equity	Adjusted Cost
1) Buy	
Investment 1,000 ($750 BV + $150 PP&E + $100 GW) Cash 1,000	Investment 1,000 Cash 1,000
2) Investee earns money	
Investment 36 (120 × 30%) Equity in Earnings 36 EIE = I/S (N) section – Not cash ⇒ back out in cash flow	No journal entry
3) Pay a dividend	
Cash 12 (40 × 30%) Investment 12	Cash 12 Dividend Income 12 DI = I/S (N) section
4) Amortization/depreciation/impairment of excess	
Purchase $1,000 Goodwill = 1,000 – 900 FV 900 = 100 BV 750 Impairment = $10 Depreciation = 900 – 750 150/10 yrs = <u>$15</u> = $25 Equity in Earnings 25 Investment 25 Taking out amortization/depreciation/impairment	No journal entry
*Investment follows equity balance of investee.	*No change to Investment.

Changes in Ownership Percentages

There are a variety of ways in which an investor may gain the ability to exercise significant influence over the investee. The investor may do so by acquiring additional shares of the investee's stock; as a result of the retirement of shares by the investee; by establishing a significant business dependency, such as becoming a significant customer or supplier; or by obtaining greater representation in the investee's governance.

When an investor *gains the ability* to exercise significant influence over the activities of an investee, the investment qualifies for the equity method and it is required to be applied prospectively.

- The carrying value of the investment is not adjusted.
- The cost of additional shares of the investee acquired by the investor, if any, is added to the carrying value of the investment.
- The equity method of accounting is applied to the investment from that point forward, using the percentage of the investee that is owned by the investor

An investor entity may also *lose the ability* to exercise significant influence over the activities of the investee. This may result from the disposal of a portion of the investment; the issuance of additional shares by the investee, reducing the investor's ownership percentage; the termination of a business dependency, such as discontinuing being a significant supplier or customer; or by reducing the investor's representation in governance.

When an investor loses the ability to exercise significant influence over the activities of the investee, it no longer qualifies for use of the equity method of accounting for the investment. The investor will:

- Apply the equity method up until the date on which the investment no longer qualifies for its use.
- The carrying value of the investment is considered its new cost.
- The investor applies the appropriate method other than the equity method:
  - If the market value of the investee is readily determinable, the investment will be adjusted to its fair value on each balance sheet date with unrealized gains and losses reported in earnings for the period.
  - If the market value of the investee is not readily determinable, the investor may elect the adjusted cost method and so indicate in the summary of significant accounting policies.

In all cases, the change in methods is applied **prospectively**.

Fair Value Option

As previously discussed, ASC 825, *Financial Instruments*, includes a provision that allows an entity to choose to report almost any of its financial instruments, including both its financial assets and financial liabilities, at fair value. This is referred to as the fair value option and may be applied to **eligible financial instruments** (eg, receivables, payables, derivatives, securities, etc.) on specified **election dates** on a **security-by-security basis** and may be applied to some or all of a group of securities.

The **election dates** on which an entity may elect the fair value option include:

- When the eligible item is first recognized.
- When an eligible firm commitment is entered into.

- When items previously presented at fair value due to specialized accounting principles, with unrealized gains or losses recognized in earnings, no longer qualify for the specialized accounting principles.
- When an investment becomes subject to the equity method.
- When an item is required to be measured at fair value on a one-time basis but is not required to be adjusted to fair value on subsequent financial statement dates.

On a given election date, the entity may elect to report the item or items at fair value or may apply the election to only some of the items, with the decision being made on a *security-by-security basis*.

- An entity with numerous firm commitments may elect to report some, all, or none of them at fair value.
- An entity with several investments accounted for under the equity method may elect to report some, all, or none of them at fair value.

Once made, a fair value election is irrevocable. It may, however, be changed on a subsequent election date. When the fair value option election is made, the eligible item will be measured at its **fair value on each balance sheet date**. Any unrealized gains or losses will be recognized as a component of **income.** If the fair value option election were applied to:

- An equity method investment, it would be measured at fair value on each balance sheet date and any changes, net of dividends received, will be recognized as a gain or loss.
- An available for sale (AFS) investment in debt securities, will be reported at the same value as before the election but the unrealized gains and losses will be reported as a component of income rather than other comprehensive income.
- A held to maturity (HTM) investment in debt securities, it would continue to be accounted for under the amortized cost method, applying the effective interest method, but after amortization of discount or premium, the carrying value will be increased or reduced to fair value at the balance sheet date and the unrealized gain or loss will be recognized in income.
- A firm commitment, such as a foreign currency forward exchange contract, an asset or liability would be recognized at fair value as the subject of the commitment, such as the foreign currency exchange rate, changes.

UWorld
YOUR WORLD OF LEARNING
ROGER
CPA Review

FAR 4 – Derivatives & Hedge Accounting

FAR 4 – Derivatives & Hedge Accounting

Table of Contents

Derivatives & Hedge Accounting

Lecture 4.01 – Derivatives

Financial Instruments

Financial instruments are defined under ASC 815 to include:

- Cash
- Ownership interests in an entity (eg, stock)
- Contracts that create **both:**
  - An **obligation** to transfer one or more financial instruments by one entity
  - A **right** to receive one or more financial instruments by another entity (eg, derivatives, debt securities, accounts receivable/payable, loans, etc.)

Some financial instruments, including notes and loans receivable or payable, are generally reported at amortized cost. Investments in the equity securities of nonpublic companies are usually accounted for at cost or under a valuation approach, such as the equity method. Many financial instruments, including investments in certain marketable securities and all derivatives, should be reported on the financial statements (F/S) at fair value.

Derivatives

Entities acquire derivatives for *three reasons.* They acquire them as investments, for arbitrage, or as hedges. (ASC 815)

1. Investments – An entity may invest its excess working capital, or amounts set aside in sinking funds, in derivatives such as stock options to increase its return on investment. When an entity's stock options are publicly traded, they generally sell for substantially less than the security they provide the option to acquire. An increase in the value of the stock will result in a comparable increase in the value of the stock option.

- Based on a lower investment amount, the return is greater.
- If the value of the stock decreases, of course, there is a comparably disproportionate decrease in the value of the derivative, making it a relatively high-risk investment.

2. Arbitrage – Arbitrage is the ability to take advantage of price differentials in separate markets allowing the entity to enter transactions that are potentially profitable without significant risk of loss.

If, for example, the six-month future price of a commodity was $1, the entity may enter a futures contract requiring it to buy 100,000 units at $1 at the end of six months. In another market, the six-month future price may be $1.05 and the entity may enter into a futures contract requiring it to sell 100,000 units at $1.05 after six months. In reality they will neither buy nor sell the commodity. Instead:

- If the market price is below $1, the entity will pay the difference between $1 and the market price to the counterparty in the buy contract. At the same time, the entity will receive the difference between $1.05 and the market price from the counterparty to the sell contract. As a result, the entity will earn the difference, $.05 per unit.

- If the market price is above $1.05, the entity will receive the difference between $1 and the market price from the counterparty in the buy contract. At the same time, the entity will pay the difference between $1.05 and the market price to the counterparty to the sell contract. As a result, the entity will earn the difference, $.05 per unit.
- If the market price is between $1 and $1.05, the entity will receive the difference between $1 and the market price from the counterparty in the buy contract. At the same time, the entity will receive the difference between $1.05 and the market price from the counterparty to the sell contract. As a result, the entity will earn the difference, $.05 per unit.

3. Hedge – A hedge is the use of a derivative to reduce or eliminate a risk that the entity is subject to either as a result of an asset or liability recognized on its F/S or a future transaction.

If, for example, an entity has a commitment for an asset being manufactured for it that is expected to be delivered in six months at a cost of 100,000 Foreign Currency Units or FCU (such as Euros or Pesos), which has an exchange rate of $1.25. In other words, 1 FCU will cost $1.25 and the cost of the machine is $125,000.

If the exchange rate of the FCU increases to $1.30, the asset will cost the entity $130,000 instead of $125,000, which may be more than the entity has budgeted for the acquisition. The entity may enter into a derivative such as a forward exchange contract under which it is required to acquire 100,000 FCUs at the end of six months at the exchange rate of $1.25 per FCU.

- If the exchange rate increases above $1.25, the entity will pay more for the asset but will receive the difference from the counterparty.
- If the exchange rate decreases below $1.25, the entity will pay less for the asset, but will be required to pay the difference to the counterparty.

As indicated, derivatives are acquired to increase potential gains when used as investments but may also produce losses. Derivatives are used as hedges to reduce or eliminate the risk of an adverse change in circumstances, but also eliminate the opportunity to take advantage of a favorable change.

- Derivatives may be assets or liabilities.
- Derivatives are always reported at their *fair values.*
- Unrealized gains and losses are generally recognized in income.
  - Unrealized gains and losses on cash flow hedges are temporarily recognized in other comprehensive income (OCI) instead of income.
  - Unrealized gains and losses on fair value hedges are recognized in income along with offsetting losses or gains on the hedged item.
  - All other unrealized gains and losses on hedges are recognized in income in the period of the increase or decrease in value.

Derivatives are financial instruments that have the following three characteristics (**NUNS**):

- **<u>N</u>o net investment** – To be considered a derivative, there must either be no initial net investment or an initial net investment that is smaller than would normally be required for an instrument that would respond similarly in the market.
  - Derivatives such as interest rate swaps, futures contracts, and forward exchange contracts often require no initial net investment or an investment that is limited to fees paid to attorneys and others to establish the derivative.

- Derivatives such as stock options require a smaller investment than the shares underlying the derivative yet will respond similarly to the shares as the value of the shares increase or decrease.

- **An Underlying and a Notional amount** – The notional amount is basically the number of units (units, bushels, pounds) and the underlying is the factor that affects the derivative's value (specified price, interest rate, exchange rate). In a forward exchange contract, for example, the notional amount would be the number of FCUs and the underlying would be the future exchange rate.

- **Net Settlement** – The derivative can be settled in a net amount. In the case of a forward exchange contract, for example, the entity does not actually buy or sell the FCUs but, instead, receives or pays the difference between the agreed upon exchange rate and the market rate. In the case of an interest rate swap, the parties do not pay each other the contractual interest amounts but the difference is paid from one party to the other.

Since one of the characteristics of a derivative is the requirement that it can be settled on a net basis, a derivative will always be settled by the transfer of a financial instrument. As a result, a derivative is always considered a financial instrument for financial reporting purposes.

- Examples of Derivatives include:
  - **Option contract** – Has *right* but *not obligation* to purchase/sell in the future. Put-option, right to sell shares, call-option, right to acquire shares in the future.
  - **Futures contract** – Has *right and obligation* to deliver/purchase foreign currency or goods in the future at a price set today. Similar to a forward contract normally traded on a national exchange.
  - **Forward contract** – Has *right and obligation* to buy or sell a commodity at a future date for an agreed-upon price.
  - **Interest rate or foreign currency swap** – A forward-based contract or agreement between two counterparties to exchange streams of cash flows over a specified period in the future.

- Note that these instruments create **off-balance sheet risk**, due to the possible changes in amounts owed.
  - Disclose the **credit risk**—ie, risk that a loss occurs because another party fails to perform according to the terms of a contract.
  - Required disclosures about each significant concentration
    - Activity, region, or economic characteristic
  - The maximum amount of loss due to credit risk
  - The entity's policy of requiring collateral or other security
  - The entity's policy arrangements to mitigate the credit risk.
  - Optional to disclose **market risk**—ie, the risk a loss may occur as a result of changes in the market value of financial instruments due to economic circumstances.

Someone who wants to make a large investment in the stock market can do so without buying any stocks through the use of **stock index futures**. Let's select a popular index of stock market prices, the Standard and Poor's 500 index based on the market value of 500 large U.S. corporations (commonly known as the S&P index).

Assume for the moment that a corporation wants to make a $10,000,000 investment in the U.S. stock market on October 1 at a time the S&P index is 1,000. The company can buy a stock index futures contract for 10,000 units of the S&P index. With an underlying of 1,000 and a notional amount of 10,000, this is the equivalent of making an investment of 1,000 × 10,000 = $10,000,000. The company does not, however, put up any cash.

Let's assume that the futures contract has a settlement date on January 2 of the following year, and that the S&P index has risen to 1,200 as of the end of the current year. The increase of 200 in the underlying multiplied by the 10,000 notional amount means that the company expects to receive a check for 200 × 10,000 = $2,000,000 from the party that took the other side of the futures contract.

There is no entry on October 1, since no exchange of cash took place. At the end of the year, the expectation of receiving a settlement of $2,000,000 in a couple of days is reported as follows:

12/31	Receivable on derivative	2,000,000	
	Gain on derivative		2,000,000

This is a gain on the **speculative** use of derivatives since the company acquired the derivative purely as an attempt to profit from stock market increases.

If, instead, the S&P dropped to 800 during that time period, the company would have to pay $2,000,000 to the other side. A payable and loss would be recorded for the cash expected to be paid at settlement. Notice that no actual stock needs to be involved: the derivative is settled by a transfer of cash from one side to the other.

Popular derivatives such as stock index futures are easily available through public securities markets, but derivatives can also be created privately. A common example of a private derivative is an **interest rate swap agreement**.

For example, Bank 1 that has made many loans with variable interest rates might contract with Bank 2 that has made many loans with fixed interest rates. Bank 1 is concerned about a drop in interest rates that would reduce its interest income. Bank 2 is concerned about a rise in interest rates that it could not benefit from with fixed rate loans. They sign a contract agreeing that each party will pay the other amounts based on the interest rates of the loans each bank has outstanding with customers.

In the specific case of the interest rate swap, there are two risks that cannot be reflected on the F/S (**off-balance-sheet risk**) but need to be disclosed in connection with such an agreement:

- The risk of exchanging a lower interest rate for a higher one.
- The risk that the other bank might default on the agreement (**credit risk**).

Generally, any financial instrument with off-balance-sheet risks requires disclosures in the notes to the F/S. In addition, for all financial instruments, the client must disclose **concentration of credit risk**, which is a special risk of multiple defaults when a client is depending on the performance of many different parties who are affected by common issues.

For example, a bank which lends only to farmers in a certain area has a concentration of credit risk associated with the possibility of weather-related crop failures or general declines in agricultural prices affecting all of the bank's customers at once.

Finally, the client may hold investments whose fair value cannot be reasonably estimated. When this is true, any information that might assist the F/S user in determining the value of the investments must be disclosed. An explanation of the reason the value cannot be estimated is also needed.

As indicated, all derivatives are required to be reported at fair value. When accounted for as a cash flow hedge, unrealized gains and losses are initially reported in OCI. Unrealized gains/losses on fair value hedges and derivatives that are not designated as hedges are reported in net income.

In many cases, the fair value of a derivative is readily determinable. When it is not, the intrinsic value of the instrument is often used.

- An option to purchase a share of stock for $30 when its market value is $30 has no intrinsic value because it provides no benefit to the holder.
- An option to purchase a share at $30 when its market value is $35, however, has an intrinsic value of $5.
- In addition, depending on the length of the exercise period remaining, there may be a time value, which would be added to the intrinsic value in determining the value of the option.

Lecture 4.02 – Fair Value vs. Cash Flow Hedge

When a derivative contract has been made to **hedge** against the risk associated with another contract or planned activity, the method of accounting for changes in the fair value of the derivative depends on the type of hedge involved:

- **Fair value hedge** – If the derivative is hedging against a recognized asset/liability or a firm purchase commitment, then changes in the value of the derivative are reported in **income from continuing operations**.
  - An example is the purchase of put options to protect against a possible decline in the market price of a stock portfolio. Should the market decline, the losses on the stock should be offset by gains on the puts.
  - Fair value hedges can be used to hedge against the value of inventories, the value of a fixed-income investment, the value of a fixed-rate debt obligation, and a firm commitment.
- **Cash flow hedge** – If the derivative is hedging against a forecasted transaction that is expected to take place in the future, but which is not yet a legal commitment, then changes in the value of the derivative are reported as direct adjustments to stockholders' equity and are included in **other comprehensive income** (OCI) until the transaction is complete and the cash flows have actually occurred.
  - An example is the purchase of a futures contract on steel by a company that believes it will need to make large steel purchases in the near future. An increase in the price of steel will cause the value of the futures contract to rise, helping the company pay the increased costs. Since those costs are not yet reflected in income, the increase in the futures contract is not reflected either.

Assume the client is an oil distributor and has purchased 100 million gallons of gasoline from its supplier refinery on October 1 at a cost of 70 cents per gallon. They plan to sell the oil to various airlines in early January, but are concerned that, in the meantime, the price of oil might drop considerably from the current selling price of 80 cents.

To protect the inventory, the client sells a gasoline futures contract based on a wholesale gasoline price index per gallon (the underlying) times 100,000,000 gallons (the notional amount), with a settlement date of January 2.

Assume the price of the index drops 4 cents per gallon by the end of the year.

The purchase of the inventory by the distributor from the refinery is recorded as follows (assume immediate payment and entries in millions of dollars):

<u>**10/1**</u>	Inventory	70	
	Cash		70

When the futures contract is established, there is no entry since no cash is involved. This is a **fair value hedge** since the distributor is hedging against an existing asset.

As of the end of the year, the decline of 4 cents per share in the price of oil results in a loss on the inventory of $4,000,000. The futures contract, however, is now expected to result in a collection of $4,000,000 upon settlement. The entries are:

12/31	Loss on market decline in inventory	4	
	Inventory		4
	Receivable on derivative	4	
	Gain on fair value hedge		4

Both the loss on inventory and gain on the fair value hedge are included in the computation of net income, so there is no net income effect. This, of course, was the goal of the hedge.

Let's now go back to October 1 and look at the side of the airline that is planning on purchasing the gasoline in early January. This client might enter the very same contract to hedge against a price increase, but it would be a **cash flow hedge**, since there is no asset, liability, or fixed commitment yet for the purchase.

On October 1, the airline enters a derivative based on the gasoline index with the same notional amount of 100,000,000 gallons. There is **no entry** on that date.

On December 31, the price decline of 4 cents per gallon in the index means that the airline expects to have to pay $4,000,000 on the settlement date. The entry is:

12/31	OCI – loss on cash flow hedge	4	
	Payable on derivative		4

Note that the loss is not included in the calculation of net income. The reason is that the decline in gasoline is expected to reduce the cost of inventory in the next period, so this loss will be offset by reduction of cost of sales in the next period. Since the offsetting event is not yet reflected in net income, neither can the hedge.

Some hedges do not entirely protect a company against the risk that the hedge is intended to mitigate. A fair value hedge, for example, may not offset all changes in the fair value of the hedged item. Likewise, a cash flow hedge may not offset all changes in the cash flows associated with the hedged item.

The degree to which a change in the value of a fair value hedge offsets the change in the value of the hedged item, and the degree to which a change in the cash flows of a cash flow hedge offset changes in the cash flows of the hedged item is called the hedge's **effectiveness**.

- A hedge is **perfectly effective** if all changes in the fair value or cash flows of the hedged item are offset by corresponding changes in the hedge.
- A hedge is **highly effective** if most changes in the fair value or cash flows of the hedged item are offset by corresponding changes in the hedge. The portion not offset is the degree to which the hedge is **ineffective**.
- A hedge is considered **ineffective** if relatively few or none of the changes in the fair value or cash flows of the hedged item are offset by changes in the hedge.

Changes in the fair value of a hedging instrument, including both the effective and ineffective portions, are reported as follows:

- **Fair value hedges** – Recognized in *income* on the same line as the corresponding gain or loss on the hedged item in the income statement.

- **Cash flow hedges** – Recognized in *OCI*, to be taken into income in the same period in which changes to the hedged item affect income.
  - **Net investment hedges** (ie, a foreign currency cash flow hedge designed to mitigate foreign currency exposure due to a net investment in a foreign operation)—Recognized in *the currency translation adjustment section of OCI*

To summarize, when derivatives are used as speculation or fair value hedges, gains and losses are reported in net income (in the case of a fair value hedge, there will be offsetting amounts on the asset or commitment being hedged). When derivatives are used as cash flow hedges, gains and losses are reported in OCI (they are transferred to net income when the expected events occur and offsetting amounts are reported in net income).

Derivatives Summary

Speculation (nonhedge)
- Acquired to take on risk in the hopes of profit.
- Gain or loss in income from continuing operations. **(I/S)**

Fair value hedge
- Acquired to hedge against a recognized asset or liability or a firm purchase commitment.
- Gain or loss in income from continuing operations. **(I/S)**
  Should be offset by loss or gain on hedged item.

Cash flow hedge
- Acquired to hedge against a forecasted future transaction.
- Gain/loss in OCI **(B/S)**
- Nothing included in net income until forecasted activity occurs.

Net investment hedge—Foreign currency hedge against an investment in foreign operations
- Acquired to hedge against currency risk from a major investment in a company with a functional currency (ie, the currency in which books are maintained) other than the U.S. dollar.
- Gain/loss in OCI **(B/S)**
- Offsets translation losses or gains from investment in foreign operations.

Alternative Accounting Approach for Nonpublic Entities (Interest Rate Swaps)

The Private Company Council (PCC) of the FASB established an alternative accounting approach that is available to nonpublic entities when accounting for certain interest rate swaps, often referred to as "plain vanilla" interest rate swaps, and which have become very common among large and small entities.

This Simplified Hedge Accounting Approach gives nonpublic companies the option to use this simpler approach to account for certain types of interest rate swaps that are entered into for the purpose of economically converting variable-rate interest payments to fixed-rate payments.

An interest rate swap to which the alternative accounting approach applies is one related to the following circumstances:

- The entity has an obligation that bears interest at a variable rate.

- The entity enters into a derivative contract known as an interest rate swap under which:
  - The entity will receive payments from the other party at a variable rate
  - The entity will make payments to the other party at a fixed rate
- As a result of the swap, the net interest paid by the entity is equivalent to what would have been paid if the obligation had interest at a fixed rate.

In order to qualify for the alternative treatment, the variable rate in the swap must vary according to changes in the same index that causes changes in the rate on the related obligation. In addition:

- The terms must be virtually identical such that they mirror the terms of the underlying obligation.
- The settlement date on which payments are exchanged for the swap are very close to the dates on which payments are made on the underlying obligation.
- The initial fair value of the swap is zero, indicating that the interest rates are comparable on the date it is entered into and that the parties have different views on anticipated future changes in the index rate.
- The notional amount of the swap, the amount on which the swapped interest rates are calculated, must be equal to, or lower than the principal balance of the hedged instrument.
- All interest payments must be designated as hedged, in proportion to the ratio of the notional amount of the hedge and the principal balance of the underlying obligation.

If all conditions are met and the entity elects to apply the alternative accounting approach, there are several differences in the requirements. First, *documentation* and other elements are not required to be completed in advance. They may be completed any time until the first set of F/S on which the alternative accounting approach is applied are either issued or available to be issued, whichever is earlier.

The remaining differences are included in the *alternative accounting approach* which will be applied as follows:

- It is assumed that the swap is perfectly effective and the debt obligation is accounted for as if it bore interest at a fixed rate.
- The hedge, the interest rate swap, is reported at its *settlement amount* rather than its fair value.
- Any difference between reported amounts and payments made or received are reported in *OCI*.

The accounting for an interest rate swap under the alternative approach will result in the following:

- Interest expense will be debited for an amount calculated by applying the fixed rate to the principal balance, adjusted for the amount of time elapsed since the previous calculation.
- Principal will be debited for the amount by which it is reduced as a result of applying the terms of the obligation to any payments made.
- An asset or liability will be debited or credited to adjust the amount reported as the balance of the derivative to the settlement value of the interest rate swap.
- Cash will be credited for the net amount paid, including the payment on the underlying obligation adjusted for the net amount received from the counterparty or paid to the counterparty to the swap, depending on whether the index rate has increased or decreased, respectively.
- The amount required to balance the entry will be reported as a debit or credit to *OCI*.

Lecture 4.03 – Embedded Derivatives

Some instruments are not derivatives but include features that have the characteristics of a derivative. An investment in bonds has two inherent risks.

- There is **credit risk** because the issuer of bonds may or may not perform, which will affect the interest rate.
- There is **market risk** because the bonds will bear interest at a fixed rate and market interest rates may change, making the bonds more or less desirable and causing increases or decreases in their fair values.

Convertible bonds have an added feature in that they can be converted into common stock. As a result, increases in the stock price mitigate market risk as the bondholders can convert their bonds into shares of stock if the value of the stock exceeds that of the bonds. As a result, the value of the bonds will fluctuate as interest rates fluctuate and as the value of the stock fluctuates.

- The convertible bond would be considered a compound or **hybrid** instrument.
- The bond is the **host instrument**.
- The conversion feature would be considered an **embedded derivative**.

Since all derivatives are required to be reported at fair value, the entity will account for a hybrid instrument in one of two manners:

- If the host instrument is reported at fair value, the derivative is also reported at fair value.
- If the host instrument is not reported at fair value, the derivative will be separated or **bifurcated** from the host instrument and accounted for separately.
    - This would only be appropriate if the features have the characteristics of a derivative.
    - The derivative should have characteristics that respond to market influences differently from the host instrument

An example of an embedded derivative that can be separated from its host is a detachable stock purchase warrant that was acquired with an investment in bonds to be held to maturity. An example of an embedded derivative that **cannot** be separated from its host is the convertibility provision obtained with an investment in convertible bonds.

ASC 815 was issued to improve the financial reporting of certain hybrid financial instruments by requiring more consistent accounting that eliminates exemptions and provides a means to simplify the accounting for these instruments. Specifically, it allows financial instruments that have embedded derivatives to be accounted for as a whole if the holder elects to account for the whole instrument on a fair value basis.

Qualitative **disclosures** are required, regarding:

- How and why an entity uses derivative instruments
- How derivative instruments and related hedge items are accounted for
- How derivative instruments and related hedge items affect an entity's financial position, financial performance, and cash flows
    - **Additional Disclosures**
        - Objectives for holding or issuing such instruments, and strategies for achieving those objectives
        - Context to understand the instrument

- Risk management policies
- A list of hedged instruments
- Disclosure of fair value of financial instruments required when practicable to estimate fair value

Transfer and Servicing of Financial Assets

Entities, particularly financial institutions, will often dispose of financial instruments by transferring them to another entity. In many cases, these instruments are relatively favorable investments and the transferring entity may desire the ability to reacquire it. In other cases, the instrument may entail certain risks and the acquiring entity may desire the ability to dispose of it.

- A transfer of financial assets in which the transferor retains either the right or the obligation to reacquire the instrument, prior to its maturity, for an amount determined at the transfer date, is accounted for as a financing transaction, rather than a sale.
- In order to recognize the transfer as a sale, allowing the transferor to derecognize the instrument and recognize a gain or loss on disposal, three conditions must be satisfied:
  - The asset must be beyond the reach of the transferor and its creditors.
  - The transferor cannot place any restrictions on what the transferee can do with the asset.
  - There is no repurchase or redemption agreement that might allow the transferor to force a return of the asset.

Fair Value Option for Reporting Financial Assets & Financial Liabilities

ASC 820 defines fair value as "the price that would be received to sell an asset or paid to transfer a liability in an orderly transaction between market participants at the measurement date (at exit price)." An orderly transaction is a transaction that allows for normal marketing activities that are usual and customary, so they are NOT a forced transaction or sale.

Fair value measurements are required in certain circumstances:

- Derivatives are always reported at fair value.
- Identifiable assets acquired and liabilities assumed in a business combination are originally measured at fair value.
- Investments in marketable securities that are classified as either trading or available for sale.
- Most investments in equity securities.
- Impaired assets are written down due to their fair values.
- Nonmonetary transactions are measured at the fair value of the consideration exchanged.

In addition, there is a fair value option that allows an entity to elect to report virtually any or all of its financial assets and liabilities at fair value. When this irrevocable election is made, the item is remeasured at fair value on each balance sheet date and unrealized gains and losses are recognized in income.

UWorld
YOUR WORLD OF LEARNING
ROGER
CPA Review

FAR 5 - Foreign Operations

FAR 5 – Foreign Operations

Table of Contents

Foreign Operations

Lecture 5.01 – Foreign Currency Transactions, Receivables & Payables

Overview of Foreign Currency Matters

There are several ways in which an entity may be involved in foreign operations (ASC 830):

- They may enter into **foreign currency transactions** with an entity in a foreign country that involves a receipt or payment in a foreign currency. The entity must determine how that transaction will be reported in U.S. dollars.
- An entity may have **financial instruments denominated in a foreign currency** (eg, a *receivable or payable*), meaning it will be settled by the receipt or payment of some amount of foreign currency. The amount of the receivable or payable must be converted into U.S. dollars for inclusion on the reporting entity's financial statements (F/S).
- An entity may get involved in **foreign currency exchange transactions**, such as forward exchange contracts. These transactions may be entered into for a variety of reasons but, regardless, often result in a net amount being paid or received to settle the contract, representing a liability or asset.
- An entity may have a **foreign investee** *(ie, a foreign division or subsidiary)* that maintains books and records in a foreign currency but will be included in the reporting entity's consolidated F/S. The F/S must be converted into U.S. dollars to include them.

Foreign Currency Transactions

When an entity enters into a transaction that will be settled through the payment or receipt of foreign currency, it is initially recognized in the **functional currency** of the entity using the exchange rate in effect on the *date of the transaction.* The exchange rate that is effective on a particular date is referred to as a **spot rate**.

An entity's functional currency is the currency that has the greatest economic impact on the entity's financial performance. A company based in the northern part of Washington, for example, may obtain all of its raw materials from Canadian suppliers, may assemble its product in the United States, and then sells all of its output to Canadian customers. Even though the company might maintain its books and records in U.S. dollars, its functional currency would be the Canadian dollar.

Various factors will be considered when identifying the functional currency. Some may be more important than others, depending on the circumstances and not all will necessarily apply.

These factors may include, for example, which currency may have the greatest influence on:

- Cash flows
- Sales prices
- Demand for the company's products or services
- Expense
- Financing and financing costs
- Intra-entity arrangements

In general, an entity's functional currency is its local currency. Usually, it is also the currency in which it maintains its books and records, but that is not always the case.

- When a transaction occurs in some currency other than the functional currency, it is **remeasured** as if the transaction had originally occurred at the functional currency.
- When the functional currency is not the same as the currency used for reporting, amounts are **translated** from the functional currency into the reporting currency.

Transactional Currency = Local currency (Usually the currency in which books and records are kept)

Remeasurement (I/S)

Functional Currency = Greatest economic impact on company (Currency in which entity generates and expends cash)

Translation (B/S) (Comprehensive Income)

Reporting Currency = Currency in which the entity prepares its F/S

For example, a company's functional currency, the U.S. dollar, is also its reporting currency. On December 15 of the current year, the company enters into a transaction in which it purchases a printing press from X Company in Heidelberg, Germany at a cost of €250,000 at the time when the exchange rate was 1.30 (€1.00 = $1.30). The balance is due on January 15 of the following year.

The transaction would be remeasured into U.S. dollars by determining the U.S. dollar equivalent of €250,000, which is (€250,000 × 1.30) $325,000 and the transaction would be recorded as follows:

Equipment	325,000	
Due to X Company		325,000

Financial Instruments Denominated in a Foreign Currency

When an entity has financial instruments, such as accounts receivable or payable, or notes and loans receivable or payable, that are denominated in a foreign currency, they are adjusted for changes in exchange rates as of each balance sheet date.

- The carrying value of the financial instrument will be remeasured based on the *spot rate* on the balance sheet date.
- Any increase or decrease is generally recognized in *income or loss* as a foreign currency transaction gain or loss.

For example, when the company prepares its financial statements as of December 31, the exchange rate has increased to 1.35. It will now require (€250,000 × 1.35) $337,500 to settle the obligation. The liability will be increased to that amount as of the balance sheet date and a loss will be recognized.

Foreign currency exchange loss	12,500	
Due to X Company		12,500

Note that the loss can also be calculated by multiplying the amount of the payable in Euros by the change in the exchange rate (€250,000 × .05 = $12,500).

When the instrument is settled, an additional gain or loss may be recognized if the exchange rate has changed since the last balance sheet date. When it is settled, the entity will pay or receive some amount of money and will either convert dollars into a foreign currency to make a payment or receive a foreign currency and convert it into dollars to deposit it into its U.S. bank account.

For example, when the company remits payment on January 15 of the following period, the exchange rate has decreased to 1.20. It will now only require (€250,000 × 1.20) $300,000 to settle the obligation. The entity will buy 250,000 Euros for $300,000 and repay the liability, resulting in the recognition of a gain.

Due to X Company	337,500	
Foreign Currency Exchange Gain		37,500
Cash		300,000

Lecture 5.02 – Foreign Currency Exchange Transactions

An entity may enter into a transaction in which they agree to exchange one currency for another at a specific exchange rate at a specific future point in time. These foreign currency exchange transactions are often referred to as **forward exchange contracts**. There are many reasons an entity may enter into a forward exchange contract.

Some companies enter into forward exchange contracts as **hedges**. This would be the case if the entity has an "exposure" that is denominated in a foreign currency and it desires protection from fluctuations in exchange rates.

Using the same example, the company may have budgeted exactly $325,000 to purchase the printing press based on the exchange rate at December 15. Although it would be to its benefit if the exchange rate decreases, resulting in a gain, it may create financial difficulties for the entity if the exchange rate increases, requiring a larger payment.

To avoid this risk, the company may enter a forward exchange contract with another entity, referred to as a counterparty. The company will agree to buy 250,000 Euros at the exchange rate of 1.30 on January 15 of the following year.

- If the exchange rate increases above 1.30, the company will benefit from the transaction by being able to purchase the Euros for $1.30 per Euro, which is below market, and realize a gain.
- If the exchange rate decreases below 1.30, the company will be adversely affected as it will have to purchase the Euros for $1.30 per Euro, which is above the market price, and incur a loss.
- Regardless of whether the exchange rate increases, decreases, or remains unchanged, the company will buy 250,000 Euros for $325,000 and give them to Company X in exchange for the press. In essence, the company has eliminated the market risk associated with changes in the exchange rate.

The fact that an entity enters into a transaction for the purposes of mitigating some risk, using a hedge, does not necessarily mean that they will report the transaction using hedge accounting. ASC 815 establishes strict requirements that must be met in order for a transaction to be accounted for as a hedge.

Other companies may enter into forward exchange contracts for **speculation** purposes. If a company has some reason to believe, for example, that an exchange rate is going to change in the future, it may enter into a forward exchange contract:

- To *buy* that currency at a future date at a predetermined exchange rate if they believe that rate will be higher on that date.
- To *sell* that currency at a future date at a predetermined exchange rate if they believe that rate will be lower on that date.

Another reason companies may enter forward exchange contracts is to **"protect"** the reported value of an investment on their F/S. A company, for example, may have an investment in a foreign entity that is reported as a single amount on its balance sheet. In addition to the effects of the entity's performance, the carrying amount of the investment may be affected by changes in exchange rates. To isolate the effects of performance and eliminate the effects of a change in exchange rates, the company may enter a forward exchange contract as the seller.

- If the reported value of the investee decreases due to a decrease in the exchange rate, the forward exchange contract would increase in value due to the company's ability to sell the foreign currency at the higher contract exchange rate.
- If the reported value of the investee increases due to an increase in the exchange rate, the forward exchange contract would decrease in value, resulting in a liability, since the company will be required to sell the foreign currency at the lower contract exchange rate.

Speculation

Unless an entity qualifies for and chooses to account for its forward exchange contracts as hedges, they will all be accounted for as if entered into for speculation purposes. Forward exchange contracts are forms of **derivatives** and all derivatives that are not designated as hedges are required to be reported at their fair values, with gains or losses resulting from fluctuations of those values reported in profit or loss (I/S).

The fair value of a forward exchange contract is determined by the exchange rate that is used to value it. The types of exchange rates that might be used are:

- The **spot rate**, which is the actual exchange rate on a particular date; or
- The **forward rate**, which is what the exchange rate is expected to be at some point in the future.
    - There might be, for example, 30-day, 60-day, or 90-day forward rates.
    - A 60-day forward rate would indicate the exchange rate that is expected to be in effect 60-days from that date.

A forward exchange contract is generally entered into at the appropriate forward rate as of the date of the contract.

For example, on June 1 of the current period, a company enters into a forward exchange contract in which they agree to buy 100,000 Euros 90 days in the future. They prepare quarterly financial statements and, as a result, their next financial statements will be prepared as of June 30. The contract will be settled with a net payment on August 29, at the end of 90 days.

Applicable exchange rates are:

	June 1	June 30	August 29
Spot rate	1.30	1.33	1.29
60-day forward rate	1.35	1.39	1.28
90-day forward rate	1.37	1.42	1.30

On June 1, when the contract is entered into, it will be based on the 90-day forward rate, since that is the rate that is expected to apply when the contract will be settled at the end of 90 days. In essence, the company is agreeing to buy 100,000 Euros for $137,000 ($1.37) on August 29, and the counter party is agreeing to sell 100,000 Euros for $137,000.

Since each party is basically required to exchange currencies that are expected to be equal in value and as a result, the forward exchange contract would have no value at that time. *No entry would be recorded*, although both parties would have disclosures to make.

On June 30, the forward exchange contract will be adjusted to at its fair value for financial statement purposes. Although the actual fair value may differ due to the time value of money, volatility, and other factors, the fair value would approximate the difference between the expected values of the currencies that will be exchanged as of the balance sheet date.

As of June 30, the contract will now be settled at the end of 60 days. On June 30, the 60-day forward rate is 1.39 indicating:

- The buying party will be paying $137,000 for Euros that are expected to be worth $139,000. The fair value of the forward exchange contract would be approximately $2,000.
- The selling party will be receiving $137,000 for Euros that are expected to be worth $139,000. The forward exchange contract represents an obligation to be reported as a liability for approximately $2,000.
- *The buying party will recognize a gain and the selling party will recognize a loss.*

The buying party's entry may be:

Forward exchange contract	2,000	
Gain on forward exchange contract		2,000

The seller's entry may be:

Loss on forward exchange contract	2,000	
Forward exchange contract		2,000

The contract will be settled on August 29, when the spot rate is 1.29. The buyer would theoretically pay $137,000 to the seller for Euros that are actually only worth $129,000. In reality, however, the buyer will pay the seller the difference of $8,000. Since the exchange rate has gone from 1.39 at June 30 to 1.29 at August 31, the buyer will incur a loss, and the seller will have a gain, of 100,000 × the difference of $.10 or $10,000.

The buying party's entry may be:

Loss on forward exchange contract	10,000	
Forward exchange contract		2,000
Cash		8,000

The seller's entry may be:

Cash	8,000	
Forward exchange contract	2,000	
Gain on forward exchange contract		10,000

Lecture 5.03 – Foreign Currency Exchange Transaction Hedging: Fair Value Hedge

Hedging Overview

When a forward exchange contract is entered into for the purposes of mitigating or eliminating a risk, it is referred to as a **hedge**. In order to account for a derivative such as a forward exchange contract as a hedge, it must designate the derivative as a hedge and must meet certain requirements. This includes:

- Documenting the relationship between the hedge and the hedged risk,
- Indicating that the hedge is expected to be highly effective, and
- Explaining how the entity measures the hedge's effectiveness.

Assuming a forward exchange contract does qualify as a hedge and hedge reporting is elected, the entity will have to determine if it is a fair value hedge or a cash flow hedge.

Fair Value Hedges

As the name implies, a fair value hedge protects a company against risks associated with changes in fair values, such as the fair value of a reported asset or liability (hedging against a **recognized** asset or liability on the balance sheet or a **firm purchase commitment**). Since all derivatives are required to be reported at fair value, on each balance sheet date, the carrying value would be increased or decreased, as appropriate.

- The increase or decrease will be recognized as a **gain or loss in the income statement (I/S)**.
- A corresponding loss or gain will be recognized on the hedged item in the same period.

The corresponding loss or gain on the hedged item will be recognized, regardless of the normal accounting for the item.

For example**,** a company is doing business with an unrelated entity that is located in Europe. To enhance the relationship, the company has purchased 100,000 units of the European Company's debt securities, which are publicly held but not actively traded.

- The market price of the debt securities, which has not changed for many years and is not expected to change any time in the future, is €20.
- The spot rate on the date of the investment was 1.30 and the total cost of $2,600,000 was recorded as an available for sale investment (100,000 × €20 × 1.3 = $2,600,000).

The company wishes to protect itself from fluctuations in the fair value of the investment that result from changes in the exchange rate. If, for example, the exchange rate was to drop to 1.20, even though the securities are still selling for €20, their carrying value would be reduced to $2,400,000. Since these are available-for-sale securities, the loss would be an unrealized loss that would be reported, net of tax, in other comprehensive income (OCI).

To protect itself, the company enters into a forward exchange contract to sell 2,000,000 Euros (100,000 units at €20) in the future for $2,600,000. When the company enters into the contract, the exchange rate is 1.30 and the contract has no value.

On the next balance sheet date, the securities are still selling for €20 per unit, but the forward exchange rate has dropped to 1.25. The following would occur as a result:

- The forward exchange contract would now have a fair value of approximately $100,000 since the company has the ability to sell Euros worth $2,500,000 for $2,600,000.
- The fair value of the available for sale investment would be reduced to $2,500,000, which is the fair value of the investment in dollars. The entries would be:

Forward exchange contract (B/S)	100,000	
Gain on forward exchange contract (I/S)		100,000
Loss due to decline in value resulting from change in exchange rate (I/S)	100,000	
Investment in AFS debt securities (B/S)		100,000

Even though the loss due to decline in value of the available for sale securities would ordinarily go into OCI, it is reported on the income statement due to the use of hedge reporting.

If, as an alternative, the securities had changed in value due to both a change in the securities price and a change in the exchange rate, only the portion related to the change in the exchange rate would be reported using hedge accounting. The residual gain or loss would receive the accounting treatment that was normal for the hedged item.

If, for example, in addition to the exchange rate dropping to 1.25, the share price increased to €21, the securities would now have a value of (100,000 × 21 × 1.25) $2,625,000.

The entries would be:

Forward exchange contract (B/S)	100,000	
Gain on forward exchange contract (I/S)		100,000
Loss due to decline in value resulting from change in exchange rate (I/S)	100,000	
Investment in AFS securities (B/S)	25,000	
Unrealized gain due to increase in value of AFS securities (OCI)		125,000

Lecture 5.04 – Foreign Currency Exchange Transaction Hedging: Cash Flow Hedge

As the name implies, a cash flow hedge protects an entity from fluctuations in cash flows. If an entity enters into a contract involving a receivable or payable that will be settled in a foreign currency at some point in the future (ie, a **forecasted transaction** or **anticipated transaction**), the entity may enter into a forward exchange contract to make certain that the number of dollars required to settle the contract do not fluctuate as the exchange rate changes.

When a derivative such as a forward exchange contract is accounted for as a cash flow hedge, it too, like all derivatives, must be adjusted to its fair value on each balance sheet date. The change in value, however, is not reported in profit or loss but, rather, it is reported in **other comprehensive income (OCI)**. The amount in OCI is reversed when the effect is recognized on the hedged transaction.

For example, in performing its analysis of capital budgeting for the next few years, a company decides it will be purchasing an expensive piece of equipment from a European supplier in 6 months. The cost is €200,000 and the 6-month forward exchange rate is 1.30. As a result, the company budgets $260,000 for the purchase.

To avoid changes in the dollar amount of the purchase price due to changes in the exchange rate, the company enters into a forward exchange contract to purchase 200,000 Euros at the 6-month forward exchange rate of 1.30.

After 2 months, when the company is preparing its year-end financial statements, the 4-month forward exchange rate is 1.35. As a result of an increase in the exchange rate of .05, the fair value of the forward exchange contract will be approximately $10,000.

Since the company has not contracted to purchase the equipment, it has nothing to report on its balance sheet in relation to it. The gain on the forward exchange contract would be reported in OCI and reclassified when the hedged transaction is affected.

The entry on the balance sheet date would be:

Forward exchange contract	10,000	
Unrealized **gain** due to Increase in value of forward exchange contract (**OCI**)		10,000

Assume the exchange rate remains at 1.35 when the company purchases the equipment.

The combined entry would be:

Equipment	260,000	
Unrealized **gain** due to Increase in value of forward exchange contract (OCI)	10,000	
Cash (received from counterparty)	10,000	
Forward exchange contract		10,000
Cash (paid to equipment vendor)		270,000

Lecture 5.05 – Foreign Investees

When a company has an investment in a foreign division or subsidiary that will be included in the company's consolidated F/S, it must convert the foreign entity's financial information from its local currency, the currency in which it maintains its books and records, into the parent's reporting currency, presumably the U.S. dollar.

The process by which the entity will convert the F/S from the local currency into U.S. dollars will depend on the functional currency.

- If the functional currency is the local currency, the process is referred to as **translation**.
- If the functional currency is the U.S. dollar, the process is referred to as **remeasurement**.

It is also possible that there will be three currencies involved.

- The subsidiary or division may be maintaining its books and records in its local currency.
- Because of the nature of its operations, its functional currency is a different one, but not the U.S. dollar.
- The company is included in the parent's F/S prepared in the reporting currency, the U.S. dollar.

As a result:

- The entity will **remeasure** its financial information from the local currency to the functional currency.
- The entity will then **translate** its financial information from the functional currency to the reporting currency.

Transactional Currency = Local currency (Usually the currency in which books and records are kept)

Remeasurement (I/S)

Functional Currency = Greatest economic impact on company (Currency in which entity generates and expends cash)

Translation (B/S)
(Comprehensive Income)

Reporting Currency = Currency in which the entity prepares its F/S

Translation of Financial Statements

When the local currency is the functional currency, in order to prepare consolidated F/S that are expressed in dollars, the parent will translate the F/S of the subsidiary into U.S. dollars. The basic principles of translation are:

- **Assets and liabilities** are translated at the *current exchange rate*, which is the exchange rate at the balance sheet date.
- **Income statement** items are translated at the *exchange rates effective on the date that those items are recognized* on the F/S.
    - Sales that occurred uniformly throughout the year, for example, would be translated at the **weighted average** exchange rate.
    - A gain on the sale of a piece of equipment will be translated using the rate in effect on the **date the gain** was realized.

- Intra entity income and expense items that are eliminated in consolidation are translated at the exchange rate in effect on the **date of the intra entity exchange**.

▪ The amount required to balance the entry is referred to as a **translation adjustment**.
  - The translation adjustment occurs because items are being translated at different exchange rates and the result is not likely to balance.
  - The translation adjustment is not recognized in income but is included in **other comprehensive income (OCI)**.

The normal process for performing a **translation** involves the following steps:

1. Translate all income statement items (weighted average). This will provide a translated amount for net income.
2. Translate items on the balance sheet as follows:
   a. Assets and liabilities are translated using the rates at the **balance sheet date** (end).
   b. Contributed capital accounts (C/S & APIC) are translated using **historical rates**.
   c. Retained earnings is "rolled forward." Net income derived from translating the income statement is added to the ending balance from the prior period. Dividends are translated using the rate in effect on the date of the dividend. The result is the current period's ending balance of retained earnings.
3. The difference will be the translation adjustment recognized in OCI on the balance sheet.

Generally, the cumulative translation adjustment remains in accumulated other comprehensive income (AOCI) until such time as the investment in the foreign investee is either disposed of or substantially liquidated.

The entity may, however, lose a controlling interest in a foreign investee without disposing of it or substantially liquidating it. This might be true, for example, when an entity obtains a controlling financial interest in a foreign VIE and subsequently loses that controlling financial interest due to a change in the relationship or other circumstances.

When this is the case, it will be considered equivalent to a disposal and the cumulative translation adjustment is reclassified out of AOCI and will be recognized in income.

Remeasurement of Financial Statements

When the functional currency is the reporting currency, presumably the U.S. dollar, in order to prepare consolidated F/S that are expressed in dollars, the parent will remeasure the F/S of the subsidiary into U.S. dollars. Remeasurement is intended to present financial information as if all transactions had originally been recorded in the functional currency.

The basic principles of remeasurement are:

▪ Certain **balance sheet** items (**nonmonetary** assets/liabilities) are remeasured at **historical rates,** the rates that were in effect when the assets were acquired; the liabilities were incurred, or when contributed capital was actually contributed. This includes:
  - Marketable securities and inventory carried at cost.
  - Prepaid expenses
  - Property, plant, and equipment and its accumulated depreciation

  - Intangibles
  - Deferred charges, credits, and deferred income
  - Preferred stock carried at issuance price and common stock
  - Revenues and expenses that are nonmonetary in nature such as cost of sales, depreciation, and amortization

- **Monetary assets and liabilities** are remeasured using the exchange rate at the **balance sheet date.**
- Remeasurement of revenues, expense, gains, or losses (**I/S**) will be determined by their natures.
  - Many revenues and expenses that are incurred throughout the period will be remeasured at the **weighted average** exchange rate.
  - Gains and losses will be remeasured using the **rates in effect on the dates** of the transactions generating the gains and losses.
  - Revenues and expenses that are nonmonetary in nature, such as cost of sales, depreciation, and amortization are remeasured using **historical rates**.
    - Depreciation and amortization are remeasured using the same rates that are applied to the items being depreciated and amortized.
    - Cost of sales is remeasured by remeasuring beginning and ending inventory at their historical rates and purchases at the weighted average rate.
- The amount required to balance the entry is referred to as a **remeasurement adjustment**.
  - The remeasurement adjustment occurs because items are being remeasured at different exchange rates and the result is not likely to balance.
  - The remeasurement adjustment is recognized in **income (I/S)**.

The normal process for performing a **remeasurement** involves the following steps:

1. Remeasure items on the balance sheet as follows:
   a. *Monetary assets and liabilities* are remeasured using the rates at the **balance sheet date.**
   b. *Nonmonetary assets and liabilities* and *contributed capital* are remeasured using **historical rates** based on when assets were acquired, liabilities were incurred, and capital was contributed.
   c. The difference is ending retained earnings. The beginning balance will be rolled forward from the previous period and dividends, remeasured using the rate in effect on the dividend date, are deducted. The difference between that amount and the ending balance is the current period's **net income or loss**.
2. Remeasure all income statement items.
3. The difference between net income or loss and the result of remeasuring all income statement items will be the **remeasurement adjustment recognized in income.**

When the functional currency is in a **highly inflationary economy**, which is defined as one that has cumulative inflation of 100% or more over a 3-year period, the reporting currency will be considered the functional currency and F/S will be remeasured rather than translated.

UWorld
YOUR WORLD OF LEARNING
ROGER
CPA Review

FAR 6 - Inventory

FAR 6 – Inventory

Table of Contents

Inventory

Lecture 6.01 – Cost of Inventory

Overview

The cost of inventory is capitalized (ie, debited) to an inventory account. The cost of inventory includes all costs of acquisition and preparation for sale (ie, its **intended use**):

- Warehousing costs prior to sale
- Insurance, repackaging, modifications
- Freight-in paid by the buyer
- Transportation costs paid by the seller on consignment arrangements

Do **not** include:

- *Abnormal costs* for idle factory expense, unallocated fixed overhead costs, excessive spoilage, double freight, and rehandling costs (these should be *expensed* immediately).
- *Financing costs* – Financing costs should be reported as interest expense. This will include interest on loans obtained to purchase inventory, as well as payments made to the seller for interest on unpaid balances or early-payment discounts not taken.
- *Selling costs* – Costs incurred at the time of sale, such as freight-out paid by the seller and sales commissions, are generally recognized as selling expenses at the time of sale, consistent with the matching principle.

Returns

If goods that have been sold are returned, the seller should reduce net sales and add the cost of the items back to inventory. This should take place as soon as the seller has authorized the goods for return, so long as the actual return of the item is considered probable.

The FAR exam normally deals with merchandise inventory only. Raw materials, work in process, and finished goods inventory are usually tested in cost accounting, which is part of the BEC exam.

Inventory Costing Methods

- Heterogeneous items
  - Specific identification
    - Items that are very different, very unique, very expensive (eg, a car).
    - Must be able to identify each unit sold.
- Homogeneous items
  - FIFO – First in, First out (LISH – Last in, still here)
  - LIFO – Last in, First out (FISH – First in, still here)
  - Average inventory methods
  - Dollar value LIFO

Goods in Transit

FOB Shipping Point

- Title passes to the buyer when the seller delivers the goods to a common carrier (shipped).
- Included in buyer's books at year end.

FOB Destination

- Title passes to the buyer when the buyer receives the goods from the common carrier (received).
- Included in seller's books until received by buyer.

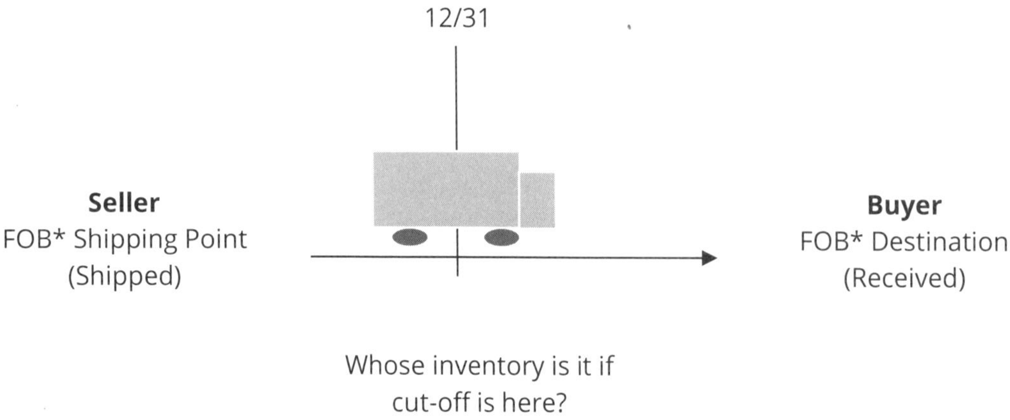

**FOB = Free on Board*

Cost of Goods Sold (COGS)

GAAP I/S		COGS
Operating income	Sales	Beg inventory
Nonoperating income (other)	**(COGS)**	**Net purchases**
Taxes	Gross margin	Goods available for sale
Income continuing ops	(SGA)	(Ending inventory)
Discontinu**e**d ops	Operating income	**COGS**
Net Income		
OCI		
Comprehensive income		

Consignment Inventory Consign**or** → Consign**ee**

Occasionally, a seller and buyer will enter a consignment arrangement. This takes place when a buyer is acquiring goods for resale but only wants to purchase those goods once they have been able to arrange the resale. In these circumstances, the potential seller (consignor) arranges for the goods to be delivered to the potential buyer (consignee) but retains legal ownership of the goods.

The consignor usually pays the transportation costs, which are added to the consignor's inventory cost (not the same as freight-out costs since no sale has occurred yet). Actually, the consignee never owns the goods since their purchase only occurs at the time they are able to resell them, at which point they are immediately reported as cost of sales.

Consignor

- Includes inventory in his balance sheet.
- Has ownership, but not possession of the goods.
- Costs incurred by consignor in transferring goods to the consignee are considered inventory costs until sold. They include:
  - The cost of the goods
  - Freight paid on shipments to consignee
  - Warehousing costs
  - In-transit insurance
- Selling costs, such as commissions and reimbursements (eg, advertising, credit card fees) paid to the consignee, are expensed in the period the revenue is recognized.

Consignee

- Items are not included in his inventory balance.
- Has possession, but not ownership of the goods.
- When sold, the sales price is given to the consignor after deducting any reimbursable costs and commissions earned by the consignee.

Two Systems for Measuring Inventory Quantities

Periodic Inventory System (physical inventory count)

Inventory quantity is determined by a physical count, usually done at year end.

- Inventory purchases are debited to purchases.
- No adjustment is made to inventory until the end of the period, when a physical inventory count is made and ending inventory is calculated.
- COGS is the plug and the exact amount of inventory shortages cannot be determined since it is buried in COGS.

	<u>At time of purchase</u>	
Purchases	X	
A/P		X
	<u>At year end</u>	
Ending Inventory	X	
COGS (plug at year end)	**X**	
Purchases		X

Perpetual inventory system (ongoing, real-time count)

Inventory purchases are debited to Inventory. The quantity on hand can be determined at any point in time.

At time of purchase

Inventory	80	
A/P		80

As sales occur

A/R	100	
Sales Rev		100
COGS	**80**	
Inventory		80

One advantage of a perpetual inventory system is that it enables the entity to determine how much inventory is on hand at any given point in time. Not only does this assist in the management of inventory but, by performing an inventory reconciliation, comparing the recorded amounts to physical counts, management will be able to identify errors in the recording of transactions involving inventory and find indicators of potential theft.

The exam has included problems and questions calling for an **inventory reconciliation** in which the candidate is expected to compare recorded amounts to physical counts and determine the reasons for differences and whether adjustments should be made to the recorded amount.

To reconcile from recorded amount to physical count:

1. Begin with recorded amount
2. Add goods held on consignment
3. Add goods sold fob shipping point and set aside but included in the count
4. (Subtract goods in transit that were sold fob destination)
5. (Subtract goods in transit that were purchased fob shipping point)

   The result should be equal to the **physical count**.

   (Any differences will be due to errors or fraud)

To reconcile from physical count to recorded amounts, the process will be reversed:

1. Begin with the physical count
2. Add goods in transit that were purchased fob shipping point
3. Add goods in transit that were sold fob destination
4. (Subtract goods sold fob shipping point that are set aside but included in the count)
5. (Subtract goods held on consignment)

   The result should be equal to the **amount recorded**.

   (Any differences will be due to errors or fraud)

Lecture 6.02 – Inventory Costing Methods

Specific Identification

- Must be able to identify each unit sold.
- Used when inventory is few in number, very expensive and can be clearly identified, very heterogeneous items.

FIFO: First-in, First-out

- FIFO assumes that goods are sold in the order of acquisition (ie, first items acquired are the first items sold).
  - The inventory remaining on hand is presumed to consist of the most recent purchases; that is, last items acquired are still here in ending inventory (LISH – Last in, Still Here).
  - This closely relates to the actual *physical flow of goods*.
- In periods of rising prices, FIFO results in the:
  - Highest ending inventory,
  - Lowest cost of goods sold (COGS), and
  - Highest net income.
- Perpetual and periodic inventory systems are the *same*.

LIFO: Last-in, First-out

- The most recent costs are expensed and matched with current revenues (ie, last items acquired are the first items sold).
  - The inventory remaining on hand is presumed to consist of the goods acquired first; that is first items acquired are still here in ending inventory (FISH – First in, Still Here).
  - This better represents the *flow of cash*.
    - LIFO does not assume goods are sold in the reverse order of acquisition. Instead, using the most recently acquired item as COGS approximates the replacement cost of the item. That is, the true cost of an inventory item that has been sold is the cost of replacing it.
- In periods of rising prices LIFO results in the:
  - Lowest ending inventory,
  - Highest COGS, and
  - Lowest net income.
- Perpetual and periodic inventory systems are *different*.
- *LIFO conformity rule* – If used for tax purposes, must also be used for financial reporting purposes.

FIFO = COGS (LISH = Ending Inventory)	**LIFO** = COGS (FISH = Ending Inventory)
If costs are going up ↑	
COGS understated	COGS ok
NI overstated	Profits ok – I/S is fair
Ending inventory - ok	Ending inventory - understated
Balance sheet ok (I/S not ok)	**Income statement ok** (B/S not ok)

Average Inventory Methods

- Assign the same unit price to similar goods available during the period.
  - Moving Average (Perpetual) – This method computes the average after each purchase.
  - Weighted Average (Periodic) – This method takes total costs of all inventory purchases during the year and divides them by the total number of inventory units available during the year.

Assume a company had the following activity in the month of January:

Date	Units Purchased (Sold)	
Beginning inventory, 1/1	2	A, B
Purchase, 1/5	2	C, D
Sale, 1/12	(1)	
Purchase, 1/19	2	E, F
Sale, 1/26	(1)	
Ending inventory, 1/31	4	

To make it easier to follow, let's name the first two units in inventory, A and B, the two units purchased on 1/5, C and D, and the two units purchased on 1/19, E and F.

Assuming the **perpetual** approach is used, each transaction is processed as it happens. Let's see which units are left in inventory after each transaction, using FIFO and LIFO:

Units after transaction	FIFO	LIFO
Start of Month	A+B	A+B
January 5, Plus 2	A+B+C+D	A+B+C+D
January 12, Minus 1	B+C+D	A+B+C
January 19, Plus 2	B+C+D+E+F	A+B+C+E+F
January 26, Minus 1	C+D+E+F	A+B+C+E

If a **periodic** approach is used, all the purchases are recorded first, then the sales:

Units after transaction	FIFO	LIFO
Start of Month	A+B	A+B
Purchases, Plus 4	A+B+C+D+E+F	A+B+C+D+E+F
Sales, Minus 2	C+D+E+F	A+B+C+D

Lecture 6.03 – Dollar Value LIFO

In certain industries, inventory is measured at current prices with increases added to the historical cost of beginning inventory, using current prices, and decreases measured on the basis of the most recent goods purchased, at their historical cost.

- Inventory is measured in terms of dollars, not units, and is adjusted for changing price levels.
- Inventory is combined into natural groups called "Inventory Pools" and each pool is valued separately. A price level index is used to convert the inventory value from LIFO to Dollar-value LIFO.

For most companies, the inventory method best matching their pricing policy is LIFO. Most companies price goods for sale based on replacement cost, and LIFO results in the most recent purchases being treated as cost of sales, coming closest to replacement cost of all GAAP methods.

Nevertheless, there are **two potential difficulties** that arise from the application of the LIFO method:

- The company needs to keep track of the different unit costs for items acquired on different dates, going all the way back to the date the company first adopted the method, which could be the date the company was founded. This need to keep cumulative accurate records will result in increasing record-keeping costs over time. When a client has several different types of products in its inventory, the **costs can be enormous**.
- When inventory levels decline temporarily, older costs previously inventoried will become a part of cost of goods sold, causing a distortion of that account if there have been substantial price changes over time. This is because the unit costs in inventory that are several years old are likely to be radically different from the approximation of replacement cost represented by the most recent purchases.

A useful solution is a method known as **Dollar-Value LIFO (DV LIFO)**. Under this approach, related inventory items are grouped in **pools**, and an overall price index is used to approximate changes in inventory costs. It addresses both difficulties mentioned above:

- It is only necessary to **keep track of annual layers** of inventory cost and price indexes for each inventory pool, instead of retaining detailed records of each unit cost of each item purchased over the life of the company. As a result, the record-keeping costs of this method are substantially lower than traditional LIFO.
- Since related items are grouped together and layers are computed annually, reductions in the level of a certain type of item in inventory that are offset by increases in the level of other items in the pool, or reductions at interim periods that are compensated by year-end, won't result in the use of older costs in the calculation of cost of goods sold (COGS). As a result, this method substantially reduces the probability that older inventory layers will be liquidated and reported in COGS.

To apply the DV LIFO method, **two figures are needed**:

- The **total current cost** of the inventory in the pool at the end of each year (this would usually be the replacement cost or the ending inventory under a FIFO approach).
- A **price index** indicating the overall price level compared to the base date (the date the method was first adopted).

Dollar Value LIFO

Beginning inventory (BI) = 2 pens @ $1 = $2

Ending inventory (EI) = 3 pens @ $1.20 =$3.60

} $1.60 Difference

Price Level Index = 1.20 → 20% Inflation

EI / **Inflation Factor**	= 3.60/1.20 = **$3** EI @ base year $

→ **$3** = EI @ beginning of year prices OR base year $
(Base Year = Year started DV LIFO)

Adding Layers

- LAYER
- LAYER
- BASE

$3 =	EI @ beginning of year prices OR Base Year $
(2) =	Subtract Base
$1 =	Increase in inventory @ base year $
× 1.20 =	Multiply by inflation factor
1.20 =	Layer @ current costs
+ 2.00 =	Still around (old inventory) @ base cost
3.20 =	EI @ current cost

Yr	Inventory @ Y/E $ ÷	Price level Index	EI @ Base Yr $	Add'tl Layer	X2 (1.0)	X3 (1.2)	X4 (1.3)	X5 (1.4)	X6 (1.5)
X2	$2.00	1.0	$2.00		$2.00				
X3	3.60	1.2	3.00	$1.00		~~$1.00~~ 0.90			
X4	4.30	1.3	3.30	0.3			~~0.30~~		
X5	4.06	1.4	2.90	(0.4)				0 (0.40) Sold	
X6	5.25	1.5	3.50	0.6					0.60
					$2.00	$1.20	$0.39		$0.90

What you sold comes out of LIFO

- **Price level index (approaches)**
  - Simplified (CPI for your industry – given)
  - Link chain (single cumulative index, compare with previous year)
  - Double extension (extend back to base year)
- **Ending inventory**
  - X2 = $2.00 2 × 1.0
  - X3 = $3.20 2 + 1.2 (1 × 1.2)
  - X4 = $3.59 2 + 1.2 + .39 (.3 × 1.3)
  - X5 = $3.08 2 + 1.08 (.9 × 1.2)
  - X6 = $3.98 2 + 1.08 + .9 (.6 × 1.5)

For example, assume that the method was adopted on 12/31/X1, and the following facts applied to the first year in which the method was applied:

Date	Current Cost (CC)	Price Index (PI)
12/31/X1	$1,000	1.00
12/31/X2	$1,320	1.10

Notice that the price index is automatically set at 1.00 on the date the method is adopted, and the above information indicates that prices increased by 10% in 20X2.

Our first step is to determine if inventory rose or fell after eliminating the effects of price changes. We do this by factoring out inflation, which is accomplished by dividing the current cost by the price index each year:

Date	Current Cost	Price Index	Base Cost (BC)
12/31/X1	$1,000	1.00	$1,000
12/31/X2	$1,320	1.10	$1,200

In a sense, we can think of the price index as the unit cost of the items, not in physical units but in units of base cost. Thus, at the end of 20X1 (beginning of 20X2), the company held 1,000 base units at $1.00 each, and at the end of 20X2, the company held 1,200 base units at $1.10 each, so that the inventory went up in real terms by 200 base units, or 20%. The rest of the increase in the dollar value of inventory was the result of inflation.

Once the increase at base cost is computed, it must be adjusted back to current prices, since the increase occurred in the current year. This results in different layers of inventory at different price indexes:

Date	CC	PI	BC	Layer	PI	DV LIFO
12/31/X1	$1,000	1.00	$1,000	$1,000	1.00	$1,000
12/31/X2	$1,320	1.10	$1,200	$200	1.10	$220
Total						$1,220

If inventory at current cost is $1,560 at 12/31/X3, and the price index has increased to 1.20, representing 20% of cumulative inflation since 12/31/X1, the next year's computation is as follows:

Date	CC	PI	BC	Layer	PI	DV LIFO
12/31/X1	$1,000	1.00	$1,000	$1,000	1.00	$1,000
12/31/X2	$1,320	1.10	$1,200	$200	1.10	$220
12/31/X3	$1,560	1.20	$1,300	$100	1.20	$120
Total						$1,340

Finally, if inventory declines in 12/31/X4 to a current cost of $1,430 while the index rises to 1.30, we will be removing some of the layers from the previous years as follows:

Date	CC	PI	BC	Layer	PI	DV LIFO
12/31/X1	$1,000	1.00	$1,000	$1,000	1.00	$1,000
12/31/X2	$1,320	1.10	$1,200	$100	1.10	$110
12/31/X3	$1,560	1.20	$1,300			
12/31/X4	$1,430	1.30	$1,100			
Total						$1,110

Compare this table to the previous one, and notice that, to account for the $200 decline at base cost from $1,300 to $1,100, we removed the 20X3 layer of $100 at 1.20, and then removed $100 from the 20X2 layer at 1.10, leaving the layers noted in the last chart.

In all the examples so far, the price index has been provided. There are **three different methods** for arriving at an index:

- **Simplified**
- **Double Extension** (extend back to base year)
- **Link-Chain** (cumulative index, compare with previous year)

The **Simplified** method refers to the use of a generally available index of prices, typically a government index such as the Consumer Price Index for Urban Consumers (**CPI**).

The **Double Extension method** requires the client to count the inventory and then extend inventory prices twice (which is the reason the term "double" is used). Then the two results are compared to determine a price index:

- Current Quantity × Current Unit Cost = Current Cost
- Current Quantity × Base Date Unit Cost = Base Cost
- Current Cost / Base Cost = Price Index

Notice that the three numbers calculated are the same three figures as in earlier examples. The difference is that the earlier examples used Current Cost / Price Index = Base Cost, but since division is transitive (if A / B = C then A / C = B), either approach is acceptable.

Let's look at an example of computing the index using the double extension method. Assume a company has two products, X and Y, with the following inventory quantities and unit costs at the end of each year:

Year	X Quantity	Y Quantity	X Unit Cost	Y Unit Cost
20X1 (base)	26	12	$20	$40
20X2	30	15	$26	$44
20X3	36	18	$28	$64

The 20X3 current cost and base cost amounts are computed as follows:

Product	Quantity	Unit Cost	Total Cost	Aggregate
X	36	$28	$1,008	
Y	18	$64	$1,152	
Current Cost				$2,160
X	36	$20	$720	
Y	18	$40	$720	
Base Cost				$1,440

The index for 20X3 is then $2,160 / $1,440 = 1.50

The **Link-Chain method** is similar to the Double Extension method, except that year-to-year price changes, rather than cumulative changes, are computed, then the annual changes are linked (multiplied) together to determine a price index. To determine the year-to-year changes, the calculation is:

- Current Quantity × End-of-year Unit Cost = Current Cost
- Current Quantity × Start-of-year Unit Cost = Prior Year Cost
- Current Cost / Prior Year Cost = Annual Cost Index

For example, use the same facts as in the previous example:

Year	X Quantity	Y Quantity	X Unit Cost	Y Unit Cost
20X1(base)	26	12	$20	$40
20X2	30	15	$26	$44
20X3	36	18	$28	$64

The 20X2 annual index calculation is:

Product	Quantity	Unit Cost	Total Cost	Aggregate
X	30	$26	$780	
Y	15	$44	$660	
Current Cost				$1,440
X	30	$20	$600	
Y	15	$40	$600	
Prior Cost				$1,200
Annual Index				1.20

The 20X3 annual index calculation is:

Product	Quantity	Unit Cost	Total Cost	Aggregate
	36	$28	$1,008	
Y	18	$64	$1,152	
Current Cost				$2,160
X	36	$26	$936	
Y	18	$44	$792	
Prior Cost				$1,728
Annual Index				1.25

The price index for 20X3 is the result of linking these indexes together:

Year	Annual Cost Index	Overall Price Index
20X1		1.00
20X2	1.20	1.20
20X3	1.25	1.50

The overall price index at the end of 20X3 is the result of multiplying the annual cost indexes for 20X2 and 20X3 (1.20 × 1.25 = 1.50).

Lecture 6.04 – Lower of Cost or Market or Lower of Cost or NRV Rule

Overview

Conservatism & Matching

Regardless of the choice of inventory costing method, a company must account for declines in the market value of unsold inventories. (ASC 330) To do this, we have two methods:

- **Lower of Cost or Market (LCM)** – This somewhat complicated approach applies only to inventory accounted for under the *LIFO* or *retail inventory methods*.
- **Lower of Cost or Net Realizable Value (LCNRV)** – This simplified approach applies to all other inventory.

Regardless of the costing or valuation method used, if the prices of goods in inventory have been consistently:

- *Rising*, then the valuation will usually be at *cost*.
- *Falling*, then the valuation will usually be at *market value*.

Inventory *valuation* may be based upon:

- Individual items
- Categories
- Total inventory

Losses are recognized immediately on the income statement. Once inventory is written down, there is **no recovery** from the write down until the units are sold.

Loss on Inventory (market decline)	X	
Inventory		X

Lower of Cost or Market (LCM)

There are three different numbers that need to be computed to determine "market" under LCM:

- **Net realizable value (NRV)** – the estimated selling price of the goods less costs of disposal (eg, necessary costs to complete the goods, freight-out, and sales commissions)—**Ceiling**
- **Replacement cost** – the estimated cost to purchase or reproduce the goods
- **NRV less normal profit margin** – the price at which no profit would be made—**Floor**

Normally, replacement cost is used as market because it is generally lower than the NRV (ie, the ceiling) and higher than the NRV less normal profit margin (ie, the floor). However, when replacement cost is:

- Higher than NRV, the NRV (ie, the ceiling) is used as market.
- Lower than the NRV less normal profit margin (ie, the floor), NRV less normal profit margin is used as market.

Thus, the amount to be used as market will always be the amount in the middle. If market is lower than the original cost, the inventory must be written down.

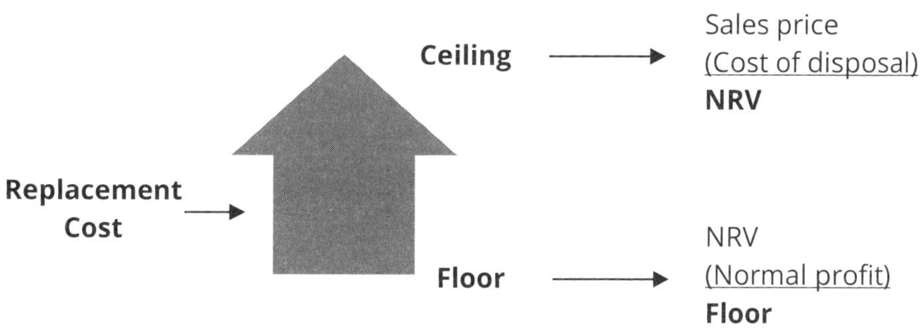

Assume the following facts:

Replacement cost	100
Estimated selling price	120
Estimated selling expenses	30
Normal profit margin	20

From the above information, we can determine the normal, ceiling, and floor amounts for market:

Normal: Replacement cost	100
Ceiling: Net realizable value	90
Floor: NRV – normal profit margin	70

Since the replacement cost of 100 exceeds the ceiling of 90, market is 90, and that number will be compared with historical cost to determine the lower of cost or market.

Lower of Cost or NRV (LCNRV)

Under LCNRV, the amount to be used as the market value will always be NRV. If the NRV is lower than the original cost, the inventory must be written down.

Summary	
LIFO & retail Inventory methods	**All other inventory costing methods**
LCM – Lower of: ▪ Cost = original cost ▪ Market = middle of three numbers: o Net Realizable Value (NRV)—Ceiling o Replacement cost o NRV less normal profit margin—Floor	**LCNRV** – Lower of: ▪ Cost = original cost ▪ NRV = Sales price – cost of disposal

Lecture 6.05 – Inventory Estimation Methods

Gross Profit (Margin) Method

Gross profit can be used to prepare interim financial statements or as an estimate if ending inventory is missing or destroyed. First, calculate an estimate of COGS by using the *Historical Gross Profit Percentage,* then back into ending inventory.

Beginning Inventory		100
+ Purchases		300
Goods Available for Sale		400
(Ending Inventory)	??	**220 (plugged)**
Cost of Goods Sold		**180**

Gross Profit % = 40% so if Sales = 300 (60%) = **180 COGS**

COGS % = 60% (estimated)

Retail Inventory Methods

These are rarely used and extremely complicated techniques for estimation of inventory.

Conventional Retail Inventory method

The company keeps track of inventory costs at both cost and retail. Sales, theft losses and employee discounts during the year are recorded at retail and at the end of the year, the co. converts ending inventory from retail back to cost by using a cost/retail percentage. This method approximates the results that would be obtained by taking a physical inventory and pricing the goods at the lower of cost or market (LCM).

- Net mark-ups are included in the cost to retail percentage calculation
- Net mark-downs are not included in the cost to retail percentage calculation.

	Cost		Retail
Beginning Inventory	X		X
+ Purchases	X		X
+ Freight in	X		
+ **Net Markups**			X
Goods available for sale	**X**	**/**	**X = C/R %**
– **Net Markdowns**			(X)
Sales price of goods available for sale			X
– Losses			(X)
– Sales @ Retail			(X)
Ending Inventory @ **Retail**			X
× C/R%			
Equals ending inventory at cost	X		

- **Net mark-ups** = mark-ups – mark-up cancellations
- **Net mark-downs** = mark-downs – mark-down cancellations

LIFO Retail Inventory method

The LIFO Retail method approximates the **original cost** of the merchandise as opposed to the conventional retail method which approximates LCM. The two differences are that:

- Net mark-ups and net mark-downs are **both included** in the cost to retail percentage calculation.
- Beginning inventory is **not** included in the cost to retail percentage calculation.

Firm Purchase Commitments

A non-cancelable agreement to buy inventory in the future. If it is expected that a loss will occur in the future, the loss is recognized at the time of the decline in price. The loss is the difference between the contract price and the market price of the minimum required amount of inventory that must be purchased in the future.

Estimated Loss (I/S)	X	
Estimated Liability		X

UWorld
YOUR WORLD OF LEARNING
ROGER
CPA Review

FAR 7 - Property, Plant & Equipment (Fixed Assets)

FAR 7 – Property, Plant & Equipment (Fixed Assets)

Table of Contents

Property, Plant & Equipment (Fixed Assets)

Lecture 7.01 – Property, Plant & Equipment: Fixed Assets

Property, Plant and Equipment (PP&E) are tangible assets acquired for long-term use in the normal course of business. They are not for resale and are generally subject to depreciation. (ASC 360)

Asset	X	
Cash		X

Acquisition Costs (Intended Use)

Acquisition costs, which are capitalized as part of the cost of the asset, include not only the purchase price of the asset, but also costs associated with obtaining it and preparing the asset for its intended use.

- Include all costs of acquisition or construction as well as preparation for use.
  - Purchase price
  - Legal fees
  - Delinquent taxes
  - Title insurance
  - Transportation (freight in)
  - Installation
  - Test runs
  - Sales taxes

The **cost of land** includes:

- Purchase price (including any existing building that is to be demolished)
- Surveying
- Clearing, grading, and landscaping
- Costs of razing or demolishing an old building are added to the land cost.
- Proceeds from the sale of any scrap (old bricks) are subtracted from the land cost.

For example, assume that a piece of land with an existing building on it is acquired, with the following facts applying:

Purchase Price	$300,000
Cost of razing old building	50,000
Sale of scrap from clearing old building	8,000

The cost of the land is $300,000 + $50,000 - $8,000 = $342,000. Notice that nothing is allocated to the old building, since it is being demolished. No benefits are being derived from the old building, so the matching principle indicates that none of the costs should be allocated to it.

Lump-Sum Purchases

If land and a building are acquired for a lump sum, use the **relative fair value method** to allocate the value between the assets.

For example, if property is acquired for $600,000, and the only available information to allocate is the tax appraisal, which allocates $100,000 to the land and $400,000 to the building, for a total of $500,000 tax value, then the cost of the property will be allocated 100,000 / 500,000, or 20%, to land, and 400,000 / 500,000, or 80%, to building. The entry to record acquisition of the property is:

Land	120,000	
Building	480,000	
Cash		600,000

If land is acquired along with a depleting asset, such as oil in the ground, then the land is normally allocated its estimated residual value assuming all oil had been removed, and the remainder is allocated to the oil itself. One complication, however, is that the cost of the property includes all costs of acquisition and preparation of the property for drilling, as well as any estimated restoration costs for the property following the completion of drilling.

Lecture 7.02 – Asset Retirement Obligations

Asset Retirement Obligations

Asset retirement obligations (ARO), such as estimated restoration costs, that are expected to be paid at the end of the period of usage, should be recorded as a liability at **fair value**. This is the amount at which that obligation could be settled today. (ASC 410) If fair value cannot be determined, an estimate should be made based on the **present value of the expected future costs** using credit-adjusted risk-free rate of return.

The liability will have to be increased each year based on the discount rate and reported as accretion expense. Accretion is the growth of the liability over time so that when the liability is satisfied, it is reported at its total nondiscounted value. The liability is considered **long term** and is amortized using the effective interest method.

Assume an oil field is acquired at a cash price of $100,000. It is estimated that, following the extraction of oil, it is expected to cost approximately $20,000 to restore the property to an acceptable condition when extraction is completed (estimated to be 12 years from now), and that the land will, at that point, have a $30,000 value.

Assume further that the fair value of the restoration costs cannot be determined, but that a discount rate of 6% is considered appropriate.

The present value of 1 at 6% for 12 years is 0.50, so the restoration costs of $20,000 have a present value (ie, an estimated fair value) of $20,000 × 0.50 = $10,000. The entry to record acquisition of the property is:

Land	30,000	
Oil reserves	80,000	
Cash		100,000
ARO liability (Est rest costs)		10,000

The estimated restoration costs are classified as long-term liabilities since they won't be paid until drilling is completed (ie, in about 12 years). The oil reserves, which result from a plug in the above entry, are depleted and inventoried as oil is removed from the ground, then expensed as oil is sold.

The ARO liability (estimated restoration costs) is increased each year by the incremental rate of 6%, so that the liability will be increased by a credit of $10,000 × 6% = $600 in the first year, with an offsetting debit to accretion expense.

Accretion expense	600	
ARO liability		600

Disclosures

- Description of the obligation and related asset
- Description of how fair value was determined
- The funding policy
- A reconciliation of the beginning and ending carrying value

Lecture 7.03 – Capitalization of Interest

Interest cost incurred during the construction period needs to be capitalized. (ASC 835) The amount capitalized is considered the avoidable interest (could have avoided had you not built the building). This amount is added to the cost of building the asset. Interest incurred on construction loans should be included, but only to the extent the funds have been spent on construction.

- Capitalize interest cost if asset is:
  - Constructed for company's **own use** (ie, built by self or outsider).
  - Assets manufactured for resale resulting from a **special order** (eg, ships).
- Do **not** capitalize interest if:
  - Costs are incurred *after* completion of construction.
  - Inventory manufactured in the ordinary course of business.
- Amount to be capitalized is:
  - **Weighted average accumulated expenditures** × interest rate = capitalized portion of interest.
  - Interest on other debt that could have been avoided by repayment of debt.
  - Never to exceed actual interest cost incurred.

Assume that a client takes out a 12% loan of $1,000,000 on 1/1/X1 to finance construction of a building for the company's own use. Construction begins immediately, and $600,000 is spent at an even pace during 20X1. The remaining $400,000 is spent at an even pace during 20X2, with construction completed on 12/31/X2. The capitalized interest is computed as follows:

	20X1	20X2
Annual expenditure	$600,000	$400,000
Prorated over year	50%	50%
Avg current expenditure	300,000	200,000
Prior year spending	---	600,000
Avg accumulated expend	300,000	800,000
Interest rate	12%	12%
Capitalized interest	36,000	96,000

The capitalized interest of $36,000 for 20X1 and $96,000 for 20X2 represent a portion of the total interest paid by the company each year.

Let's assume that the $1,000,000 12% loan requires annual interest payments at the end of each year. The entries to record the interest payments would be:

12/31/X1	Building WIP	36,000	
	Interest expense	84,000	
	Cash		120,000

12/31/X2	Building WIP	96,000	
	Interest expense	24,000	
	Cash		120,000

Once construction is finished, the building is no longer a work-in-process, but a completed asset, and the entire balance of Building WIP is transferred to Building. Any interest incurred after 12/31/X2 is expensed immediately, in accordance with the matching principle, since the building is now being used and providing benefits to the company. The capitalized interest will now be a part of the depreciation expense on the building over its useful life.

Lecture 7.04 – Costs Incurred After Acquisition

Repairs and Maintenance Expense

Revenue Expenditure

This includes costs incurred to keep or restore an asset to its normal operating condition (eg, repairing a damaged truck or routine maintenance, such as engine tune-ups and oil changes). These costs are **expensed** as incurred.

Capital Expenditure

If, however, the cost makes the asset bigger, better, or last longer, that's good, since one would rather capitalize the cost than expense it.

- **Bigger** – additions, new capacity, new functions (eg, a hospital wing)

Asset	X	
Cash		X

- **Better** – a betterment or improvement (eg, a rearrangement improving efficiency, replacing a wooden floor with a concrete floor)

Asset	X	
Cash		X

- **Longer** – extension of an asset's useful life (overhaul)
    - Costs that extend the useful life of the asset are subtracted from accumulated depreciation thereby increasing the carrying value (ie, book value).

Accumulated Depreciation	X	
Cash		X

Refurbishment

Replace a part of the asset.

- **Identifiable** – Account for as if the old part was sold and it was replaced with a new part.

Accumulated Depreciation	X	
Loss	X	
Asset		X
Asset	X	
Cash		X

- **Not Identifiable**
    - Enhances the asset (similar to an addition or betterment)

Asset	X	
Cash		X

- Increasing the asset's useful life (similar to an extension)

Accumulated Depreciation	X	
Cash		X

Lecture 7.05 – Depreciation Methods

Depreciation is a systematic and rational method of allocating the cost of an asset to the periods benefited.

Matching Concept

Straight-Line Method (S/L)

- Used when assets give equal benefits to the company throughout their useful lives (eg, a building).
- Depreciation expense is the same amount each year.
- Depreciation rate = 1/useful life (1/5 years = 20%)
- Considers depreciation a function of time instead of a function of usage.

$$\frac{\text{Cost} - \text{Salvage Value}}{\text{Useful Life}} = \text{Depreciation Expense}$$

- To record depreciation:

Depreciation Expense (I/S)	X	
Accumulated Depreciation		X

Accumulated Depreciation ← Contra-asset account (reduces asset)

Accelerated Methods

Accelerated methods are used when an asset gives greater benefits in earlier years than in later years (eg, office equipment).

Sum of the Years Digits (SYD)

SYD is an accelerated depreciation method that is considered less aggressive than the double-declining balance method.

- Numerator = The number of years left in the asset's useful life.
- Denominator = The sum of the years in the asset's useful life. The formula is **N(N+1)/2.**

$$(\text{Cost} - \text{Salvage Value}) \times \left(\frac{\text{\# of years left in asset's life}}{\text{Sum of years in asset's life}}\right) = \text{Depreciation Expense}$$

Assuming a 3-year asset, in year 1 the numerator would be 3, then 2, then 1. The denominator would be 3+2+1, or 3(3+1)/2 = 6. In year 1, depreciation will be the basis multiplied by 3/6. For year 2, multiply the basis by 2/6. For year 3, multiply by 1/6.

Straight-Line	SYD	Y1	Y2	Y3
1/3 = Rate	3	3/6	2/6	1/6
	2			
	1			
	= **6**			

= **6** → $\frac{3\,(3+1)}{2}$

Double-Declining Balance (DDB)

- DDB is depreciation rate that is twice the straight-line rate is applied against the book value of the asset. For example, 1/5 = 20% (S/L rate) × 2 = 40% (DDB rate)
- Salvage value is ignored.
- Depreciation expense should not be reduced below the salvage value. In the final year either:
  - Calculate depreciation expense in the last year as the amount to reduce the carrying value to the salvage value.
  - Switch from DDB to either SYD or S/L toward the end of the asset's useful life, depreciating the asset to its salvage value.
- Balance declines; DDB rate stays the same.

Depreciation Expense Yr 1

$$\text{Cost} \times \left(\frac{1}{\text{\# of Years}}\right) \times 2$$

Depreciation Expense Yr 2

$$(\text{Cost} - \text{Depreciation Expense Yr 1}) \times \text{DDB\%}$$

Units of Production (UOP) – Activity Method

(Variable Charge approach or Physical usage depreciation)

- Assumes depreciation is a function of use (machine hours) or productivity (finished widgets) instead of the passage of time.

$$(\text{Cost} - \text{SV}) \times \frac{\text{hours this year}}{\text{Total estimated hours}} = \text{Depreciation expense}$$

Benefits of Accelerated Methods

- Better **matching** since asset is more productive in earlier years.
- Minimize loss due to **obsolescence.** Since the asset was depreciated more quickly, the carrying value is lower; therefore, the loss is smaller.
- **Helps to even out expenses**. Since repairs and maintenance in the earlier years is lower, if we take more depreciation earlier on, the total expenses would be more constant over time.

Lecture 7.06 – Depreciation Example & Other Depreciation Methods

To review the basic methods of depreciation, let's use the following example of a machine, and calculate depreciation expense for each of the **first 2 years**:

Purchase date	1/1/X1
Cost	$1,000
Estimated useful life	5 years
Estimated salvage value	$100
Estimated total output	1,000 units
20X1 output	250 units
20X2 output	300 units

Straight-line (SL) depreciation allocates the depreciable basis (cost – salvage) over the useful life:

- 20X1 Cost 1,000 – Salvage 100 = Basis 900 / Life 5 years = $180
- 20X2 Cost 1,000 – Salvage 100 = Basis 900 / Life 5 years = $180

Units of Production (UOP) depreciation multiplies the basis by a fraction whose numerator is the current output and whose denominator is the estimated total output.

- 20X1 Basis 900 × Current Output 250 / Total Output 1,000 = 225
- 20X2 Basis 900 × Current Output 300 / Total Output 1,000 = 270

Sum of Years Digits (SYD) depreciation multiplies the basis by a fraction whose numerator is the number of the years left in the life of the asset as of the beginning of the year and whose denominator is the sum of the number of years in the life of the asset.

- 20X1 Basis 900 × Ratio 5 / (1+2+3+4+5) = 900 × 5 / 15 = 300
- 20X2 Basis 900 × Ratio 4 / (1+2+3+4+5) = 900 × 4 / 15 = 240

Double-Declining Balance (DDB) depreciation multiplies the book value (cost – accumulated depreciation) at the beginning of each period by a fraction that is double the straight-line depreciation rate.

- 20X1 Cost 1,000 × Multiplier 2 / SL rate 5 = 1,000 × 2 / 5 = 400
- 20X2 Cost 1,000 – A/D 400 = Book value 600 × 2 / 5 = 240

Other declining balance approaches work the same way as the double-declining balance approach, except that the multiplier of the straight-line rate is different.

Partial period depreciation – In computing depreciation expense for partial periods, it is necessary to determine the depreciation expense for the full year and then to prorate the depreciation expense between the two periods involved. Continue this process throughout the useful life of the asset.

When an asset is bought on some date other than the beginning of the fiscal year, depreciation in the year of acquisition needs to take into account the fractional time period for all methods except the UOP method (which is based on output rather than the passage of time).

Assume the same facts applied as in the previous example, except that the purchase date was later in the year:

Purchase date	7/1/X1
Cost	$1,000
Estimated useful life	5 years
Estimated salvage value	$100
Estimated total output	1,000 units
20X1 output	250 units
20X2 output	300 units

Since the asset was purchased in the middle of the year, first year depreciation is based on one-half of a year, and the second year is affected as well:

SL depreciation:

- 20X1 Cost 1,000 – Salvage 100 = Basis 900 / Life 5 years × ½ = $90
- 20X2 Cost 1,000 – Salvage 100 = Basis 900 / Life 5 years = $180

UOP depreciation:

- 20X1 Basis 900 × Current Output 250 / Total Output 1,000 = 225
- 20X2 Basis 900 × Current Output 300 / Total Output 1,000 = 270

SYD depreciation:

- 20X1 Basis 900 × Ratio 5 / (1+2+3+4+5) × ½ = 900 × 5 / 15 × ½ = 150
- 20X2 Basis 900 × Ratio 4.5 / (1+2+3+4+5) = 900 × 4.5 / 15 = 270

Note: Using SYD, the numerator is the amount of life remaining at the start of the year. For a 5-year asset that is 6 months old, the remaining life is 4.5 years at the start of the second year.

DDB depreciation:

- 20X1 Cost 1,000 × Multiplier 2 / SL rate 5 × ½ = 1,000 × 2 / 5 × ½ = 200
- 20X2 Cost 1,000 – A/D 200 = Book value 800 × 2 / 5 = 320

Charting the Results

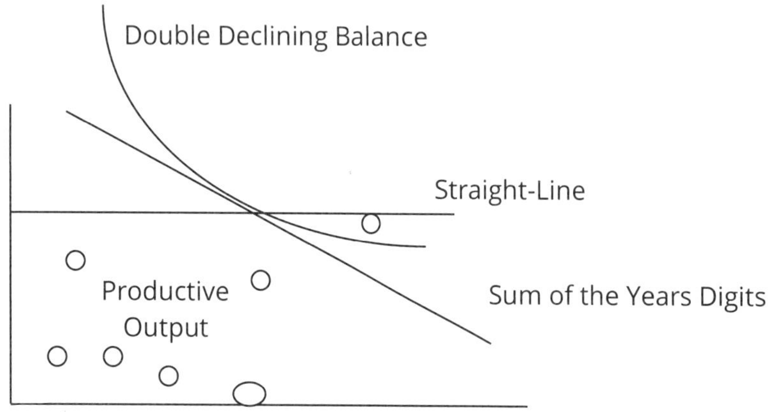

Group or Composite

- Depreciate as a group (eg, a fleet of trucks)
- *Group* refers to a collection of assets that are *similar* in nature, fairly homogeneous and have approximately the same useful lives.
- *Composite* refers to a collection of assets that are *dissimilar* in nature, fairly heterogeneous and have different lives.
- Problem occurs when you sell one of the assets in the group. Accumulated depreciation is not known.
  - Assume cash received = carrying value
  - Assume no gain/loss
  - Plug accumulated depreciation

Cash	20		
Accumulated Depreciation	**80** ← plug		
Loss	NONE		20 = BV
Asset		100	
Gain		NONE	

Under the *composite method* of depreciation, a building that is furnished with tables, chairs, and other items might elect to determine a weighted average life for all of the furnishings, and depreciate the total over this life. In the first year, the company determines the individual depreciation amounts for the items, totals them, and then divides this amount into the total cost to determine an average life that is then used from that point forward.

Assume a company acquires a desk, chair, and lamp to furnish an office and that these items will be of approximately equal usefulness each year, with no salvage at the end of their individual lives:

Item	Cost	Estimated life in years	Annual depreciation
Desk	$1,000	10	$100
Chair	$200	5	$40
Lamp	$100	4	$25
Total	$1,300	7.88	$165

Under the composite approach, the furnishings for the room are carried on the depreciation schedule at a single cost of $1,300, and depreciated over a life of 7.88 years ($1,300 / $165).

Of course, this example doesn't show the value of the composite method, which often involves hundreds of items being depreciated together instead of separately. The savings in bookkeeping effort can be enormous.

If this method seems strange, consider that it is actually being used in almost all depreciation already. An automobile, for example, actually includes an engine, transmission, axle, belts, and other parts that don't all have the exact same life, yet an automobile is depreciated as a single asset. This is a form of the composite approach.

Appraisal or Inventory Method of Depreciation

This method is rarely used. Under this approach, an estimate is made at the end of each year of the value of the assets, and sufficient depreciation expense is recorded to reduce the carrying value to that amount. Since this approach doesn't systematically match costs to benefits, it is only used when the loss in value is directly related to productivity, such as for property being rented to others.

Depletion

While assets like property, plant, and equipment have limited useful lives, some assets actually get used up. Mining companies and others in what are referred to as *extractive industries* will buy, or otherwise obtain rights to real property that is expected to have some natural resource, such as *oil, minerals, precious metals, or other commodities*.

When property with a natural resource is acquired, the cost is allocated to the property and the natural resource based on their relative estimated fair values. As the natural resource is extracted from the property, the cost is transferred from the natural resource to inventory and, ultimately, to cost of sales when the inventory is disposed of.

Depletion is recognized each period in a three-step process that is similar to the process used to calculate depreciation and is also often referred to as the **activity method**.

1. The total volume of the resource is estimated
   - The volume is measured in terms of number of units such as barrels of oil, tons of coal, or cubic feet of natural gas
   - In the initial period, the estimate will be the total of the estimated reserves
   - In subsequent periods, it will be the estimated amount remaining as of the beginning of the period, which includes the amount extracted during the period plus the amount estimated to be remaining at the end of the period.
2. The total volume is divided into the remaining cost, referred to as the **depletion base**, to get a cost per barrel, ton, cubic foot, or other unit.
   - In the initial period, this will be the total amount allocated to the resource (Cost + additional costs + restoration costs – Salvage/Residual value)
   - In subsequent periods, it will be the carrying value of the resource, which will be the original amount minus any depletion taken in previous periods.
3. The amount per unit is multiplied by the amount extracted during the period to determine the depletion for the period.

$$Depletion = \frac{\text{Depletion base}}{\text{Total volume at beginning of year}} \times \text{Units Extracted}$$

As the natural resource is extracted, the depletion represents the cost of the resource itself. The depletion, along with other direct costs such as labor and overhead, are reported as inventory. Once the inventory is sold, the cost is transferred from inventory to cost of sales.

- An entity in the oil and gas industry may incur costs when evaluating property to determine whether or not a sought natural resource is present and to develop an estimate of the volume. These costs, referred to as **exploration costs**, may be accounted for in one of two ways: Under the **full-cost approach**, all exploration costs are capitalized and become part of the cost of depleted resources that are found. As a result, depletion includes all of these costs.

- Under the **successful efforts approach**, exploration costs are attributed separately to each property and only those that yield an extractable resource are capitalized.
  - Exploration costs attributable to unsuccessful efforts are recognized as expense in the period.
  - Exploration costs attributable to successful efforts become part of the cost included in the depletion base.

Amortization, depreciation and depletion, like many areas of accounting, require the use of numerous estimates. These include estimates used in allocating costs when assets are acquired, estimates of salvage values and useful lives of property, plant, and equipment and certain intangibles, and estimates of volumes of remaining reserves of natural resources. These estimates are subject to scrutiny every period and, as they change, they are accounted for as changes in accounting estimates. As such:

- Prior period financial statements are not adjusted
- The new estimate is applied prospectively, in the current and future periods

When an entity **changes its method of depreciation, amortization, or depletion** of an asset, it is a change in accounting principle, but it is also a change in the estimate of how the entity is obtaining benefits from the use of that asset. As a result:

- A change in depreciation, amortization, or depletion method is accounted for **prospectively** like a change in estimate
- Since it involves a change in accounting principle, the entity must *justify the change* on the basis that the new method is preferable.

Lecture 7.07 – Impairments

Impairment of Long-Lived Assets Held for Use

Impairment of long-lived assets held for use occurs when the carrying amount of an asset is not recoverable and a write-off is needed. (ASC 360)

Examples

- A significant decrease in the market value of an asset.
- A significant change in an asset's physical condition or the extent or manner in which it is used.
- A significant adverse change in legal factors or in the business climate that affects the value of an asset.
- An accumulation of costs significantly in excess of the amount originally expected to acquire or construct the asset.
- A projection or forecast that demonstrates continuing losses associated with an asset.
- An expectation that it is more likely than not that the asset will be disposed of before the end of its expected useful life.

Impairment Testing

Impairment testing applies to asset groups as well as individual assets. The impairment is applied proportionately to all of the long-lived assets in the asset group (but no asset is reduced below its fair market value).

The process of determining an impairment loss is as follows:

1. Review events or changes in circumstances for possible impairment (above). If none are identified, no further testing is required.
2. If the review indicates impairment, apply the **recoverability test**: if the sum of the **expected future net cash flows** from the long-lived asset is **less than** the **carrying amount** of the asset, an impairment has occurred.
3. The **impairment loss** is the amount by which the **carrying amount** exceeds the **fair value** of the asset. The fair value is the market value or the present value of future expected cash flows.

Note that estimated *future cash flows* are used to determine if impairment has occurred, but the asset is adjusted to its *estimated fair value*, **not** estimated future cash flows, once the determination has been made. The impairment loss, which appears on the income statement in income from continuing operations, may **NOT be restored** for an asset *held for use*.

Assume an asset has a carrying value of $600, the expected future net cash flows is $580, and the market value is $525. Since the $580 expected cash flow is less than the $600 carrying value, an impairment has occurred. The amount of the loss is 75 (ie, 600 carrying value – 525 market value). Now we calculate the future depreciation from the new $525 carrying value.

Impairment Loss (I/S)	75	
Accumulated Depreciation		75

Disclosures

- Description of impaired assets and circumstances which led to impairment
- Amount of impairment and manner in which fair value was determined
- Caption in income statement in which impairment loss is aggregated, if it is not presented separately

Impairment of Long-Lived Assets to Be Disposed of—Held for Sale

When assets are no longer being used in operations, they are reclassified on the balance sheet. They are taken out of property, plant, and equipment and are reported in ***Other assets*** and described as held for sale.

- When first transferred to the held-for-sale category, the amount is the *lower of* the asset's **carrying value** and its **net realizable value** (NRV), which is its estimated selling price less costs of disposal.
  - If NRV is lower, it becomes the new carrying value (CV) and a loss is recognized on the income statement in continuing operations.
  - If the old CV is lower, it remains as the CV and no loss is recognized.
- Assets held for sale are *not* depreciated.
- In subsequent periods, increases or decreases in the NRV are recognized:
  - The asset is increased or decreased to its NRV at the balance sheet date, provided it is not increased to an amount that exceeds its CV before the transfer.
  - The increases or decreases are recognized as gains or losses.
  - Thus an asset held for disposal **can be written up or down** in future periods as long as the write-up is never greater than the carrying amount of the asset before the impairment.

Loss on planned disposition	700	
Equipment to be disposed of (other assets)	1,500 (NRV)	
Accumulated Depreciation	3,800	
Equipment		6,000

Disposal of Fixed Assets

When a company disposes of a fixed asset, they will normally remove the original cost and accumulated depreciation, record any amounts received or due to them as a result of disposal, and recognize a gain or loss for the difference. The gain or loss is reported in continuing operations as part of other items.

If a client owns a machine with a cost of $10,000 and carrying amount of $3,000, and it is sold for $2,500 cash, the entry is:

Cash	2,500	
Loss on sale	500	
Accumulated depreciation	7,000	
Machinery & equipment		10,000

Involuntary Conversion

Disposals include *destruction of property* as well as seizure by government entities as a result of condemnation or eminent domain actions. The accounting for these events is **identical to voluntary sales**, and GAAP does not allow deferral of gains or losses as a result of subsequent replacement of such property.

Assume that, on 9/15/X1, a fire destroyed a client's warehouse with an original cost of $1,000,000 and accumulated depreciation on the date of destruction of $225,000. Removal of debris cost $20,000. On 1/20/X2, the insurance company issued a check to the client for $1,200,000, and a new warehouse was built and completed on 6/30/X2 at a cost of $1,300,000. In 20X1, entries to account for the effects of the fire will have the following effect:

Due from insurance	1,200,000	
Accumulated depreciation	225,000	
Involuntary conversion gain		405,000
Warehouse		1,000,000
Cash		20,000

In 20X2, the collection of the insurance payment and construction of the new warehouse result in the following:

Cash	1,200,000	
Due from insurance		1,200,000
Warehouse	1,300,000	
Cash		1,300,000

In determining the accumulated depreciation balance at the time of a disposal, the asset should reflect any depreciation in the current period prior to the time of the sale. Also, in determining the gain or loss, all costs associated with the sale should be included.

If an asset that is part of a group being depreciated under the composite method is sold or removed from service before the entire group has been fully depreciated, determining the asset's cost and accumulated depreciation may be impossible. In this case, the carrying value of the group is simply reduced by net proceeds (if any) resulting from disposal, and no gain or loss is recorded.

Lecture 7.08 – Nonmonetary Exchanges

Overview

In some cases, there may be an exchange of assets between entities that does not involve cash or cash equivalents, receivables, or payables. When these transactions are related to a contract with a customer, the guidelines for revenue recognition are followed, with the nonmonetary assets received treated as nonmonetary consideration. Otherwise, these transactions, referred to as *nonmonetary exchanges*, are generally recognized at **fair value**.

This general rule applies when the transaction has **commercial substance**. ASC 845 considers an exchange to have commercial substance whenever the *risk, timing, and/or amount of cash flows* are affected by the exchange.

There are three exceptions to the general rule, including when an exchange **lacks commercial substance**. In these circumstances, such nonmonetary exchanges are handled differently.

Exchanges with Commercial Substance (General Rule)

A nonmonetary exchange with commercial substance is treated as if it were two unrelated events:
1. Sale of the asset surrendered
2. Purchase of the asset received

The sales price of the **asset surrendered** is considered its fair value.
- If the fair value of the asset given is not readily determinable, the assumed sales price will be the fair value of the asset received plus any monetary consideration received or minus any monetary consideration given.
- If neither fair value is readily determinable, the assumed sales price will be the carrying value of the asset surrendered.

The **asset received** will be recognized at the sales price, minus any monetary consideration received, or plus any monetary consideration given. As a result, a **gain/loss** is recognized on the difference between the fair value and book value of the asset surrendered.

Nonmonetary Exchanges with Commercial Substance

- Recognize *all* gains and losses.
- Record new asset at FMV. If know #1 below, use it as the debit to the new asset. If #1 not known, use #2. If #2 not known, use #3.
  1. FMV given up + cash paid (– cash received)
  2. FMV of asset received
  3. Book Value (BV) given up + cash paid (– cash received)

Exchanges Lacking Commercial Substance (Exceptions)

Since nearly all exchanges will result in *some* change in future cash flows, **assume commercial substance** on all exam questions involving nonmonetary exchanges **unless**:
- The fair value of the assets received/relinquished cannot be determined within a reasonable limit.

- It's an exchange of assets sold in the *ordinary course of business* for assets sold in the same line of business (eg, inventory for inventory) to facilitate sales to third-party customers.
    - Usually such exchanges take place with a competitor or vendor merely to facilitate future sales to unrelated customers.
- The exchange lacks commercial substance (ie, cash flows are expected to be substantially unchanged as a result of the exchange).

In all three of these exceptions, the *carryover basis* (ie, book value, adjusted for the cash paid/received) is used to measure the transaction instead of the fair value. Gains are not recognized unless boot is received (discussed later). **Losses**, however, are reported in full.

Nonmonetary Exchanges Lacking Commercial Substance*

- Recognize all losses.
- Defer all gains, unless boot is received.
- Record at *lowest* of:
    1. FMV given up + cash paid (– cash received)
    2. FMV of asset received
    3. Book Value (BV) given up + cash paid (– cash received)

Debit asset for lowest of these three

**Includes all exeptions to the general rule.*

Four Examples: 2 examples with commercial substance and 2 lacking commercial substance.

- Cash paid out for Example A = $10.
- Cash paid out for Example B = $20.
- FMV of asset given up is unknown.
- FMV of new asset = $30.
- Book Value of asset given up = $15.

Example A: Substance			Example B: Substance		
New	30		New	30	
Old		15	Loss	5	
Cash		10	Old		15
Gain		5	Cash		20

Example A: Lack Substance			Example B: Lack Substance		
New	**25**		New	**30**	
Old		15	Loss	5	
Cash		10	Old		15
			Cash		20

Example A: 1) ? 2) 30 **3) 25**

Example B: 1) ? **2) 30** 3) 35

Lacks Commercial Substance – *BOOT Received*

There is one type of exchange lacking commercial substance in which **gain is recognized**, however, and that is when boot is received in a exchange. The reason for this difference is that the cash received results in a small amount of commercial substance, and that part of the transaction must be reported differently from the portion of the exchange that lacks it.

- Defer all gains unless boot is received, then recognize the gain up to the proportionate share of boot received to total consideration received. The ratio to use is: total boot received / total consideration received (boot + FV of asset received), multiplied by the gain.
- When the boot received is ≥ 25% of the total consideration received (including the boot), the transaction is viewed as a monetary exchange and all of the gain is recognized.

Assume a company receives inventory with an FMV of $8,000 and cash of $2,000, by giving up similar inventory with a book value of $6,000.

FMV Received	8,000	
+ Cash (boot) Received	2,000	= 2,000/10,000 (boot to total consideration rec'd)
Total consideration rec'd	**10,000**	
– Book Value (BV) given up	(6,000)	= 20% of proceeds are boot, so recognize 20% of gain
Realized Gain	**4,000**	
	× 20%	
	800	

New (plugged)	4,800	
Cash	2,000	
Old		6,000
Gain		**800**

Summary

A nonmonetary exchange is recognized at fair value *unless:*

- Fair value is not determinable,
- The exchange is to facilitate sales to customers, or
- The exchange lacks commercial substance.

There are six different situations that need to be distinguished in determining whether *gains* (FMV exceeds carrying amount) and *losses* (carrying amount exceeds FMV) are recognized:

	Commercial Substance			**Lacks Commercial Substance***		
Boot	None	Paid	Received	None	Paid	Received
Gain	Yes	Yes	Yes	No	No	Part
Loss	Yes	Yes	Yes	Yes	Yes	Yes

**Includes all exeptions to the general rule.*

Donations

On occasion, a company will receive an **asset as a donation** (ie, a nonreciprocal transfer). The receipt of the donated asset is generally treated as ordinary income for the fair market value of the asset. For example, if an individual donates land worth $3,000,000 to the company, the entry is:

Land	3,000,000	
Other income (Contribution Revenue)		3,000,000

UWorld
YOUR WORLD OF LEARNING
ROGER CPA Review

FAR 8 – Intangibles

FAR 8 – Intangibles

Table of Contents

Intangibles

Lecture 8.01 – Intangibles

Overview

Intangible assets refer to assets of a company which **lack physical substance** and provide economic benefits through the rights and privileges associated with their possession. They may be *identifiable* or *unidentifiable*. They also may be externally acquired (purchased at fair value) or internally developed (ASC 350). They come in 3 basic forms:

- Knowledge
- Legal rights & identifiable intangibles
- Goodwill (unidentifiable intangible)

Knowledge

Knowledge is developed by a process of **research and development (R&D)**.

- **Research** is aimed at the discovery of new knowledge that will result in a new product or process or a significant improvement to an existing product or process.
- **Development** is the conversion of that new knowledge into a plan or design for a new product or process.

Matching R&D costs to benefits is virtually impossible, since much of the work will result in failure, or the benefits are of indefinite value and duration. As a result of this tremendous uncertainty, R&D costs are **expensed** as incurred, in accordance with the conservatism principle.

The only **exception** is for the acquisition of fixed assets to be used in research. When such assets have possible **future benefits**, they should be **capitalized** initially, and the costs amortized into R&D over their useful life. Equipment purchased only for current R&D projects should be immediately expensed as R&D. (ASC 730)

Costs should **not** be treated as **R&D** when they are directly related to current revenue. The following costs are considered part of cost of sales and will be capitalized and recognized as appropriate:

- Research performed for others for a fee.
- Periodic design changes to existing products.
- Costs for setting up production of a commercially viable product.

Legal Rights & Identifiable Intangibles

These types of intangible assets include patents, copyrights, trademarks, franchises, and licenses.

Patents – Protection for product and process ideas resulting from R&D.

- The **capitalized cost** of a patent includes the **legal costs** of **obtaining** it and, if necessary, **successfully defending** it in court against infringement by other companies. If a legal defense of the patent is unsuccessful, all costs should be expensed since no legal benefit exists in that case.

- A patent that has been purchased from another party is capitalized at the purchase price.
- Patents have a maximum 20-year life but should be **amortized** over the **shorter of** the **useful** or **legal life**.
- Do not include research & development of product or process.

In general, the cost of the following other legal rights is determined similarly to patents: purchase prices to the extent the benefits were obtained from other parties plus legal expenditures associated with protecting them.

- **Copyright** – Protection of artistic works, including books, recordings, and computer software. The copyright period is for the life of the creator plus 70 years (or 95 years total for works made for hire), but the costs should be amortized over its useful life.
- **Trademark** – Exclusive use of an identifying name for a product or process. External acquisition costs are amortized over their useful life. Indefinite number of renewals for periods of 10 years each.
- **Franchise** – Operation of a business unit under contractual arrangements with another party.

After Acquisition

Finite Useful life Intangibles (subject to amortization) – Intangible assets with definite lives (ie, finite useful life) are amortized over their estimated useful lives, in accordance with the matching principle. When a range of lives is possible, the shortest alternative should be used, in accordance with the conservatism principle. The amount to be amortized is its cost minus residual value.

Similar to PP&E, these assets are evaluated **annually** to determine if events or conditions indicate a likelihood of **impairment**. If there is no indication, no further testing is required. If, however, events or conditions indicate it is likely that the asset is impaired, the **recoverability test** is applied.

- If the sum of the expected future net cash flows from the asset is less than the carrying amount of the asset, an impairment has occurred.
- The **impairment loss** is the amount by which the **carrying amount** of the asset is *greater than* the **fair value** of the asset.

In **determining** the **useful life**, consideration should be given to any legal limits on the existence of the right. *Patents and copyrights* have legal limits on their lives set by law. *Franchises* have legal limits based on the related contracts. To determine the useful lives, one must consider:

- The expected use of the asset by the entity
- Legal, regulatory, or contractual provisions that may limit the useful life
- The effects of obsolescence, competition, and other economic factors
- The expected maintenance expenditures required

There are three different **methods of amortization** that can be used. The method of amortization chosen should be the most conservative, meaning the one that reduces the carrying value of the intangible to the lowest amount (ie, highest amount of amortization).

- **Straight-line** – Costs are recognized equally over the useful life.
- **Units of sales** – Costs are allocated based on the sales to date as a percentage of estimated total sales.

- **Net realizable value** – Sufficient amortization is recorded to reduce the carrying value of the intangible to the estimated remaining future benefits.

Indefinite Useful Life Intangibles (not subject to amortization) – Intangible assets and goodwill with indefinite useful lives are NOT amortized, but rather are **tested** at least **annually** for **impairment**. If no legal, regulatory, contractual, competitive, economic, or other factors limit the useful life, it is considered to be indefinite.

Before testing an identifiable intangible with an indefinite useful life for impairment, an entity has the *option* to perform a qualitative analysis. If the qualitative analysis does not indicate impairment, no further testing is generally required until the next assessment anniversary date. There are several factors that may adversely affect the fair value of an intangible asset, indicating possible impairment:

- *Cost factors* – An increase in costs associated with the use of the intangible, such as raw materials or labor
- *Financial performance* – A decrease in cash flows, revenues, or earnings associated with the use of the intangible
- *Environment* – A change in the legal, regulatory, contractual, political, or business environment
- *Entity-specific events* – Changes in management or key personnel, strategy, or customers, and events like potential litigation or bankruptcy
- *Industry and market considerations* – An increase in competition, the effects of obsolescence, a change in demand, or a change in other economic factors
- *Macroeconomic conditions* – Changes in general economic conditions, limitations on the access to capital, fluctuations in foreign currency exchange rates, and other changes to the equity and credit markets

If the entity believes that one or more of these factors indicates that it is *more likely than not* that the intangible has been impaired, the intangible will be tested for impairment. Intangibles with an indefinite useful life, other than goodwill, are tested for impairment by comparing the carrying value of the asset to its fair value. As previously discussed, **fair value** is determined based on one of the following approaches **(MIC)**:

- **Market approach** – Uses prices and other relevant information generated by market transactions involving identical or comparable assets, liabilities, or groups of assets and liabilities.
- **Income approach** – Converts expected future amounts, such as revenues or cash flows, to a single current amount applying present value concepts.
- **Cost approach** – Measures the amount that would be currently required to replace the service capacity of an asset.

If the asset is **impaired**, a **loss** is **recognized** in an amount equal to the excess of the asset's carrying value over its fair value. Subsequent **reversal** of a previously recognized impairment loss is **prohibited**.

Intangibles with indefinite lives (such as trademarks) are not amortized but are tested for impairment on an annual basis.

Lecture 8.02 – Goodwill

Overview

Goodwill is known as the unidentifiable intangible since its value cannot be directly determined. It is, however, represented by the excess of what a buyer is willing to pay for a business over and above the value of the net identifiable assets on the books of the acquired company.

Since it is impossible to verify the value of goodwill in the absence of an actual transaction, it may only be recorded on the balance sheet when it results from the purchase of another business. A company may not record as goodwill the internal costs of developing or restoring it.

Measuring Goodwill

If one entity acquires 100% of another entity, it is assumed that the fair value of the consideration given is the fair value of the entity reported. That amount will be compared to the net of:

+ The fair value of all identifiable tangible and intangible assets acquired, which may include assets that are not on the financial statements of the acquired entity, minus
- The fair value of all liabilities assumed

In most cases, the fair value of the consideration given will exceed the fair value of the underlying net assets, in which case the difference would be goodwill. In rare circumstances, the fair value of the underlying net assets exceeds the fair value of consideration given, in which case the difference is recognized as a gain on bargain purchase by the acquiring entity.

Assume one entity acquires all of the stock of another entity for $1,000,000. The acquired entity has the following assets and liabilities:

	Book value	Fair value
Current assets	$ 350,000	$ 350,000
Plant and equipment, net	600,000	850,000
Intangibles, excluding goodwill	0	100,000
Total identifiable assets	$ 950,000	$ 1,300,000
Liabilities assumed	500,000	500,000
Value of underlying net assets	$ 450,000	$ 800,000
Total consideration		1,000,000
Goodwill		$ 200,000

In a business combination, goodwill is assigned to one or more reporting units. A reporting unit can be an operating segment or one level below. The amount assigned to an individual reporting unit is the excess of the fair value of that reporting unit over the fair value of the net underlying assets in the reporting unit.

- The acquired entity may be *integrated into the acquiring entity* without maintaining separate books and records for the acquired entity.
  - The assets and liabilities of the acquired entity, including goodwill, are recorded on the books and records of the acquiring entity.
  - The entity, as a whole, is considered the reporting unit with the goodwill.
- The acquiring entity may *maintain separate books and records* for the acquired entity.

  - The acquiring entity will recognize an investment in subsidiary on its books.
  - Consolidated financial statements will be prepared each period.
  - The acquired entity will be considered the reporting unit with the goodwill.
- The acquiring entity may not only maintain separate books and records for the acquired entity but may actually maintain more than one set of books and records if the acquired entity consists of more than one department, operation, or other natural business unit.
  - The acquiring entity, for example, may maintain separate units for a research division, a manufacturing division, and a sales and distribution division.
  - Each division would be considered a separate reporting unit.
  - Goodwill would be allocated among the reporting units based on the differences between the value of each reporting unit and the fair value of its underlying net assets.

Impairment

Goodwill has an indefinite useful life and, similar to other intangibles with indefinite useful lives, it is **tested** for impairment at least **annually**. Goodwill is considered impaired when the carrying value of the reporting unit with which it is associated exceeds that reporting unit's fair value.

Interim Testing

The goodwill associated with each reporting unit is required to be evaluated separately. In addition to the annual impairment tests, the entity may have reason to believe that goodwill has been impaired between impairment dates. If the entity does determine that it is more likely than not that goodwill has been impaired between the most recent evaluation date and the date of the financial statements, an additional interim impairment test will be performed.

Optional Qualitative Assessment

Various qualitative factors can be evaluated to determine whether it is *more likely than not* that the carrying value of a reporting unit exceeds its fair value, indicating that goodwill may be impaired.

- Macroeconomic conditions, such as general limitations on the availability of capital
- Industry and market considerations, such as an increase in the competitive environment
- Cost factors, such as increases in the costs of raw material or labor
- Overall financial performance, such as declining profits or cash flows
- Events specific to the entity, such as changes in management
- Events affecting the reporting unit, such as a change in the composition of its assets
- In some cases, a sustained decrease in the price of shares of stock
- Other relevant events or circumstances that affect a reporting unit's carrying value or fair value of net assets

Quantitative Impairment Test

If the optional qualitative assessment above indicates that goodwill is *unlikely* (ie, less than 50% chance) to be impaired, then further testing is *not required*. If, however, the qualitative assessment indicates that goodwill is more likely than not impaired, or the qualitative assessment is not performed, then a *quantitative assessment* of goodwill (ie, impairment testing) is required.

Goodwill is tested for impairment by comparing the carrying value of the reporting unit (including goodwill) to its fair value. The carrying value of the reporting unit will be known to the entity since it is the amount reflected in the books and records being maintained for the reporting unit. The fair value will represent the amount that the entity would be able to sell the reporting unit for in an orderly transaction between market participants.

- If the fair value of the reporting unit is equal to, or greater than, its carrying value, it is generally assumed that goodwill is not impaired.
  - Note that deferred taxes are included in the carrying value of a reporting unit.
- If, however, the carrying value of the reporting unit is greater than the fair value, there is an impairment loss equal to the excess of the carrying value over the fair value, but it is limited to the amount of goodwill recorded.
  - Note that any other assets subject to impairment testing at the same time should be tested and written down, if necessary, prior to testing goodwill.

Once goodwill has been written down due to impairment, the adjusted amount becomes the goodwill's new carrying value. This amount is used for comparison in future assessments. Even if it is later determined that goodwill has increased in value, **recoveries are not recognized**.

Impairment loss (I/S – continuing ops)	X	
Goodwill		X

In a business combination, Push Corporation acquired all of the outstanding stock of Shove, Inc. for $7,500,000 at a time when Shove's underlying net assets had a fair value of $6,900,000 in the transaction. As a result, **goodwill of $600,000** was recognized. Push maintains separate accounting records for Shove, which is considered a separate reporting unit.

During the current period, due to some very aggressive marketing tactics, Shove's reputation was damaged, and Push has determined that it is more likely than not that the goodwill has been impaired. As a result, Push will perform an impairment test in relation to Shove's goodwill. Push will compare Shove's carrying value (CV) to its fair value (FV).

- The carrying value on the date of the test is readily determinable from the separate accounting records being maintained:

Cash	$ 350,000
Accounts receivable	1,250,000
Inventories	3,000,000
Other current assets	200,000
Plant and equipment	5,750,000
Intangibles	2,000,000
Goodwill	600,000
Total	$13,150,000
Current liabilities	(950,000)
Long-term debt	(4,100,000)
Carrying value of reporting unit	$ 8,100,000

- The fair value, determined using an appropriate valuation technique, most likely employing the same approach(es) used to determine how much Push would originally purchase Shove for, turned out to be $7,900,000.
- $8,100,000 CV – $7,900,000 FV = $200,000 impairment loss

Goodwill would be written down from $600,000 to $400,000, and an impairment loss of $200,000 would be recognized in income.

Alternative Accounting Approach for Nonpublic Entities (Goodwill)

The Private Company Council (PCC) of the FASB established an alternative accounting approach that is available to nonpublic entities when accounting for goodwill to reduce the burden associated with testing goodwill for impairment. The PCC decided to simplify the process due to the cost and complexity of testing goodwill for impairment under the old 2-step approach.

When the alternative accounting approach is elected, the entity will begin amortizing its goodwill. It will be *amortized* on a **straight-line basis** over its ***useful life*** not to exceed **10 years.** Since goodwill will be amortized, the carrying value decreases each period, making it less likely that its carrying amount will exceed its fair value and that goodwill will be impaired.

- Goodwill will be **tested for impairment** at the company-wide level only when a **triggering event** occurs indicating that the fair value of the entity has fallen below its carrying amount.
- Like a publicly held entity, the nonpublic entity will perform a **qualitative assessment** to consider such factors as economic conditions, competition, changes in costs, and changes to the regulatory environment to determine if there is reason to believe that it is more likely than not, or, in other words, that there is a greater than 50% probability that goodwill has been impaired.
- If the entity determines that it is NOT more likely than not, no further testing is required. If, however, it appears that it is more likely than not that goodwill has been impaired, the entity will test goodwill for impairment.

A nonpublic entity performing an impairment assessment has the **option** of performing it on the **entity level or the reporting unit level**. If the entity level is elected, which would also be disclosed in the Summary of Significant Accounting Policies, along with the election to apply the alternative accounting approach, the entity will combine all components of goodwill and perform a one-step impairment test for the entity as a whole.

- The fair value of the entity is compared to its carrying value.
- If the fair value is lower than the carrying value, the entire difference is attributed to goodwill and recognized as an impairment loss.

Since goodwill cannot be reduced below zero, if the amount of the impairment loss exceeds the carrying value of goodwill, the entity will have to evaluate its other assets to determine what additional impairment losses should be recognized.

Lecture 8.03 – Computer Software Costs & Other Assets

Costs to Develop Computer Software to Sell, Lease or Market

In the case of computer software developed to sell, lease or market as a product, these costs associated with converting a technologically feasible program into final commercial form are **capitalized**. (ASC 985)

- Costs **prior** to **technological feasibility** are **expensed** as research and development (R&D).
- Costs incurred **after** software **sales** begin are inventoried and included in **cost of sales**.

Costs incurred during phases

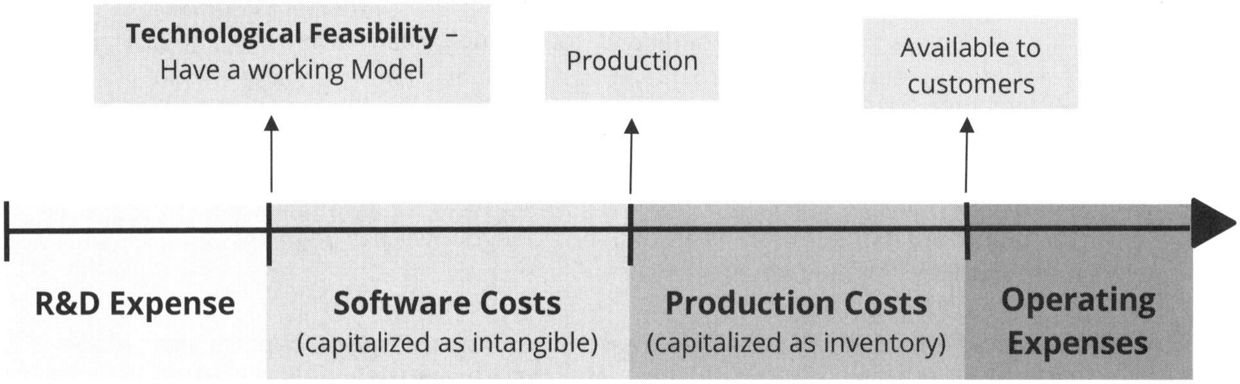

R&D Expense	Software Costs	Production Costs	Operating Expenses
- Planning	- Coding & testing after technological feasibility	- Duplication	- Maintenance
- Designing	- Producing product masters	- Training materials	- Customer support
- Coding & testing		- Packaging	

Amortization of capitalized software costs, which is **charged to cost of sales**, is calculated using a two-step process:

1. Amortization is calculated using the more conservative of **straight-line** and the **relative sales value approach**; that is, the **larger** of the two amounts will be recognized as amortization expense:
   - The *straight-line* amount is calculated by *dividing* the remaining *carrying value by* the remaining *useful life,* as of the beginning of the period.
   - The amount under the *relative sales value approach* is calculated by establishing a ratio with the current period's sales in the numerator and the total estimated sales for the remaining life of the software, including the current period's sales, in the denominator. Amortization is equal to the *ratio multiplied by* the *carrying value* of the software as of the beginning of the period.

$$\frac{\text{Current Period's Sales}}{\text{Current Period's Sales} + \text{Estimated Future Sales}}$$

2. The new **carrying value** of the software, **after amortization** from Step 1, is **compared to** the **net realizable value (NRV)** of the software. If the carrying value is greater, the **excess** is also **written off** as amortization expense. For purposes of this calculation, the *NRV* of the software *is* the amount expected to be generated from *future sales less* the costs associated with *completion, disposal, maintenance, and customer support*.

Example:

- 5-year useful life
- S/L = 1/5 = 20%
- Ratio = 100 revenue / 400 expected total revenue = 25%
- Amortization will be 25% of carrying value.
- If new carrying value is $285 and NRV is $240, write off extra $45 amortization expense.

Software Developed for Internal Use Only

- If computer software is developed for internal use only, costs incurred in the **preliminary project stage** and costs incurred in training, data conversion, reengineering and maintenance should be **expensed**.
- Costs incurred during the **application development stage** and for **upgrades** and **enhancements** should be **capitalized** and amortized on a straight-line basis.
- Capitalization of costs should cease when the software project is substantially complete and ready for its intended use (ie, **postimplementation stage** costs should be **expensed**).
- If the entity later decides to market the software to outsiders, net proceeds received should be applied first to the carrying amount of the software until it reaches zero, then recognized as revenue.

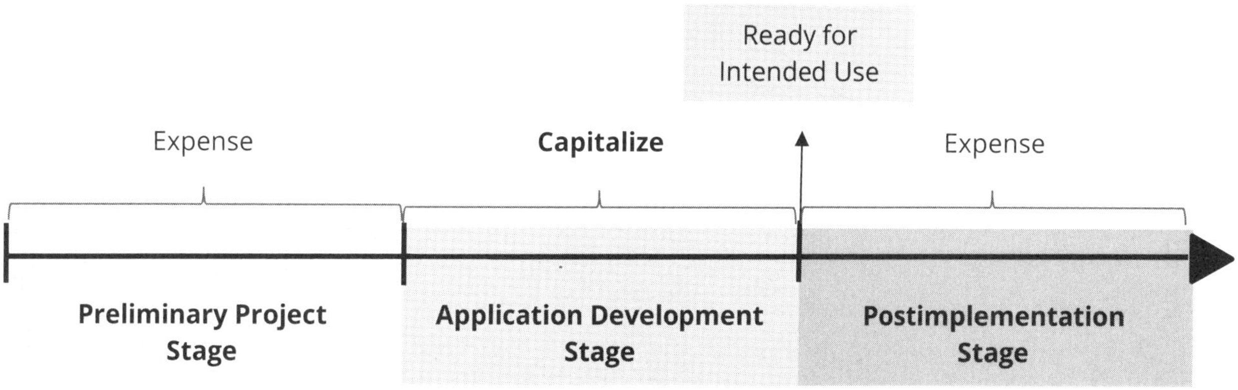

Preliminary Project Stage
- Planning
- Design

Application Development Stage
- Costs to develop or obtain software.
  - Coding & testing
  - Interest
- Implementation costs*

Postimplementation Stage
- Operating costs
  - Training
  - Maintenance

**Capitalized implementation costs do not include costs for training, data conversion, reengineering, and maintenance; these costs must be expensed.*

Cloud Computing Arrangements

When an entity enters a cloud computing arrangement (aka, hosting arrangement), an analysis is performed to determine whether some or all of the arrangement represents a software license:

- If the entire arrangement is considered a **software license**, the entire cost, including the present value of future payments, is treated as an intangible and accounted for similar to other licenses. It will be **capitalized,** and a determination will be made as to whether or not it has a finite useful life.
- If the arrangement does not include a software license, the entire amount is treated as a **service contract** with the **expense** recognized in the period in which the benefit is derived.
    - Note, however, that **implementation costs** (ie, implementation, setup and other upfront costs) incurred during the **application development phase** for such service contracts are **capitalized** depending on the nature of the costs. This does not include costs for *training, data conversion, reengineering, and maintenance*; these costs must be *expensed* (ie, same treatment as internal-use software).
- If the arrangement represents a *combination*, the total cost will be *allocated* between the software license and the service contract.

YOUR WORLD OF LEARNING

ROGER CPA Review

FAR 9 - Receivables

FAR 9 – Receivables

Table of Contents

Receivables

Lecture 9.01 – Receivables

Accounts Receivable

Trade accounts receivable (A/R) result from sales of goods or services in the ordinary course of business, covered in ASC 606, *Revenue from Contracts with Customers*. Receivables that are not related to normal operations, such as amounts due from officers, employees or stockholders, are reported separately from trade A/R (ASC 310).

Trade A/R are reported in an amount equal to the consideration recognized in the transaction that has not been collected as of the date the revenue is recognized. The amount is recorded net of **trade discounts**.

Trade discounts are the difference between the amount that the entity's customer would normally sell the product or service to its customers for and the amount for which the reporting entity is selling the goods/services. This gives the entity's customers the ability to earn a margin upon the sale to its customers. The discounts also may be subject to increases as a customer's volume increases.

There are several other provisions often included in sales contracts that also potentially reduce the amount of consideration. These are referred to as **variable consideration** in a sales contract. They are estimated according to the guidelines for revenues from contracts with customers and reduce revenues recognized upon sale. They include:

- Discounts for prompt payment (ie, sales discounts)
- Reductions for returned goods
- Reductions for defective or nonconforming goods

Discounts for prompt payment are often expressed in terms of a formula, such as 2/10, net 30. This indicates that the customer may take a 2% discount if payment is made within 10 days. If not, no discount is taken, and the amount is due in 30 days. Those customers who are able will generally take advantage of these discounts because they represent a very high effective interest rate.

- With terms of 2/10, net 30, the customer is receiving a 2% discount for paying 20 days earlier than the entire amount is due.
- With approximately 360 days in a year, there are 18 20-day periods.
- The result is an effective rate of roughly 36% per year.

Many times, customers are allowed to **return goods** that they are unable to sell within a reasonable period of time. The customer will return the goods and receive a reduction of the amount to be paid or a refund of amounts paid. In such cases, since the goods are being returned, the reduction of the consideration to be recognized as revenue is net of the value of the goods being returned.

When an entity sells **damaged or nonconforming goods**, the customer may retain the goods and obtain a discount due to the defects or nonconformity. This enables the customer to discount their sales price so that they may sell them, rather than bear the inconvenience of returning them.

While all these items reduce consideration recognized as revenue, **they do not reduce the receivable**. They are, instead, recognized as **contract liabilities**. This is true if the entity has already received payment, in which case the liability represents a refund to be paid. If the revenues have not yet been received, the liability represents a reduction of the amount to be received.

Since these amounts are estimated when consideration is measured, they are subject to change. As a result, the contract liability is evaluated at each reporting date and adjusted as necessary.

Credit losses, as previously discussed, are the portion of trade receivables the seller does not expect to collect due to the customers' inability to pay. They are estimated considering the seller's experience, industry standards, economic conditions, and other factors that may affect customers' ability to pay. They are reported by recognizing credit losses on the income statement and reducing trade receivables with an allowance for credit losses, a contra-asset account.

In performing the evaluation of credit losses, a variety of methods may be applied, such as the following:

- *Discounted cash flow method* – Losses are estimated by determining the present value of the expected future cash flows.
- *Loss-rate method* – Losses are estimated as a percentage of total exposure.
- *Aging method* – The instruments are stratified, often on the basis of when they will mature, and different percentages are applied to each stratum.

(Loss-rate and aging methods: Most likely to be tested with respect to A/R on the CPA exam.)

- *Roll-rate method* – Losses are estimated on the basis of the time required for the conversion cycle, the period required for instruments to be realized.
- *Probability-of-default method* – Losses are estimated by multiplying a likelihood that an instrument will be defaulted upon by the balance of the instrument.

After the initial acquisition and recognition of a financial asset, a current estimate of expected losses is measured each reporting period, using the same measurement technique as was used originally. The allowance is adjusted to the appropriate amount and the related increase or decrease in the allowance is recognized as an additional credit loss expense or a reversal.

In some cases, the amount that is unlikely to be collectible cannot be estimated. This could be for a variety of reasons, such as economic conditions or industry circumstances that are atypical. Under the guidelines in ASC 606, the inability to estimate collectibility indicates that a contract does not exist. An alternative accounting method specified by the standard involves recognizing amounts received as a liability until such time that the credit loss amount can be estimated, or certain other conditions are met.

The inability to estimate credit losses precludes recognition of the receivable. When there is significant uncertainty as to collection, other methods of accounting may be used. These may include the cash basis, the cost recovery basis, or some other method. Under the **cost recovery method**, all payments received, including those designated as interest, are considered recoveries of cost and are not recognized as revenue or profit. When the cost has been recovered in its entirety, further payments will be recognized in income.

If, for example, an entity has sales of $2,000,000, they expect half of their customers to take advantage of the 2% discount for early payment, and based on their past experience and industry knowledge specific to the industry, they expect uncollectible amounts will be 2 ½% of credit sales, they would record the events as follows:

A/R	2,000,000	
Credit loss expense	50,000	
Allowance for credit losses		50,000
Contract liability		20,000
Revenue		1,980,000

The balance in A/R is also reduced by collections on account and amounts written off.

Notes (Loans) Receivable

When an entity makes a loan to another entity or individual, it recognizes a note receivable, representing a **current** asset for portions expected to be collected **within one year** or one accounting cycle, whichever is longer, and a **noncurrent** receivable for the **remainder**.

If the **loan consists exclusively of cash**, it is assumed that the net proceeds are equal to the present value of the future payments to be received.

- When proceeds are below the face value, the difference is a discount, increasing the effective interest rate to the market rate.
- When proceeds are above the face value, the difference is a premium, reducing the effective interest rate to the market rate.
- The discount or premium is recognized in a valuation account and is amortized over the life of the receivable using the effective interest method.

Loans receivable also may result from a transaction involving some cash and some **goods and services**, or may involve only goods and services. (These are discussed later in this section.)

Loans also may be **purchased**. In many cases, the amount paid for a purchased loan will include a premium or will be reduced for a discount such that the effective interest rate is equal to the market rate.

Accounting Options

Loans and trade A/R are financial assets and an entity may elect the **fair value option**, as previously discussed. They also may be reported at the **lower of amortized cost basis or fair value**. When neither of these options is elected, however, the loan will be reported applying the **amortized cost basis**.

Initial Measurement

A note receivable is originally measured as the principal balance of the loan, reduced by an allowance for credit losses, adjusted for any discount or premium. Loan origination fees and costs are deferred and included in the carrying value of the loan on the balance sheet.

Interest Income

In each subsequent period, interest is calculated on the carrying value of the loan using the *effective interest rate*. The difference between that calculation and the amount paid, which is calculated on the face value using the *stated interest rate*, is the discount or premium. Reductions due to pricing may be **sales discounts**, in which case, they are accounted for as a **reduction to the sales price and a contract liability**.

- Amortization of a discount increases interest expense and results in an increase in the carrying value of the loan.
- Amortization of a premium reduces interest expense and results in a decrease to the carrying value.
- Amortization of loan origination fees and costs is also reported as an adjustment to interest income.

Loans also may be purchased in which the debtor's credit is deteriorated (**PCD assets**). The purchase price will be discounted to take into account the likelihood that some or all payments may not be collected due to the deteriorated credit. This discount, which is accounted for as an allowance for credit losses, does not affect the amount of interest income to be reported. Only the amortization of the portion of discount or premium that is not related to credit losses is included in the calculation of interest.

In order to recognize income on loans that are purchased with credit deterioration, the entity would need to have a reasonable expectation as to the amount that is expected to be collected. If that is not the case, the loan may be placed on nonaccrual status, indicating that interest income is not accrued. The entity may use the cost recovery method or the cash basis for income recognition. Although interest may not be recognized, the discount due to credit deterioration will be recognized as a credit loss. Under the cost recovery method or the cash basis, the carrying value of the financial asset may exceed the payoff amount. When that is going to occur, interest income may not be recognized to the extent that the net investment will exceed the payoff amount.

Balance Sheet Presentation

Loans and trade receivables are often presented in the aggregate on the balance sheet. That would not include, however, receivables that are *held for sale* rather than for the purpose of receiving the cash flows. Receivables held for sale are required to be reported in a separate line item on the balance sheet.

Troubled Debt Restructuring

Unless the creditor has elected the fair value option, when a debtor is unable to make payments on a receivable as they come due, the debt may be restructured to assist the debtor in making payments. This usually provides the creditor with the greatest amount achievable under the circumstances.

Exclusions

Certain modifications to a receivable are **not** considered **troubled debt restructures (TDRs)**, including:

- Lease modifications
- Changes to employment agreements
- A debtor's failure to make payments or a delay in taking legal action by the creditor unless there is an agreement to restructure the debt between the debtor and creditor

In addition, the standards exclude the following debt restructurings from the TDR category:

- A transfer of cash, other assets, or equity to the creditor when the fair value of the consideration equals or exceeds the creditor's amortized cost basis
- A transfer of cash, other assets, or equity to the creditor when the fair value of the consideration equals or exceeds the debtor's carrying value of the obligation
- The creditor reduces the effective interest rate to reflect changes to the market rate to discourage the debtor from obtaining funds from another source at the lower market interest rate
- The debtor replaces the debt with new marketable debt with an effective interest rate at or near the market rate for instruments with maturities and interest rates similar to debt issued by debtors that are not troubled

Assets Received in Full Satisfaction

A TDR may provide the creditor with assets or an equity interest in the debtor in *full satisfaction of the receivable*.

- The assets or equity interest received are measured at their **fair values** (less costs to sell if the creditor intends to sell the assets).
- The total recognized for cash, other assets, and equity interests received reduces the amortized cost basis of the receivable.
- The **remaining amortized cost basis** of the loan is eliminated and a **loss on troubled debt restructuring** is recognized for that amount.

If the fair value of the receivable being satisfied is more readily determinable than the assets transferred to the creditor, it may be used instead. Once recognized, the assets received are accounted for as if they had been purchased for cash.

Assets Received in Partial Satisfaction

When the transfer of cash, other assets, and equity is in *partial satisfaction of the receivable*, the terms may be modified in relation to the remaining balance of the receivable. In some cases, the terms are modified without a transfer of assets or equity. Regardless of whether the terms are modified, the remaining collections that are expected to be received on the remaining amortized cost basis under the modified or unmodified terms are measured at their present values.

- The rate used to calculate the present value of future collections is the rate specified in the original contract.
- The market rate at the time of restructure is not used because the loan, as modified, is not considered a new loan but rather an attempt by the creditor to recover its investment.
- The **excess** of the **amortized cost** of the loan **over** the **present value** of the **collections expected** to be received is **recognized** as a **loss**.

Writing Off Receivables

Financial assets are required to be written off (partially or in full) in the period in which it is determined that they are **uncollectible**. The asset is reduced to zero and the allowance for credit losses is decreased by the same amount.

Allowance for credit losses	X	
A/R		X

Recoveries of amounts written-off should be credited back to the allowance for credit losses.

Cash	X	
Allowance for credit losses		X

The result is the same as if the account was first reinstated and then credited with the collection:

A/R	X	
Allowance for credit losses		X
Cash	X	
A/R		X

Direct Write-off Method

Under the direct write-off method (used for tax purposes), bad debt expense is recognized when a specific account is determined to be uncollectible. No valuation account is used.

- A/R is reduced when accounts are written off and recorded as bad debt expense:

Bad debt expense	X	
A/R		X

- **Violates GAAP** in two ways:
  - **Not Matching** – Bad debt (ie, credit loss) expense is not recorded at the time of sale.
  - **Not Conservative** – A/R is carried at its face amount, which will overstate the A/R balance in the balance sheet.

Lecture 9.02 – Sale & Pledging of Receivables

On occasion, a client will want to generate cash from a receivable without waiting until it is collected from the customer. There are **4 basic techniques** available:

- **Pledging** – The client borrows the necessary cash, and "pledges" (offers) the receivable to the lender as collateral to secure the loan. When this occurs it must be *adequately disclosed* in a footnote in the financial statements (F/S).
- **Assigning** – The client borrows the necessary cash, and agrees to use the proceeds from the receivable to repay the lender. Sometimes, the customer is notified to make payment directly to the lender instead of the client.
- **Factoring** – A company converts its A/R into cash by assigning or selling it either with or without recourse to a factor
    - **Sale without recourse** – The client sells the receivable to another party (a factor), with the buyer assuming the risk that the receivable may not be collectible.
    - **Sale with recourse** – The client sells the receivable to another party, with the buyer retaining the right to demand the client make good on the receivable if the customer does not pay as promised.

Transfers & Servicing of Financial Assets

Entities in general, and financial institutions in particular, transfer financial assets to other entities. The transfer may involve a single entire financial asset, such as a mortgage loan receivable; a group of financial assets, such as an entity's A/R; or a participating interest in a financial asset, such as a percentage of the entire financial instrument. (ASC 860)

- When a component of a financial asset that is not considered a participating interest is transferred, it will be accounted for as a secured borrowing with pledge of collateral.
- A component of a financial instrument is **a participating interest** if it has certain characteristics:
    - It represents a proportionate interest in the entire instrument.
    - All cash flows from the instrument, other than those allocated as compensation for services, are divided proportionately among participating interest holders.
    - The rights of all participating interests have the same priority and are not subordinated to one another.
    - All participating interests must agree in order for a party to pledge or exchange the entire financial instrument.

The accounting for a transfer of a financial instrument, group of financial instruments, or a participating interest in a financial interest is determined on the basis of whether or not the transferor has surrendered control of the instrument.

- If control has been surrendered, the transfer will be recognized as a sale, along with a related gain or loss.
- If control has NOT been surrendered, the transfer will be recognized as a secured borrowing with the financial instrument pledged as collateral.

Control of a financial instrument has been surrendered (considered a **sale**) only when all of the following three conditions are met:

1. The transferred financial instruments have been *isolated* from the transferor and *beyond the reach of the transferor* or its creditors, including creditors in bankruptcy.
2. Transferees have the *right to pledge or exchange* the asset it received without restrictions and without providing more than a trivial benefit to the transferor.
3. The transferor does *not maintain effective control* over the financial instrument, considering all of the transferor's continuing involvements with the instrument. The transferor does maintain effective control when:
   a. An agreement, entered into contemporaneously with the transfer, both entitles and obligates the transferor to repurchase or redeem the transferred financial assets at a fixed or determinable price.
   b. An agreement allowing the transferor the unilateral ability to require the transferee to return specific financial assets.
   c. An agreement allowing the transferee to require the transferor to repurchase the transferred financial assets at a price significantly favorable to the transferee.

Unless all 3 of these conditions are satisfied, the financial asset is considered to have been merely **pledged or assigned** as collateral for a loan (**borrowing** transaction).

In the cases of **pledging or assigning**, the company remains the legal owner of the financial asset, and simply records a liability for the amount borrowed:

Cash	X	
Note Payable		X

Notes to the F/S will indicate the dollar amount of the financial assets that have been pledged or assigned. Alternatively, the company can identify these amounts on the face of the balance sheet:

A/R Assigned	X	
A/R		X

The remaining entries include normal entries to record interest and principal payments on the note, and collection of the receivables.

If control is surrendered and the transfer is **accounted for as a sale**, two other issues should be considered.

- A **factor's holdback** (also referred to as *"Due from factor"*) is an amount which provides a margin of protection against sales discounts, sales returns and allowances, and disputed accounts.
- A **recourse obligation** (*probable uncollectible accounts*) is an amount included as *protection for the transferee* against uncollectible accounts; such obligations result in a continuing interest in the asset.

To illustrate, assume an entity with A/R that are expected to have a net realizable value of $35,000 transfers them to another entity for $30,000.

If control is not surrendered, the transaction will be recognized as a secured borrowing:

Cash	30,000	
Interest expense	5,000	
Note payable		35,000

If control is surrendered, and the transferee withholds $5,000 from the proceeds for protection against future reductions resulting from returns, allowances, or disputed amounts, the transaction will be reported as a sale:

Cash	25,000	
Due from factor (withheld amount)	5,000	
Loss on sale of receivables	5,000	
A/R		35,000

- **Factoring** - The sale of short-term A/R. A factoring fee is applied by the buyer and is a straight percentage of the factored receivables.
- **Discounting** - The sale of long-term notes receivable. A discount rate is applied by the buyer and is an annualized rate that will vary depending on the length of time until collection is due.

In the case of sales, the buyer of the receivable becomes the legal owner of it, and the client reduces the carrying value of the receivables to zero, reporting a gain or loss for the difference between the proceeds from sale and the carrying value of the receivable. There is, however, a major difference between the treatment of sales without recourse (as most, though not all, factoring involves) and sales with recourse (as most, though not all, discounting involves).

In the case of a **sale without recourse**, the seller is relieved of any obligation on the receivable. Thus, if the buyer of the receivable is unable to collect from the customer, they cannot require the seller of the receivable to compensate them.

- The transferee (buyer) bears the risk of uncollectible accounts.
- The transferee does not, however, bear the risk of goods being returned, allowances made for nonconforming goods, or disputed balances.

Assume the client has gross A/R of $100,000, and an allowance for credit losses of $8,000. On that date, the client **factors all of the receivables without recourse**, and the buyer charges a factoring fee of 9% of the face amount ($100,000 × 9% = $9,000). The entry is as follows:

Cash and Amount due from Factor (holdback)	91,000	
Loss on factoring	1,000	
Allowance for credit losses	8,000	
A/R		100,000

Notice that the client removes the entire allowance for credit losses, since the risk of collectability has been transferred to the buyer of the receivables (w/o recourse).

When receivables are **factored with recourse**, the client is liable for uncollectible accounts, and must report an estimated liability for the additional amounts that are expected to be paid to the buyer.

If $100,000 A/R with an allowance for credit losses of $8,000 has been **factored with recourse**, and the buyer is charging a 3% factoring fee on the face value ($100,000 × 3% = $3,000), the entry is:

Cash and Amount due from Factor (holdback)	97,000	
Loss on factoring	3,000	
Allowance for credit losses	8,000	
Liability on Transferred receivable		100,000
Estimated recourse liability		8,000

If the buyer is subsequently able to collect only $91,000, and the client is required to pay $9,000 on the uncollectible accounts, an additional loss is recorded as follows:

Estimated recourse liability	8,000	
Loss on factoring	1,000	
Cash		9,000

If the company sells the A/R to a factor in a transaction considered a *borrowing transaction*, this would be considered factoring with recourse.

Cash	X	
Factor's holdback	X	
Interest expense (discount)	X	
Liability on transferred		X

When an interest-bearing note receivable is sold to a bank, the usual process is known as **discounting**. The bank first determines the maturity value of the note, meaning the total payment of principal and accrued interest that is due at maturity. This amount is then reduced by a discount rate, and the bank pays the net result. Notes receivable that have been discounted *with recourse* are reported on the balance sheet with a corresponding contra account (notes receivable discounted). Notes receivable discounted *without recourse* have essentially been sold and should be removed from the balance sheet.

For example, assume the client sells inventory on 6/30/X1 for $100,000, and receives a one-year note for $100,000 bearing interest at 10% (the market rate of interest). The entry for the sale (we'll ignore cost of sales for this illustration) is:

6/30/X1	Note receivable	100,000	
	Sales		100,000

That same day, the client discounts the note at a bank at a 10% discount rate. The amount to be received is calculated as follows:

Face value	100,000
Interest at maturity (10%)	10,000
Maturity value	110,000
Discount (10%)	11,000
Net paid by bank	99,000

Notice the client is not collecting the face value, even though the bank rate is the same as the effective rate on the note, because bank interest is computed on the maturity value. The entry for the discounting activity is:

6/30/X1	Cash	99,000	
	Loss on discounting	1,000	
	Note receivable		100,000

If the note has been **discounted with recourse**, the client should disclose a contingent liability for the amount that might have to be paid if the customer defaults to the bank.

Both the interest rate on a note and the discount rate charged by a bank are annual rates, so the calculations are affected by the holding period.

	Face amount
+	**Interest (**Interest = Face × Interest rate × Term)
=	**Maturity value**
-	**Discount (**Discount = Maturity value × Discount rate × Time Remaining)
=	**Proceeds**

Accounting for Transfers of Participating Interests

An entity may have only a **participating interest** in a financial instrument. To be considered a participating interest, certain characteristics must apply:

- The interest represents a proportionate interest in the entire instrument.
- All cash flows from the instrument are divided proportionately among all participating interests.
- Each participating interest is given the same priority.
- No entity has the ability to pledge or exchange the entire instrument without the consent of all participating interest holders.

When a transfer of a participating interest qualifies as a sale, the transaction is accounted for as follows:

1. Consideration received is recognized at its fair value.
2. The carrying value of the entire instrument is allocated between the participating interest transferred and the interests retained on the basis of their relative fair values.
   a. The portion allocated to the participating interest sold is eliminated.
   b. The difference between that and the fair value of consideration received is recognized as a gain or loss in earnings
3. The remaining carrying value becomes the carrying value of the retained interests.

For example, assume a company has a note receivable with a face and carrying value of $580,000. The entity decides to transfer 40% of the note for $260,000 to another entity at a time when the fair value of the receivable is $650,000. As a result, the fair value of the 40% participating interest being transferred is $260,000 and the fair value of the retained interests is $390,000. The carrying value will be allocated as follows:

- Participating interest transferred - $260,000/$650,000 × $580,000 = $232,000
- Retained interests - $390,000/$650,000 × $580,000 = $348,000

There would be a gain on sale:

Sales price	$260,000
Basis	$232,000
Gain	$ 28,000

The resulting entry would be:

Cash	260,000	
Gain on sale		28,000
Note receivable		232,000

Servicing of Financial Assets

Financial assets, notes receivable in particular, require what is referred to as **servicing**. Servicing of a note receivable includes such administrative functions as sending debtors monthly statements, collecting payments, allocating payments between principal and interest, and sending tax information forms to the debtor. It is fairly common for the seller of a financial asset or a participating interest in a financial asset to retain the obligation to service the receivable, referred to as servicing rights.

- The entity with the servicing rights may not receive any compensation or may receive compensation that is below the fair compensation for performing the servicing obligations, in which case the entity has a *servicing liability*.
- The entity may receive compensation that exceeds the fair compensation for performing the servicing obligations, in which case the entity has a *servicing asset*.

In addition to recognizing a service asset or liability when servicing rights are retained upon the sale of a financial instrument or a participating interest in one, an entity will also recognize a servicing asset or liability when it acquires or assumes a servicing obligation for a financial instrument in which it has no direct interest.

A **servicing asset or servicing liability** is initially recognized at its **fair value**, regardless of whether or not consideration was received. Once recognized, servicing assets or liabilities may be accounted for under either of two methods:

- **Amortization method**
  - The asset, when revenues will exceed costs, or liability, when costs will exceed revenues, is amortized over the period during which servicing income (asset) or loss (liability) will be recognized.
  - The amortization will be in proportion to the amount of income or loss.
  - The asset or liability is assessed for impairment (asset) or increased obligation (liability) at each reporting date.
- **Fair value method**
  - The servicing asset or liability is adjusted to fair value on each reporting date.
  - Increases or decreases are reported in earnings.
  - Selecting the fair value method involves an irrevocable election.

In addition to servicing assets and liabilities, there are other ways in which financial instruments are divided with some of the various components being transferred and others retained. One component is referred to as an **interest-only strip (i-o strip).** Sometimes they are retained as part of the consideration for the portion of the instrument transferred. In other cases, they are considered compensation for the service obligations.

- I-o strips are considered financial instruments, not servicing assets.
- The entity receives a proportionate amount of each interest payment received.
- They are reported at fair value when received.
- They are subsequently accounted for as available for sale securities or trading securities, as appropriate.

Securitization

Financial assets may be securitized in order to make them easier to transfer. Securitization is the process of converting financial assets into securities. It is accomplished when a group of homogeneous securities are combined into a pool and transferred into an entity referred to as a securitization mechanism. A group of mortgage notes receivable, for example, may be transferred to a real estate investment trust (REIT). Shares in the trust can then be sold to investors as securities.

Payments received by the securitization mechanism may be classified as either:

- Payments used to pay off debt securities, referred to as *pay-through*; or
- Payments attributed to investors, referred to as *pass-through*.

In certain circumstances, referred to as *revolving period securitizations*, receivables are transferred at the inception and also periodically thereafter. During the term, referred to as the revolving period, cash collections are used to purchase additional receivables from the transferor.

Assume an entity sells a loan for $44,000, retaining servicing rights and a 1% interest only strip. The loan has a book value of $45,000 and, on the date of transfer, the fees that will be received for the servicing is expected to exceed the cost of performing the servicing, resulting in a servicing asset with a fair value of $4,100. The i-o strip has an estimated fair value of $2,200 at the date of transfer.

Proceeds consist of:

Cash	$44,000
Servicing rights (at fair value)	4,100
I-O strip (at fair value)	2,200
Total	$50,300

Since the carrying value of the receivable was $45,000, there would be a gain on sale of $5,300. The journal entry would appear as follows:

Cash	44,000	
Servicing rights	4,100	
I-O strip	2,200	
Note receivable		45,000
Gain on Sale		5,300

Accounting for Collateral

When a debtor provides a creditor with collateral for a loan, the accounting for it will depend on who retains control of the collateral. In most circumstances, the transferor (debtor) retains control of the collateral.

- It remains as an asset on the debtor's F/S.
- The fact that it is collateral for a debt is disclosed.
- The transferee (creditor) does not recognize the asset in its F/S.

Upon default, the creditor will take control of the collateral.

- The debtor will eliminate the carrying value of the asset, the carrying value of the debt and related accounts, such as accrued interest, and recognize a gain or loss for the difference.
- The creditor will recognize the asset at fair value, derecognize the receivable, and recognize a gain or loss (generally a loss), as appropriate.

When the transferee has control of the collateral, it recognizes an asset and a corresponding liability, recognizing the obligation to return the collateral upon settlement of the debt instrument. Since the transferor will no longer have possession of the collateral, it will be reported as a receivable. If the debtor defaults:

- The debtor will eliminate the liability and the receivable with the difference representing a gain or loss.
- The creditor will eliminate the receivable and the liability to return the collateral, with the difference representing a gain or loss.

Lecture 9.03 – Interest on Receivables

- A/R occurs in the ordinary course of business, so record at **Face value**. (ASC 310)
- L/T receivables are not in the ordinary course of business, so record at **Present Value (PV).**
- The **future value factor** is equal to 1 divided by the present value factor. For example, an investment of $10,000 in two years at 10% would accumulate to the principal multiplied by the future value factor. In this case the $10,000 × 1/0.826 = $12,107.
  - **Notes received solely for cash** (assume rate is fair)

N/R	10,000	
Cash		10,000

  - **Notes received for goods or services**

1. Note receivable at a **reasonable rate**. The PV of the note is the same as the Face amount. Assume the asset book value is 6,000.

Notes receivable	10,000		
Discount on N/R		0	> **cv = 10,000**
Asset		6,000	
Gain on sale		4,000	

Noninterest-bearing notes (Zero-Interest-Bearing Notes)

2. If the interest rate is not stated or is unreasonable, use the **FMV of the goods or the FMV of the note,** whichever is more easily determinable. Assume the FMV of the asset is 9,000.

Notes receivable	10,000		
Discount on N/R		1,000	> **cv = 9,000**
Equipment		6,000	
Gain on sale		3,000	

3. If the interest rate is not stated, the FMV of the goods or the FMV of the note is not determinable, **IMPUTE** an interest rate. Use a reasonable rate for a note of this type. PV of a note in 2 years at 10% is .8265 × 10,000 = 8,265.

Notes receivable	10,000		
Discount on N/R		1,735	> **cv = 8,265**
Equipment		6,000	
Gain on sale		2,265	

- When interest rate isn't fair, the fair rate must be imputed
  - Receivable is carried at the present value of payments discounted at fair interest rate.
  - Periodic interest income accrues based on fair rate.

As a general rule, businesses don't bother charging interest on A/R expected to be collected within 30 days, and the AICPA permits a company to **ignore the interest component** or choose an unusual rate so long as **two conditions** are satisfied:

- The entire receivable will be collected within a year.
- The terms of the sale are customary in the trade.

For long-term receivables and short-term sales **not** consummated under **customary trade terms,** however, the entity is normally required to compute interest income using a fair rate of interest.

If the client is not assessing a fair interest rate on a receivable resulting from a sale, we must impute interest, which means determining the implicit rate of interest being charged. In such a case, it is assumed that some or all of the interest may have been included in the quoted sales price.

It may also be necessary to impute interest on a receivable obtained in connection with a loan, if the repayment includes provisions requiring the borrower to provide goods or services or other consideration in addition to cash payments. It is assumed that some or all of the interest may be represented by the value of the consideration provided.

Imputing interest is not appropriate when a loan involves a straight repayment of the cash with no other conditions, since there is no account to which the interest can be attributed.

Let's look at an example of imputing interest on a sale. Assume that the client sells a product on 1/1/X1 for $1,000, with payment not due for 3 years and no interest to be assessed. Since the period of collection exceeds one year, we must assume that a portion of the quoted selling price actually represents interest, rather than being part of the true sales price of the product.

There are two reasonable approaches to determining the true sales price:

- **Cash selling price** - The price being charged by the client for sales to customers who pay in full on the date of sale.
- **Present value** - The cash flow of the receivable discounted at a fair interest rate.

Normally, the first approach is preferred, since cash selling price is more verifiable and, therefore, a more reliable measurement. The latter approach requires the determination of a fair rate of interest, and there can be reasonable disagreement as to the appropriate rate to utilize.

Assume, however, that the cash selling price is not determinable, and that a fair interest rate of 10% is determined. The present value of $1 for 3 years at 10% is .751, so that the present value of $1,000 payment due in 3 years is $751. The sale is recorded as follows:

1/1/X1	Note receivable	1,000	
	Discount on note		249
	Sales		751

The discount on note, which is simply the difference between the gross receivable and the present value of the receivable, is a form of unearned interest income.

Once a receivable is recorded, it will bear interest using the appropriate rate.

In the previous example, after recording a note receivable of $1,000 with a discount of $249 at 1/1/X1, the company will report interest over the 3 years until the note comes due. The interest is based on the carrying value of the note, which is the gross note less the unamortized discount. Since the imputed interest rate is 10%, the original note of $1,000 - $249 = $751 will result in interest income of $75, recorded as follows:

12/31/X1	Discount on note	75	
	Interest income		75

This will increase the carrying value of the note by $75 for the subsequent period, so that interest income will also increase. A schedule showing the interest income in each period follows:

	20X1	**20X2**	**20X3**
Gross receivable	1,000	1,000	1,000
Unamortized	249	174	91
Carrying value	751	826	909
Interest rate	10%	10%	10%
Interest Income	75	83	91

Interest Amortization

CV	×	Effective Int. Rate	=	Interest Income		(face × stated × time) cash payment =		Amortization of Disc/Prem
8,265	×	10%	=	826	-	0	=	826
+826								
9,091	×	10%	=	909	-	0	=	909
+909								
10,000								

UWorld
YOUR WORLD OF LEARNING
ROGER
CPA Review

FAR 10 - Bonds & Present Value Tables

FAR 10 – Bonds & Present Value Tables

Table of Contents

Bonds & Present Value Tables

Lecture 10.01 – Bond Terminology

A bond is a borrowing agreement in which the issuer promises to repay a certain amount of money (Face/Par value) to the purchaser, after a certain period of time (term), at a certain interest rate (Effective, Yield, Market rate). (ASC 470 and 835)

- **Term bond** – a bond that will pay the entire principal upon maturity at the end of the term.
- **Serial bond** – a bond in which the principal matures in installments.
- **Debenture bonds** – unsecured bonds that are not supported by any collateral.
- **Stated, face, coupon, nominal rate** – the rate printed on the bond. Represents the amount of cash the investor will receive every payment.
- **Carrying amount** – this is the net amount at which the bond is being reported on the issuer's balance sheet, and equals the face value of the bond plus the **premium** (when the bond was issued above face value) or minus the **discount** (when the bond was issued below face value) and minus any **bond issue costs**. It is also called the book value or reported amount. It will initially be the same as issue price, net of issue costs, but gradually approaches the face value as time passes, since the premium or discount and the bond issue costs are amortized as an adjustment to interest expense over the life of the bond.
- **Effective rate**, **Yield, Market Interest rate** – this is the actual rate of interest the issuer is paying on the bond based on the issue price. The effective rate is often called the market rate of interest or yield.
- When the bond is issued at a **premium**, the effective rate of interest will be lower than the stated rate, since the cash interest and principal repayment are based on face value, but the company actually received more money than that.
- When the bond is issued at a **discount**, the effective rate of interest will be higher than the stated rate, since the issuer must pay cash interest and principal based on a higher amount than the funds actually received upon issuance.
- **Convertible bond** – a bond that is convertible into common stock of the debtor at the bondholder's option.
- **Callable bond** – a bond which the issuer has the right to redeem prior to its maturity date.
- **Covenants** – restrictions that borrowers must often agree to.

When an entity issues bonds, or incurs any debt, it may incur costs in the form of fees paid to a financial institution, sometimes referred to as "points" or other fees, to an attorney for drawing up documents, or to regulators or others in order to be able to print up and issue its bonds. These costs, referred to as issue costs, are treated as a contra-liability, reducing the carrying value of the debt. Issue costs are amortized with the amortization treated as an adjustment to interest expense.

ASC 825 provides that a company may elect the fair value option for reporting financial assets and financial liabilities. If the fair value option is elected for a financial liability (bonds), the requirements of ASC 470 no longer apply. Instead, the financial liability is reported at fair value at the end of each reporting period, and the resulting gain or loss is reported in earnings of the period.

If an entity does not elect the fair value option, the bond is recorded at its issue price, and the effective interest method is used to amortize any premium or discount on the bond and any bond issuance costs. The remainder of this section will focus on the pricing of the bond using the effective interest method of amortizing a bond as required by ASC 470.

Issuance of Bonds (Examples)

Face value of bonds	$1,000,000
Term	5 years
Stated interest rate	8%
Effective rate/Market rate/Yield	**a)** 8%, **b)** 10%, **c)** 6% (3 examples)

a. Bond issued at **par value** where market rate of interest (8%) equals the stated rate (8%).

Cash	1,000,000	
Bonds Payable		1,000,000

Each year interest will be paid for $1,000,000 (face) × 8% (stated rate) = $80,000 per year

Interest expense	80,000	
Cash		80,000

b. Bond issued at a discount, since the stated rate of 8% is lower than the market rate of 10%, the only reason an investor would purchase this bond is if it would effectively yield 10%. To do so, the issuer must sell the bond at a **discount** (the actual cash proceeds must be precisely computed using present value factors and are only estimated in this journal entry).

Cash	900,000	
Discount	100,000	
Bonds Payable		1,000,000

The **discount must be amortized** over the life of the bond. Let's assume we are using straight-line amortization of $20,000 year (100/5yrs = 20).

Interest expense	100,000	
Discount		20,000
Cash		80,000

c. Bond issued for a premium since the stated rate of 8% is higher than the Market rate of 6%. Investors are paying a **premium** to acquire this bond (the actual cash proceeds must be precisely computed using present value factors and are only estimated in this journal entry).

Cash	1,100,000	
Premium		100,000
Bonds Payable		1,000,000

The premium must be amortized over the life of the bond. (100/5 = 20)

Interest expense	60,000	
Premium	20,000	
Cash		80,000

The next consideration is how to calculate the proceeds from the issuance of the bonds. The above examples assumed the proceeds were given at 900,000 to 1,100,000. To calculate the **present value (PV) of the proceeds,** two amounts need to be PV.

- **PV of the Face** of the bonds (Face × PV of a lump sum using the effective interest rate)
- **PV of the interest** as an annuity (Face × stated rate × time = interest × PV of an Ordinary annuity at the effective interest rate)
  - The sum of these two amounts represents the PV of the bonds.
  - If **semi-annual** interest is being paid, take the years × 2 and the interest rate/2
    - Eg, 5-year bonds at 10% semi-annual. Use the PV table for 10 periods @ 5%.

In some circumstances, a problem will not require the use of present value to calculate the proceeds from issuance. It may instead express the sales price of the bond in terms of a **percentage of face value**.

- When bonds are issued at *101*, for example, the proceeds would be 101% of face value.
- If they are issued at *98*, the proceeds would be 98% of face value.

Lecture 10.02 – Present Value Tables: Time Value of Money

To determine the exact selling price of a bond requires the use of present value concepts. (ASC 835) Money that is received at a future date is less valuable than money received immediately, and present value concepts relate future cash flows to the equivalent present dollars. Present value is defined as the current measure of an estimated future cash inflow or outflow, discounted at an interest rate for the number of periods between today and the date of the estimated cash flow. Many decisions require adjustments related to the time value of money:

- **Present Value of Amount (lump sum)** – This is used to examine a single cash flow that will occur at a future date and determine its equivalent value today. The amount one needs to invest today, for how many years, at what interest rate, to get $1 back in the future.
- **Present Value of Ordinary Annuity** – This refers to repeated cash flows on a systematic basis, with amounts being paid at the *end* of each period (it may also be known as an **annuity in arrears**). Bond interest payments are commonly made at the end of each period and use these factors.
- **Present Value of Annuity Due (Now)** – This refers to repeated cash flows on a systematic basis, with amounts being paid at the *beginning* of each period (it may also be known as an **annuity in advance** or special annuity). Rent payments are commonly made at the beginning of each period and use these factors.
- **Future Values (compound interest)** – These look at cash flows and project them to some future date and include all three variations applicable to present values. This is the amount that would accumulate at a future point in time if $1 were invested now. The future value factor is equal to 1 divided by the present value factor. For example, an investment of $10,000 in two years at 10% would accumulate to the principal multiplied by the future value factor. In this case the $10,000 × 1/0.8265 = $12,100.

Present and Future Value Tables*

Future Value (Amount) of $1

(n) Periods	6%	8%	10%	12%	15%
1	1.060	1.080	1.100	1.120	1.150
2	1.124	1.166	1.210	1.254	1.323
3	1.191	1.260	1.331	1.405	1.521
4	1.262	1.360	1.464	1.574	1.749
5	1.338	1.469	1.611	1.762	2.011
10	1.791	2.159	2.594	3.106	4.046
15	2.397	3.172	4.177	5.474	8.137
20	3.207	4.661	6.728	9.646	16.367
30	5.743	10.063	17.449	29.960	66.212
40	10.286	21.725	45.259	93.051	267.864

Present Value of $1

(n) Periods	6%	8%	10%	12%	15%
1	0.943	0.926	0.909	0.893	0.870
2	0.890	0.857	0.826	0.797	0.756
3	0.840	0.794	0.751	0.712	0.658
4	0.792	0.735	0.683	0.636	0.572
5	0.747	0.681	0.621	0.567	0.497
10	0.558	0.463	0.386	0.322	0.247
15	0.417	0.315	0.239	0.183	0.123
20	0.312	0.215	0.149	0.104	0.061
30	0.174	0.099	0.057	0.334	0.015
40	0.097	0.046	0.022	0.011	0.004

Future Value (Amount) of an Ordinary Annuity of $1

(n) Periods	6%	8%	10%	12%	15%
1	1.000	1.000	1.000	1.000	1.000
2	2.060	2.080	2.100	2.120	2.150
3	3.184	3.246	3.310	3.374	3.473
4	4.375	4.506	4.641	4.779	4.993
5	5.637	5.867	6.105	6.353	6.742
10	13.180	14.486	15.937	17.549	20.304
15	23.276	27.152	31.772	37.280	47.580
20	36.786	45.762	57.275	72.052	102.444
30	79.058	113.283	164.494	241.333	434.745
40	154.762	259.056	442.592	767.091	1779.090

Present Value of an Ordinary Annuity of $1

(n) Periods	6%	8%	10%	12%	15%
1	0.943	0.926	0.909	0.893	0.870
2	1.833	1.783	1.736	1.690	1.626
3	2.673	2.577	2.487	2.402	2.283
4	3.465	3.312	3.170	3.037	2.855
5	4.212	3.993	3.791	3.605	3.352
10	7.360	6.710	6.144	5.650	5.019
15	9.712	8.559	7.606	6.811	5.847
20	11.470	9.818	8.514	7.469	6.259
30	13.765	11.258	9.427	8.055	6.566
40	15.046	11.924	9.779	8.243	6.642

Present Value of an Annuity Due of $1

(n) Periods	6%	8%	10%	12%	15%
1	1.000	1.000	1.000	1.000	1.000
2	1.943	1.926	1.909	1.893	1.870
3	2.833	2.783	2.736	2.690	2.626
4	3.673	3.577	3.487	3.402	3.855
5	4.465	4.312	4.170	4.037	3.855
10	7.802	7.247	6.759	6.328	5.772
15	10.295	9.244	8.367	7.628	6.724
20	12.158	10.604	9.365	8.366	7.198
30	14.591	12.158	10.370	9.022	7.550
40	15.949	12.879	10.757	9.233	7.638

** All values rounded to the nearest thousandth of a percent*

Converting From One Annuity to Another

In some cases, when attempting to determine the present value of a stream of interest payments, an ordinary annuity, the only table available may be for an annuity due. To determine the present value of the ordinary annuity, either:

- Use the factor for 1 more period and subtract 1.0 from it, or
- Use the factor for the appropriate number of periods and divide it by 1 + the interest rate
  - The factor for an ordinary annuity for 4 years at 8% is 3.312.
  - This can be derived by using the factor for 5 years for an annuity due, 4.312, and subtracting 1.0 to get 3.312.
  - This can also be derived by dividing the factor for an annuity due of 4 years, 3.577, by 1 + the interest rate, or 1.08, to get 3.312.

In other cases, when attempting to determine the present value of a stream of rent payments, an annuity due, the only table available may be for an ordinary annuity. To determine the present value of the annuity due, either:

- Use the factor for 1 less period and add 1.0 to it, or
- Use the factor for the appropriate number of periods and multiply it by 1 + the interest rate
  - The factor for an annuity due for 4 years at 8% is 3.577.
  - This can be derived by using the factor for 3 years for an ordinary annuity, 2.577, and adding 1.0 to get 3.577.
  - This can also be derived by multiplying the factor for an ordinary annuity of 4 years, 3.312, by 1 + the interest rate, or 1.08, to get 3.577.

Actual factors for $1 are typically provided in tables to be multiplied by the cash flows in exam problems.

Assume that a company can earn 10% on its money. If it had to wait one year to receive a dollar, that would be the equivalent to them of 91 cents today (rounding all information to the nearest penny). The reason is that 91 cents invested at 10% would earn approximately 9 cents over the next year and become a dollar. The way this relationship is expressed is by saying that the present value of 1 at 10% for 1 period = 0.91.

For multiple years at 10%, the factors (rounded) are:

Years	Factor
1	0.91
2	0.83
3	0.75
4	0.68
5	0.62
Ordinary Annuity	**3.79**

An ordinary annuity refers to payments being made at the end of each period and is simply the sum of the value of each of the payments. In the above, the present value of an ordinary annuity of 1 at 10% for 5 periods = 3.79, meaning that getting one dollar each year for the next 5 years is the equivalent of getting $3.79 immediately. Another way to express it is to say that a person who paid $3.79 today to obtain an annuity of $1 per year for the next 5 years is earning a 10% rate of return on their investment.

Assume the following facts on the issuance of a single bond:

Face Value	$1,000
Stated Rate	8%
Effective Rate	10%
Issue Date	1/1/X1
Pay Dates for Interest	12/31
Due Date for Principal	12/31/X5
PV of 1 at 10% for 5 periods	0.62
PV of ordinary annuity at 10% for 5 periods	3.79

To determine the selling price of this term bond on 1/1/X1, the interest payments of $1,000 × 8% = $80 per year and the principal payment of $1,000 due in 5 years will be discounted at the effective rate of return of 10%, as follows:

Item	Amount	PV Factor	Present Value
Principal	$1,000	0.62	$620
Interest (Annuity)	$80	3.79	$304
Total			$924

Notice that, as expected, the selling price of the bond is less than face value, because the effective rate of interest of 10% exceeds the stated rate of 8%.

The entry to record the issuance is as follows:

1/1/X1	Cash	924	
	Unamortized discount	76	
	Bond payable		1,000

Occasionally, a company will issue a zero-coupon bond, which refers to a bond that pays no periodic interest (0% coupon rate of interest). The bondholder only receives the face value of the bond at maturity.

Lecture 10.03 – Issuance of Bonds: Journal Entry

3. Cash [% face + Accrued Interest – BIC]
4. BIC (a contra-liability, will be absorbed into discount or premium)
5. Discount (plug, increased by any BIC)
    1. Bond Payable (Face)
    2. Accrued Interest Payable = [face × (stated rate) × (time – since last interest paid)]

    5. Premium (plug, decreased by any BIC)

Carrying Value = Face Net of BIC & Discount or Premium

Note: The carrying value (CV) of the bonds is Bonds Payable (1), net of the discount or premium (5), and net of BIC (4).

The bond payable is reported in **noncurrent liabilities**, net of bond issue costs and either net of unamortized discount or including unamortized premium.

The FASB has not yet provided practical guidance for recording BIC given the requirements of ASU 2015-03. It is unlikely that BIC will be tested closely on the exam before such guidance is provided. Just in case, here are examples of how BIC would most likely be recorded at issuance.

BIC and Discount Example

Roger Co. issues $1,000,000 in 3% 10-year bonds when the market rate of interest is 5%. Bond issue costs are $20,000. Interest is paid annually, and there is no accrued interest.

- Present value of lump sum at 5% after 10 periods: 0.6139
- Present value of ordinary annuity at 5% over 10 periods: 7.7217

The cash proceeds will be (($1,000,000 × 0.6139) + ($30,000 × 7.7217)), or $845,551.

The discount is $1,000,000 - $845,551, or $154,449. Instead of the $20,000 in BIC being entered as a separate debit, it will be added to the discount amount, causing the discount to be reported as $154,449 + $20,000, or $174,449. This will balance because the $20,000 cash paid in BIC reduces the cash proceeds by $20,000, to $845,551 - $20,000, or $825,551.

Journal entry at issuance:

Cash, net of BIC paid	825,551	
Discount including BIC	174,449	
Bonds payable		1,000,000

BIC and Premium Example

Roger Co. issues $1,000,000 in 5% 10-year bonds when the market rate of interest is 3%. Bond issue costs are $20,000. Interest is paid annually, and there is no accrued interest.

- Present value of lump sum at 3% after 10 periods: 0.74409
- Present value of ordinary annuity at 3% over 10 periods: 8.5302

The cash proceeds will be (($1,000,000 × 0.7441) + ($50,000 × 8.5302)), or $1,170,610.

The premium is $1,170,610 - $1,000,000, or $170,610. Instead of the $20,000 in BIC being entered as a debit, it will be netted against the premium amount, causing the premium to be reported as $170,610 - $20,000, or $150,610. This will balance because the $20,000 cash paid in BIC reduces the cash proceeds by $20,000, to $1,170,610 - 20,000, or $1,150,610.

Journal entry at issuance:

Cash, net of BIC paid	1,150,610	
Premium, net of BIC		150,610
Bonds payable		1,000,000

Accrued Interest Payable

A bond isn't always sold when it is dated.

For example, the 8% bond dated 1/1/X1 in our earlier example might not be issued to the public until 4/1/X1. Even so, interest accrues from the date on the bond, so the buyer is immediately credited for 3 months of interest ($1,000 × 8% × 3/12 of a year = $20), and will receive a full year of interest ($1,000 × 8% = $80) on 12/31/X1. To be equitable, the buyer will be required to pay an additional $20 on 4/1/X1 when purchasing the bond, and the issuer will report the amount as accrued interest payable, reported as a current liability.

Assume that the bond itself sells for 93 (ie, %). The entry to record the issuance on 4/1/X1 is:

4/1/X1	Cash	950	
	Unamortized discount	70	
	Bonds payable		1,000
	Accrued interest payable		20

The bond payable will be reported at $1,000 – $70 = $930. Notice that the reported amount refers to the carrying value of the bond and is equal to the face value of the bond payable plus the unamortized premium or minus the unamortized discount. Accrued interest, like deferred bond issue costs, is not included in the carrying value of the bond.

Bond Issue Costs (BIC)

Costs directly associated with the issuance of the bonds are a deduction from the carrying amount *(Contra Liability) of the bonds* and are amortized over the period of time the bonds are outstanding using the effective interest method. As a general rule, BIC are amortized, along with discount or premium, as an adjustment to interest expense. BIC may include:

- Printing and engraving of the bond certificates
- Legal and accounting fees
- Underwriter commissions
- Promotion costs (printing the prospectus)

Due to the simplification initiative, BIC had been recognized as a deferred charge, thus creating different balance sheet presentation requirements for debt discounts, premiums and issue costs. As shown in the examples above, BIC will most likely be added to a discount or netted against premium, then amortized along with the discount or premium using the effective interest method. By simplifying it, it eliminated the conflicts with FASB concept statement No. 6, Elements of F/S.

As mentioned earlier, the discount or premium may be amortized over the time period that the bonds are *outstanding* using the straight-line method (not GAAP), or the effective interest method (interest method). The Interest method is preferred and is GAAP. The straight-line method may be used only if it is not materially different from the effective interest method.

Discount Amortization

Face	-	Discount	=	CV	×	Effective interest rate	-	Interest expense		(face × stated × time) cash payment		Amortization of Discount
$1,000,000	-	100,000	=	900,000	×	10%	=	90,000	-	80,000	=	10,000
	-	10,000		+10,000								
1,000,000	-	90,000	=	910,000	×	10%	=	91,000	-	80,000	=	11,000
	-	11,000	=	+11,000								
1,000,000	-	79,000	=	921,000	×	10%						

		Debit	Credit
JE 1)	Interest expense	90,000	
	Discount		10,000
	Cash		80,000
JE 2)	Interest expense	91,000	
	Discount		11,000
	Cash		80,000

Note: When amortizing a discount, the interest expense increases each year, and the amortization of the discount increases each year.

Premium Amortization

Face	+	Premium	=	CV	×	Effective interest rate	-	Interest expense		(face × stated × time) cash payment		Amortization of Premium
$1,000,000	+	100,000	=	1,100,000	×	6%	=	66,000	-	80,000	=	14,000
	-	14,000		-14,000								
1,000,000	+	86,000	=	1,086,000	×	6%	=	65,000	-	80,000	=	15,000
	-	15,000	=	-15,000								
1,000,000	+	71,000	=	1,071,000	×	6%						

		Debit	Credit
JE 1)	Interest expense	66,000	
	Premium	14,000	
	Cash		80,000
JE 2)	Interest expense	65,000	
	Premium	15,000	
	Cash		80,000

Note: When amortizing a premium, the interest expense decreases each year, but the amortization of the premium increases each year.

Lecture 10.04 – Bond Retirement

Bonds may be called or retired prior to maturity (aka, early extinguishment of debt). When this happens, the difference between the net carrying amount of the debt and the amount paid to retire the debt is reported as a gain/loss on the issuer's income statement as part of continuing operations (ASC 470). The journal entry is basically the opposite of the original issuance. The plug to balance the entry is the **gain/loss**.

Bonds Payable (face)	X	
Premium (unamortized)	X	
Loss (plug)	X	
BIC (unamortized)		X
Discount (unamortized)		X
Cash (amount to retire)		X
Gain (plug)		X

Note that if the fair value option under ASC 825 is elected, the net carrying value of the debt retired will equal the fair value of the debt at retirement. Any related gains/losses accumulated in other comprehensive income will be recognized in net income in the year of retirement.

Bond Sinking Funds

A fund set up for the retirement of bonds. The balance is treated as a noncurrent asset until the bonds mature. Any interest or dividends earned are added to the sinking fund balance and reported as income.

Lecture 10.05 – Bonds with Detachable Warrants

A warrant is a security that can be sold or exercised by the bondholder, while still keeping the bond. Since it is separable, it is as if two securities were issued, therefore a value must be given to both securities. The value for the warrant is included in APIC.

- If the FMV of both securities is known, the **relative FMV approach** is used.
- If the FMV of only one security is known, the other is a plug.
- The amount for warrants is recorded in **APIC-Warrants**.
- If *Non-detachable* stock purchase warrants, no separate value is given
- If the warrants expire, close them out into APIC.

For example: $800 par value of bonds with warrants is issued for $900. The relative FMV of bonds to warrants is 80% bonds, 20% warrants.

Bonds with Warrants

-FMV of Bond *without* warrant	X		80%
-FMV of Warrants		X	20%
Total FMV		X	

		Cash proceeds	
Bond	80% ×	900 =	720
Warrant	20% ×	900 =	180
			900

			Looks like a premium but isn't
Cash	900		
Discount	80		720
Bond Payable		800	
APIC – Warrants		180	

Disclosures should be made regarding the combined aggregate amount of maturities and sinking fund requirements for all long-term-borrowings for each of the **next 5 years** and in the aggregate.

UWorld
YOUR WORLD OF LEARNING
ROGER
CPA Review

FAR 11 - Accounting for Leases

FAR 11 – Accounting for Leases

Table of Contents

Accounting for Leases

Lecture 11.01 – Overview of Lease Accounting

ASC 842 defines a **lease** as "a contract, or part of a contract, that conveys the right to control the use of identified property, plant , or equipment (an identified asset) for a period of time in exchange for consideration." This is an extremely important definition since anything considered a lease generally must now be recognized by the lessee as a lease asset and liability on the balance sheet; there is an exception for short-term leases (ie, 12 months or less), however.

Depending on the nature of the lease, a lease generally may be classified as either an **operating lease** (ie, a true rental) or a **finance / sales-type lease**, which transfers substantially all the rights and risks of ownership (ie, more like a purchase/sale). In this section, we will begin by taking a look at the big picture, exploring some important general definitions, and covering the lease accounting basics.

Lessor	Lessee
Operating	Operating
Nonoperating • Sales-type o with selling profit o without selling profit • Direct financing – rare	Finance

Lease Term

The lease term is the period of time during which the lease is expected to be in force. It begins at the commencement date and is the sum of the following:

- **Initial lease term** – This is the original *noncancelable* term of the lease that does not include any renewal periods.
- **Periods for which a renewal option is likely to be exercised by the lessee**
- **Periods for which an option to terminate is unlikely to be exercised –** This might be the case when a lease contains a provision that requires the lessee to pay a significant penalty to the lessor for not renewing the lease.
- **Periods for which a renewal option** (or option not to terminate) **is controlled by the lessor**

Initial Measurement of Lease Payments

Lease payments represent the amount that the lessee will likely pay for the use of the underlying asset (NOT including amounts allocated to nonlease components, see below) under the terms of the lease during the lease term, as defined above. Such payments may include:

- **Fixed Payments –** This is the amount the lessee is required to pay the lessor over the lease term, minus any lease incentives paid/payable to the lessee. Lease incentives may include:
  - Payments made to or on behalf of the lessee.
  - Losses incurred by the lessor to assume the lessee's preexisting lease with another party.

- **In Substance Fixed Payments –** These are payments the lessee is required to pay the lessor that appear to be variable, but they really aren't. For example, a clause is written in the lease to create variability of payments, but it has no economic substance.
- **Certain Variable Lease Payments** – These are rent increases based on a change in an index, interest rate, or comparable external factor (eg, CPI, Federal funds rate, etc.). Note: Other types of variable lease payments are NOT included in "lease payments."
- **The Exercise Price of a Purchase Option Reasonably Certain to Be Exercised** – Determining whether any option (ie, renewal, purchase, termination, etc.) is reasonably certain to be exercised is based on all relevant economic factors, such as:
    - Contractual terms/conditions compared with the market.
    - Leasehold improvements that are expected to have significant economic value to the lessee.
    - Costs relating to terminating the lease and obtaining a new lease.
    - The importance of the underlying asset to the lessee's operations.

For purposes of calculating PV of lease payments, a purchase option reasonably certain to be exercised will be treated as a lump sum paid at the end of the noncancelable lease term.

- **Penalties** – If the lease term reflects the lessee exercising an option to terminate the lease, then any penalties for such termination should be included in lease payments.
- **Amounts Likely to Be Owed under Residual Value Guarantees (for Lessee Only) –** In some cases, the lessee guarantees that the property will be worth at least a certain amount when it is returned to the lessor at the termination of the lease and, thus, must make up for certain deficiencies; this is referred to as a "residual value guarantee."
    - A lease provision that requires the lessee to make up for damage, extraordinary wear and tear, or excessive usage would NOT be considered a lessee guarantee of the residual value and would be treated similar to variable lease payments.
    - Amounts paid by the lessee to obtain a third-party guarantee of residual value would NOT be included in lease payments.
    - Guarantees of the lessor's debt are also NOT included.

Lease and Nonlease Components

Some contracts that contain leases will have various components, some of which are lease components and some of which are nonlease components. When that is the case, lease components and nonlease components are accounted for separately, and lease payments are allocated to each of the separate components proportionately based on the **standalone price** of each lease and nonlease component.

- For example, **nonlease components** such as *maintenance service obligations* (ie, the lessor is required to maintain the property) are separated from the lease components of a contract and are generally recognized as incurred, depending on the entity's accounting policy for maintenance.
- Generally, only lease components are accounted for under ASC 842. There are, however, **practical expedients** for both lessees and lessors under ASC 842 to account for lease and nonlease components together, if elected. For *lessors* to take advantage of the option to not separate the components in a contract, both of the following tests must be met:
    - The timing and pattern of revenue for both components are the same.
    - The combined single lease component is classified as an operating lease.

- Some items specified in a lease, however, are *not considered components* and, thus, no portion of the lease payments are allocated to them. An item in a contract is a **component** if it conveys some benefit (ie, a *good/service)* to the lessee. Neither the administrative cost of setting up the lease nor the direct payment/reimbursement to the lessor of *costs associated with ownership* (aka, **lessor costs**), such as payment of **taxes/insurance** on the underlying asset, convey a good/service to the lessee that is separate from the right to use the property.
  - If taxes/insurance are billed to the lessee or the payments otherwise vary from year to year, the payments are treated like variable lease payments and, thus, are *not* part of the lease liability.
  - However, if taxes/insurance are included in the lease payment, the entire payment is still just treated as a lease payment—there is no allocation (even if the amounts are itemized in the contract). For example, if $500 of a $4,000 annual lease payment is itemized in the contract as payment to the lessor to cover taxes and insurance; the $500 is still included as part of total $4,000 annual lease payment; it's not allocated separately.
  - Lessors are generally required to include any such amounts (ie, lessor costs) collected from the lessee in lease revenue and then expense them accordingly.
    - Any lessor costs the **lessee pays directly to a third party** are **excluded** from the lessor's revenue/expenses.
    - Lessor costs paid by a lessor and **reimbursed by the lessee** are accounted for as variable payments (ie, **included** in lessor's revenue/expenses).
    - Also, due to the complexity of determining whether certain sales taxes and other similar taxes are considered lessor costs, there is an **election** for lessors to simply **exclude amounts collected for sales taxes** (and other similar taxes) from lease revenue/expenses. If elected, disclosure is required.

Disclosure Requirements

Disclosures for leases by both lessor and lessee are very comprehensive. (If in doubt, disclose.) Generally, the overarching requirement is to show disclosures that enable users of financial information to assess the amount, timing and uncertainty of cash flows from leases. Disclosure requirements are both qualitative and quantitative.

Qualitative disclosures for both **lessee and lessor** include a general description of the following: lease arrangement, variable lease payments, options, nonlease payments and residual values. Quantitative disclosures for **lessees:**

- Interest and amortization costs for finance leases
- Lease costs disclosed separately for operating and short-term leases
- Any variable lease costs
- Weighted average lease term
- Discount rate used in calculation of present value
- Reconciliation of beginning and ending balances of right-of-use asset
- Contractual obligations and options that the lessee is expected to exercise for each of the next five years, and a total for the remaining years in the aggregate.
- Future lease payments by type of lease for each of the next five years and a total for all remaining years, undiscounted.
- Lease transactions with related parties

Quantitative disclosures for **lessors:**

- Explanation of assumptions and judgments
- Lease revenues received
- Lease sales (vs. regular sales)
- For each type of lease, future lease payments for each of the next five years and the total for all remaining years in the aggregate.
- A reconciliation of sales-type lease receivables with total balance sheet receivables
- Gross investment and net investment in leases
- Description of assets under operating leases, risks associated with residual values and important changes in unguaranteed residual values

Lecture 11.02 – Operating Leases

An operating lease is any lease that is not a finance / sales-type lease or direct-financing lease.

Lessor Accounting

- **Recognition**
  - At the commencement date, the lessor must defer initial direct costs (eg, commissions or payments made to an existing tenant to get them to terminate their lease early). Note: Initial direct costs do NOT include costs that would have been incurred regardless of whether the lease was obtained (eg, advertising, certain legal fees, cost to evaluate a prospective lessee's financial condition, etc.).
  - After the commencement date, both of the following are generally recognized on a straight-line (S/L) basis over the lease term:
    - Fixed **lease payments** are included in income. When there is a difference between the cash received and the amount to be recognized, it is recorded as either Rent Receivable or Deferred Rent, depending on whether the payment received is higher or lower than the lease income to be recognized. Total lease payments / years in lease term = Annual Rent Revenue.
    - **Initial direct costs** are expensed.
  - Variable lease payments are included in income as circumstances occur that fix the lessor's right to such payments (similar treatment for *early termination penalties*).
- Lessor depreciates the actual asset (ie, even though the lessee records a right-of-use asset, the leased property itself remains on the lessor's balance sheet as an asset).
- Rent received in advance is considered unearned (deferred revenue).
- Security Deposits
  - Nonrefundable – unearned revenue until earned
  - Refundable – liability until returned
- Uneven rental payments (eg, free rent) are recognized *uniformly* (evenly) over the lease term.

Lessee Accounting

Right-of-use asset and corresponding liability are recorded; no more off-balance sheet financing, except for short-term leases (≤ 1 year).

- **Right-of-Use Asset**
  - Includes:
    - The initial measurement of the lease liability (at PV of lease payments)
    - Any lease payments made at or before the commencement date, less any lease incentives (eg, lease-signing bonus) received
    - Any initial direct costs incurred (eg, commissions, certain legal fees, etc.)
  - *Amortized unevenly* over the term of the lease for the difference between the total lease expense and accreted interest for each period.
- **Lease liability** is recorded at **PV of lease payments.**

- Variable lease payments are included in the lease liability in the period in which the obligation is incurred.
- Likewise, early termination penalties are included in the lease liability as a lease payment at PV when it is reasonably certain that early termination will be exercised. This also shortens the lease term used.
- To determine the PV of the lease payments, the lessee should use the *rate implicit in the lease*, or if it is not readily determinable, the *incremental borrowing rate* can be used.
  - Lessee uses the implicit rate if it is known; this is true even if the implicit rate is higher than the incremental borrowing rate.
  - The incremental borrowing rate is the rate the lessee would otherwise pay to borrow the same amount of money over the same amount of time in a similar economic environment.
  - Note: The *lessor* always uses the rate implicit in the lease.

- **Recognition** – After the commencement date, lease payments are expensed over the lease term, generally on a S/L basis. Total lease expense is comprised of accreted interest expense and amortization of the right-of-use asset. While these may be calculated separately, they are reported as a **single straight-line lease expense** each year on the income statement.
- **Leasehold improvements** are reported with PP&E and amortized over the *shorter* of:
  - Remaining lease term
  - Useful life
- **Deposits** – Refundable maintenance deposits, or security deposits, are assets (ie, receivables) if it is probable that they will be returned to the lessee. Maintenance expenses, however, should be expensed in the period incurred or capitalized in accordance with the lessee's maintenance accounting policy.

Assume the client has signed a 5-year rental contract (with no renewal option) for office equipment on 1/1/X1. The economic useful life is estimated to be 10 years. The client has an incremental borrowing rate of 6% and the payments are $10,000 per year, due at the end of each year. As an inducement to enter the agreement, the client has been offered the first six months free and a $1,000 signing bonus. The lessee has incurred $1,000 in initial direct costs. The PV factor for a lump sum @ 6% for 1 year is 0.943, and the PV factor for an ordinary annuity @ 6% for 5 years is 4.212. The payment schedule will be as follows:

12/31/X1	5,000
12/31/X2	10,000
12/31/X3	10,000
12/31/X4	10,000
12/31/X5	10,000
Total	**45,000**

In 20X1, the initial entry is:

Right-of-Use Asset*	37,405	
Lease Liability		37,405

*The right-of-use asset is calculated as follows:

Lease liability at PV of lease payments ($37,405, see calculation below)
+ Lease payments made at or before the commencement date ($0)
– Lease incentives (eg, lease-signing bonus) received (– $1,000)
+ Initial direct costs incurred (eg, commissions) (+$1,000)
Right-of-use asset ($37,405)

The PV of the lease payments is calculated as follows:

- The lump sum of $5,000 at 6% in year one ($5,000 x 0.943 = $4,715).
- The PV of an ordinary annuity of $10,000 at 6% over 5 years, minus the first-year lump-sum value of $10,000 at 6% [($10,000 x 4.212 = $42,120) – ($10,000 x 0.943 = $9,430)] = $32,690.

Total: $4,715 + $32,690 = **$37,405**

Now, since the total of lease payments is $45,000, lease expense will be recognized on a S/L basis at $9,000 each year (ie, $45,000 / 5 years). There are essentially two components of lease expense for a lessee in an operating lease: **accreted interest expense** and **amortization expense.** While these may be calculated separately, they are reported as a **single straight-line lease expense** each year on the income statement. Thus, for the first year, the entries will be as follows at 12/31/X1:

	Debit	Credit
Lease Expense	9,000	
Lease Liability*		2,244
Right-of-Use Asset**		6,756
Lease Liability	5,000	
Cash		5,000

$5,000
– 2,244
$2,756

- *Lease Liability is increased for accreted interest: 6% × $37,405, or $2,244.
- **Right-of-Use Asset is reduced for the amount amortized (ie, the difference between the lease expense and the accreted interest): $9,000 – $2,244, or $6,756.

Again, notice that the total lease expense here is equal to the accreted interest expense of $2,244, plus amortization expense of $6,756, for a total of $9,000 lease expense.

Entries at end of 12/31/X2:

	Debit	Credit
Lease Expense	9,000	
Lease Liability*		2,079
Right-of-Use Asset**		6,921
Lease Liability	10,000	
Cash		10,000

$10,000
– 2,079
$7,921

- *Lease Liability is increased for accreted interest on the 20X2 beginning lease liability amount of $34,649 (ie, $37,405 + $2,244 accreted interest – $5,000 payment): 6% × $34,649, or $2,079.
- **Right-of-Use Asset is reduced for the amount amortized: $9,000 – $2,079, or $6,921

Total lease expense will still be $9,000, consisting of accreted interest expense of $2,079 and amortization expense of $6,921.

The following table shows how the lease liability will change over the life of the lease under the effective interest method:

Lease Liability	Interest Rate	=	Accreted Interest Expense	–	Lease Payment	=	Net Reduction in Lease Liability
37,405	6%	=	2,244	–	5,000		2,756
(2,756)							
34,649	6%	=	2,079	–	10,000	=	7,921
(7,921)							
26,728	6%	=	1,604	–	10,000	=	8,396
(8,396)							
18,332	6%	=	1,100	–	10,000		8,900
(8,900)							
9,432	6%	=	566	–	10,000		9,434
(9,434)							
0*							

**Note that there is a $2 difference due to rounding for simplicity purposes.*

Short-Term Leases

A short-term lease is one that **does not exceed one year** and does not include an option to purchase the asset that the lessee is reasonably certain to exercise. The lessor's accounting is the same as for an operating lease. The lessee, however, has a choice. The lessee may choose to treat such leases the same as operating leases, or, if the lessee so chooses, no asset or liability need be recorded, and lease payments are simply recognized as lease expense.

Lecture 11.03 – Finance Leases – Lessee Accounting

A finance lease is generally one in which the rights and risks of ownership have essentially transferred from the lessor to the lessee. That is, in substance it's a purchase, although in form it's a lease. Just as with an operating lease, the lessee recognizes both a right-of-use asset and a liability at the PV of the lease payments.

While an operating lease liability would generally not be considered debt for purposes of ratios, debt covenants, etc., a finance lease liability is considered part of the lessee's total debt—eg, it is part of "Debt" in the Debt-to-Equity ratio. Another key difference is that the right-of-use asset will normally be amortized on a S/L basis, not unevenly as with an operating lease. Note: The lessor will account for such a lease as a sales-type lease, either with or without profit (discussed in another section).

Finance Lease Criteria

If the lease meets one of the following five criteria **(Special-PO-T-75-90)**, the lessee accounts for the lease as a finance lease, as if he OWNS it. If not, it is considered an operating lease.

1. Due to its ***(S)*pecialized nature**, the leased property has no foreseeable alternative use to the lessor at the end of the lease term.
2. The lease contains a "***(P)*urchase *(O)*ption reasonably certain to be exercised.**"
3. The lease **transfers *(T)*itle**, *ie, ownership,* of the property to the lessee by the end of the lease term.
4. The lease term is for the **"major part"** ***(75%)*** of the remaining economic life of the property. ASC 842 suggests 75% or more of the estimated economic life of the property at inception as meeting this "major part" criterion; however, this is no longer a bright-line test.*
5. The PV of lease payments and any residual value guaranteed by the lessee that is not already reflected in the lease payments is equal to **"substantially all"** ***(90%)*** of the FMV of the property at inception. ASC 842 suggests 90% of FMV as meeting this "substantially all" criterion; however, this is no longer a bright-line test.*

*If the beginning of the lease term falls "at or near the end" of the estimated economic life of the leased property, criterion #4 and #5 cannot be used for purposes of classifying the lease. ASC 842 suggests within the **last 25%** of the economic life as a reasonable guideline for assessing the property to be "at or near the end" of its useful life.

Recognition

After the commencement date, the lessee will report **interest expense** on the liability and **amortization of the right-of-use asset** (generally on a *S/L basis* unless another basis is more representative of the lessee's consumption pattern) in the income statement.

- The lessee must amortize the right-of-use asset over the **shorter of the useful life or the lease term,** unless there is a purchase option that is reasonably certain to be exercised (PO) or the title transfers at the end of the lease (T). When this is the case, the property is amortized over the useful life of the asset even if it is longer. This same rule applies to **leasehold improvements** under a finance lease.
- Variable lease payments that are not already included in the lease liability are expensed as incurred.

Now, let's take the same example we used for operating leases, except that the economic useful life of the equipment is 5 years instead of 10. Since the lease consumes 100% of the economic useful life of the asset, the lease must be accounted for as a finance lease. So, to reiterate, assume the client has signed a 5-year rental contract for office equipment on 1/1/X1. The client has an incremental borrowing rate of 6% and the payments are $10,000 per year, due at the end of each year. As an inducement to enter the agreement, the client has been offered the first six months free and a $1,000 signing bonus. The lessee has incurred $1,000 in initial direct costs. The PV factor for a lump sum @ 6% for 1 year is 0.943, and the PV factor for an ordinary annuity @ 6% for 5 years is 4.212.

In 20X1, the initial entry is the same ($37,405 PV of $45,000 in lease payments – $1,000 bonus + $1,000 initial direct costs):

Right-of-Use Asset	37,405	
Lease Liability		37,405

The accounting changes when we get to the recognition of lease expense, which must be reported separately as **interest expense** and **amortization expense** (which is generally reported on a S/L basis) in the income statement. Thus, for the first year, the entries will be as follows at 12/31/X1:

Amortization Expense	7,481	
Right-of-Use Asset*		7,481
Interest Expense**	2,244	
Lease Liability	2,756	
Cash		5,000

- *Right-of-Use Asset is reduced for the amount amortized (ie, S/L over 5 years): $37,405 / 5 = $7,481
- **Interest expense is 6% x $37,405, or $2,244 and Lease Liability is reduced to $34,649 for the difference between the payment and the interest expense (ie, $5,000 – $2,244, or $2,756).

Entries at end of 12/31/X2:

Amortization Expense	7,481	
Right-of-Use Asset*		7,481
Interest Expense**	2,079	
Lease Liability	7,921	
Cash		10,000

- *Right-of-Use Asset is reduced for the amount amortized (ie, S/L over 5 years): $37,405 / 5 = $7,481.
- **Interest expense is 6% x $34,649 lease balance, or $2,079, and Lease Liability is reduced for the difference between the payment and the interest expense (ie, $10,000 – $2,079, or $7,921).

Let's do another example to see how the calculations and entries change when the first payment is made on day 1, rather than the end of the year. In this case, the entire first payment reduces the lease liability. Remember: when the first payment is made at year end, that payment will include interest expense.

Assume the client has signed an 8-year equipment lease with payments of $75,000 per year, due at the beginning of the year. The estimated economic life of the equipment is 10 years. The depreciation method is straight-line, and there is no residual value. Title to the equipment passes at the end of the lease. The lessee's incremental borrowing rate is 12%, but the lessor has made it known to the lessee that the rate implicit in the lease is 11%.

Since the 1st payment of $75,000 is due on day 1 (ie, annuity due), the PV of the 8 lease payments @ 11% (5.7122 PV factor) = $428,415.

Lease Liability	Interest Rate	=	Accreted Interest Expense	–	Lease Payment	=	Reduction in Lease Liability
428,415					75,000		75,000
(75,000)							
353,415	11%	=	38,876	–	75,000	=	36,124
(36,124)							
317,291	11%	=	34,902	–	75,000	=	40,098
(40,098)							
277,193							

Initial entry to record the asset and lease liability at PV of lease payments (note that there are no other payments or initial direct costs in this example):

Right-of-Use Asset	428,415	
Lease Liability		428,415

First Payment at beginning of year 1:

Lease Liability	75,000	
Cash		75,000

Amortization at the end of year 1 (428,415/10 year useful life since title transfers at end of lease):

Amortization expense	42,842	
Right-of-Use Asset		42,842

Second Payment at beginning of year 2:

Lease Liability	36,124	
Interest Expense	38,876	
Cash		75,000

Note: Of the remaining $317,291 Lease Liability at the end of year 2, the next payment of $40,098 represents a current liability (ie, due within 1 year) and the rest ($277,193) is a long-term liability.

Lecture 11.04 – Sales Type Leases – Lessor Accounting

If the lease meets one of the five criteria as a finance lease (ie, **Special-PO-T-75-90**), the lease is accounted for by the *lessor* as a sales-type lease, either with or without profit.

Recognition

At the commencement date, the lessor must:

- **Derecognize the leased asset** (so long as collectibility of lease payments is probable)
- Recognize:
  - Net investment in the lease, which includes:
    - *Lease Receivable*, measured at PV of future lease payments and any amount expected from a residual value guarantee.
    - *Unguaranteed Residual Asset*, measured at PV.
  - Selling profit or loss =
    - Fair value of asset (or, if lower, Lease Receivable + Prepaid Lease Payments)
    - Less: Carrying amount of asset net of unguaranteed residual asset
    - Less: Deferred initial direct costs
  - Initial direct costs, which are either:
    - *Expensed immediately* when the lease includes a selling profit, or
    - *Deferred over the lease term* as an increase in Lease Receivable and decrease in overall Interest Revenue when there is no selling profit.

After the commencement date, the lessor must recognize:

- **Interest income** on the net investment in the lease
- **Variable lease payments** (that are not already included in the Lease Receivable) in the period in which the circumstances that fix the payments occur
- **Credit losses** on the net investment in the lease

Sales-Type Lease With Selling Profit

A lease where the seller is usually a manufacturer or dealer of the asset and uses the lease as a way of selling the asset on an installment basis. The fair value of the leased property differs from the cost, which creates a dealer's profit or loss.

Let's take a look at how that last finance lease example would look from the lessor's perspective.

Assume the lessor has leased equipment to a lessee with the following terms:

- 8 years with payments of $75,000 per year, due at the beginning of the year.
- The estimated economic life of the equipment is 10 years.
- Title to the equipment passes at the end of the lease
- There is no residual value.
- The rate implicit in the lease is 11%.
- The lessor's cost of the equipment is $300,000.

Since the 1st payment of $75,000 is due on day 1 (ie, annuity due), the PV of the 8 lease payments @ 11% (5.7122 PV factor) = $428,415.

Lease Liability	Interest Rate	=	Interest Expense	–	Lease Payment	=	Reduction in Lease Liability
428,415					75,000		75,000
(75,000)							
353,415	11%	=	38,876	–	75,000	=	36,124
(36,124)							
317,291	11%	=	34,902	–	75,000	=	40,098
(40,098)							
277,193							

Initial entry to remove the asset from the books and record the Lease Receivable at PV of lease payments (note that there are no other payments, initial direct costs, or residual value in this example):

Lease Receivable	428,415	
Equipment		300,000
Gain on Sale		128,415

Or if the lessor is a merchant/dealer:

Lease Receivable	428,415	
COGS	300,000	
Inventory		300,000
Sales Revenue		428,415

First Payment at beginning of year 1:

Cash	75,000	
Lease Receivable		75,000

At the end of year 1, interest income is recognized, but the payment hasn't been received yet:

Interest Receivable	38,876	
Interest Revenue		38,876
[11% x ($428,415 – 75,000)]		

Second Payment at beginning of year 2:

Cash	75,000	
Lease Receivable		36,124
Accrued Interest Receivable		38,876

Sales-Type Lease Without Selling Profit

A lease where the lessor is financing the acquisition of an asset by the lessee but is not earning a profit. (This commonly happens when the lessor is a financial intermediary whose business model hinges on earning interest revenue.) The PV of the lease payments will be **equal** to the fair value of the property, and the lessor will earn only interest income. This makes our example a little simpler, since there is no profit, COGS, or Inventory to account for.

Assume the same facts as the last example, except that the lessor's cost of the equipment is $428,415 (ie, equal to the PV of the lease payments). Only the initial entry is different here since there is no profit to recognize; the rest of the entries are the same.

Initial entry to remove the asset from the books and record the Lease Receivable at PV of lease payments:

Lease Receivable	428,415	
Equipment		428,415

Direct-Financing Lease

A lease where the lessor is financing the acquisition of an asset by the lessee but is generally not earning a manufacturer's or dealer's profit. The present value of the lease payments will be equal to the fair value of the property and the lessor will earn only interest income. A direct financing lease is a rare situation in which none of the five criteria (ie, Special-PO-T-75-90) are met, but it's also not an operating lease since:

- Collectibility of the lease payments is probable, and
- There is a **residual value guaranteed by a compensated third party** (eg, an insurance company), and the combined present value (PV) of the following constitute *substantially all* of the leased asset's fair value:
  - The lessee's lease payments
  - The lessee's guaranteed residual value
  - The third party's guaranteed residual value

The accounting for a direct financing lease is generally similar to a sales-type lease without selling profit, but in cases where there is a selling profit, the accounting varies a little: instead of immediately recognizing the selling profit, it is *deferred and recognized as interest income when payments are received*. This is accomplished by reducing the Lease Receivable with a contra asset credit entry to **Deferred Profit**. Due to the rare nature of this type of lease, it is unlikely to be tested to a depth beyond remembering and understanding how such a lease is classified.

Lecture 11.05 – Sale-leaseback Transactions

The property owner sells the property, then immediately leases all or part of it back from the new owner. Most of the time a company does a sale-leaseback to raise cash. This transaction is accounted for in one of two ways:

- **As a sale (with gain or loss) + an operating lease** – if normal revenue recognition conditions are met and the lease portion meets none of the Special-PO-T-75-90 criteria.
- **As no sale, just a loan** – if the lease portion meets **at least one** of the Special-PO-T-75-90 criteria, indicating the property owner sold the property then essentially bought it back, meaning no genuine sale to an external party occurred.
    - In this situation, where the leaseback would qualify as a finance lease, the accounting is simple:
        - The asset remains on the seller-lessee's books.
        - No sale or gain (loss) is recorded.
        - No lease accounting is applied.
        - The transaction is accounted for as a Note Payable.

Candy Co. needs cash. On December 31, year 1, Candy Co. sells a building with an adjusted basis of $80,000 and a fair value of $100,000 to Kahuna Co. for $100,000 @ 10% interest rate, then immediately leases back the building from Kahuna Co. The PV of the lease payments totals $100,000 and the title transfers back to Candy at the end of the lease term. The first lease payment is due December 31, year 2.

In this situation, Candy didn't really sell the building to Kahuna, because the leaseback terms (Special-PO-T-75-90) allow the seller-lessee, Candy, to retain substantially all the rights and risks of ownership. The transaction allowed Candy to raise a lump sum of cash—the $100,000 selling price—in exchange for paying back the $100,000 over the course of the lease term. The transaction is, in substance, a **loan**.

Assuming a 10% interest rate and yearly payments of $20,000, Candy's journal entries on the sale date and for the first payment would be:

December 31, year 1

Cash	100,000	
Note payable		100,000

December 31, year 2

Interest expense (10% x $100,000)	10,000	
Note payable (difference)	10,000	
Cash		20,000

Now, let's see how the accounting changes for a sale-leaseback that does not meet any of the five criteria (ie, the leaseback is an operating lease).

On December 31, year 1 Candy Co. sells equipment to Kahuna Co. for $10,000, then immediately leases it back. The equipment has an original cost of $12,000, a carrying value of $9,000, and a fair value of $10,000. The lease term is 10 years and requires annual payments of $1,184, starting on the sale date. The estimated remaining useful life of the equipment is 15 years. With an implicit rate of 10%, known to both parties, the PV of the lease payments is $8,000.

None of the Special-PO-T-75-90 criteria are met, so the leaseback is an operating lease. The situation is therefore considered both a sale and an operating lease, resulting in the following seller-lessee journal entries for Candy Co.:

December 31, year 1 – to record the sale of asset

Cash	10,000	
Accumulated depreciation	3,000	
Equipment (cost)		12,000
Gain on sale-leaseback		1,000

December 31, year 1 – to record the operating lease

Right-of-use asset	8,000	
Lease payable		8,000

December 31, year 1 – to record the initial payment

Lease payable	1,184	
Cash		1,184

This initial principal-only payment reduces the remaining lease liability to $8,000 - $1,184, or $6,816.

December 31, year 2 – to record annual lease payment and amortization of the ROU asset

Lease expense *	1,184	
Lease payable**	502	
Cash		1,184
Right-of-use asset		502

*Lease expense = interest exp. ($6,816 × 10%) + amortization exp. ($1,184 – $682)
** Lease payable reduction and ROU asset amortization = $1,184 payment – $682 interest exp.

UWorld | ROGER CPA Review

YOUR WORLD OF LEARNING

FAR 12 - Liabilities

FAR 12 – Liabilities

Table of Contents

Liabilities

Lecture 12.01 – Current Liabilities

Overview

Current liabilities are liabilities that will be settled within one year or the operating cycle whichever is longer. Current liabilities are valued at their net realizable value (NRV) or settlement value. They include[1]:

- Accounts payable
- Accrued expenses
- Dividends payable
- Income taxes payable
- Current portion of long-term (L/T) debt

Accounts Payable

Accounts payable generally represents amounts due to vendors resulting from the purchase of merchandise.

- Liabilities incurred in obtaining goods and services from vendors in the ordinary course of business
- **Discounts** for prompt payment (eg, 2/10, N/30)
  - **Gross method** – Purchases are shown at gross; if the discount is taken, it is considered a reduction of Cost of Sales.

Purchases	100	
A/P		100
A/P	100	
Cash		90
Discount		10 (COGS ↓)

  - **Net method** – Purchases are shown at net, if the discount is not taken, considered interest expense.

Purchases	90	
A/P		90
A/P	90	
Expense	10	
Cash		100

[1] ASC 210/405

Goods in Transit

FOB shipping point

- Title passes when *shipped* by seller (placed with carrier).
- Included in buyer's books at year-end as both Inventory and an A/P.

FOB destination

- Title passes when *received* by buyer (tendered to buyer).
- Included in seller's books until received by buyer. Not included in buyer's books as an A/P until the goods are received.

Seller
FOB* Shipping Point
(Shipped)

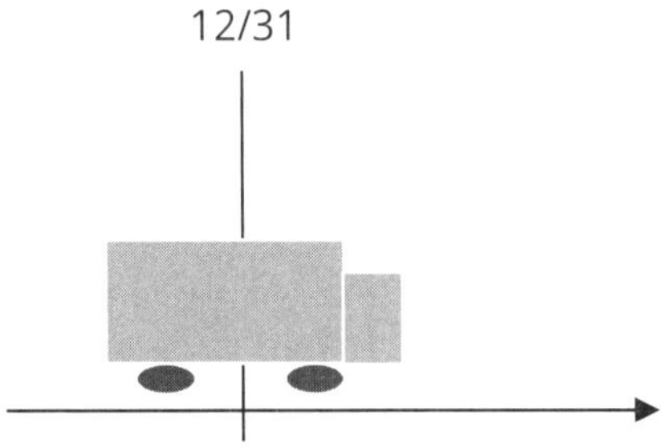

Buyer
FOB* Destination
(Received)

**FOB = Free on Board*

Estimated & Accrued Amounts

Accrued Liabilities/Expenses (Current Liability)

- An expense that is **incurred but not yet paid** in cash (eg, unpaid salaries or taxes at year end).
  - **Employee's share** of taxes that the employer withholds are not an expense of the employer, even though they are a liability.

Expense (I/S)	X	
Accrued Liability (Salaries payable) (B/S)		X
Accrued Liability	X	
Cash		X

Prepaid Expenses (Current Asset)

- Expenses paid in cash, but not yet incurred (eg, prepaid rent).

Prepaid Expense	X	
Cash		X
Expense (I/S)	X	
Prepaid Expense		X

Deferred Revenues (Current Liability)

- Revenue collected but not yet earned (eg, rent collected or subscriptions collected in advance or gift certificates issued, but not yet redeemed).

Cash	X	
Unearned Revenue (B/S)		X
Unearned Revenue	X	
Revenue (I/S)		X

Revenue Receivable (Current Asset)

- Revenue earned but not yet collected (eg, revenue earned but still due from customer).

Receivable	X	
Revenue (I/S)		X
Cash	X	
Receivable		X

Assume a company paid $65,000 in expenses. Its beginning balance in accrued expenses was $7,500 and the ending balance was $9,000. The beginning balance in prepaid expenses was $3,800 and the ending balance was $4,100.

Using a journal entry approach, we know that there was a cash payment, recognized with a credit to cash, of $65,000. Accrued expenses increased by $1,500. An increase in a liability is a credit. Prepaid expenses increased by $300. Prepaid expenses are assets and an increase is a debit. The amount required to balance the entry is $66,200, representing the amount of expenses incurred.

Expenses (plug)	66,200	
Prepaid expenses ($4,100 - $3,800)	300	
Cash (given)		65,000
Accrued expenses ($9,000 - $7,500)		1,500

Warranty Costs

Products sold by the client often include warranties promising repairs or replacement for a limited time period. In most cases, it is impossible to determine how much of the sales price is for the product, and how much for the warranty commitment. As a result, revenue is recognized in its entirety on the date of sale, and the estimated warranty cost accrued at the same time.

The method of estimation to be used is the percentage of sales approach. It is similar to the equivalent approach for credit losses (ie, bad debts).

Assume a client has cash sales of $1,000 in 20X1, its first year of operations. The products are covered by a 2-year warranty, and the client estimates that costs equal to 1% of sales will have to be spent in the first year of the warranty, and 3% of sales in the second and final year of the warranty (repairs are expected to increase as the products get older). Let's also assume the client has spent $6 on warranty repairs in 20X1.

The entry to record sales is:

Cash	1,000	
Sales		1,000

At the same time, warranty costs estimated to total 4% of sales over the warranty periods are reported:

Warranty expense	40	
Estimated warranty liability		40

The amount spent on actual repairs is applied to the liability:

Estimated warranty liability	6	
Cash		6

Service Contracts

Many retail stores offer service contracts in connection with goods sold. Unlike warranties, service contracts are priced and sold separately, so it is possible to identify the revenue associated with them. As a result, proceeds from the sale of a service contract are systematically allocated over the period of the contract. In this case, actual repair costs are simply recorded as they occur in expenses.

One problem with the allocation of revenue, however, is that a straight-line approach isn't justified, since the amount of repairs and replacements will normally increase as products get older, so more of the revenue is earned later in the contract period.

Assume a 4-year service contract is being sold to customers. Rather than expect that 25% of servicing will take place in each year, it might be more reasonable to expect a steady increase over time, so that 10% of total service is rendered in the first year of the contract, 20% in the second year, 30% in the third year, and 40% in the final year of the contract. Although there will even be a difference between the first 6 months and the last 6 months of each year, let's assume that the pace of repairs within each year is even. If $100 of contracts are sold in 20X1 throughout the year, the entry for the collection of contract money is:

	Cash	100	
	Deferred service revenue		100

At the end of the year, revenue for the time that has elapsed on the average contract is:

12/31/X1	Deferred service revenue	5	
	Service revenue		5

Notice that only 5%, not 10%, has been earned by the end of 20X1. This is because the service contracts were sold throughout the year, not all on 1/1/X1, so the average contract is only one-half of a year, not a full year, old at 12/31/X1.

Coupons or Premiums

Many companies issue coupons for discounts on their products, distributing them through newspapers, mailings, and other means. The costs associated with these coupons are uncertain since many of the coupons will never actually be used. For those that are used, the actual cost to the issuer will usually be greater than the face value of the coupon, since merchants redeeming coupons are usually reimbursed for handling costs associated with processing them.

To determine the estimated liability for unredeemed coupons at the balance sheet date, take the following steps:

1. Determine the total face value of the coupons issued.
2. Add the handling fee percentage promised to merchants.
3. Multiply by the percentage of coupons expected to be redeemed.
4. Subtract payments already made to merchants for redeemed coupons.

In determining the estimated liability for unredeemed coupons, ignore any coupons that expired long enough before the balance sheet date so that redemption is no longer considered to have any reasonable chance of occurring.

Assume the client has issued the following coupons, and is attempting to determine the liability for unredeemed coupons at 12/31/X1:

Face value	$500
Expiration date	12/31/X1
Handling fee paid to merchants	20%
Normal time merchants take to process coupons	One month
Payments to merchants in 20X1	$300
Total coupons expected to be redeemed	60%

In applying the steps indicated the results are:

1. There are $500 in coupons.
2. The handling fee of 20% adds $100 to the possible cost, making it $600.
3. 60% of coupons are expected to be redeemed, costing $360.
4. $300 has already been paid out, so that a remaining liability for unredeemed coupons of $60 exists.

Accrued Vacation Pay

In addition to regular pay, many employees are entitled to future compensated absences such as vacation. Recognition of the cost of these compensated absences must take into consideration two accounting issues (ASC 710):

- **Matching** – Costs should be recognized at the time employees render the services that entitle them to compensated absences.
- **Faithful Representation (Neutrality)** – Costs should only be recognized if they have been paid or are likely to be paid in the future.

Generally, a company will report a liability for future compensated absences if **all four** of the following conditions are met:

- The obligation for compensation for future absences results from services already provided.
- The right to compensation for future absences either vests or accumulates.
- Payment is probable.
- The amount of the payment can be reasonably estimated.

When employees have performed the services, they are typically credited for a specific number of days of compensation, which should be computed at the wage rate expected to be in effect when these days are utilized. If wage rates are adjusted, the liability should also be adjusted.

For vacation days, the recognition of costs is required if the days accumulate or vest. **Accumulation** means that days not taken in the current period may be used in a future period. **Vesting** means that days not used will be paid in cash at the time of the employee's termination of service with the company. Accumulated vacation days are almost certain to be used by an employee at some time if they are in danger of losing them.

Assume that a company pays its employees an average of $100 per day, and that there are 50 unused vacation days at 12/31/X1 which accumulate but do not vest. Also assume that the company is giving a 10% raise to all employees, effective 1/1/X2. The company must accrue the vacation pay:

12/31/X1	Vacation pay expense	5,500	
	Liability for unused vacation days		5,500

Refundable Deposits

Finally, a client may receive **refundable deposits** on containers for products sold by the company. The deposit must be reported as a liability when collected but may later become revenue if there is an expiration date on the right of the customer to claim the refund.

Assume the company collects deposits of $1 on containers used to transport the company's product to customers, and that customers must return the containers by the end of the calendar year following the year of the sale to receive a refund on the deposit. The following information applies to the first two years in which this policy applies:

Number of sales in 20X1	50
20X1 containers returned in 20X1	30
20X1 containers returned in 20X2	15
Number of sales in 20X2	60
20X2 containers returned in 20X2	40

In 20X1, entries are made for containers delivered and returned:

Cash	50	
Liability for refundable deposits		50
Liability for refundable deposits	30	
Cash		30

In 20X2, similar entries are made:

Cash	60	
Liability for refundable deposits		60
Liability for refundable deposits	55	
Cash		55

Additionally, an entry is made at 12/31/X2 for the expiration of the time allotted for the return of the remaining 20X1 containers (50 – 30 – 15 = 5):

Liability for refundable deposits	5	
Container revenue		5

Accrued & Deferred Amounts

Some companies pay **bonuses** to top-level executives based on the overall results of the organization. The calculation of these bonuses can get complicated, because they often are based on income in excess of certain amounts, and sometimes the bonus percentage is based on what income will be after the bonus is paid rather than before.

A company may pay the president a bonus equal to 10% of income in excess of $400 after the bonus is deducted. Expressed using basic algebra, the bonus (B) on income (I) before deducting the bonus is:

- B = 10% (I – B – 400)

If income before deduction of the bonus is $510, the bonus formula will be solved as follows (10% will be expressed as .1):

- B = .1 (510 – B – 400)

The dollar amounts inside the parentheses can be combined:

- B = .1 (110 – B)

The items inside the parentheses can be individually multiplied by .1:

- B = 11 - .1B

Then .1B is added to both sides:

- 1.1B = 11

Then both sides are divided by 1.1:

- B = 10

Some companies collect **subscriptions on publications** to be delivered in the future. On the exam, these commonly involve directories or other annual or semi-annual publications. As deferred revenues, these must be reported as earned only when the publications are delivered to customers.

Let's say the client publishes a directory twice a year, sending the May 15 edition to subscribers that have paid by April 30, and the November 15 edition to those who have paid by October 31. At 12/31/X1, unearned revenue of $190 exists. During 20X2, the client collects $1,200 evenly through the year, and publishes as promised.

To determine the subscription revenue in 20X2, consider that the 5/15/X2 publication earns the money collected up to 4/30/X2. Based on the information, cash collections in 20X2 are at the rate of $1,200 / 12 = $100 per month. Thus, $400 came in during the first 4 months, and this was earned along with the $190 from the start of the year (which presumably represented collections in 20X1 after 10/31/X1), for a total of $590 revenue recognized on 5/15/X2.

The 11/15/X2 publication earns money collected between 5/1/X2 and 10/31/X2, which at the rate of $100 per month comes to $600 for those six months. The total revenue in 20X2 is $590 + $600 = $1,190. A single entry reflecting all of the year's activity in 20X2 is:

Cash	1,200	
Unearned subscription revenue (balance)		10
Subscription revenue		1,190

Payroll taxes need to be accrued at the time related payroll expenses are recognized. It is important, however, to distinguish employer taxes from the employee taxes on payroll. The latter are not costs of the company, but instead represent withholdings from the gross pay of the employees. As a result, only employer taxes meet the definition of accrued expenses (costs recognized on the income statement before payment).

Let's assume social security taxes under FICA are assessed at an 8% rate for employers with an equal amount withheld from the paycheck of employees, that the employer pays unemployment taxes under FUTA at a 3% rate, and that federal income taxes are withheld from employee paychecks.

If an employee earns $100 gross pay for a period, and is required to have $15 withheld for federal income taxes, the entry to account for the paycheck and related taxes is as follows:

Payroll expense	100	
Payroll tax expense	11	
Cash		77
Accrued payroll taxes liability		11
Withholdings due to IRS		23

Dividends Payable

Dividends are considered a **current liability** when they are **declared** whether related to common stock or preferred stock. Dividends in arrears on cumulative preferred stock are not a liability but must be disclosed in the notes to the financial statements.

Lecture 12.02 – Contingencies

A contingency is a gain or loss that may occur in the future as a result of an existing condition. (ASC 450)

Contingent Liabilities

The event occurs before the balance sheet date, but the resolution is contingent upon a future event. We are concerned with the existence of the liability. Examples include:

- Obligations related to product warranties.
- Pending or threatened litigation.
- Obligations related to product defects.
- Threat of expropriation of assets.

Loss Contingencies

- **Remote** – slight chance of occurring
  - Don't disclose
  - Don't accrue
- **Reasonably Possible** – more than *remote*, less than *probable*.
  - Disclose nature and range of loss
  - Don't Accrue – Fair presentation
- **Probable** – "Likely" to occur
    - If **not Estimable**
      - Disclose nature and range of loss
      - Don't Accrue
    - If **Estimable**
      - Disclose nature and range of loss
      - Do Accrue
        - Conservatism / Matching

A **remote** contingency is a loss that is reasonably certain not to occur. There are virtually unlimited numbers of different things that can go wrong in a business, and to attempt to identify all of them in the financial report would actually defeat the attempt to fairly present the company. It would distract the user from more significant risks with greater chances of occurring. Although disclosure of remote contingencies isn't forbidden, it is only required in one circumstance: when the client has guaranteed the debt of another party.

If a loss is **reasonably possible**, it must be disclosed in the notes to the financial statements, including the nature of the contingency and the range of possible losses. Accrual of the loss on the financial statements is forbidden, since the loss is still not probable. Accrual would bias the presentation of the financial numbers to the downside, violating the **neutrality** ingredient of **Faithful representation**, one of the primary qualitative characteristics of accounting information. The client may, however, appropriate a portion of retained earnings for reasonably possible losses so as to indicate that these amounts are not available to pay dividends to shareholders.

When a loss is **probable** it will, of course, be disclosed. In addition, though, we should accrue the expected amount of loss. The problem is that it is difficult to establish a verifiable number for the loss. If it is possible to estimate an amount, this will be reported on the income statement and reduce net assets on the balance sheet. For example, if the client is being charged with breach of contract in a case which the client's attorney believes is probably going to be lost, and the contract in question specified the monetary damages for breach at $300,000, or the client has insurance coverage that will limit their loss to $300,000 in any event, the entry might be:

Estimated losses from legal claims	300,000	
Estimated liability from legal claims		300,000

- **If a Range of Loss**
  - Accrue amount "most Likely" to occur.
  - If any amount is as likely as the rest, accrue the minimum amount in the range and disclose the range.
- **Unasserted Claims** (eg, potential lawsuit – not yet initiated)
  - If not probable that claim will be asserted
    - No disclosure, no accrual
  - If Probable that the claim will be asserted
    - Look at likelihood of loss
    - Remote, Reasonably Possible, Probable
- **Uninsured Losses** – potential loss for which company has no insurance.
  - If don't expect condition to occur, do nothing
  - If expect to occur, Disclose.
  - If occurred, Accrue and Disclose.

Gain Contingencies

- Disclose if Reasonably possible or Probable, the nature and amount.
- Never accrue until realized
  - Conservatism

Loss Contingency	Disclose	Accrue
Remote – Slight	No	No
Reasonably Possible	Yes	No
Probable & Estimable	Yes	**Yes**
Probable & Not Estimable	Yes	No

Estimated Loss (I/S)
Estimated Liability (B/S)

Gain Contingency	Disclose	Accrue
Remote = Slight	No	No
Reasonably Possible	Yes	No
Probable & Estimable	Yes	**No**

Subsequent Events

Events occurring during the time interval between the balance sheet date but before the date that the financial statements are issued or are available to be issued, may have an impact in one of **two ways:**

- **Type 1** – Some events provide evidence of **conditions existing** at the balance sheet date that require **adjustment (recognized)**. For example, the bankruptcy filing of a customer on January 4, 20X1 may indicate that a receivable from that customer at December 31, 20X0 ought to be written off. Another example might be the settlement of a litigation for an amount different than the amount that had been accrued.
- **Type 2** – Some events do not affect the balance sheet, as the **condition did NOT exist** at the balance sheet date, but still represent important information that should be **disclosed (nonrecognized)** to assist users of the financial statements in interpreting them. For example, a fire that destroyed the company's main warehouse on January 4, 20X1 does not change the inventory balance at December 31, 20X0, but would affect the significance of that inventory and suggest possible future difficulties. Other examples include sale of bonds or issuance of stock, purchase of a business, fire or flood loss, receivable loss.

Summary

Subsequent to B/S date but before issue financial statements.

- **Type I**
  - Condition **Existed at B/S date (**eg, Lawsuit is settled or IRS assessment).
  - Accrue and disclose (recognized). Use original report date 3/1.
- **Type II**
  - Condition **did not Exist** at B/S date (eg, Issue bonds after year end).
  - **Disclosure (nonrecognized)**, but do not Accrue. Either dual date report or date report as of event date (if after field work date).

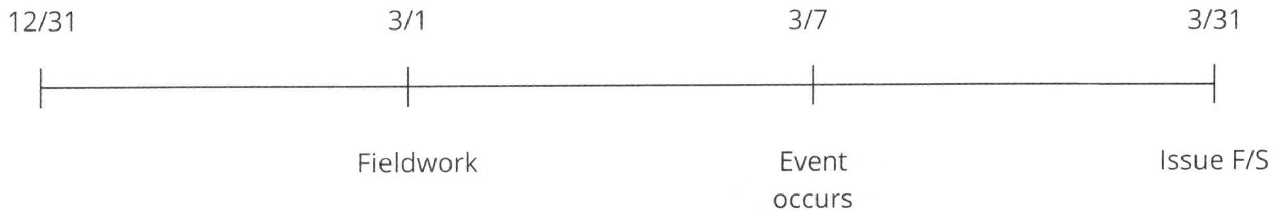

Lecture 12.03 – Interest on Notes Payable

Interest on notes payable is calculated similarly to interest on notes receivable.

- If N/P occurs in the ordinary course of business, record at **face value**. (Don't present value)
- L/T payables are recorded at **present value (PV).**
- If Long-term notes are payable in installments, the principal amounts that are due within the next 12 months or the operating cycle whichever is longer, must be reported as current liabilities, called **current portion of long-term debt.**

Note: When violation of a debt covenant gives the lender the right to call the debt, and the lender does not waive this right, this violation should typically result in the classification of the entire debt as ***current*** *by the borrower.*

Notes payable may be noninterest bearing, interest bearing, or bear a rate of interest that is not considered a fair rate. When this is the case, the same rules that apply to notes receivable also apply to notes payable.

- **Notes received/paid solely for cash** (assume rate is fair)

N/R	X		Cash	X	
Cash		X	**Notes payable**		**X**

- **Notes received/paid for goods or services**
  - Note receivable at a **reasonable rate**. The PV of the note is the same as the Face amount. (face)

Notes receivable	10,000		Asset	X	
Asset		X	**N/P**		**X**
Gain		X			

- **Noninterest-bearing notes**
  - If the interest rate is not stated or is unreasonable, use the **FMV of the goods or the FMV of the note,** whichever is more easily determinable. Assume the FMV of the asset is 9,000.

Notes receivable	10,000		
Discount on N/R		1,000	> CV = 9,000
Equipment		6,000	
Gain on sale		3,000	

Asset	9,000		
Discount on N/P	1,000		> CV = 9,000
N/P		10,000	

- If the interest rate is not stated, the FMV of the goods or the FMV of the note is not determinable, **Impute** an interest rate. Use a reasonable rate for a note of this type. PV of a note in 2 years at 10% is .8265 × 10,000 = 8,265.

Notes receivable	10,000		
Discount on N/R		1,735	> cv = 8265
Equipment		6,000	
Gain on sale		2,265	

Asset	8,265	
Discount on N/P	1,735	
Notes Payable		**10,000**

- When interest rate isn't fair, the fair rate must be **imputed.**
  - Receivable/Payable is carried at the present value of payments discounted at fair interest rate.
  - Periodic interest income/expense accrues based on fair rate.

In some cases, an entity may generate cash by issuing a note payable and discounting it with another entity or a financial institution. An entity, for example, may issue a noninterest-bearing note that matures in one year, discounted at a bank at a rate of 8%.

- The maturity value will be equal to the face value since it is a noninterest-bearing note.
- A discount will be computed by multiplying the maturity value (face value in the case of noninterest-bearing notes) by the discount rate.
- The result, adjusted for the length of time from the date of discounting to maturity, will be recorded as a discount.

The entry will be:

Cash (for net proceeds)	X	
Discount on note payable (maturity amt x discount rate x time)	X	
Note payable (face amount)		X

The discount is then amortized according to the entity's policies. The effective interest method is generally preferred but straight-line is also used.

Refinancing of Short-Term Obligations on a Long-Term Basis

Obligations maturing within one year or the operating cycle, whichever is longer are considered short term. If the company **intends** to refinance the obligation on a long-term basis, it is classified as long term.

- **Intent & Ability:**
  - Actually **issuing long-term debt** or Equity securities after the balance sheet date, but prior to the issuance of the financial statements.
  - Signing a **firm agreement** to refinance the obligation with a lender or investor that has the financial ability to provide the financing.

Special Loss Contingencies

- **Unconditional Purchase Obligation (Purchase Committments)**
  - If obligated to purchase goods for a period of time at a fixed price, the liability is disclosed for each of the 5 years following the Balance Sheet date.
    - Accrue loss if the market value of the item falls below the purchase price. The loss will be for the Minimum quantity required to be purchased.

Assume the client signed a 3-year contract at 1/1/X1 agreeing to purchase 1,000 units per year of particular goods at 10 cents per unit. At 12/31/X1, the notes must disclose the fixed obligations for the remaining contract:

- 20X2 100
- 20X3 100

Assume, however, that the goods in question become obsolete during 20X1, and at the time the financial statements for 20X1 are being issued, the client estimates that the best alternative available will be to sell the goods for scrap for 2 cents per unit.

In addition to writing down any inventory on hand at 12/31/X1 to market, the client must accrue a liability for the 8-cent loss expected on the unconditional obligation to purchase 2,000 additional units over the next two years:

Estimated loss on purchase commitment	160	
Estimated liability on purchase commitment		160

Lecture 12.04 – Troubled Debt Restructuring

When a debtor cannot pay a debt as it comes due, the debt is considered a *troubled debt*. (ASC 470) In evaluating whether a restructuring constitutes a troubled debt restructuring, a creditor must separately conclude that *both* of the following exist:

1. The restructuring constitutes a *concession.*
2. The debtor is experiencing *financial difficulties.*

There are three ways to restructure the debt. Following are the descriptions and procedures from the perspective of the debtor. Note that all cases refer to a gain on restructuring. If the debtor transfers property that equals or exceeds the carrying value of the debt, it would be a repaid in full, which is not considered a troubled debt restructuring. Since the value will be lower than the carrying value, the debtor is relieved of a portion of the loan, which results in a gain.

- **Transfer of Property**
    - **Gain on restructuring** of payables is recognized for the difference between the carrying value of the liability and the fair value of the asset transferred.
    - **Gain/loss on transfer** of asset is recognized for the difference between the asset's carrying value and its fair value on the date of the restructuring.
- **Equity Interest in Debtor**
    - Debtor records **equity** as if it was issued for its **fair value** with increases to common stock and additional paid-in capital, as appropriate.
    - **Gain on restructuring** of payables is recognized for the difference between the carrying value of the debt and the fair value of the equity.
- **Modification of Terms**
    - Interest **rate** is **reduced**, reducing the payments and, in some cases, allowing the debtor to make payments as they fall due.
    - **Due date** of one or more payments is **delayed**, giving the debtor more time to obtain the resources necessary to repay the debt.
    - **Face amount, accrued interest,** or both are **reduced**, reducing payments and, in some cases, allowing the debtor to make the remaining payments.

    When debt is restructured by modifying the terms of the debt:

    - If total future **payments** are **less than** the **carrying value** of the obligation, including accrued interest, the debtor will reduce the carrying value of the obligation to the total of the payments. This will result in a **gain** on restructuring of payables and all future payments will be treated as reductions of the principal, with no amounts recognized as interest expense.
    - If total future **payments** are **equal** to or **greater than** the **carrying value** of the debt, the effective interest **rate** will be **reduced** such that the present value of remaining payments will be equal to the carrying value of the debt. As payments are made, the effective interest method is applied, using the reduced effective interest rate. The **debt** is **not adjusted** and payments in excess of the revised principal balance over the remaining term will be recognized as interest.

A. I have debt of 600; will give up an asset with a FMV of 500 and a BV of 300.
B. Give stock with a par value of 200 and a FMV of 300.
C. Modify the terms.

	Debtor	Creditor
CV Debt = 600 }	100 Gain on restructuring	(100) Loss on restructuring
FMV of asset giving = 500 }		
BV of asset giving up = 300 }	200 Gain/Loss on disposal of asset	

A. Transfer Asset

Debtor	Dr	Cr	Creditor	Dr	Cr
N/P	600		**Loss** - restructuring	100	
Asset		300	Asset	500	
Gain on restructuring		100	N/R		600
Gain on transfer		200			

B. Transfer Equity

Debtor	Dr	Cr	Creditor	Dr	Cr
N/P	600		Investment in stock	300	
Common Stock		200	**Loss** - restructuring	300	
APIC		100	N/R		600
Gain on restructuring		300			

C. Modify Terms

Assume the client has a $500 note payable outstanding, with interest payments of 10%, or $50, due at the end of each calendar year until the note matures. At 12/31/X1, the client is unable to make the required annual interest payment, and the creditor agrees to restructure the debt by forgiving the missed payment, reducing the principal on the note to $400, and requiring 10%, or $40, interest payments on 12/31/X2 and 12/31/X3, with the note principal due 12/31/X3.

On 12/31/X1, prior to restructuring, the client had a $500 note payable and $50 accrued interest payable, for a total liability of $550. The restructured loan will require two interest payments of $40 each and principal of $400, for a total of $480 in future payments. The difference of $550 - $480 = $70 is the gain on restructuring, recorded as follows:

Date	Account	Dr	Cr
12/31/X1	Note payable	500	
	Accrued interest payable	50	
	Note payable		480
	Gain on restructuring of payables		70

Notice that the new note doesn't distinguish principal and interest. This is because the client isn't even going to repay $550 owed before restructuring, so there really isn't any additional interest being paid. All future payments are applied to the note payable.

The accounting by the creditor is different. To be conservative, the payments under the new arrangement are discounted at a fair interest rate before comparing them with the liability.

Assuming the 10% rate in this example is fair, the new note has a present value of $400, and is recorded as such:

12/31/X1	Note receivable	400	
	Loss on restructuring of payables	150	
	Note receivable		500
	Accrued interest receivable		50

Normal interest income of $40 per year will be recognized over the next two years.

Fair Value Option

According to ASC 825, an entity has the option, but not the requirement, to report some or all of its financial instruments at fair value. Among those financial instruments that may be reported at fair value are recognized financial assets and financial liabilities.

A debtor may elect the fair value option for some of its liabilities without making the election for others, even if they are similar. When a debtor elects the fair value option for a liability, that liability will be reported at its fair value on any given balance sheet date. Any decrease or increase required to adjust the liability to its fair value is recognized as a gain or loss in the income statement in the period of change.

The election of the fair value option by a debtor does not affect the accounting by the creditor. The creditor has a similar option to recognize the receivables at fair value.

If the fair value option is not elected for liabilities, a debtor will account for them using traditional approaches covered in this section.

Bankruptcy ($16,750)

- Concerned with the distribution of assets in a liquidation.
  - **Secured Creditors** – perfected security interest
    - Fully secured – the value of the collateral covers the debt owed.
    - Partially secured – the value of the collateral is less than the debt owed. The remaining balance becomes an unsecured claim.

  - **Priority Claims** (paid one level at a time / **STOP-IT Drunk Driver)**
    - **S**upport and alimony payments
    - **T**rustee, attorney and accountant fees
    - **O**wed to involuntary gap creditors
    - **P**ayroll within 180 days up to $13,650
    - **I**ndividual consumer deposits up to $3,025
    - **T**ax claims within 3 years of the filing
    - **Drunk Driver** injury claims

  - **General (unsecured) creditors**

UWorld

YOUR WORLD OF LEARNING

ROGER
CPA Review

FAR 13 - Acctg for Income Taxes (Deferred Taxes)

FAR 13 – Accounting for Income Taxes (Deferred Taxes)

Table of Contents

Accounting for Income Taxes (Deferred Taxes)

Lecture 13.01 – Accounting for Income Taxes: Permanent Differences

Financial statements (F/S) are governed by GAAP, and income taxes are governed by the Internal Revenue Code. Because of the differences between the recognition and measurement of book and taxable income, the amount of income tax expense and the amount of income taxes payable allocable to continuing operations are often different. These differences may result in future taxable amounts, deferred tax liabilities, or could result in future deductible amounts, deferred tax assets (DTAs).

Deferred Income Taxes

Deferred income taxes (ASC 740) result from differences between the carrying values for book purposes and the tax bases of assets and liabilities of the client. Some of these differences will result in future taxable amounts, requiring the recognition of deferred tax liabilities, and others will result in future deductible amounts, requiring the reporting of DTAs.

The **Liability method** is used to report deferred income tax expense. Calculate the current and deferred income tax asset/liability (Balance Sheet Approach), and the plug is income tax expense.

Taxes → Current / Deferred

Assume the client is reporting income before taxes on the 20X1 financial statement of $200 and has an effective tax rate of 20% in the current year and 30% in future years. They received municipal bond interest of $60, and MACRS deductions exceeded depreciation on the financial statements by $40. The calculation of current income tax expense is as follows:

Income Tax **Expense**	**32 (Current 20, Deferred 12)**
Current Tax Liability	20 (100 × 20%)
Deferred Tax Liability	12 (40 × 30%)

O
N
Taxes

(Like M-1 for Tax)

Pretax Book Income	200	
± Permanent Difference	60	
= **Book Taxable**	**140**	
± Temporary Difference	40	40 × 30% = 12
= **Taxable Income**	**100**	
× Current tax Rate	20%	
= **Current Tax Liability**	**20**	
Less: Prepayment	(15)	
= **Tax payable**	**5**	

Notice the current tax liability/payable is based on the current tax return income of $100 × the current tax rate of 20%. The deferred tax liability/payable is based on the change in the deferred income tax asset or liability from the beginning to the end of the reporting period of $40 × 30%, which is the future enacted tax rate.

There are **two types of differences** between pretax GAAP income and taxable income, Permanent differences and Temporary differences.

Since books are generally maintained by a corporation on a GAAP basis, certain adjustments will have to be made from book income in order to determine taxable income. Some of these differences are the result of **Permanent differences** in reporting, which refers to items on the income statement that are not taxable or deductible under present law.

There are also differences between GAAP and taxable income that result from items being taxable or deductible in a different period than the item is reported on the income statement. These are called **Temporary Differences.**

Permanent Difference

A permanent difference is a difference that will appear on either the F/S or the tax return, but not both. They do not result in deferred tax differences since they will never reverse. Some examples:

- Municipal bond interest (not taxable)
- Dividends received deduction (DRD) (not a book deduction)
- Life insurance expense, when the company is the beneficiary (not tax deductible)
- Life insurance proceeds
- Fines or penalties (not tax deductible)
- 50% meals for tax (100% for book)
- Entertainment (generally not tax deductible)
- Federal income tax payments

Lecture 13.02 – Accounting for Income Taxes: Temporary Differences

Temporary differences represent differences between the tax bases of assets or liabilities and their reported amounts in the F/S (books) that will result in taxable or deductible amounts in the future. These differences will reverse over time. Goodwill is considered a temporary difference. The differences are reported as an asset or liability, resulting either in taxable or deductible amounts.

Deferred tax *Liabilities* (*taxable temporary difference* – **TTD**) are expected future tax liabilities that arise because future Taxable income is expected to be **greater** than future Book income due to these temporary differences. Examples include:

- Depreciation methods for tax and book may be different (accelerated depreciation for tax)
- Investments accounted for under the equity method for book, and cost method for tax. (More income for book today, so owe government money later)
- Accrual Sales for book, and installment sales method for tax (more book income today, owe government money later)
- Prepaid expenses (cash basis for tax).
- Goodwill (15 yr amortization for tax and tested annually for GAAP)

Deferred tax *Assets* (*deductible temporary difference* – **DTD**) are expected future tax-deductible differences that arise because future Taxable income will be **less** than future Book income due to temporary differences. Examples include:

- Warranty expense for book today, but deductible for tax when you pay it (Tax expense is less today, so income is higher)
- Rent, Royalty & Interest received in advance is taxed when received, but for book, when earned.
- Credit loss expense – for tax, use direct write-off, for books an allowance approach.
- Contingent Liabilities

Book Expense < Tax Expense
Book Income > Taxable Income
} **Liability** (**T**axable **T**emporary **D**ifference)

Book Expense > Tax Expense
Book Income < Tax Income
} Deferred Tax **Asset** (**D**eductible **T**emporary **D**ifference)

Lecture 13.03 – Deferred Tax Liabilities

Rog Co. prepays a $50 expense at the start of the year that is for the next 5 years. For book purposes our expense is $50/5 = $10/yr as we are using accrual accounting. For tax purposes, we deduct all $50 today as we are using the cash basis. Assume the current tax rate is 20%, and the future rate is 30%.

	Book			Tax		
X1	Expense	10		Expense	50	
	Prepaid expense	40		Cash		50
	Cash		50			
X2	Expense	10		Expense	0	
	Prepaid		10	Cash		0

If income in X1 was $150 before this $50 expense and $200 in X2,

X1
$150

Book	Tax	
150	150	
–10	–50	
140	100	× 20% = $20 current tax liability

X2
$200

Book	Tax	
200	200	
–10	–0	
190	200	× 30% = $60

Difference is $40 which will reverse at $10 per year, if future tax rate is 30%, $40x30% = **$12 deferred tax liability**

Difference is $10, so the difference starts to reverse out. We then measure the remaining Liability of $30 (40-10) at the future tax rate of 30%, and that gives us a new **Target Liability of $9.**

Note: The cumulative difference is analyzed over time to determine the amount needed in the deferred tax liability account at year end.

The Journal entries would be:

X1	Income tax expense	32		(20 current/12 def'd)
	Deferred tax Liability		12	
	Current tax Liability		20	
X2	Income tax expense	57		(60 current/3 def'd)
	Deferred tax liability	3		(to get to target of $9)
	Current tax Liability		60	

The calculations of current and deferred taxes for 20X1 are:

Year	**20X1**	**20X2**	**20X3**	**20X4**	**20X5**
Taxable	100	0	0	0	0
Accounting	140	(10)	(10)	(10)	(10)
Difference	(40)	10	10	10	10
Rate	20%	30%	30%	30%	30%
Current tax	20				
Deferred tax		3	3	3	3 = 12

The current income tax expense on the $100 of taxable income at the effective 20% rate is $20, and is recorded as follows (assuming no prepayments):

Presentation on the Income Statement:	**X1**		**X2**
Provision for income taxes			
Current	($20)	Current	($60)
Deferred	($12)	Deferred	$ 3
Total provision for income taxes	($32)		($57)

Note: The tax rate used is the **enacted tax rate**. That is the rate expected to be in effect when the temporary difference is paid or realized.

The *Effective Tax Rate* is the Average rate at which pretax profits are being taxed. It is calculated by taking the income tax expense divided by its net income before taxes.

Changes in Tax Law

ASC 740 requires any impact on deferred taxes due to changes in tax law (eg, change in tax rates) to be recognized in the reporting period that includes the **enactment date**. If a change is made during an *interim period*, an entity reflects the change in the estimated annual rate in the period of enactment instead of in the period that includes the effective date (a prospective transition approach).

Lecture 13.04 – Deferred Tax Assets

Rog Co. receives rental revenue in advance of $50 at the start of the year that is for the next 5 years. For book purposes our revenue is $50/5 = $10/yr, as we are required to use the accrual method. For tax purposes all $50 would be recognized today as we are a cash basis taxpayer, so we have prepaid the tax due, creating a deferred tax asset (DTA). Assume the current tax rate is 20%, and the future rate is 30%.

	Book			**Tax**		
X1	Cash	50		Cash	50	
	Rent rev		10	Rent rev		50
	Unearned rev		40			
X2	Unearned rev	10		Unearned	0	
	Rent rev		10	Rent rev		0

If income in X1 was $150 before this $50 revenue and $200 in X2,

X1 $150			**X2** $200		
Book	**Tax**		**Book**	**Tax**	
150	150		200	200	
+10	+50		+10	+0	
160	200	× 20% = $40 current tax liability	210	200	× 30% = $60

Difference is $40 which will reverse at $10 per year, if future tax rate is 30%, $40 × 30% = **$12 DTA**

Difference is $10, so the difference starts to reverse out. We then measure the remaining asset of $30 (40 – 10) at the future tax rate of 30%, and that gives us a new **Target Asset of $9.** That means we need to reduce the DTA from 12 down to 9.

Note: The cumulative difference is analyzed over time to determine the amount needed in the DTA account at year end.

Journal Entries

X1	Income tax expense	28		(current 40/defd 12)
	Deferred tax asset	12		
	Current tax liability		40	
X2	Income tax expense	63		(current 60/defd 3)
	Deferred tax asset		3	(to get to target of $9)
	Current tax liability		60	

Valuation Allowance

When a company has a **deferred tax asset**, it must determine if it is **more likely than not** (ie, 50% or more likelihood) that some or all of the asset will not be realized (eg, due to insufficient future taxable income). If that is the case, a DTA valuation allowance is established for the portion that is not expected to be realized. This is a contra-asset to the DTA, thus reducing it.

If, for example, we had a deferred tax asset of $12, but we only expect to use $8, that means it is more likely than not that $4 will not be realized. Therefore, a DTA valuation allowance must be established for $4. By recording this allowance, we are increasing our income tax expense by $4 from $28 to $32.

Income tax expense	32	
Deferred tax asset	12	
Current tax liability		40
DTA valuation allowance		4

Uncertain Tax Positions

FASB defines a **tax position** as a position previously taken on a tax return (or expected to be taken in the future) that is reflected in determining current or deferred income tax assets and liabilities. An entity may have **uncertain tax positions** (UTPs) related to deductions, credits, or income that have not yet been resolved with the tax authorities. These UTPs must be reviewed to determine if potential accruals and disclosure are required in the F/S.

The **tax benefit** from a UTP may be recognized or unrecognized on the F/S.

- ASC 740 requires that a tax benefit resulting from a UTP can be **recognized** only if there is a **more-likely-than-not** (greater than 50%) **chance** the tax position will be sustained. The tax benefit recognized is limited to the estimated outcome with the largest dollar amount associated with a *greater than 50% cumulative probability* of occurring.
- An **unrecognized** tax benefit is reported as a **liability** representing the potential income taxes a company may have to pay in the future due to UTPs. The journal entry would be:

Income tax expense	XX	
Unrecognized tax benefit liability*		XX

**The unrecognized tax benefit can be realized when the tax position is settled or can no longer be challenged.*

Assume an entity took a tax position on its current year tax return resulting in a $20,000 deferred tax benefit. Based on technical merits, it is determined that the position has a greater than 50% chance of being sustained. The amounts and possible outcomes of the position being allowed are as follows:

Possible estimated outcome	Individual probability of occurrence	Cumulative probability of occurrence
$20,000	25%	25%
15,000	35%	60%
10,000	30%	90%
5,000	10%	100%
	100%	

Since the entity has determined the more-likely-than-not threshold has been met, the tax benefit qualifies for recognition. Determining the amount to be recorded requires an analysis of the cumulative probability of occurrence. Although three of the possible outcomes each have a cumulative probability of occurring that is greater than 50%, the entity records the outcome with the largest dollar amount (not percentage) as the tax benefit (ie, $15,000).

Lecture 13.05 – Equity Method, NOL & Classification

Equity Method Effects on Deferred Taxes

If an investment is accounted for under the **Equity method**, two differences need to be accounted for. There would be a Dividend Received Deduction (DRD) difference and also a deferred tax difference.

The calculation of taxes on significant investments in the common stock of other companies is unusually complex. This results from the use of the equity method of accounting for book purposes and the dividends-received deduction on dividends taxed when received.

For example, assume the client has made a 40% investment giving them significant influence over the activities of the investee, and that the following information applies to 20X1, the first year the investment is held:

Investee net income	$500
Investee dividends paid	$100
Dividends-received deduction	65%
Investor taxable income	$714
Investor pretax accounting income	$900
20X1 effective tax rate	21%
Expected tax rate in 20X2 and beyond	21%

All undistributed earnings are expected to be distributed and reported as dividend income in future years.

The difference of $186 ($900 – $714) between the taxable and accounting income results from the difference in treatment of the income from the investment. For GAAP purposes, the equity method of accounting caused the investor to pick up their share of the earnings of the investee, which is $500 × 40% = $200 (ie, $700 + $200 = $900). The dividend on the tax return is $100 × 40% = $40, but due to the 65% dividends-received deduction, only 35% of that $40 dividend, or $14, is taxed (ie, $700 + $14 = $714 taxable income).

In future periods, the $400 of undistributed earnings of the investee will be distributed, with 40%, or $160, going to the investor. Due to the 65% dividends-received deduction, only $56 (35%) of those dividends will be in future taxable income. The schedule to compute current and deferred taxes follows:

Year	20X1	Future
Taxable income	$714	$56
Accounting income	$900	0
Difference	($186)	$56
Rate	21%	21%
Current tax	$150 (rounded)	
Deferred tax		12 (rounded)

Notice that the $186 difference in the current year is not the same as the future taxable amounts of $56, since most of the dividends will not be taxed in future periods.

160 = Difference
65% → DRD → $104
35% → $56 Taxable Income → **DTL** → × 21% = $12

Income	Investment in S	200	
	Equity in Earnings		200
Dividends	Cash	40	
	Investment in S		40

Note: The difference of $160 will be distributed in the future, therefore resulting in future cash receipts. A taxable temporary difference (TTD) of $160 results, but is subject to a 65% DRD, so only $56 (ie, 35%) will be taxable at the future rate of 21% = $12 (rounded) Deferred Tax Liability.

Net Operating Losses

Due to the Tax Cuts and Jobs Act of 2017 (TCJA), a Net Operating Loss (NOL) is generally carried **forward indefinitely** and is limited to 80% of taxable income for the year to which it is carried. When an operating loss is carried forward, the tax effects are recognized to the extent that the tax benefit is *more likely than not* to be realized. Tax carryforwards should be recognized as deferred tax assets (DTA) in the period they occur.

DTA = Carryforward × Enacted Tax Rate

For example, in 20X1, the taxpayer has a loss of $500 and carries it forward to offset the following years' income; thus, they would have a deferred tax asset of $500 (carryforward) × 21% (ie, the enacted tax rate) for the benefit they get to use in following years. The journal entry would be:

Deferred tax asset	105 (B/S)	
Income tax benefit		105 (I/S)

Note: Since an NOL can be carried forward indefinitely, the 80% limitation would only need to be applied to determine a valuation allowance when an entity expects to discontinue operations and not have enough taxable income in the future to absorb the NOL.

The 2020 CARES Act **repealed** the **80% limitation** for tax years beginning **before 2021**; thus, for 2018 – 2020, NOLs may offset 100% of taxable income. It also provides that for taxable years beginning after 2020, the 80% limitation equals 80% of taxable income in *excess* of any pre-2018 NOL carryover. Therefore, any pre-2018 NOL carried forward to a tax year after 2020 is fully deductible, and any NOL created after 2017 carried forward to a tax year after 2020 is subject to the 80% limitation.

In addition, **NOLs incurred in 2018 – 2020** may be **carried back** to the **five** taxable **years** preceding the year of the loss. For example, an NOL created in 2020 may be carried back to 2015 – 2019 to receive refunds from each year in which there is taxable income. These refunds will reduce the DTA and may increase or decrease the income tax benefit depending on the tax rate for those years.

Knowing the details of the CARES Act is more important for the REG exam. Generally, in a FAR question on NOLs, they will provide the circumstances needed to calculate a DTA (whether they reflect current law or not). The CARES Act changes, however, could make it more likely that one may see a question with an NOL carried back within the exam.

Assume the same facts as in our example above, except that the taxpayer can carry back \$200 of the \$500 loss to tax years with a 40% tax rate. In this case, the journal entry would be:

Income tax refund receivable	80 (200 × 40%)	
Deferred tax asset	63 (300 × 21%)	
Income tax benefit		143

Classification on the Balance Sheet

All deferred tax assets and liabilities are classified as **noncurrent** amounts on the balance sheet.

The **net** amount of all deferred tax assets and liabilities, along with any related valuation allowance, is presented on the balance sheet as a **single noncurrent amount**.

Example:

Noncurrent Deferred Tax Asset	10	
Noncurrent Deferred Tax Liability		30
Noncurrent Tax Asset Valuation Allowance		5

Net balance sheet presentation: **Noncurrent** deferred tax Liability of 25

Disclosures

Certain disclosures are required in relation to the items reported on the balance sheet. In general, they may be provided on the face of the F/S, in supplementary schedules, or in the notes to the F/S. These include:

- The components of the net deferred tax asset or liability reported on the balance sheet, including:
  - The total of all deferred tax liabilities;
  - The total of all deferred tax assets; and
  - The total DTA valuation allowance recognized, along with the net change in the allowance for the period.
- The amounts of operating loss carryforwards and tax credit carryforwards along with their expiration dates.

An entity will also provide disclosures about **temporary differences**. The specific disclosures are different for public and nonpublic entities.

- Public entities will disclose the approximate tax effect of each type of temporary difference and carryforward that affects deferred tax assets or liabilities.
- Nonpublic entities will disclose the types but are not required to disclose the approximate tax effects.

For each year presented, the significant components of income tax expense arising from continuing operations are disclosed.

- Current tax expense or benefit
- Deferred tax expense or benefit
- Investment tax credits
- Government grants
- Benefits of operating loss carryforwards
- Adjustments to deferred tax assets or liabilities resulting from changes in tax laws, tax rates, or the entity's tax status
- Adjustment to the beginning valuation allowance due to changes in judgment about the realizability of deferred tax assets

In the example above, the numbers would be netted on the Balance Sheet to show a $25 noncurrent tax Liability, as a result of netting the deferred tax Asset of $10, offset by a $5 valuation allowance, with the deferred tax Liability of $30.

A client with taxable income of $500 at an effective tax rate of 30% in 20X1 and an expected tax rate of 40% in 20X2 and beyond has the following differences between book and tax reporting as of the end of 20X1, its first year of operations:

Rent collected in advance on one-year lease agreement	150
Excess of MACRS deduction on tax return over GAAP depreciation	250
Municipal bond interest	120
Prepaid insurance on policy with 3-year remaining life	300

Current income taxes are $500 × 30% = $150.

Rent collected in advance is included in this year's taxable income but is a current liability that will only be reported in revenue on the financial statement next year. Since this will cause next year's taxable income to be lower than financial statement income, it is a future deductible amount resulting in a deferred tax asset of $150 × 40% = $60.

The depreciation difference, reflected in fixed assets in the noncurrent asset section, will cause future tax deductions to be smaller, and taxable income higher, so it is a future taxable amount resulting in a deferred tax liability of $250 × 40% = $100.

Municipal bond interest does not result in any difference in carrying values and is not a part of future financial statement or taxable income.

Prepaid insurance was deducted on the tax return when paid but will result in reductions of book income equally over the next 3 years under the matching principle with no tax deductions in those years. As a result, the $300 is a future taxable amount resulting in $300 × 40% = $120 of deferred tax liabilities.

Summarizing the tax accounts from this example:

Current income taxes on taxable income	150
Deferred tax asset on rent	60
Deferred tax liability on depreciation	100

After the netting of deferred tax assets and deferred tax liabilities, the **balance sheet** will report the following:

Current Liabilities	
Current income taxes payable	150
Noncurrent Liabilities	
Deferred tax liability	160

On the **income statement**, the following will be reported in continuing operations:

- Current income tax expense 150
- Deferred income tax expense 160

UWorld
YOUR WORLD OF LEARNING

ROGER
CPA Review

FAR 14 – Stockholders' Equity

FAR 14 – Stockholders' Equity

Table of Contents

Stockholders' Equity

Lecture 14.01 – Stockholders' Equity

Presentation of Stockholders' Equity (ASC 505)—Overview

- **Preferred stock**
  - Disclose shares authorized, issued, outstanding
  - Disclose dividend and liquidation preference
  - Disclose cumulative and participation rights
- **Common stock**
  - Disclose shares authorized, issued, outstanding
  - Net treasury shares under **par value method** from total (*contra C/S*)
- **Additional paid-in capital**
  - Preferred stock
  - Common Stock
  - Treasury Stock
  - Warrants
  - Employee stock options
- **Noncontrolling Interest in "S"**
- **Retained earnings** (Appropriated/Unappropriated)
- **Accumulated other comprehensive income (DENT)** (Prominently displayed)
  - **D**erivative cash flow hedges
  - **E**xcess adjustment of Pension PBO and FV of Plan assets at year end
  - **N**et unrealized gain or loss on available-for-sale securities
  - **T**ranslation adjustments for Foreign Currency
- **Treasury stock**
  - Report only if under **cost** method (*contra-equity*)

Common Stock

A corporation begins operations by issuing stock in order to raise funds. It will obtain the authority to issue shares from the state of incorporation. All corporations will issue some form of common stock, which normally has a **par value (Certificate of Incorporation) or stated value (Board of directors)** assigned to it. The issue price of the stock, however, is virtually always greater than the par, and this excess goes to additional paid-in capital (APIC) and is identified specifically as being from common stock.

For example, if a corporation is authorized to issue $10 par value common stock, and issues a single share for $13, the entry is:

Cash	13	
Common stock		10
APIC–C/S		3

If common stock has no par or stated value, there is no allocation between Common stock and APIC; the entire amount is simply recorded in the Common stock account.

If the stock is issued in exchange for **property** other than cash, the property is recorded at **fair market value.**

If **multiple securities** are issued (stocks and bonds or common and preferred stock), the **relative Fair market value method** should be used.

If stock is **repurchased and retired**, the accounts credited at the time of issuance are debited. If the repurchase price is lower than the original issuance price, the difference is credited to APIC from stock retirements. If the repurchase price is higher, the remainder is normally debited to retained earnings (after debiting any APIC that exists from previous stock retirements that exists).

For example, if the above share is **repurchased at $12** and retired, the entry is:

Common stock	10	
APIC–C/S	3	
APIC-Retired stock		1
Cash		12

If, instead, it is **repurchased at $15**, the retirement entry is:

Common stock	10	
APIC–C/S	3	
Retained earnings	2	
Cash		15

If the client had APIC-Retired stock from previous transactions, the debit to retained earnings would have been made to that account instead. If the difference, however, was greater than the balance in APIC-Retired stock, it would be reduced to zero and the remainder would reduce retained earnings.

A company will sometimes obtain **stock subscriptions** from potential shareholders for new offers of the stock. A down payment is received at the time of the subscription, and the remainder when the stock is issued.

Assume the client is planning to issue shares of its $10 par value stock at $30 per share, and obtains subscriptions from potential buyers, who are required to make a $3 down payment with the subscription and pay the balance when the stock is issued to them. The entry when the subscription is **taken out** is:

Cash	3	
Subscriptions receivable	27	
Common stock subscribed		10
APIC–C/S		20

When the balance is paid and **stock issued**, the entry is:

Cash	27	
Common stock subscribed	10	
Subscriptions receivable		27
Common stock		10

If a company does not issue stock within a certain time period after subscription, the potential investor is entitled to a **refund** of the down payment and **cancellation of the contract.** If the company failed to issue stock, the refund entry is:

Common stock subscribed	10	
APIC–C/S	20	
Cash		3
Subscriptions receivable		27

If, on the other hand, the potential buyer breaches the subscription contract and refuses to purchase it when available, the company is normally entitled to **keep the down payment** as an estimate of damages from breach, and records the cancellation as follows:

Common stock subscribed	10	
APIC–C/S	20	
APIC-Forfeited subscriptions		3
Subscriptions receivable		27

If shareholder **donates** stock back to corporation, the entry would be:

Treasury Stock	X (@ FMV)	
APIC–T/S		X

Lecture 14.02 – Treasury Stock

Often, shares are repurchased but not retired. These **treasury shares** are *not paid dividends and are not voted*, so they reduce the number of shares outstanding. They are considered **authorized, issued, but not outstanding**. When the company intends to hold the shares indefinitely, it will account for treasury shares under the **par value method**. The entry is similar to retirement, except that the debit to common stock is instead, recorded to treasury stock, and any APIC-Retired stock is instead recorded as APIC-T/S. Treasury shares held under the par value method are not reported directly on the financial statements, but reduce the amount shown as common stock.

- **Treasury stock (two methods)**
  - Cost Method
  - Par Value Method (Legal / stated value method)

Example: Issue 20,000 shares of $5 Par value C/S @ $25 per share.

1. Cost Method (Cost In, Cost Out → Until Retire)			**Par Value Method** (Legal method) (Par In, Par Out)		
Cash	500,000		Cash	500,000	
C/S (20 ($5))		100,000	C/S (20 ($5))		100,000
APIC – C/S (20 ($20))		400,000	APIC – C/S (20 ($20))		400,000
2. Repurchase 2,000 @ $19					
Treasury Stock – Cost	38,000		APIC – C/S (2,000 (20))	40,000	
Cash		38,000	T/S (2,000 (5))	10,000	
			Cash		38,000
			APIC – T/S		12,000
3. Resell 700 @ $22					
Cash	15,400		Cash	15,400	
APIC – T/S/RE	**X**		T/S (700 (5))		3,500
T/S (19 (700))		13,300	APIC – C/S		11,900
APIC – T/S		**2,100**	*Like a new issuance*		
4. Resell 500 @ $15					
APIC – T/S	2,000		Cash	7,500	
Cash	7,500		T/S (500 (5))		2,500
T/S (500 (19))		9,500	APIC – C/S		5,000
5. Retire 300 – No longer issued or outstanding					
C/S (300 ($5))	1,500		C/S	1,500	
APIC – C/S (300 ($20))	6,000		T/S		1,500
T/S (300 ($19))		5,700			
APIC – T/S		1,800			

OR (APIC – T/S/RE or APIC – T/S)

Note: Under the cost method, T/S is considered a contra Equity account. Under the par value method, T/S is considered a contra C/S account.

If one share of $10 par value stock that was originally issued for $13 was reacquired under the **par value method** at $12, the entry would have been:

Treasury stock	10	
APIC–C/S	3	
APIC–T/S		1
Cash		12

If reacquired at $15, the entry would have been:

Treasury stock	10	
APIC–C/S	3	
Retained earnings	2	
Cash		15

APIC-T/S and/or APIC-Retired stock would have been debited instead of retained earnings to the extent that such amounts existed from previous transactions.

A subsequent resale of these shares is reported in a similar manner to a new issuance, except that treasury stock is credited for the par value of the shares instead of common stock. If the share reacquired in either of the transactions on this page is subsequently resold at $18, the entry is:

Cash	18	
Treasury stock		10
APIC–C/S		8

Notice that the credit to APIC is on common stock, not treasury stock.

When shares are reacquired with the intention of reselling them soon thereafter, the treasury shares are accounted for under the **cost method**. Using this approach, the shares are recorded at cost and reported separately on the financial statements as the last account in stockholders' equity. There is no difference between shares repurchased below the original issue price or above it. If the shares mentioned earlier are acquired for $12, the entry under the cost method is:

Treasury stock	12	
Cash		12

A subsequent resale at $18 is recorded as follows:

Cash	18	
Treasury stock		12
APIC–T/S		6

Notice that the APIC is from treasury stock. The APIC–C/S from the original issuance is not disturbed.

Lecture 14.03 – Preferred Stock & APIC

Preferred Stock

Preferred Stock refers to stock similar to a debt instrument with two advantages over common stock:

- **Dividends** – preferred shares must be paid a dividend before the company is allowed to pay the common shareholders a dividend.
- **Liquidation** – if the corporation liquidates, preferred shareholders must be paid before the common shareholders.

The **dividend preference** for preferred shares is based on a stated dividend rate that is computed on the par (or stated) value of the shares. Keep in mind that dividends are optional, however, and a company may decide not to pay any dividends at all in a particular year to any shareholders. The preferred shareholders have a dividend preference, not a dividend guarantee.

To see how the allocation of dividends is computed, assume a client has two types of stock outstanding at 12/31/X6, at which time $300 of dividends are declared:

Type of shares	Par value	Shares	Total
10% Preferred stock	$100	4	$400
Common stock	$1	100	$100

Of the $300 in dividends, the first $400 × 10% = $40 must be paid to the preferred shareholders, based on the dividend preference. The remaining $260 is paid to the common shareholders.

Along with the stated annual preference, preferred shareholders may be paid additional amounts if the shares are:

- **Cumulative** – dividends missed in earlier years must also be paid before the common shareholders receive anything.
- **Participating** – if the common shareholders get a dividend that is a higher rate on its par value than the stated rate on the preferred shares, the preferred shareholders must get the same higher rate.
- **Convertible** – the preferred shareholder has the option of converting their stock for common stock at a specified ratio.
- **Callable** – the corporation has the option of repurchasing the preferred stock at a specified price.
- **Preferred with Warrants** – the warrants are convertible into shares of common stock.

Assume, for example, that the company in the preceding example paid the same $300 in 20X6, but paid no dividends in the 5 years 20X1 to 20X5. Notwithstanding their preference, the preferred shareholders received nothing in those years. If the stock is not cumulative, the preferred shareholders will still only receive $400 × 10% = $40. If, however, the stock is cumulative, then the $40 preferences missed for 5 years result in $200 of **dividends in arrears** at 12/31/X5. In 20X6, when $300 is paid, the preferred shareholders will collect $240 and the common shareholders $60, determined as follows:

Amount	Shareholders	Reason
$200	Preferred	Dividends in arrears
$40	Preferred	Annual preference
$60	Common	Remainder

If the preferred shares are not cumulative, but are participating, they will still receive more than their annual preference when $300 is paid in 20X6. First, they receive $400 × 10% = $40 as their annual preference. Next, the common shareholders are paid, but only until they are also receiving 10% on their par value, or $100 × 10% = $10. The remaining $250 is allocated to the preferred and common shares based on their relative par values:

Type of shares	Total par value	Percentage of combined
Preferred	$400	80%
Common	$100	20%
Total	$500	100%

Thus, the preferred shares get an additional $250 × 80% = $200 and the common shares an additional $250 × 20% = $50. The preferred shareholders end up receiving $40 + $200 = $240 and the common shareholders $10 + $50 = $60. In each case, the shareholders are getting dividends equal to 60% of par value, so the preferred shares are fully participating in the large dividend.

When a company liquidates, preferred shareholders are paid first, based on the amount of their **liquidation preference**. Unless specifically stated, this is usually the same as the par value of the preferred shares. Remember, however, that a liquidating distribution is still a form of dividend, so preferred shareholders must also be paid dividends in arrears on top of their liquidation preference. The remainder is paid to common shareholders. The amount that each outstanding common share is entitled to receive is known as **book value per common share**. The calculation of BV per C/S share is Common Shareholders equity / Common shares outstanding.

To demonstrate the calculation of liquidation payments and book value, assume the stockholders' equity section of the client is as follows on 12/31/X1, and that no dividends have been paid in 20X1:

Account	**Amount**
8% Cumulative Pfd stock - 5 shares authorized and issued @ $100 par, $110 liquidation value	$500
C/S – 5,000 shares authorized, 103 shares issued @ $1 par	$103
APIC	$200
Retained earnings	$223
Treasury stock, at cost – 3 shares @ $12	($36)
Stockholders' equity	$990

The preferred shareholders are entitled to receive the liquidation preference of $110 × 5 shares = $550 and the dividends in arrears of $500 × 8% = $40, for a total of $590. The common shareholders receive the remaining equity of $990 - $590 = $400. The book value per share of preferred stock is $590 / 5 = $118, and the book value per share of common stock is $400 / 100 = $4. Notice that the book value is based on the shares outstanding.

Additional Paid-In-Capital (APIC)

There are many forms of additional paid-in capital (APIC) (contributed capital) that may be included in the stockholders' equity section of the balance sheet, including:

- **Common stock** – the portion of the issue price of common stock that exceeded the par (or stated) value of the shares.
- **Preferred stock** – The portion of the issue price of preferred stock that exceeded the par (or stated) value of the shares.
- **Retired stock** – Repurchase and retirement of shares below the original issue price.
- **Treasury stock** – Repurchase of shares below the original issue price under the par value method and resale of shares above the repurchase price under the cost method.
- **Warrants** – The amount allocated to the value of detachable warrants that are issued with bonds or preferred stock.

Companies may issue securities that give the holders the right to buy shares of stock at an established price for a specific period of time. Examples of these securities are **stock rights** which are often issued to existing shareholders, **stock options** which are often issued to officers or employees, and **stock warrants** which are often issued to bondholders.

Stock rights (sometimes called *preemptive or subscription rights*) are contractual rights held by existing shareholders to purchase a proportional share of new shares in the same class, to preserve their preexisting ownership percentage (prevent dilution of ownership).

There are, however, many other types of transactions that may affect APIC.

Lecture 14.04 – Share-Based Payment Transactions

Regardless of whether a **share-based compensation** transaction is with an **employee or nonemployee**, the entity will recognize the goods or services received when goods are obtained or services are received. In addition, the entity will recognize an increase in either *equity* or *liabilities*; thus, it is important to distinguish if the share-based payments are considered **equity** or a **liability.**

- When the transaction is for goods that provide a future value, such as inventory, an asset is recognized that is reported in earnings when the asset is sold or consumed.
- When the transaction is for services, they are recognized in income as they are consumed.

Noncompensatory Stock Options

Most stock options are considered compensatory and result in the recognition of compensation expense. Those that do not involve recognition of compensation expense are considered **noncompensatory**. To be considered noncompensatory, certain criteria must be met.

- The stock option plan must satisfy one of two conditions, **either**:
  - The terms are comparable, and no more favorable, to terms offered to shareholders holding the same class of stock that is the subject to the plan; or
  - Any purchase discount below fair value at issuance is no greater than the costs that would have been incurred in a public offering of the securities, which is assumed to be the case if the discount is 5% or less.
- The plan is available to substantially all employees meeting limited employment requirements.
- The plan provides no special option features other than:
  - Permitting employees a period not to exceed 31 days to enroll in the plan once the purchase price has been determined.
  - The purchase price is determined on the basis of the market price on the date of purchase.
    - Employees may be permitted to cancel participation before the purchase date.
    - Upon cancellation, employees would be refunded amounts previously paid.

No entry is reported for the granting of noncompensatory options nor upon their expiration, and the exercise of such options is recorded as a simple issuance of shares at the exercise price paid by the employee.

For example, if a company issues **noncompensatory options** granting all employees the right to buy shares in the company's $10 par value stock for $40 per share, the exercise of an option is reported as follows:

Cash	40	
Common stock		10
APIC-C/S		30

Initial Measurement of Share-Based Payment Transactions

According to ASC 718, all share-based compensation plans that do not meet all of the above criteria are compensatory, indicating that they will result in the recognition of compensation expense. A share-based transaction with employees/nonemployees will always be measured at the **fair value** of the equity instruments issued. The cost of goods obtained or services received from employees/nonemployees in a share-based transaction will generally be equal to either:

- The fair value of equity instruments issued as of the grant date; or
- The fair value of liabilities incurred.

If, however, the grantee pays (or is obligated to pay) an amount in exchange for the instruments granted, then that amount must be subtracted from the cost of goods obtained or services received.

Assume Grantee pays $10 at the grant date for an option with a fair value of $100 received in exchange for services provided by Grantee. The cost of the services is $90.

Share-Based Payments Classified as Equity

The date on which the amount of compensation is determined is considered the *measurement date*, which is the date on which the options are granted (ie, **measurement date = grant date**). If stock options are traded in active markets, the fair value is readily determinable. In other cases, particularly when dealing with nonpublic entities, the fair value of the stock options is not readily determinable.

When that value of stock options is not readily determinable, an option pricing model will be used to determine the fair value of the options. A reliable model will take into account such factors as the exercise price, the expected life of the option, the current value of the underlying stock and the volatility of the underlying stock's price, dividends, and the risk-free interest rate.

- Originally, the FASB suggested a preference for the **Black-Scholes model** to estimate fair value. The formula used by this method is far too complicated to be learned, and no exam questions have ever asked for it to be applied.
- Recent FASB comments indicate a preference for the **binomial distribution model,** which is based on the *expected cash flow* method. Estimates are made as to the possibility of different price changes in the stock and decisions by employees to exercise, and a weighted average expectation is generated and discounted using interest rate assumptions.

A simplified example of the calculation of fair value based on the binomial distribution method follows.

Assume that a company has stock selling at $30 at the time they issue stock options to key employees, giving them the right to purchase company stock at $30, exercisable for a period starting in two years and ending in five years. The risk-free interest rate is 5%, the present value of $1 for 2 periods at 5% is 0.91, and the present value of $1 for 5 periods at 5% is 0.78.

The company estimates that 30% of the options will expire without ever being exercised, that 50% will be exercised in 2 years, at their earliest possible date, with the stock selling at an average $40 price, and that 20% of the options will be held as long as possible and exercised in 5 years, just before expiration, at an average $50 price. The gain to the employees who exercise the options will be the amount by which the value of the stock received exceeds the exercise price on the date of exercise. The fair value of the option under the binomial distribution method is $7.67:

Result	Stock Price	Exercise Price	Gain	Factor	PV	%	Weighted Value
Expire	–	–	–	–	–	30%	–
Exer 2 Yrs	$40	$30	$10	0.91	$9.10	50%	$4.55
Exer 5 Yrs	$50	$30	$20	0.78	$15.60	20%	$3.12
Fair Value							$7.67

When fair value cannot be determined with any degree of reliability, the entity will value stock options using the **intrinsic method**. Nonpublic entities may also make a one-time election to use the intrinsic method, which is an irrevocable election. Under the intrinsic method, the options are measured on the basis of the difference between the exercise price and the fair value of the share on the measurement date.

- If the fair value of the stock is greater than the exercise price, compensation will be equal to the difference multiplied by the number of options.
- If the fair value of the stock is equal to or lower than the exercise price, there will be no compensation.

No entry is required at the time stock options are granted, although many entities will recognize deferred compensation for the total amount, the number of options multiplied by the fair value of an option, with a credit to APIC from stock options outstanding.

The entity must make an accounting policy election as to how to measure the total amount of compensation, which is based on the number of options that are expected to vest and become exercisable. The **two methods** that the entity will choose between will be:

- To estimate the number of options expected to be forfeited before becoming exercisable; or
- To account for forfeitures when they occur.

Under the **first approach**, if a company issued 100,000 options to employees that vest over 3 years with an expected turnover rate of 2% per year, the number of options expected to be exercisable will be calculated as follows:

- Year 1 – 2% will terminate employment, resulting in forfeitures of 2% × 100,000 or 2,000, leaving 98,000 options.
- Year 2 – An additional 2% will terminate employment, resulting in forfeitures of 2% of 98,000 or 1,960, leaving 96,040 options.
- Year 3 – An additional 2% will terminate employment, resulting in forfeitures of 2% of 96,040 or 1,921, leaving 94,119 options that are estimated to become exercisable.

Total compensation expense will be 94,119 multiplied by the fair value per option and will be recognized over the 3-year vesting period.

Assume the 100,000 options, issued on 1/1/X1, each give the employee the right to buy one share of the company's $10 par value common stock for $34, its current selling price. The option can be exercised after 1/1/X4 if the employee remains in service to the company, and expires on 12/31/X6. The company is using the fair value method, and the value at 1/1/X1 using the binomial distribution model is estimated at $6 per option.

On the **date of grant**, the entry is based on 94,119 options at $6:

1/1/X1	Deferred compensation	564,714	
	APIC-Stock options outstanding		564,714

Compensation expense is recognized over the period during which the employee is performing services for the entity in exchange for the compensation. This can be determined on the basis of the terms of the option.

- If the option is immediately exercisable, it indicates that the compensation is for services already rendered.
  - On the date of grant, the total amount of compensation will be recognized as compensation expense.
  - No deferred compensation is recognized.
- If the options are not immediately exercisable, the compensation will be recognized over the period from the grant date through the date on which the options become exercisable.
  - When options become exercisable, they are said to be vested on such date.
  - The period is referred to as the vesting period.

As for vesting, under a **cliff vesting** schedule, options vest all at once or 100 percent after five years of service. Under a **graded vesting schedule**, employees are 20 percent vested after three years of service and become 20 percent vested each year after that until they are 100 percent vested after seven years.

Since the employee must remain for 3 years before the option can be exercised, the **compensation expense** is allocated over that time:

<u>12/31/X1, 12/31/X2, & 12/31/X3</u>

Compensation expense	188,238	
Deferred compensation		188,238

Assuming that the entity's actual turnover is the same as estimated turnover, the same entry will be made every year. If actual turnover differs, the amounts will be adjusted prospectively.
At the time the options are exercised the journal entry would be:

Cash (94,119 × $34)	3,200,046	
APIC Stock options O/S (94,119 × $6)	564,714	
Common Stock (94,119 × $10)		941,190
APIC Common Stock (94,119 × $30)		2,823,570

Now let's look at the **second approach**, assuming the same facts and circumstances. In addition, actual forfeitures were 2,100 in year 1, 2,250 in year 2, and 1,950 in year 3.

On the **date of grant**, the entry is based on the total 100,000 options at $6:

1/1/X1	Deferred compensation	600,000	
	APIC-Stock options outstanding		600,000

To recognize compensation expense at the end of the 1st year, first, 1/3 of the total compensation, $600,000/3 or $200,000, is recognized as compensation expense:

12/31/X1	Compensation expense	200,000	
	Deferred compensation		200,000

The forfeitures are then recognized. With 2,100 options forfeited, at $6 each, total forfeitures will be $12,600, 1/3 of which relates to year 1 with the remaining 2/3 relating to years 2 and 3:

APIC-Stock options outstanding	12,600	
Compensation expense		4,200
Deferred compensation		8,400

This reduces deferred compensation to $600,000 - $200,000 - $8,400, or $391,600.

To recognize compensation expense at the end of the 2nd year, first, 1/2 of the remaining deferred compensation, $391,600/2 or $195,800, is recognized as compensation expense:

12/31/X2

Compensation expense	195,800	
Deferred compensation		195,800

The forfeitures for year 2 are then recognized. With 2,250 options forfeited, at $6 each, total forfeitures will be $13,500, 2/3 of which relates to years 1 and 2, with the remaining 1/3 relating to year 3:

APIC-Stock options outstanding	13,500	
Compensation expense		9,000
Deferred compensation		4,500

This reduces deferred compensation to $391,600 - $195,800 - $4,500 or $191,300.
To recognize compensation expense at the end of the 3rd year, first, the remaining deferred compensation, $191,300, is recognized as compensation expense:

12/31/X3

Compensation expense	191,300	
Deferred compensation		191,300

The forfeitures for year 3 are then recognized. With 1,950 options forfeited, at $6 each, total forfeitures will be $11,700, all of which will be recognized:

APIC-Stock options outstanding	11,700	
Compensation expense		11,700

Disclosures

- Vesting requirements, maximum term of options granted and number of shares authorized for grants of options
- The number and weighted-average exercise of prices of each group of options
- Weighted average grant-date fair value of options granted
- Description of methods used and assumptions made in determining fair values of options
- Total compensation cost recognized for the year
- For O/S options, range of exercise prices
- For options that are being reported under the intrinsic method (only applicable to options granted before the effective date of SFAS 123 revised), pro forma disclosures of the impact on earnings if the fair value method had been used.

Share-Based Payments Classified as Liabilities

Although stock options often provide a nice benefit to employees (or nonemployees), there are limiting factors that may make it difficult for grantees to exercise them.

- They must have the cash to pay the exercise price.
- They will be taxed in the period of exercise based on the difference between the stock's market value and the option price.

To make certain that grantees have the opportunity to take advantage of a share-based compensation plan, entities will often use an alternative, such as **stock appreciation rights** (SAR). A SAR works similarly to a stock option in that:

- It is granted to employees (or nonemployees), specifying an option price.
- It is generally not immediately exercisable and vests over a period from the grant date to the exercise date at a future time.
- It is generally exercisable for a certain length of time.

A SAR may be exercised at any time from the vesting date to the expiration date. When it is exercised, rather than purchase a share of stock for the exercise price, the employee will be compensated for the difference between the market value of the share on the exercise date and the exercise price (**measurement date = settlement/exercise date**).

For publicly held companies, compensation related to share-based plans classified as liabilities is the same as for those classified as equity in that both are recognized on the basis of fair value. The measurement date, however, is the date of settlement.

Nonpublic entities may recognize share-based payment arrangements as liabilities either at fair value or at intrinsic value and will make a policy decision as to which.

Since the share-based payment will be made in cash, rather than through the issuance of shares, the transaction results in the recognition of a liability instead of equity. Unlike stock option rights, where the total amount of compensation for the plan is determined on the grant date, compensation in a SAR plan is measured in each reporting period.

For example, assume an entity has given its president 100 stock appreciation rights on 1/1/X1, exercisable on 12/31/X3 and expiring on 12/31/X5. The stock price on various dates was as follows:

1/1/X1	$20
12/31/X1	$23
12/31/X2	$26
12/31/X3	$25
12/31/X4	$27
12/31/X5	$30

In the first year, the **stock increased $3**, indicating total compensation of $300 ($3 × 100 rights). Since only 1/3 of the vesting period has elapsed, only 1/3 of the compensation expense will be recognized:

Compensation expense	100	
Liability for appreciation rights		100

In the second year, the stock increase to $26, indicating that total compensation of $600 ($6 × 100 rights). Since 2/3 of the vesting period has elapsed, 2/3 of the compensation expense, $400, has been incurred. Compensation expense of $100 was previously recognized, requiring recognition of an additional $300 in the current period:

Compensation expense	300	
Liability for appreciation rights		300

At the end of the third year, the stock price has declined to $25 per share, indicating total compensation expense of $500 ($5 × 100). Since $400 has been incurred in the preceding two periods, and additional $100 in compensation expense will be recognized in the current period.

Compensation expense	100	
Liability for appreciation rights		100

As of the end of 20X4, the SARs have not been exercised. As a result, the liability is remeasured with any adjustment recognized in the current period as an increase or decrease to compensation expense. Since the price is now $27, total compensation is $700. This is compared to the $500 recognized to date requiring additional compensation expense of $200.

Compensation expense	200	
Liability for appreciation rights		200

Finally, on 12/31/X5, when the SARs are getting ready to expire, the president exercises them. At that point, the value of the stock is $30 per share, indicating compensation of $10 per share or $1,000. The liability has a balance of $700, requiring the following entry:

Compensation expense	300	
Liability for appreciation rights	700	
Cash		1,000

Lecture 14.05 – Retained Earnings & Dividends

Retained Earnings (RE) represents the accumulated earnings since inception of the company that have not been paid out to shareholders in the form of a dividend. At the end of each accounting year, net income is closed into retained earnings. In addition, retained earnings is periodically reduced for dividends. There are three dates relevant to each dividend:

- **Declaration date** - the board of directors commits to the dividend.

RE	X	
Dividends Payable		X

- **Record date** - The shareholders at this date are identified as the ones entitled to the dividend

  (no Journal entry)

- **Payment date** - distribution is made to the shareholders of record.

Dividends Payable	X	
Cash		X

- **Types of Dividends**
  - Cash
  - Property (FMV @ date of declaration)
  - Scrip (Interest bearing Note Payable)
  - Liquidating (return of capital)
  - Stock - Small (FMV) / Large (Par)
  - Stock split

Cash Dividend	Scrip – Give dividend but no money	Stock Dividend
RE 25 Cash 25	RE 25 Note Payable 25	**Small < 20 – 25% - FMV** RE 25 CS 20 APIC 5
	Partial Liquidating Dividend RE 15 APIC 10 Cash 25	**Large > 20 – 25% - Par** RE 20 CS 20
Property (FMV) RE 25 Asset 20 Gain 5	**Person receiving Liq Div** Cash 25 Div income 15 Investment 10	**Stock Splits – Double shares, Half par** CS (10(10)) 100 CS (20(5)) 100

Net effect on Stkhldrs equity = 20

Note: All dividends reduce Stockholders' Equity except for stock dividends and stock splits.

The corporation charges retained earnings on the **declaration date** since the liability is created at that time.

For example, if the board declares dividends totaling $500 on 4/1/X1, payable on 4/28/X1 to shareholders of record on 4/21/X1, the entries are:

4/1/X1	Retained earnings	500	
	Dividends payable		500

This records the obligation. Identifying the actual payees doesn't change any account balances, so the next entry is on the **payment date**:

4/28/X1	Dividends payable	500	
	Cash		500

When a dividend exceeds the balance of retained earnings prior to declaration, the amount of the dividend in excess of retained earnings represents a return of contributed capital and is known as a **liquidating dividend**.

For example, if the board declares the $500 dividend on 4/1/X1 as above, but the balance in retained earnings is only $400 before recording the dividend, the entry is:

4/1/X1	Retained earnings	400	
	Additional paid-in capital	100	
	Dividends payable		500

When a company pays a dividend in the form of **property** other than cash, this is known as a **dividend-in-kind**. Such dividends are treated as simultaneous sales of property and distributions of cash, and results in gains or losses.

For example, assume the client declares a dividend-in-kind of land on 7/1/X1, payable on 7/15/X1. The land originally cost $300, is worth $800 on 7/1/X1, and $820 on 7/15/X1. The entry on the declaration date is:

7/1/X1	Retained earnings	800	
	Dividends payable		800
	Land	500	
	Gain on land		500

On the payment date, the entry is:

7/15/X1	Dividends payable	800	
	Land		800

The price appreciation after the declaration date is ignored, since the commitment to distribute the land effectively sells it.

Stock dividends are not actual distributions of assets from a company but represent transfers of capital from retained earnings to contributed capital accounts. Total stockholders' equity is unchanged. There are two types of stock dividends:

- **Ordinary stock dividends** – These are small stock dividends (typically less than 20%) and are recorded at the fair market value of the stock at the time of the dividend.

- **Stock splits effected in the form of stock dividends** – These are large stock dividends (typically more than 25%) and are recorded at the par value of the stock.

For example, assume a client has outstanding 100 shares of $10 par value stock with a fair market value of $30 per share. If a **5%** (5 shares) **stock dividend** is declared and paid, it is reported at $30 per share:

Retained earnings	150	
Common stock		50
APIC-C/S		100

If a **100%** (100 shares) **stock dividend** is declared, it is reported at $10 per share:

Retained earnings	1,000	
Common stock		1,000

The reason for the difference is that the fair market value of the stock is not deemed to be a realistic estimate after a large stock dividend takes place, since it will substantially reduce the selling price of the shares. Dividends between 20% and 25% do not take place on the exam, since it is difficult to determine which classification they should have.

Stock splits in which old stock is exchanged for new stock are accounted for by adjusting the par value of the new shares for the split. If a 2-1 stock split occurred in the above situation, the 100 shares of $10 par stock would have been replaced by 200 shares of $5 par stock. Since total par value is unchanged, no entry is made. A reverse stock split does the opposite by reducing the number of shares outstanding and proportionally increases the par value.

Retained earnings are assumed to be available for the payment of dividends, so when a company faces contingent liabilities that may require large payments in the future, it will often **appropriate** a portion of the retained earnings to indicate to its shareholders its unavailability for dividend payments.

If a company wishes to appropriate $100,000 of retained earnings for possible losses related to pending lawsuits, the entry is:

Retained earnings-Unappropriated	100,000	
Retained earnings-Reserve for lawsuits		100,000

Notice that the above entry has no impact on net assets or net income, and doesn't actually change retained earnings, either. It is considered a disclosure on the face of the financial statements and is appropriate for reasonably possible costs or costs that are probable but not estimable. The above entry is not used for probable and estimable losses, which should be accrued on the income statement and reduce net assets.

When the reserve is no longer needed, the above entry is reversed. This is appropriate whether or not the costs actually occur, since the effects of the contingency will be reflected directly if and when they do result in losses.

In general, retained earnings may not be increased except when net income is closed into it. An exception is when a company has a **quasi-reorganization (fresh start)** (ASC 852). Since new companies always begin with retained earnings of $0, a company with a deficit in retained earnings has the ability to eliminate that deficit by reorganizing as a new company. Accounting principles, therefore, allow a company to restate its accounts as if they had reorganized. This requires shareholder approval.

Usually, a company involved in a quasi-reorganization will take the opportunity to adjust the carrying amount of assets to market values and may adjust the par value of the stock as well. If the entry doesn't balance, the difference adjusts APIC.

For example, assume a client has the following balance sheet:

Assets	900
Liabilities	200
$10 par common stock	800
APIC	500
Retained Earnings	(600)
Liabilities and stockholders' equity	900

They elect a quasi-reorganization. Assets are reduced to market value of $800, and the par value of the shares reduced to $5. The entry is:

Common stock	400	
APIC (balance)	300	
Assets		100
Retained earnings		600

The reason the par value of the stock is often reduced (as in this example) is that APIC cannot be debited for an amount that exceeds its balance before the quasi-reorganization.

Lecture 14.06 – Presentation

The presentation of stockholders' equity (ASC 205) in a balance sheet may include as many as **seven categories**, presented in the following order:

- Preferred stock
- Common stock
- Additional paid-in capital
- Noncontrolling interest (minority interest)
- Retained earnings
- Accumulated other comprehensive income
- Treasury stock, at cost

Stock accounts are known as the **legal capital** of the corporation and are listed from the most senior security (the one entitled to dividends first) to the most junior. If a company has one class of preferred stock and one class of common stock, the preferred stock is listed first.

Preferred stock is shown at the total par (or stated) value of shares issued less shares held in treasury under the par value method. On the face of the balance sheet as part of the account name, the company must disclose:

- Par value per share
- Liquidation value per share (if different from par value)
- Dividend preference rate or amount per share
- Cumulative (if applicable)
- Participating (if applicable)
- Shares authorized
- Shares issued
- Shares outstanding

Common stock is also shown at the total par value of shares issued less shares held in treasury under the par value method. On the face of the balance sheet as part of the account name, the company must disclose:

- Par value per share
- Shares authorized
- Shares issued
- Shares outstanding

Additional paid-in capital is listed immediately after the stock accounts and includes all contributed capital in excess of the legal capital of the company. Some of the types of APIC are from:

- Preferred stock
- Common stock
- Retired stock
- Treasury stock
- Warrants
- Employee stock options (less deferred compensation)
- Expired stock options

Noncontrolling interest, sometimes referred to as the minority interest, arises when a reporting entity prepares consolidated financial statements that include a subsidiary in which the parent owns less than 100%. This may include an entity:

- With which the reporting entity has entered a business combination in which it acquired a majority of the equity shares, in which case the noncontrolling interest represents the minority portion not owned.
- That is a variable interest entity (VIE) in which it has a controlling financial interest but does not own a majority of the equity. In this case, the noncontrolling interest represents the equity of the consolidated VIE that is not owned by the reporting entity, generally a majority.

The noncontrolling interest of a consolidated subsidiary is initially recognized at its fair value on the date of the combination. In many cases, this will be measured at the market price of a single share multiplied by the number of shares held by stockholders other than the reporting entity. It will be adjusted for the noncontrolling interest's share in income, comprehensive income, and distributions.

The noncontrolling interest of a VIE will be determined in the same manner when the VIE is not a related entity. When the VIE is a related entity, however, the consolidation is reported using the VIE's book values, rather than fair values, and the noncontrolling interest is the portion of the VIE's reported equity that is not owned by the reporting entity.

Net income includes all components of income for both the reporting entity and all consolidated entities and is allocated between the portion attributable to the reporting entity and the portion attributable to the noncontrolling interest. Other comprehensive income, including components of the reporting entity and consolidated entities, is also allocated.

The noncontrolling interest is a component of stockholders' equity and is required to be presented in the equity section of the balance sheet.

Retained earnings is reported next. The details of the changes in the account are reported in a separate **statement of retained earnings**, which might appear as follows:

XYZ Corporation
Statement of Retained Earnings
For the Year Ended December 31, 20X3

Retained earnings, 12/31/X2 – as previously reported	$600
Prior period adjustment to correct inventory, net of $80 taxes	120
Retained earnings, 1/1/X3 – adjusted	720
Net income for the year ended 12/31/X3	260
Less dividends	(100)
Retained earnings, 12/31/X3	880

The next section is for **accumulated other comprehensive income (OCI) - (DENT)**, which reflects cumulative changes in net assets resulting from certain transactions not included in net income and not affecting retained earnings including:

- **D**erivative Cash flow hedges.
- **E**xcess adjustment of Pension PBO and FV of Plan assets at year end

- **N**et unrealized changes in the value of marketable securities
- **T**ranslation gains and losses from foreign currency

Tax effects may be reported on each of the accounts or in the aggregate for the section. In certain cases, the items included in this section may be debit balances, resulting in contra-equity accounts being reported.

Treasury stock is presented last on the balance sheet, but only for stock that is being held under the cost method (treasury shares held under the par value method are netted directly against the stock accounts presented earlier). It is always a contra-equity account. Included in the account name must be disclosures of:

- Number of shares held
- An indication that the shares are reported at cost

An example of the *stockholders' equity section* of the balance sheet follows:

XYZ Corporation
Stockholders' Equity
December 31, 20X3

Preferred stock, $100 par value, $105 liquidation value, 8% cumulative, 100 shares authorized, issued, and outstanding		$10,000
Common stock, $1 par value, 4,000 shares authorized, 1,000 shares issued, 900 shares outstanding		1,000
Additional paid-in capital		5,000
Noncontrolling Interest		400
Retained earnings		12,400
Accumulated other comprehensive income:		
Foreign currency translation gains	$1,800	
Net unrealized losses on available-for-sale securities	(300)	
	1,500	
Less taxes	(600)	900
		29,700
Less common stock in treasury, 100 shares at cost		(1,200)
Total stockholders' equity		$28,500

Assuming there are no dividends in arrears on preferred stock, the **book value** of the common stock is computed as follows:

Stockholders' equity	$28,500
Preferred stock liquidation value	(10,500)
Common stock equity	18,000/
Divided by common shares outstanding	900 =
Book value per common share	$20

Statement of Changes in Stockholders' Equity

When significant changes occur in stockholders' equity, companies are required to disclose them. Here is an example of such a statement taken from the financial statements of Marriott, International:

MARRIOTT INTERNATIONAL, INC. (DEC)
CONSOLIDATED STATEMENTS OF SHAREHOLDERS' EQUITY
Fiscal Years 20X1
(In millions)

Common Shares Outstanding		Total	Equity Attributable to Marriott Shareholders: Class A Common Stock	Additional Paid-In Capital	Retained Earnings	Treasury Stock, at Cost	Accumulated Other Comprehensive Income (Loss)	Equity Attributable to Noncontrolling Interests
366.9	Balance at year-end 20X0	$1,585	$5	$3,644	$3,286	-$5,348	-$2	—
—	Net income	198	—	—	198	—	—	—
—	Other comprehensive loss	-24	—	—	—	—	-24	—
—	Dividends	-135	—	—	-135	—	—	—
9.5	Employee stock plan issuance	182	—	9	-137	310	—	—
-43.4	Purchase of Treasury stock	-1,425	—	—	—	-1,425	—	—
—	Spin-off of Marriott Vacations Worldwide Corporation	-1,162	—	-1,140	—	—	-22	—
333	Balance at year-end 20X1	($781)	$5	$2,513	$3,212	($6,463)	($48)	$—

Equity Securities Classified as Debt

Some financial instruments issued by an entity have characteristics of both debt and equity. ASC 480, *Distinguishing Liabilities from Equity*, requires financial instruments that embody an **obligation** of the issuing entity be reported as a liability. An obligation in this context is a duty or responsibility to transfer assets or issue equity shares. The obligation may be conditional or unconditional.

An example of an equity instrument that includes an obligation would be a put option issued by the entity. A put option entitles the holder to require to repurchase its equity securities. Settlement may be through:

- Physical settlement in which the full cash amount is transferred in exchange for all the shares.
- Net cash settlement in which cash is paid or received based on the difference between the option price and the fair value at exercise.
- Net share settlement in which shares are issued or reacquired with a total value equal to the difference between the option price and the fair value at exercise.

In some cases, these instruments will require the entity to issue shares for an amount greater than their fair value on the date of issuance or will be the recipient of a net settlement. In such cases, the instruments would be reported as assets.

Instruments that may be reported as liabilities or assets include:

- Mandatorily redeemable financial instruments;
- Obligations to repurchase equity shares by issuing assets; and
- Certain obligations to issue a variable number of shares.

Mandatorily redeemable instruments are always reported as liabilities unless redemption is only required upon liquidation or termination of the entity. An instrument that is redeemable only upon the occurrence of an event that is not certain to occur is not considered mandatorily redeemable. The instrument will be recognized as a liability when:

- The event has occurred;
- The condition is resolved; or
- The event has become certain to occur.

An **obligation to repurchase equity shares by transferring assets**, such as a forward purchase contract or a put option, is classified as a liability, unless it is an outstanding share, if two characteristics apply:

1. There is an obligation to repurchase the entity's equity securities or has an obligation that is calculated on the basis of the fair value of the shares; and
2. The obligation does, or may, ultimately require settlement by the transfer of assets.

An instrument that gives the holder the right to require the entity to transfer assets is always reported as a liability.

In some cases, an entity may have an **obligation to issue a variable number of shares**. These are reported as liabilities when the monetary value of the shares the entity will be required to issue is based on:

- A fixed monetary amount such that the number of shares will be determined essentially by dividing that amount by the fair value per share at settlement; or
- An index other than the fair value of the entity's equity shares, such as a financial instrument that is indexed to the Dow Jones Industrial Average; or
- A relationship that varies inversely to the fair value of the entity's equity securities, such as a written put option that can be satisfied by net share settlement.

Equity securities of an entity that are reported as liabilities are not considered in the calculation of earnings per share. This includes mandatorily redeemable securities as well as forward contracts, such as put options, to repurchase equity shares.

When all the shares of an entity are mandatorily redeemable, all will be reported in the liability section, identified as shares subject to mandatory redemption. As a result, there will be no stockholders' equity section and amounts for common stock, APIC, and retained earnings are disclosed.

A closely held corporation is formed by 5 friends, and a single class of common stock is issued. There is a provision requiring the corporation to repurchase the shares of any shareholder who dies by the payment of cash equal to the net book value of the shares on the latest financial statement date prior to the death. In such a circumstance, the common stock is treated as a liability. The balance sheet might appear as follows:

Five Buddies Corporation

Total Assets	$10,000,000
Liabilities other than shares	$ 3,000,000
Shares subject to mandatory redemption	7,000,000
Total Liabilities	$10,000,000

UWorld | ROGER CPA Review

YOUR WORLD OF LEARNING

FAR 15 - Earnings Per Share (EPS)

FAR 15 – Earnings Per Share

Table of Contents

Earnings Per Share (EPS)

Lecture 15.01 – Earnings Per Share: Basic

Reporting Earnings Per Share

A publicly held company is required to present earnings per share (EPS) for Basic and Dilutive EPS on the **face** of the income statement for (ASC 260):

- **Income from continuing operations (ONT – I)**
- **Net income**

The company must also present EPS for **discontinued operations**, which may be presented **either** on the *face* of the statement or in the *notes* to the financial statements.

A company does not present other **C**omprehensive income or total comprehensive income on a per share basis. Cash flows per share are also not disclosed.

If a company has only common stock, preferred stock, and other instruments that cannot be converted into common stock (no options or convertible securities outstanding) it has a **simple capital structure** and reports a single EPS number for each of the above categories. If a company has outstanding options or convertible securities, it has a **complex capital structure** and must present two EPS numbers for each of the above categories:

- **Basic**
- **Diluted**

Basic Earnings Per Share

The calculation of EPS in a simple capital structure (and basic EPS in a complex capital structure) follows. We'll use the calculation of net income for all of these examples.

Earnings per share is, of course, earnings divided by shares:

- **Earnings** = Net income minus preferred stock dividends.
- **Shares** = Weighted average common shares outstanding during the year.

Since EPS is being computed for the **common stock**, earnings must be reduced by dividends payable to preferred shareholders. If the preferred stock is **not cumulative**, only dividends actually declared during the year are subtracted. If the preferred shares are **cumulative**, the annual dividend preference is subtracted each year, regardless of whether or not it is declared or paid, since the amounts not paid accumulate and will never be payable to common shareholders. The effect of participating preferred shares is more complicated and appears to be beyond the scope of CPA exam testing.

Simple (Basic) Capital Structure

Net Income
– Preferred Divs (All Cumulative and Non-cumulative only if declared)
$ Available to C/S
――――――――――――――――――――
(1) Wtd avg. # c/s outstanding (divs and splits – Retroactive)

As an example of the computation of earnings for EPS purposes, assume a company has the following capital structure:

8% Preferred stock	$400
Common stock	100

The company reports net income of $932 for the year and declares no dividends. If the preferred stock is not cumulative, common stock earnings are $932. If the preferred stock is cumulative, then the missed dividend of $400 × 8% = $32 accumulates and will be paid to the preferred shareholders eventually, reducing the earnings applicable to common stock to $932 - $32 = $900. It doesn't matter if there are dividends in arrears from earlier years, since those amounts would have been subtracted in determining EPS of those earlier years, and wouldn't be subtracted again this year.

1 - Weighted Average Number of Common Stock Shares Outstanding

The determination of the **number of shares** to include in the denominator of the calculation can be very tricky. The amount to be used is the weighted average of the number of common shares outstanding during the year. As a result, shares sold to the public during the year must be prorated for the portion of the year they were outstanding.

For example, assume the following facts applied to the client for the first two years of its existence:

Issued, 1/1/X1	500
Issued, 7/1/X1	100
Issued, 10/1/X1	300
Outstanding, 12/31/X1	900

Although the number of shares outstanding at 12/31/X1 is 900, only 500 of these shares (those issued at the start of 20X0) were outstanding throughout 20X1. The 100 shares issued on 7/1/X1 were only outstanding for half of the year, and the shares issued 10/1/X1 for the final quarter of the year. The calculation of weighted average shares for 20X1 is:

500 × 12/12 =	500
100 × 6/12 =	50
300 × 3/12 =	75
Total	625

The reason for prorating shares issued during the year is that the funds received from issuance are only available for productive use by the corporation from that point on, not the entire year. This would **not** be the case, however, if shares are issued as a result of (**Retroactive**):

- Stock dividends
- Stock splits
- Delayed issuance for earlier consideration (Stock Subscriptions)

In these cases, the shares are treated as if they had always been outstanding and are included at full amount for the current year. They are also included for earlier years that are shown in *comparative financial statements.* In the case of a reverse stock split, these would retroactively *reduce* shares outstanding for all periods presented.

For example, assume that the 100 shares issued on 7/1/X1 were the result of a 20% stock dividend on the 500 shares outstanding previously. Since all shares are going to previous shareholders, they are treated as if they always had these additional shares. The calculation for 20X1 is:

500 × 1 =	500
100 × 1 =	100
300 × ¼ =	75
Total	675

Example: On 1/1, 100,000 shares of C/S are outstanding. On April 1st, 80,000 shares are issued. On July 1st, a 10% stock dividend is issued. On September 1st, 18,000 shares of Treasury Stock are repurchased. On December 31st a 2 for 1 stock split occurs. Calculate the weighted average number of shares of C/S outstanding at 12/31.

1/1 100,000 shares o/s × 100% =	100,000
4/1 80,000 shares issued × 9/12 =	60,000
7/1 10% dividend issued 160,000 × 10% =	16,000
9/1 18,000 shares of Treasury Stock repurchased × 4/12 =	(6,000)
	170,000
12/31 a 2 for 1 stock split occurs	× 2
Weighted average number of c/s outstanding at 12/31 =	**340,000**

Lecture 15.02 – Earnings Per Share: Diluted

2 - The If-Converted Method

The calculation of **diluted EPS** (assume anyone who "*could convert*" does so) for a company with **convertible Preferred stock or Convertible Bonds** starts with the computation just discussed, which is called **basic EPS.** For convertible securities, the following adjustments are made in the calculation:

- **Numerator** – earnings are increased by the dividends or after-tax interest expense that would not have been due if the securities had been converted to common stock at the beginning of the year.
- **Denominator** – shares are increased by the additional number of common shares that would have been outstanding if the securities had been converted. The convertible preferred stock or convertible debt is assumed to have been converted at the beginning of the period, or at the time of issuance, whichever is later. No weighting is "required".

If the calculation results in an EPS number which is higher than the basic EPS number, then the security is **anti-dilutive** and not included in the reported diluted EPS. To determine whether or not an item is anti-dilutive, each item is considered separately in sequence from most to least dilutive. One would normally consider options and warrants first.

Complex (Diluted) Capital Structure (Could convert)

Net Income Available to C/S

+ (2) Preferred Divs (not net of tax)
+ (2) Interest expense saved from convertible Bonds (net of tax)
+ (3) $0 (from Treasury stock)

---

(1) Wtd avg. # c/s outstanding (divs and splits – Retroactive)
+ (2) # of shares convertible security is converted into for both Pfd stock and convertible bonds (not weighted)
+ (3) Incremental # of C/S outstanding from Treasury stock method at average market price. (Not weighted)

For example, assume that a company reporting $932 net income for the year has the following capital structure, which did not change during the year:

Preferred stock, $100 par, 8% cumulative, 4 shares, each convertible into 10 shares of common stock	$400
Common stock, $1 par, 100 shares	100

<u>To calculate **basic EPS:**</u>

Earnings = Net income – PS dividends = $932 - $32 = $900
Shares = 100
Basic EPS = $900 / 100 = $9.00

If the preferred shares had been converted at the beginning of the year, the $32 in preferred dividends would not have been owed and there would have been 4 × 10 = 40 additional common shares. To calculate diluted EPS:

Earnings = $900 + $32 = $932
Shares = 100 + 40 = 140
Diluted EPS = $932 / 140 = $6.66

The **conversion of a bond ("if converted method")** requires considering the tax effect, since the reduction of interest expense is accompanied by an increase in taxable income. It is assumed that the conversion occurred at the *beginning of the earliest period reported* (or at the time of *Issuance*, if later).

For example, assume a client with $800 of net income and an effective tax rate of 30% had the following capital structure throughout the year:

6% Convertible bond, $1,000 face value, convertible into 20 shares of common stock	$1,000
Common stock, $1 par, 200 shares	200

Basic EPS is computed as follows:
Earnings = $800
Shares = 200

Basic EPS = $800 / 200 = $4.00

The conversion of the bonds would have eliminated the $1,000 × 6% = $60 in interest expense, but would have increased taxes by $60 × 30% = $18, so the net savings is only $60 - $18 = $42.

Diluted EPS is computed as follows:
Earnings = $800 + $42 = $842
Shares = 200 + 20 = 220

Diluted EPS = $3.83

Lecture 15.03 – Earnings Per Share: Treasury Stock Method

3 - The Treasury Stock Method

The effect of **options** on diluted EPS is to first increase the shares by the number that would have been issued if the options had been exercised, then decrease the shares by the number that could have been repurchased by the corporation (at the **average CS market price** during the year) with the proceeds from exercise. This is known as the **treasury stock method.** The exercise of options has no effect on earnings since options pay no dividends or interest. If market prices change in the future, previously reported EPS should not be adjusted retroactively, leave it as it was reported.

For example: If 40,000 options are issued at an option price of $15 per share when the average market price is $20 per share, what is the dilutive effect?

40,000 options which are convertible into 40,000 shares of c/s
× $15 option price
$600,000

		40,000
600,000/$20 avg. mkt price	=	- 30,000 shares of treasury stock
		10,000 shares dilutive effect.

Another method of calculating the *incremental number of shares outstanding* is:

$$\text{Number of shares} - \frac{\text{(number of shares} \times \text{exercise price)}}{\text{Average market price}} = \text{additional shares outstanding}$$

$$40{,}000 - \frac{(40{,}000 \times \$15)}{\$20} = 10{,}000$$

UWorld
YOUR WORLD OF LEARNING
ROGER
CPA Review

FAR 16 - Reporting the Results of Operations

FAR 16 – Reporting the Results of Operations

Table of Contents

Reporting the Results of Operations

Lecture 16.01 – Reporting the Results of Operations

Statement of Earnings

The current FASB presentation of Results of Operations is a Statement of Earnings and Comprehensive Income. It includes up to **3 different sections**:

- Income from Continuing Operations
- **D**iscontinued operations
- **O**ther Comprehensive income (OCI)

Income from Continuing Operations may be prepared using **two different formats**:

- Multiple-step income statement
- Single-step income statement
  - The **multiple-step** approach includes subtotals for gross profit, operating income, and income before taxes, while the **single-step** approach does not. Nevertheless, income from continuing operations is identical under the two approaches.

Sales
– Cost of Goods Sold
= Gross Margin
– Selling, General & Administrative exp.
= Operating Income

Beg Inventory
+ Net Purchases
= Goods Available for Sale
– Ending Inventory
= **Cost of Goods Sold**

Income Statement
(Stmt of Profit or Loss)
Operating Income

Nonoperating Income

Taxes – **Current** / **Deferred**

Income from continuing ops.
Discontinued Operations, net of Taxes

Net Income (Goes to Retained Earnings)
± **O**ther Comprehensive Income **(DENT)**

Comprehensive Income (Goes to B/S – an Equity Account)

Multiple Step (ON-TIDe-N-OC)

Roger Company
Statement of Earnings and Comprehensive Income
(Statement of Profit or Loss)
For the Year Ended December 31, 20X3

Sales		$2,000,000
Cost of sales		600,000
Gross profit		1,400,000
Less:		
Selling expenses	$340,000	
General & administrative expenses	260,000	
Depreciation Expense (impairment loss – public co)	100,000	700,000
Operating income (O)		700,000
Other income and (expense): (**Nonoperating**)		
Interest/Dividend income	10,000	
Interest expense/unusual and/or infrequent items	(20,000)	
Loss due to earthquake	(72,000)	
Gain on sale of equipment/Investments (imp loss –nonpublic)	30,000	(52,000)
Income before income tax		648,000
Provision for income Tax (T):		
Current	150,000	
Deferred	40,000	190,000
Income from continuing operations **(I)**		$ 458,000
Gain (loss) from operations of **Discontinued component unit, (ASC 205)** net of tax of $30,000 **(De)**		45,000
Net income (N)		$503,000
Other Comprehensive income **(OCI) (DENT)**		
Derivative Cash Flow Hedge Gain/Loss (net of tax)		xxx
Excess adjustment of Pension PBO and FV of Plan assets at year end		(xxx)
Net Unrealized holding gains (AFS) arising during period (net of tax)		xxx
Translation adjustment of Foreign currency (net of tax)		xxx
Other comprehensive income		xxx
Comprehensive Income (C)		**$xxx,xxx**
Earnings per share:		
Income from Continuing operations		$2.29
Income from Discontinued operations		.23
Net income per share		$2.52

Single step

Revenues
– Expenses
Income from continuing operations
De
Net Income

Operating Income ("O")

Sales or revenues from contracts with customers are recognized when the promised goods or services have been delivered to the customer or, when certain criteria are met, while the goods or services are being delivered. Revenues that do not arise from contracts are recognized when the entity no longer has any obligations to provide goods or services to the customer and it is not likely that revenues received will be required to be returned to the customer.

Recognize **expenses** or losses when economic benefit is used up (as **incurred**):

Cost of goods sold (COGS)
Beginning inventory
+ Net purchases (COG manufactured)
Cost of goods available for sale
– Ending inventory
= COGS

Note: Freight-in is included in net purchases.

- **Selling Expenses** – Salaries and commissions, advertising, freight out

  Note: Freight out may be included in either cost of goods sold or selling expenses.

- **General and Administrative Expenses** – Officers' salaries, accounting and legal, insurance

  Note: Credit loss expense could be either a Selling or G&A expense.

Nonoperating Items ("N") (Other Income/Expense, Gains/Losses)

- Interest income or expense, dividend income, gain/loss on sale of PP&E or Investments, foreign currency transactional gains/losses, unrealized gain/loss from Trading securities, and gains, losses, revenues, and expenses that are unusual or infrequent or both.
- The tax effects related to these items are included in the tax provision.

Taxes ("T") (Provision for Taxes)

- Current income tax expense (current taxable income × current tax rate)
- Deferred income tax expense (temporary differences × enacted tax rate)

= Income from continuing operations ("I")

Lecture 16.02 – Discontinued Operations ("De")

When an entity decides to dispose of a portion of its business, it will determine if it should be accounted for as a disposal of assets or discontinued operations. (ASC 205) A disposal of a component of an entity or a group of components is reported as discontinued operations if the disposal represents a ***strategic shift*** *that will have a significant effect on the entity's operations and financial results.*

Disposal of a component or group of components would be a **strategic shift** when:

- The entity is discontinuing operations in a major geographical region
- The entity is discontinuing a major product line
- The entity is disposing of a significant investment accounted for under the equity method
- Other major "parts" of an entity

When reported as discontinued operations, the assets of the component or group of components are reported separately in the asset section of the balance sheet and identified as assets related to discontinued operations. Liabilities of the discontinued operations are likewise separately reported in the liability section of the balance sheet. In addition, the operations of the component or components, and any gains or losses on disposals of assets and settlements of liabilities, are reported separated on the income statement, *net of tax,* after income from continuing operations and before net income.

A component or group of components that qualifies as a strategic shift, will be reported in discontinued operations if it is *disposed of* by sale or by some other means during the period; or if it qualifies to be classified as "held for sale". A component qualifies as *held for sale* if *all* of the following criteria are met:

- A plan to sell the component has been committed to by those with the authority to do so.
- The component is in salable condition and available for immediate sale
- Actions to complete the plan for disposal have been initiated and a buyer is being actively sought
- The sale is probable and expected to be completed and to qualify for recognition within one year
- The price at which the component is being marketed is reasonable
- It is unlikely that significant changes will be made to the plan or that it will be withdrawn.

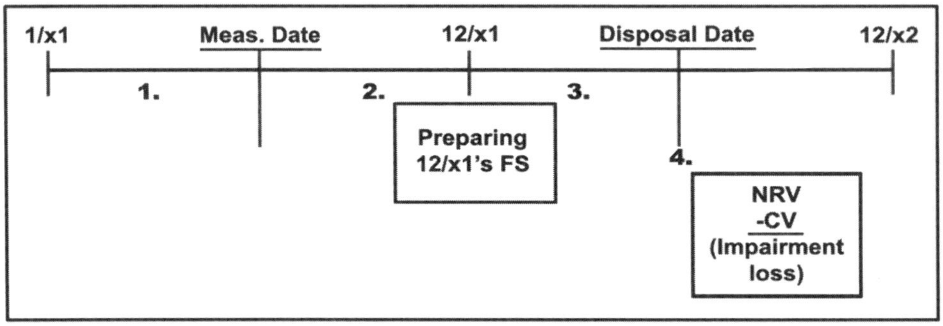

Special Items to Note

- Expected gains or losses from operations in future periods are **not** included until the period they occur.
- The expected loss on a disposal may, however, indirectly be recognized through **impairment testing** that causes the write-down of a component to its fair market value. Long-lived assets to be disposed of by sale should be measured at the lower of carrying amount or fair value less the cost of disposal (NRV). An asset held for disposal **CAN be written up or Down** in future periods as long as the write-up is never greater than the carrying amount of the asset before the impairment.
- Gain or loss is reported net of taxes with disclosure of the tax effect on the face of the income statement. EPS disclosure is also required (DE).
- Disposals of assets or asset groups that are **not** components are reported in continuing operations and included in the determination of operating profit.
- For *comparative purposes*, the income statement must be adjusted retrospectively to enhance comparability with the current year's income statement for all prior years presented. The amounts are netted into one figure for each year presented, "Income (loss) from Discontinued Operations". The Balance sheet of previous periods must also reclassify assets and liabilities of a discontinued operation.
- Regardless of when during the period the decision is made to discontinue a segment, all results of operations for that segment, as well as any gains or losses on the disposal of assets during the period, are recognized as discontinued operations.
- The costs of termination benefits, lease termination, and consolidating facilities or relocating employees related to a disposal activity that involves discontinued operations should be included in the results of discontinued operations

Disclosures

- Description of the reasons for the disposal; the means of disposal; and the expected date
- Carrying amounts of assets and liabilities included in the disposal group
- Gains and losses on assets held for sale along with an indication as to where on the income statement they appear
- Any revenues, expenses, and pretax profit or loss from discontinued operations and where it is presented on the income statement if not presented separately
- The business segment in which the assets that are part of the disposal group are reported

---

= Net Income ("N")

Lecture 16.03 – Comprehensive Income

*O*ther Comprehensive Income & *C*omprehensive Income ("OC")

The purpose of reporting comprehensive income is to report a measure of overall enterprise performance. (ASC 220) Comprehensive income includes all changes in equity during a period except those resulting from investments by owners and distributions to owners. It should be **prominently** displayed (net of tax effect) within the financial statements (F/S). It may be displayed in one of two ways:

1. As a separate statement of comprehensive income that immediately follows the income statement.
2. In a combined statement of income and comprehensive income.

Roger Company
Statement of Comprehensive Income
FYE 12/31/20X3

Net Income		$xxx,xxx
Other comprehensive income (OCI) (**net of tax**)		
Derivative, cash flow hedges	$xxx	
Excess adjustment of Pension PBO and FV of Plan assets at year end	$xxx	
Net unrealized gain/loss Avail-for-sale Securities	$xxx	
Translation gains and losses	$xxx	$x,xxx
Comprehensive income		**$xxx,xxx**

Although they also result in changes in net assets, the following items are not currently included in the reporting of OCI:

- Contributions from owners
- Distributions to owners (dividends)
- Prior period adjustments

A **prior period adjustment** actually is a form of comprehensive income, but since it doesn't relate to the current year, it isn't reported in the OCI section of the statement. Prior period adjustments, along with distributions of earnings, are reported on the **Statement of Retained Earnings**, while contributions by owners and distributions that represent a return of capital are not currently required to be reported on any of the F/S.

Accumulated Other Comprehensive Income

This is reported on the balance sheet as a component of stockholders' equity that includes the total of OCI for the current and previous periods.

Earnings Per Share (EPS)

Companies with publicly traded stock are required to include **EPS information** at the bottom of the statement for:

- Income from continuing operations (ONT)
- Net income

Additional EPS numbers must be reported either at the bottom of the statement or in the notes for discontinued operations.

No EPS information is reported for comprehensive income or for the OCI section.

The presentation of EPS information for companies with **complex capital structures** must include:

- Basic EPS
- Diluted EPS

A sample Statement of Earnings and Comprehensive Income for a publicly held company follows (we'll use the single-step format for the continuing operations section).

ABC Company
Statement of Earnings and Comprehensive Income
For the Year Ended December 31, 20X3

Sales		1,000,000
Dividend income		4,000
Total revenue		1,004,000
Cost of sales	600,000	
Selling, general, and administrative expenses	300,000	
Loss on sale of equipment	17,000	
Current income tax expense	23,000	
Deferred income tax expense	3,000	943,000
Income from continuing operations		61,000
Discontinued operations:		
Gain (loss) from operations of **discontinued component**, *net* of $12,600 taxes		29,400
Net Income		90,400
Other comprehensive income:		
Translation adjustment, net of $2,400 taxes	5,600	
Unrealized gain on available-for-sale securities, net of $9,600 taxes	22,400	28,000
Comprehensive income		118,400
Earnings per share:		
	Basic	**Diluted**
Income from continuing operations	6.10	4.88
Net income	9.04	7.01

Lecture 16.04 – SEC Reporting Requirements

Regulations S-K and S-X

Unless exempt by regulation, companies with $10+ million of assets, 2,000+ shareholders (500+ if nonaccredited investor shareholders), and securities that trade on a national securities exchange or an over-the-counter market must have their securities registered. This is governed by the 1933 Federal Securities Regulations Act. The ongoing reporting requirements are governed by the 1934 Act.

- **Regulation S-K** regulates the disclosure of *nonfinancial-statement* data.
- **Regulation S-X** regulates the disclosure of *financial-statement* data.

Note that Regulations S-K and S-X require less disclosures from **smaller reporting companies (SRCs)**. A company qualifies as an SRC if it has:

- Less than $250 million in public float (ie, equity held by nonaffiliated investors), or
- Less than $700 million in public float *and* less than $100 million in annual revenues.

1. Annual Report (Form 10-K)

Form 10-K provides a comprehensive picture of a company's business, its risks, and its performance, including audited F/S.

a. Business
   - Risk factors (not required for SRCs)
   - Comments by SEC staff regarding the entity's periodic or current reports that remain unresolved
   - Human capital resources

b. Properties
   - Disclose only those properties that are material to the company

c. Legal proceedings

d. Mine safety disclosures

e. Information related to:
   - The market for the registrant's common equity
   - Related stockholder matters
   - Issuer purchases of equity securities

f. Management's discussion and analysis (MD&A)
   - Principal objectives of MD&A
   - Financial condition and results of operations (including material changes in revenue or the relationship between costs and revenues)
   - Quantitative and qualitative disclosures about market risk (not required for SRCs)
   - Liquidity and capital resources
   - Critical accounting estimates

g. F/S and supplementary data
   - 2 years of balance sheets
   - 3 years of income statements, statements of cash flows, and statements of comprehensive income
   - No supplementary data and only 2 years of F/S required for SRCs

h. Changes in and disagreements with accountants on accounting and financial disclosures
   - Controls and procedures
     - Management's evaluation of effectiveness of disclosure controls and procedures
     - Management's annual report on internal control over financial reporting
   - Other information – anything required to be reported on Form 8-K during the fourth quarter

The **deadline** for filing the Form 10-K is within:

- **60 days** after the close of the company's fiscal year for **large accelerated filers**—companies with a market value of at least $700 million public float.
- **75 days** for **accelerated filers**—at least $75 million public float and $100 million in annual revenues.
- **90 days** for **nonaccelerated filers**—less than $75 million public float, or SRC with less than $700 million in equity and less than $100 million in annual revenues.

2. Quarterly Report (Form 10-Q)

Like Form 10-K, Form 10-Q requires F/S, management discussion and analysis, quantitative and qualitative disclosures about market risk, and information about controls and procedures. Form 10-Q is required within:

- **40 days** of the end of each of the first three quarters for *accelerated and large accelerated* filers, and
- **45 days** for nonaccelerated filers.

F/S, which are **reviewed** as opposed to audited, will include comparative balance sheets as of the end of the current quarter and the comparable quarter in the preceding year, and operating results and cash flows for the current quarter and the year-to-date for both the current and the preceding years. The 10-Q is filed for the first 3 quarters and then the final quarter is included in the annual 10-K.

While management provides its evaluation as to the effectiveness of internal controls on an annual basis, Form 10-Q requires information about changes in controls over financial reporting that are likely to have a material effect since the previous report.

3. Information Statements (Form 8-K)

Form 8-K is required to be filed within **4 business days** of an event of major significance, such as entering into or terminating a material agreement; bankruptcy; the acquisition or disposal of assets; or a change in directors, CEO or auditor.

	Market Value of Outstanding Securities	Annual Revenues	10-K	10-Q
Large Accelerated Filer	$700M and up	N/A	60 days	40 days
Accelerated Filer	$250M – $700M	$100M and up	75 days	40 days
Accelerated Filer and SRC	$75M – $250M			
Nonaccelerated Filer and SRC	$75M – $700M	Under $100M	90 days	45 days
	Under $75M	Unlimited		

Lecture 16.05 – Interim Financial Reporting

Companies that issue annual financial statements typically issue interim reports on a **quarterly** basis as well. In general, the application of **generally accepted accounting principles** to a report covering three months will be no different than for a report covering one year, since an interim period is an integral part of the overall year. Timeliness is emphasized over reliability. These statements should be marked "unaudited." As a result **(ASC 270):**

- **Revenues** are recognized in each quarter as earned and realized (for example, estimates must be made each quarter when applying the percentage-of-completion method of construction accounting to determine the profit in each period).
- **Expenses** are matched to each quarter (for example, a property tax bill covering an entire year must be allocated equally to the four quarters).
- **Accounting Changes** made in an interim period are to be reported by retrospective application.

For example, assume a client received an annual rental payment of $300 from a client on 1/2/X1 and paid a $100 property tax bill covering all of calendar year 20X1 on 3/15/X1. The effects of these items on the interim reports in the 20X1 are:

Quarter	1st	2nd	3rd	4th
Rent income	75	75	75	75
Property tax	(25)	(25)	(25)	(25)

One item that may need special consideration is the provision for income taxes. When preparing an annual report, the company already knows its taxable income for the year and can compute its income tax provision with full knowledge of the applicable tax rates and available tax credits.

When computing income taxes at an interim date, however, the company must make an estimate of the **effective annual tax rate** that it believes will be applicable for that entire year. This should take into account estimates of total taxable income for the year and any tax planning strategies the company plans to adopt during the year.

The estimate of the effective annual tax rate should be updated at each interim date, and the provision for income taxes in later quarters will be based on the current estimated rate applied to cumulative income reduced by provisions reported in early periods.

For example, if a client has income of $100 in the first quarter of 20X1 and expects the effective annual tax rate for all of 20X1 to be 25%, then the provision for income taxes in the first quarter will be $100 x 25% = $25. If the client has an additional $150 of income in the second quarter, and revises their estimate of the effective annual tax rate for all of 20X1 to 30%, then the provision for income taxes in the second quarter will be calculated as follows:

Income in 2nd quarter of 20X1	150
Income in 1st quarter of 20X1	100
Income for 6 months ended 6/30/X1	250
Expected effective annual tax rate	30%
Income taxes for 6-month period	75
Less: Amount reported in 1st quarter	(25)
Income tax provision in 2nd quarter	50

Another item requiring special handling on interim reports is **inventory**. The use of inventory estimation techniques is permissible for interim reports. A special problem, however, involves fluctuations in inventory values at interim dates.

Since interim periods are integral parts of the entire year, they must be computed in a manner that will result in consistent presentations with the full year. A company sometimes experiences declines in inventory values at interim dates that are **expected to be recovered** by year-end. In these cases, inventory should **not** be written down to market at the interim date. On the other hand, if a decline in value is not expected to be recovered before year-end, then the inventory should be written down.

For example, assume a client has suffered a substantial drop in the replacement cost of their inventory at the end of the first quarter, but believes these values will recover before the end of the year. The decline in market will not be reported in the first quarter. If the client is incorrect, and values do not recover by the end of the year, the decline will be reported in the fourth quarter.

On the other hand, assume a decline occurs in the first quarter, and the client **does not believe prices will recover** by year-end. They will write down the inventory to market in the first quarter. If the client is incorrect, and values recover in the third quarter of the year, the increase in market will have to be reported in the third quarter to offset the decline reported in the first quarter. Any increase in value in the third quarter that exceeds the decline reported in the first quarter is ignored, since inventory is not valued at market when it is higher than cost.

To Summarize:

- Property taxes, bonuses, depreciation – allocate to all quarters
- Inventory losses – in that quarter
- Major expenses - in that quarter, unless benefit future quarters then allocate.
- **D**iscontinued operations – in that quarter
- **Income tax expense** is estimated each quarter using the rate expected for the entire year.

SEC Reporting Requirements under Regulation S-K

Quarterly report (Form 10-Q) provides quarterly information similar to that in the 10-K but in less detail. Quarterly financial statements are **reviewed** by public accountants. The company files three Form 10-Qs every year and the Form 10-K contains the quarterly results for the fourth quarter. The Form 10-Q must include the following financial statements.

- An interim balance sheet as of the end of the most recent fiscal quarter, and a balance sheet as of the end of the preceding fiscal year. It will include only major captions and items representing less than 10% of total assets that have not changed by more than 25% may be combined with other items.
- Interim statements of income for (1) the most recent fiscal quarter, (2) for the period between the end of the preceding fiscal year and the end of the most recent fiscal quarter, and (3) for the corresponding periods of the preceding fiscal year. It will also include only major captions. Items representing less than 15% of average net income for the 3 most recent fiscal years that have not changed by more than 20% when compared to the corresponding preceding fiscal period's statement of income may be combined with other items.
- Interim statements of cash flows for (1) the period between the end of the preceding fiscal year and the end of the most recent fiscal quarter, and for (2) the corresponding period of the preceding fiscal year. The statement is abbreviated and reports a single figure for net cash flows from operating activities and only reports individual changes from investing and financing activities if they exceed 10% of average net cash flows from operating activities for the preceding 3 years.
- The statement of changes in equity may also be presented.

Disclosures are limited to those needed to avoid the financial information being presented from being misleading. Information that was included with the most recent annual financial statements that have not changed significantly may be omitted.

Form 10-Qs are due **40 days** after the end of the fiscal quarter for accelerated and large accelerated filers (**45 days** for all other registrants including non-accelerated filers and small reporting companies)

Lecture 16.06 – Segment Reporting

Publicly held companies (not non-public or not-for-profit) are required to report certain key information about significant segments of their business, referred to as **reportable segments**. The definition of "segment" is based on a concept known as the **management approach**, in which a segment represents any group of activities with revenues and expenses that is regularly evaluated by management as a single unit.

According to ASC 280, a segment is a component of a public entity that has three characteristics:

- It is involved in business activities that may result in earning revenues and incurring expenses, whether external or internal.
  - External activities involve transactions with other entities.
  - Internal activities involve transactions with other components of the same public entity.
- Its performance is evaluated by management for the purposes of resource allocation.
- Financial information identifiable to the component is available.

Different segments can be in the same line of operations, as long as management evaluates them separately for internal purposes. Segments may be identified, for example, by:

- *Activity*, such as manufacturing components making up one segment and distribution centers, another.
- *Product*, such as those components distributing heavy equipment making up one segment and those distributing software making up another.
- *Customers*, such as those components making sales domestically making up one segment and those selling internationally making up another.

There are three different ways to identify a reportable segment. A segment is reportable if it contributes at least **10% of the total for all segments** of one or more of the following:

- Revenues
- Assets
- Profits

The **revenue** test is based on combined revenues of all segments, including those resulting from intersegment sales. This is the case even though consolidated revenues on the income statement will eliminate intersegment activity.

Assume the client has 4 industry segments with the following revenue information:

Segment	Sales to Unaffiliated Companies (Outside)	Intersegment Sales	Total Sales
A	20	25	45
B	150	45	195
C	35	0	35
D	95	30	125
Total	$300	$100	**$400**

Although consolidated revenue on the income statement is reported at $300, the 10% test is applied to total sales of $400, so segments with total sales of at least $40 are reportable. Segments A, B, and D are reportable, and C is not.

There is also a 75% test, discussed below, that requires additional reportable segments to be included when the total external revenue reported by segments is less than 75% of total external revenues. That criterion is met in this case—75% of $300 (the unaffiliated revenue = $225). Reportable Segments A, B and D = $265, which is at least 75%.

The 10% test applying to **profits** is the most complex. First, the calculated amount for each segment represents **operating income** only (sales reduced by cost of sales and selling, general, and administrative expenses). Furthermore, expenses incurred at the overall corporate level (such as the salaries of the company's top officers) are excluded from the computations. Common costs, however, must be included and allocated among the various segments, using an appropriate technique (always identified in exam questions).

Assume that the company had total sales of $1,000, of which $300 occurred in Segment C. Segment C had operating expenses of $90. The company as a whole had $200 of common expenses, and allocates common costs based on sales. The operating profit of Segment C is computed as follows:

Sales	300
Operating expenses	90
Income before common costs	210
Common costs – 200 × (300 / 1,000)	60
Operating profit	$150

All segments having **operating profits** are combined, and all segments having operating losses are combined. The **10% test** is applied to the **higher** of the combined profits or combined losses. In performing this test, absolute values are considered. This means it does not matter if the larger total is the total of the segments with profits or losses. Ten percent of the number represented by the larger total is the threshold. In addition, it does not matter if the segment earned a profit or incurred a loss. If the amount of component's profit or loss is at least equal to the threshold amount, it is a reportable segment.

Let's assume the four industry segments of a business have the following operating income figures:

Segment	Operating Profit (Loss)
A	1,850
B	(190)
C	150
D	(310)

The combined operating profits are $1,850 + $150 = $2,000, and the combined operating losses are $190 + $310 = $500. Since $2,000 is higher, the 10% test requires a segment to have $200 or higher net profit or loss, so that segments A and D are the reportable segments.

The 10% test applied to **assets** includes identifiable assets only, not goodwill. There are no special complications and this is rarely tested.

In addition to reporting significant segments based on the management approach, a public company should also report data for **foreign operations** (geographic areas) if such operations contributed at least 10% of total revenues or total identifiable assets. Reporting of revenues should separately identify sales to unaffiliated customers and intersegment sales.

Finally, a company should report revenues from **major customers**, referring to those that individually provided at least 10% of consolidated revenues.

There must be enough segments separately reported so that at least *75% of unaffiliated revenues (to outsiders)* is shown by reportable segments. If the 75% test is not satisfied, additional segments must be designated as reportable (even if don't meet the three tests) until the test is satisfied.

- Don't exceed 10 reported segments; combine the smaller segments. There is a practical limit to the number of segments reported (ie, reporting too many segments may make information needlessly detailed).
- Report aggregate information for all nonkey segments.
- Not required to disclose allocated costs and expenses of reportable segments.
- An enterprise may consider *aggregating two or more* operating segments if they have similar economic characteristics and if the segments are similar in each of the following areas:
  - Nature of products and services
  - Production process
  - Type of customers
  - Methods used to distribute their products or services
  - Nature of regulatory environment

Disclosure – An enterprise must disclose the following general information:

- General information, including how reportable segments are identified and the types of products and services from which each reportable segment derives its revenues.
- Certain info about the basis of measurement for reported segment profit or loss and segment assets.
  - Internal and external revenues

- Interest income and expense
- Depreciation, depletion, and amortization expense and other significant noncash items
- Unusual items
- Equity in net income of equity method investees

- Income tax reconciliations of the segment amounts to the enterprise amount, including revenues, profit or loss, and assets
- Interim period information
- Enterprise-wide disclosures
    - External product and service revenue
    - Geographic area revenue including both domestic and foreign revenue.
    - Geographic area Long-lived assets.
    - Information about major customers (> 10% revenue).

Reportable Segment ≥ 10%

a. **Operations in Different Industries** (test #1,2,3) → Meet any of 3 tests, disclose ALL 3

b. **Foreign Operations** (Geographic areas) (test #1 & 3) → Meet any 1, disclose ALL 3

c. **Major Customer or Export Sales** (test #1) → Meet, disclose ONLY 1

Three Tests

1) **Revenue** = If segment's revenues ≥ 10% of Company's total revenue (includes intercompany/intersegment sales & transfers)

2) **Profit/Loss** = If segment's P/L ≥ 10% of Combined operating Profit/Loss of all segments that had a Profit/Loss.
    - Includes allocated common costs
    - Excludes Corporate level expenses
        - Interest
        - Income taxes
        - Gain/loss from discotinued ops

3) **Segments asset test** = If segments assets ≥ 10% of Company's identifiable assets

75% Test

There must be enough segments separately reported so that at least *75% of unaffiliated revenues (To outsiders)* is shown by reportable segments. If the 75% test is not satisfied, additional segments must be designated as reportable (even if don't meet the 3 tests) until the test is satisfied. NOTE: In the first example, 75% of 300 (the unaffiliated revenue = $225.) Reportable Segments A, B and D = $265, which is at least $225, so the 75% rule is met.

UWorld | ROGER CPA Review

YOUR WORLD OF LEARNING

FAR 17 - Accounting Changes & Error Corrections

FAR 17 – Accounting Changes & Error Corrections

Table of Contents

Accounting Changes & Error Corrections

Lecture 17.01 – Accounting Changes: Principle & Estimate

ASC 250 defines an accounting change as a change in accounting principle, a change in estimate, or a change in the reporting entity. The correction of an error in previous financial statements (F/S) is not an accounting change.

The **three types** of accounting changes are:

1. Change in accounting principle
2. Change in accounting estimate
3. Change in reporting entity

ASC 250 is the result of a broader effort to improve the comparability of cross-border financial reporting by working with the *International Accounting Standard Board (IASB)* toward developing a single set of high-quality accounting standards.

1 - Change in Accounting Principle (Retrospective approach)

A change in accounting principle is:

- A change from one generally accepted principle to another one that is also generally accepted when there are two or more acceptable alternative accounting treatments.
- A change to a generally accepted principle when the one previous in use is no longer acceptable.
- A change in the method of applying an accounting principle.

An entity may only change an accounting principle if either the change is required as a result of an authoritative pronouncement or the entity can justify the change in that it is preferable. In many cases, authoritative pronouncements that require a change in accounting principles provide transition guidance indicating how the change is to be implemented. When provided, those guidelines are required to be followed.

A change in accounting principles, assuming no transition guidance is provided, is accounted for by applying the new principle **retrospectively**. This is accomplished as follows:

- The cumulative effect of the change on periods prior to the earliest period presented is reflected in the carrying values of assets and liabilities as of the beginning of the earliest period presented.
- An offsetting adjustment, if necessary, is generally made to the opening balance of retained earnings but may be to another component of equity or net assets, as appropriate.
- F/S for each period presented will reflect application of the new accounting principle.

To account for the change in accounting principle under ASC 250:
The F/S for all years impacted should be **retrospectively restated.** A retrospective application is the application of a different accounting principle to previously issued F/S, as if that principle had always been used. This is done as of the **beginning of the first period presented**.

1. F/S for each individual prior period presented are adjusted to reflect the **period-specific effects** of applying the new accounting principle.

2. An offsetting adjustment is made to the opening balance of retained earnings for that period (the beginning of the first period presented).

Note that this change in treatment removes the accounting change from the Income Statement and moves it to the Statement of Retained Earnings.

Change from GAAP to GAAP

- Change in the valuation method for inventory (FIFO, etc.)
- Change to or from the full-cost method in the extractive industry
- Changes in construction accounting (ex: completed contract to percentage of completion).
    - A change in depreciation method is considered not distinguishable from a change in estimate and is treated as a change in estimate and accounted for on a *prospective basis*. It is called *a change in accounting principle inseparable from a change in accounting estimate.*

Only the **direct effects** of the change are recognized. An example of a direct effect is an adjustment to an inventory balance due to a change in inventory valuation method. Related changes, such as the effect on deferred taxes or impairment adjustment are also considered direct effects and must be recognized.

Indirect effects are any changes to current or future cash flows that result from making a change in accounting principle. An example of an indirect effect is a change in a profit sharing or royalty payment based on revenue or net income. Any indirect effects of the change are reported in the period in which the accounting change is made.

If it is impracticable to determine the cumulative effect to any of the prior periods, the new accounting principle is applied as if the change was made **prospectively** at the earliest date practicable.

Footnote disclosures to the F/S are required for a change in accounting principle. They include:

- The nature and reason for the change, and explanation as to why the new method is preferable
- The method of applying the change
- A description of the prior period information that is retrospectively adjusted
- The effect of the change on income from continuing operations, net income, and any other affected financial statement line item, and any affected per share amounts for the current period and all periods adjusted retrospectively
- The cumulative effect of the change on retained earnings or other components of equity or net assets as of the earliest period presented
- If retrospective application is impracticable, the reason, and a description of how the change was reported
- A description of the indirect effects of the change, including amounts recognized in the current period, and related per share amounts
- Unless impracticable, the amounts of indirect effect of the change and the per share amounts for each prior period presented

For example, showing both methods, assume a client operating on a calendar year used the weighted average method for inventory costing through the end of 20X1, and that ending inventory at 12/31/X1 was $700. In 20X2, the client changed to the FIFO method. Had FIFO always been in use, inventory at 12/31/X1 would have been $900.

Assume the change is also being made for tax purposes (if not, use Deferred tax liability instead of Current tax liability), and that the client's effective tax rate in 20X1 and 20X2 is 40%.

Since the change must be made as of the *beginning* of the fiscal year, an entry is required on 1/1/X2 to adjust inventory to the method and record the related tax effect:

Inventory	**From Weighted Average**	**To FIFO**
12/31/X1	700	
1/1/X2		900

1. To record the change to the FIFO method of inventory costing using **ASC 250**, the following journal entry would be prepared in 20X2:

Inventory	200	
Current income tax liability		80 (200 x 40%)
Retained Earnings		120 (200 x 60%)

2. To record the change to the FIFO method of inventory costing using **APBO 20 (old method)**, the following journal entry would be prepared in 20X2 (no longer GAAP):

Inventory	200	
Current income tax liability		80 (200 x 40%)
Cumulative effect on prior years of accounting change (I/S)		120 (200 x 60%)

Note that this change in treatment removes the accounting change from the Income Statement and moves it to the Statement of Retained Earnings.

The tax effect of a change in principle occurs even if the change is not made for tax purposes. The only difference is that the tax effect will be reported as a deferred income tax liability instead of current.

If it is *impracticable* to determine the cumulative effect to any of the prior periods, the new accounting principle is applied as if the change was made **prospectively** at the earliest date practicable.

If, for example, a company changed inventory valuation from FIFO *to LIFO* and it is impracticable to determine the cumulative effect of applying this change retrospectively because records of inventory purchases and sales are no longer available for all prior years, then prior periods are presented as if it had carried forward the 20X0 ending balance in inventory (measured on a FIFO basis) and begun applying the LIFO method to its inventory beginning January 1, 20X1.

2 - Change in Accounting Estimate (Prospective Method)

A **change in estimate** has the effect of adjusting the carrying value of an existing asset or liability or affecting the subsequent accounting for existing or future assets or liabilities.

- Changes in accounting estimates result from the availability of new information.
- Examples may include credit losses (ie, bad debts); inventory obsolescence; sales discounts and sales returns and allowances, service lives and salvage values of depreciable or amortizable assets, and warranty obligations.

A change in accounting estimate is not applied to prior periods but is instead applied *prospectively*. It may affect the current period only, such as the writing off of a receivable that had not previously been reserved against; or may affect the current and future periods, such as a determination that a higher percentage of credit sales than expected are proving uncollectible.

It may be difficult to distinguish between a change in accounting principle and a change in accounting estimate, such as a change in the **method for depreciating or amortizing an asset**. Such a change is a change in the method of applying a generally accepted accounting principle, indicating it is a change in accounting principle. It is also recognition of the fact that the estimate of the pattern of benefits to be derived from the asset has changed. When *a change in accounting principle is inseparable from a change in accounting estimate*, it is accounted for as a **change in accounting estimate** (**Prospectively**).

When making the change:
1. Prior periods are NOT adjusted.
2. Current year, use the New Basis (new number of years, new percentages, etc.) and future periods if the change affects both. (called Prospective)

Note: If the accounting change is inseparable from a change in principle, treat as a change in estimate.
Disclose – the impact of the change on the current accounting period.

Since estimates, by their nature, are not exact figures, it can be expected that changes in estimate will occur on a continuous basis. As a result, no special reporting is needed: the new estimate is simply used from the **date of revision** onward. In the case of allowance accounts, the amount is simply adjusted with the other side of the entry being reported in continuing operations. For example, if the allowance for credit losses is revised, an entry to adjust the allowance will be offset by a change to the credit loss expense account. There are no special disclosures required.

Lecture 17.02 – Accounting Changes: Entity & Error

3 - Change in Reporting Entity – (Retrospective Adjustment)

A **change in reporting entity** results in F/S that are essentially those of a different reporting entity, consisting primarily of:

- Presenting consolidated F/S in place of individual F/S for each entity.
- Changing the specific subsidiaries making up groups for which consolidated F/S are prepared.
- Changing the entities included in combined F/S.
- Changes between the use of the equity method of accounting and consolidation of a subsidiary without a change in the ownership percentage of stock.

A change due to a change in ownership, such as a business combination reported under the acquisition method, is not a change in reporting entity. It is a change in the actual entity and subject to different accounting and reporting guidelines.

A change in reporting entity is applied retrospectively and all prior periods' F/S that are presented are modified to reflect the new reporting entity as if that had been the reporting entity as of the beginning of the earliest period presented.

When making this change:

1. Prior periods presented are corrected.
2. Any remaining balance affects beginning Retained Earnings (net of tax), as a prior period adjustment.

The accounting for these changes requires the use of the **retrospective approach**, meaning that the presentation of all items in current and comparative previous years' F/S will be as if the combination of companies in the current F/S were always the same. Since these changes affect virtually every account on the balance sheet and income statement, computational problems on this type of change are generally beyond the scope of the exam.

Correction of an Error / Prior Period Adjustment – (Retroactive Adjustment)

Although a **correction of an error** is not considered an accounting change, it is accounted for in a manner similar to a change in accounting principle. When an error that had been made in a prior period's F/S is discovered, it is reported as an error correction and the prior F/S are restated. Although restatement is accomplished in the same manner as the recognition of a change in accounting principles, there is a distinction in the presentation and disclosure.

To report a correction of an error:

- The cumulative effect of the error on periods prior to the earliest period presented is reflected in the carrying values of assets and liabilities as of the beginning of the earliest period presented.
- An offsetting adjustment, if necessary, is generally made to the opening balance of retained earnings as a **prior period adjustment** but may be to another component of equity or net assets, as appropriate.

- F/S for each period presented will reflect the correction of the effects of the error on that period's F/S.

Examples include:

- Change from Non-GAAP to GAAP (cash to accrual, direct write-off method for credit losses to an allowance approach)
- A mathematical error
- Mistakes in applying GAAP (failure to record depreciation expense)
- Inventory Errors

Statement of Retained Earnings

Beginning RE	$xxx
+/-**Prior period adjustment** (net of tax)	**xx**
Adjusted beginning RE	xxx
+ Net income	xx
- Dividends	(xx)
Ending Retained earnings	$xxx

If it is discovered in the current year that an error has been made in accounting in a prior one, the affected accounts are adjusted as of the beginning of the current year, and reported as a prior period adjustment to beginning retained earnings. It will be reported on the Statement of Retained Earnings of the current year, unless comparative F/S are being issued, in which case the accounting of the prior years will be corrected directly.

If only some of the prior years affected are being presented, the presented ones are corrected and the remaining effects are shown on the Statement of Retained Earnings of the earliest year being presented. The approach to correction of an error is an example of the retroactive approach. Retroactive application is the restatement of previously issued F/S to correct an error.

Inventory errors correct themselves after 2 years. If, however, an inventory error is found in the first and or second year, an adjustment may be required to both the balance sheet and the income statement. For example, if ending inventory of X1 is overstated, that means COGS for X1 is understated, so NI for X1 is overstated. In X2, the beginning inventory will now be overstated (since X1 ending inventory is now X2 beginning), so X2 COGS is overstated and NI for X2 is now Understated. Therefore, RE at the end of X2 is now correct (X1 income Over and X2 is Under, so it is a wash).

Required **Disclosures** for a Correction of an Error include:

- The effect of the correction on each financial statement line item and any per-share amounts for all prior periods presented.
- The cumulative effect of the restatement on retained earnings or other components of equity as of the beginning of the earliest period presented.
- A statement that previously issued F/S have been restated.

Lecture 17.03 – Financial Statement Disclosures

F/S must be accompanied by informative disclosures which will assist in understanding and interpreting the F/S. (ASC 235)

Summary of Significant Accounting Policies

One note that is always included is the **summary of significant accounting policies** (**1st footnote**). This note identifies the choices made by the client for those items that have more than one acceptable approach under GAAP. This discusses the accounting principles selected where GAAP allows alternatives, the methods of applying those principles, as well as other information about unusual or innovative principles that the client is applying.

Examples include:

- Revenue recognition policies
- Inventory costing system (eg, FIFO, LIFO)
- Depreciation method (eg, straight-line, sum-of-the-years' digits)
- Long-term construction accounting method
- Criteria for classification of investments (eg, cash equivalents, trading securities)

There is no disclosure of methods required when only one method is acceptable, such as the use of expensing for research and development costs or the inclusion of cash in bank at the reconciled account balance. The user of the F/S only needs to be informed when there was a different approach that might have been used, so as not to be confused by differences resulting from accounting methods that vary from company to company.

Long-Term Obligations

Another disclosure that is necessary in the notes to the F/S for almost every company is for **long-term obligations**. To assist the user in identifying potential cash flow problems in future years, this disclosure must report legal commitments to cash payments in connection with:

- Notes and bonds payable (including obligations to make payments to a sinking fund)
- Leases (both operating and finance)
- Unconditional purchase obligations extending more than 1 year

All **fixed and determinable** payment obligations of the client as of the balance sheet must be disclosed, but a distinction is made between those payments due within 5 years of the balance sheet date and those not due until after that time:

- Payments due within the **next 5 years** will be identified year by year.
- All payments due after that are **aggregated** into a single amount.

For example, if a client signs an 8-year lease agreement on 7/1/X1 requiring payments of $10,000 per year beginning with the date of signing, a disclosure of the long-term obligations in the notes to the 12/31/X1 F/S would appear as follows:

20X2	$10,000
20X3	$10,000
20X4	$10,000
20X5	$10,000
20X6	$10,000
After 12/31/X6	$25,000
Total	**$75,000**

Related parties – This discusses major transactions with related parties (owners, management, employees, affiliates) and identifies all parties who control or are controlled by the entity, even if no transactions have occurred with them. Special disclosure is not required when a transaction is obviously with a related party, such as dividends (that are obviously being paid to owners), and wages (that are obviously being paid to employees in the ordinary course of business).

There is **no requirement to disclose** related-party transactions if they are either:

- Compensation arrangements with employees (including management) arising in the ordinary course of business, or
- Eliminated in the preparation of combined or consolidated F/S.

The AICPA has stated that coverage of related party transactions will be exclusive to the AUD exam as of April 1, 2017.

Special Purpose Frameworks

F/S may be prepared in conformity with a comprehensive basis of accounting other than GAAP (OCBOA), referred to as a special purpose framework. Some different methods include:

- Cash receipts and disbursements basis
- Income tax basis
- A method prescribed by a regulatory agency

In addition to normal disclosures, a description of the basis being used and its major differences from U.S. generally accepted accounting principles should be provided in the notes to the F/S.

Prospective Financial Statements

Prospective financial information is any information about the future, and is considered an Attestation engagement, discussed in the Audit exam. There are 2 types of statements:

- **Forecast** – what management **expects** to occur in the future (General or Limited use).
- **Projection** – what management believes will occur given certain **hypothetical** assumptions (Limited use only).
    - Must perform work using due professional care and in accordance with GAAP.
    - A summary of significant accounting policies and assumptions must be disclosed.
    - The services that may be performed include an Examination, Compilation or Agreed-upon-procedures report.

UWorld
YOUR WORLD OF LEARNING

ROGER
CPA Review

FAR 18 - Statement of Cash Flows

FAR 18 – Statement of Cash Flows

Table of Contents

Statement of Cash Flows

Lecture 18.01 – Statement of Cash Flows

The statement of cash flows is consistently tested on the CPA exam, usually as either several multiple-choice questions or as part of a simulation.

The statement of cash flows is a **required** financial statement whenever a company is presenting the results of operations for a year (ASC 305). The primary **purpose** is to provide detailed information about an entity's cash inflows and outflows (Sources and Uses). We are also interested in their Investing and Financing activities.

In the statement of cash flows, we measure the change in cash and **cash equivalents.** A Cash equivalent is a financial instrument that is *both*:

- Easily convertible into a known amount of cash (**highly liquid**), and
- **Original maturity of 3 months or less** from the date of purchase. Since it is so close to maturity, this presents very little risk of change in value, due to changes in interest rates. (Eg, Treasury bills, commercial paper and money market funds)

There are **three categories of activities** in the statement of cash flows:

- **Operating activities** – Inflows and outflows of cash related to the production of income from continuing operations. All transactions that are NOT investing and financing activities are considered operating.
  - Collections on sales from customers
  - Cash payments for COGS and SGA
  - Interest received and paid
  - The portion of a settlement of zero-coupon debt instruments attributable to the accreted interest related to the debt discount.
  - Dividends received
  - Acquisition and disposal of trading securities
  - Payments for income taxes
  - All other receipts/disbursements that do not stem from transactions defined as Investing or Financing activities.
- **Investing activities –** Investing in yourself or others.
  - Principal collections or **L**oans made by the entity (interest and dividends received are Operating)
  - Acquisition or disposal of available-for-sale or held-to-maturity **I**nvestments (Not Trading)
  - Acquisition or disposal of **P**roperty, plant & equipment and intangibles
  - Cash received in settlement of corporate-owned life insurance policies
  - Cash received from payments on receivables transferred in exchange for a beneficial interest in a securitized transaction

Acquisition			Disposal		
PP&E	47		Cash	15	
Cash		47	Accumulated Depreciation	37	
			Equipment		47
			Gain on sale		5

- **Financing activities** – Issuing Debt or Equity
  - Proceeds from issuing or payments for retiring Bonds (interest is Operating)
  - Issuance or Reacquisition of stock or Treasury stock
  - Borrowing or repaying a loan
  - Debt prepayment or debt extinguishment costs
  - The portion of a settlement of zero-coupon debt instruments attributable to principal
  - Dividends paid to shareholders (dividends received is Operating)

Examples of **Financing activities**

Cash	X	
Common stock		X
Preferred stock		X
APIC		X
N/P		X
Bonds Payable		X

The classification of some items is determined based on the nature of the payment and the circumstances under which it is received or paid. For example:

- Contingent consideration related to a business combination that is paid in a period after that of the business combination:
  - If made soon after the acquisition, it is an outflow for investing activities
  - If paid to settle a contingent consideration liability that was recorded at the acquisition date, it is an outflow for financing activities to the extent that it reduces the contingent liability with any excess classified as an outflow for operating activities.
- Cash proceeds from the settlement of insurance claims are classified on the basis of the nature of the loss.
- Cash payments for insurance premiums on corporate-owned policies may be reported as outflows for investing activities, for operating activities, or some combination of the two.
- Distributions from equity method investments may be treated using either of two approaches:
  - Under the **cumulative earnings approach** – distributions received are cash inflows from operating until the cumulative amount recognized equals the cumulative equity in earnings recognized by the investor. Any excess is an inflow from investing activities.
  - Under the **nature of distribution approach** – distributions are classified based on the nature of the activity that generated the distribution, with returns **on** investment classified as cash inflows from operating activities and as cash inflows from investing activities when a return **of** investment.

Cash receipts and payments that have characteristics associated with more than one classification may be subject to specific requirements identified in the FASB Accounting Standards Codification, indicating how they should be classified on the statement of cash flows. If not, cash flows related to each separately identifiable source should be classified based on the nature of the underlying cash flows. When cash flows with characteristics of more than one classification cannot be separated by source, they should be classified based on the most predominate characteristic.

Roger Company
Statement of Cash Flows
FYE December 31, 20X3

	Dr.	Cr.	Change
Cash flows from **Operating** activities			
Net cash *provided (used)* by operating activities			**$135**
Cash flows from **Investing** activities			65
Net cash provided (used) by investing activities			
Cash flows from **Financing** activities			
Net cash provided (used) by financing activities			(50)
Net Increase or Decrease in cash			$150
+ **Beginning** cash balance			+100
Ending cash balance			$250

Lecture 18.02 – Statement of Cash Flows – Direct Method

Operating Activities

There are two acceptable approaches to preparing the Operating activities section of the statement of cash flows:

- **Direct method** – (direct cash approach – preferred method) Cash sources and uses related to each account in income from continuing operations are listed individually.
  - Sales are adjusted for changes in A/R
  - COGS are adjusted for changes in both Inventory and A/P.
  - Selling expenses may be adjusted for changes in allowance for credit losses (A/R) and accumulated depreciation if they are included in selling expense.
  - Interest expense is adjusted for amortization of bond discount or premium.
  - Income tax expense is adjusted for changes in current and deferred taxes.

    Note 1: Gains and losses from sale of Investments (other than trading), and expenses not requiring the use of cash (depreciation, amortization) are not reported.

    Note 2: If selling expense includes depreciation or credit loss expense, they should be deducted since they do not involve the payment of cash.

- **Indirect method** – (reconciliation approach) Income from continuing operations is reconciled to net cash flow from operating activities by adjusting for differences related to changes in balance sheet operating accounts (such as accounts receivable, inventory, and accounts payable) and noncash income items (such as depreciation, amortization, and deferred income taxes).
  - Both are acceptable methods, but if the statement is prepared using the direct method, the indirect method MUST be presented as a supplementary schedule.

Roger Company
Income Statement
FYE December 31, 20X3

Sales	$600
COGS	(200)
Selling expense (Includes $20 credit loss expense)	(100)
General & administrative expenses	(40)
Depreciation expense	(50)
Interest expense	(30)
Equity in earnings of Investee	10
Income tax expense	(60)
Gain on sale of Avail-for-sale security (AFS)	10
Net Income	**$140**

Selected Balance Sheet account changes for the year

Increase in A/R	$80
Increase in investment under Equity method	10
Increase in Inventory	30
Increase in A/P	20
Increase in Allowance for credit losses (A/R)	20
Increase in Accumulated Depreciation	50
Decrease in Bond Discount	5
Decrease in deferred tax liability	10
Increase in Taxes Payable	40

Changes in the selected Balance Sheet accounts during the year:

Account	Debit	Credit
A/R	80	
Investment - Equity	10	
Inventory	30	
A/P		20
Allowance A/R		20
Accum. Depreciation		50
Bond Discount		5
Def. tax liability	10	
Taxes Payable		40

Direct Method (Direct Cash Approach)

Take every income statement item and convert from the accrual method of accounting back to Cash.

1. **Cash collected from Customers** (A/R increased by 80)

CASH (Plug)	520	
A/R (Change in A/R)	80	
Sales		600

2. **Payments for Purchases** (Inventory increased by 30 and A/P increased by 20)

COGS	200	
Inventory (change)	30	
A/P (change)		20
Cash (plug)		210

3. **Payments for Selling expenses** (Allowance for credit losses increased by 20; credit losses is considered a selling expense.)

Selling expenses	100	
Allowance for credit losses		20
Cash		80

4. **Payments for G&A expense**

G&A expense	40	
Cash		40

5. **Depreciation expense –** Ignore under the direct method, since there was no effect on cash.

Depreciation expense	50	
Accumulated depreciation		50

6. **Interest expense** (amortization of Discounts or Premiums changed by 5. Is covered in more detail in the Bond section).

Interest expense	30	
Amortization of discount		5
Cash		25

7. **Equity in earnings** – when an investment is accounted for under the Equity method, as the Investee earns income, the investor recognizes their share of the income on their Income Statement, even though they have not yet received cash.

Investment under the equity method	10	
Equity in earnings of Investee		10

8. **Income tax expense** (Deferred tax liability decreased by 10, taxes payable increased by 40)

Income tax expense	60	
Deferred tax liability	10	
Income taxes payable		40
Cash		30

9. **Gain on sale of investment** – Assume an Available-for-sale (AFS) investment that had an original cost of $50, was sold for $60. The cash proceeds would be considered an Investing activity, so the gain is a nonoperating gain and should not be part of Operating activities.

Cash	60	
Investment		50 (cost)
Gain on sale of AFS		10

Operating activities (direct method)	Dr.	Cr.	Change
Cash collected from customers	$520		
Payments for purchases		$210	
Payments for selling expenses		80	
Payments for G & A expenses		40	
Payments for **Interest**		25	
Payments for **Taxes**		30	
Net cash **provided** by Operating activities	$520	$385	**$135**

Note: Under the direct method, nonoperating Gains and losses are ignored. Noncash items such as depreciation, credit loss expense, amortization expense and Equity in Earnings are also ignored unless already included in Selling expense (credit loss expense in this example), then adjust.

Lecture 18.03 – Statement of Cash Flows – Indirect Method

Indirect Method (Reconciliation Approach)

When applying the indirect method, begin with **Net Income** and make 3 types of adjustments.

1. **Noncash items are adjusted** (Depreciation and Amortization expense is added back, equity in earnings is deducted)
2. **Nonoperating items** are adjusted (deduct the gain from sale of an Available-for-sale security, since this is an Investing activity)
3. Changes in the balances of **accrual related accounts are adjusted** (A/R, Inventory, A/P, Allowance for credit losses (A/R), Amortization of Discount, and taxes)

Operating activities (indirect method)	Dr.	Cr.	Change
Net income	**$140**		
Depreciation expense	50		
Equity in earnings		$10	
Gain on sale of AFS investment		10	
Increase in A/R		80	
Increase in Inventory		30	
Increase in A/P	20		
Increase in Credit losses (allowance)	20		
Amortization of Discount	5		
Decrease in Deferred tax liability		10	
Increase in tax payable	40		
Net cash ***provided*** by operating activities	$275	$140	**$135**

Indirect method:
Begin with **Net Income of $140.** The following adjustments are then made:

1. **Noncash items are adjusted**. Since Depreciation and Amortization expense did not result in the use of any cash but was deducted from Net Income, the depreciation expense is added back to Net income ($50). Income from the investment held under the Equity method was also received, but it did not result in the inflow of any cash. Since the income recorded as "equity in earnings" was included as income, but did not result in the inflow of any cash, the income is deducted from Net income ($10).(Note: under the direct method, these were ignored)
2. **Nonoperating items are adjusted.** The sale of the AFS investment resulted in a $10 gain. The cash proceeds from the sale of an investment is an Investing activity, however, the gain would have been included in the Income Statement. Since the gain was NOT from Operating activities, it must be deducted from Net Income ($10). (Note: under the direct method, this was ignored)

Cash	60	
Investment		50 (cost)
Gain on sale		10

3. **Changes in the balances of accrual related accounts are adjusted**. As we did for the direct method, all the changes in the balances must be accounted for. For example, A/R increased by $80. Therefore, the amount included for sales was $600, but the actual cash inflow was only $520, so we must take out the $80. Basically, if an **asset Increased, it is a deduction** on the indirect method, if a **Liability increased, such as A/P of $20, it is an addition** to the indirect method.

Note: Net cash provided/used by operating activities should be the **same** under either the Direct or the Indirect method. The Direct method is preferred by the FASB.

Supplementary Disclosures

- If **direct method** is used:
  - Schedule to **reconcile net income** to cash flow from operations
    - Identical to indirect method of preparing operating activities section.
  - Schedule of **noncash** investing and financing activities
    - Transactions having no effect on cash
      - Conversion of bonds to stock.
      - Purchase financed entirely by loan.

- If **indirect method** is used:
  - Cash payments for Interest and Income Taxes must be **Disclosed.**
  - Schedule of **noncash** investing and financing activities.
  - If cash or cash equivalents are restricted, the restricted amount is included in the total of cash and cash equivalents when reconciling the beginning and ending balances
  - If reported separately on the balance sheet, statement of cash flows required to identify amounts of cash, cash equivalents, and restricted cash or restricted cash equivalents, on the balance sheet as well as the line items on the balance sheet where they are located
  - The sums of the line items identified in the beginning and ending balance sheets should agree with the beginning and ending balances reported on the statement of cash flows
  - Disclosures may be in the footnotes or on the face of the statement of cash flows and may be in a narrative or a tabular form.

- **Cash flows per share** are *NOT Disclosed*

Cash to Accrual

Another topic regularly tested on the exam is the conversion of cash basis financial statements to the accrual basis. Many questions will provide the amount of cash paid for an expense, or received for a revenue item. The increases and decreases in related accrual accounts such as accounts receivable, accounts payable, prepaid expenses, or accrued expenses, are also provided. The question will require the calculation of the appropriate accrual basis amount.

A similar approach should be used to solve these questions as is used for solving questions calling for items to be reported on a statement of cash flows under the direct method, referred to as the journal entry approach. In applying this approach:

- Debit or credit cash for the amount given
- Debit or credit the related accrual accounts for the increase or decrease
- The amount required to balance the entry will be the accrual basis amount for the revenue or expense item.

Assume that a company reported cash receipts from customers of $345,000. Accounts receivable had a beginning balance of $29,000 and an ending balance of $31,000. Sales can be calculated by adding the $31,000 ending accounts receivable to cash receipts of $345,000 and deducting $29,000, resulting in sales of $347,000.

- Revenues = Cash received + increase (or - decrease) in accounts receivable
- Revenues = $345,000 + $2,000 = $347,000

Cash Receipts (given)	345,000	
Increase in A/R	2,000	
Sales (plug)		347,000

The same methodology is applied when converting cash paid for merchandise into cost of goods sold. Cash paid for merchandise is increased by the ending accounts payable balance, representing goods purchased in the current period but not yet paid for, and reduced by the beginning balance to exclude payments made in the current period for goods purchased in previous periods. The result will be goods purchased during the period, but not cost of goods sold.

Purchases will be increased by beginning inventory, representing goods purchased in previous periods that may have been sold in the current period, and decreased by ending inventory, representing goods purchased in the current period or prior periods but that is not yet sold. The result will be cost of sales.

- Cash payments for merchandise + increase (or - decrease) in accounts payable = purchases
- Purchases - increase (or + decrease) in inventory = cost of goods sold

Cost of Goods Sold (plug)	X	
Inventory (Increase in Inventory)	X	
Cash paid (given)		X
A/P (Increase in A/P)		X

Lecture 18.04 – Preparing a Statement of Cash Flows

The CPA exam will periodically require candidates to prepare a statement of cash flows. The problem will generally provide:

- A comparative balance sheet with beginning and ending balances and a column showing the increase or decrease in the individual accounts
- A summarized income statement
- Additional information about specific transactions

These problems can best be solved when a systematic approach is applied. The following approach can be used to solve any such CPA exam problem and will enable you to complete the problem easily within the time allotted and provide the maximum points.

The procedures to be followed are:

1. Set up the statement of cash flows in a 3-column format.
   - The 1st column will be for increases, the 2nd for decreases, and the 3rd for the net change to an item.
   - Leave ample space for each category of cash flows, with operating activities generally having the most transactions.
   - If the problem calls for the use of the direct method and a supplementary schedule reconciling net income to cash flows, set up the supplementary schedule using a similar 3-column format.
   - At the bottom of the statement, fill in the amounts for the net increase or decrease in cash and the beginning and ending balances of cash.

2. Set up T-accounts for each balance sheet account, other than cash.
   - The increase or decrease can be placed on the appropriate debit or credit side of the T-account.
   - Leave room above the increase or decrease to enter transactions

3. Analyze the additional information provided, preparing journal entries for the transactions. Post the debits and credits in the appropriate schedules.

   Begin with net income. Put the amount in the increase column of the operating activities section of the statement of cash flows. If the direct method is used, enter it in the increase column of the supplementary schedule. In either case indicate that it is "Net income". In addition, enter the same amount on the credit side of the retained earnings T-account.

   For all additional entries:
   - Entries to balance sheet accounts other than cash will go into the T-accounts
   - Debits or credits to cash will go into the appropriate section of the statement with debits in the increase column and credits in the decrease column.
   - Debits or credits to income statement accounts will go into the operating activities section of the statement. If the problem calls for the direct method, these entries will go into the supplementary schedule instead.

4. Any unreconciled differences in the balance sheet T-accounts should be eliminated with the offsetting debit or credit going into the appropriate section of the statement of cash flows.

5. If the problem calls for the direct method, complete the operating activities section of the statement by using the income statement and the related balance sheet accounts. In all cases, complete the statement with subtotals for each section.

Class Example

The comparative balance sheet for Ruiz Corporation at December 31, 20X1 and 20X0 is as follows:

Ruiz Corporation
Comparative Balance Sheet
December 31, 20X1 and 20X0 (000's omitted)

	20X1	**20X0**	**Increase (Decrease)**
Assets			
Cash	$ 550	$ 430	$ 120
Short-term investments	400	100	300
A/R, net	100	100	--
Inventory	540	460	80
Long-term investments	1,500	1,600	(100)
Plant assets	4,100	3,400	700
Accum Dep	(1,200)	(1,200)	--
Total Assets	$5,990	$4,890	$1,100
Liabilities & S/E			
A/P	$ 170	$ 175	$ (5)
Dividends payable	400	240	160
Short-term bank debt	325	--	325
Long-term debt	510	400	110
C/S, $10 par	700	600	100
APIC	820	700	120
R/E	3,065	2,775	290
Total Liab & S/E	$5,990	$4,890	$1,100

The following additional information is available:

- Net income was $790.
- A long-term investment was sold for $135. There were no other transactions affecting long-term investments. All investments are classified as available-for-sale securities.
- Cash dividends of $500 were declared.
- Building costing $600 and having a carrying amount of $350 was sold for $350.
- Equipment costing $110 was acquired through issuance of long-term debt.
- 10,000 shares of common stock were issued for $22 a share.

Required:

Prepare a statement of cash flows using the indirect method. Do not prepare schedules for supplementary disclosures.

Class Solution

The quickest way to solve the problem is to prepare the journal entries that must have taken place during the year to explain the changes in all the accounts, then post to the statement of cash flows those debits and credits that involve income statement accounts to the operating activities section (O), entries to cash associated with asset acquisitions and disposals in the investing activities section (I), and entries to cash associated with creditor and shareholder transactions in the financing activities section (F). In the journal entries below, each item that would be posted to the statement of cash flows is identified by section in parentheses. The entries that are most obvious are those based on the additional information.

1. To report net income of $790, the entry is:

Net income (O)	790	
Retained earnings		790

2. The long-term investment sold for $135 must have had a cost of $100 based on the decrease in the investment account, so the entry is:

Cash (I)	135	
Gain on sale of investment (O)		35
Long-term investments		100

3. The declaration of $500 in dividends is recorded as follows:

Retained earnings	500	
Dividends payable		500

4. The sale for $350 of the building that cost $600 and has a carrying value of $350 is reported as follows:

Cash (I)	350	
A/D	250	
Plant assets		600

5. The acquisition of $110 of equipment by issuing long-term debt is as follows:

Plant assets	110	
Long-term debt		110

6. The issuance of 10,000 shares of stock at $22 per share is recorded as follows:

Cash (F)	220	
CS, par $10		100
APIC		120

At this point, it is clear that more entries are needed, since the changes in several of the accounts have not yet been explained. Look at each account on the balance sheet that hasn't yet been explained by the previous six entries and prepare the most logical entry to explain the change.

7. The short-term investments increased by $300, presumably by purchase. The likely entry is:

Short-term investments	300	
Cash (I)		300

Accounts receivable didn't change, so no entry is needed.

8. Inventory increased by $80 during the year. This is probably the result of a large number of entries for purchases and sales and isn't easy to determine. Using the indirect method, however, it is only necessary to identify the net change in inventory as an adjustment to cost of sales in the operating section, so the entry is as follows:

Inventory	80	
Increase in inventory (O)		80

The decrease in long-term investments of $100 was already explained with entry (5) above.

9. Plant assets already were reduced in entry (3) by $600 and increase in entry (4) by $110, for a net decrease of $490. Since, however, plant assets ended the year $700 higher than they began, there must have been purchases totaling $1,190 that weren't identified previously, (1,190 – 600 + 110 = 700). The likely entry is:

Plant assets	1,190	
Cash (I)		1,190

10. Accumulated depreciation didn't change during the year, but entry (4) required a decrease of $250 when the building was sold, so there must have been an increase of $250 not yet identified. Clearly, this is from the normal depreciation entry:

Depreciation expense (O)	250	
A/D		250

11. The decrease in accounts payable is the result of multiple transactions and under the indirect method can simply be assumed to be an adjustment to cost of goods sold in the operating section:

Accounts payable	5	
Decrease in accounts payable (O)		5

12. Dividends payable increased $500 when dividends were declared in entry (2), but the net change for the year was an increase of only $160, so there must have been a decrease of $340 resulting from dividends payments (500 – 340 = 160):

Dividends payable	340	
Cash (F)		340

13. The only reason for short-term debt to increase by $325 is borrowing:

Cash (F)	325	
Short-term bank debt		325

The increase of $110 in long-term debt was explained by entry (4) already. The increases in common stock and APIC were explained by entry (6). The increase of $290 in retained earnings was explained by entries (1) and (2) (790 – 500 = 290).

Now that all of the accounts have been explained, all necessary entries must have been prepared. The resulting statement of cash flows is:

Ruiz Corporation
Statement of Cash Flows
December 31, 20X1

<u>DESCRIPTION</u>	<u>DEBITS</u>	<u>CREDITS</u>	<u>NET CHANGE</u>
<u>OPERATING ACTIVITIES</u>			
Net income	790 (1)		
Gain on sale of investment		35 (2)	
Increase in inventory		80 (8)	
Depreciation expense	250 (10)		
Decrease in accounts payable		5 (11)	
Net from operating activities	**1040**	**120**	**920**
<u>INVESTING ACTIVITIES</u>			
Proceeds from building sale	350 (4)		
Proceeds from sale of investment	135 (2)		
Cost of short-term investments		300 (7)	
Payments for plant asset purchase		1,190 (9)	
Net from investing activities	**485**	**1,490**	**(1,005)**
<u>FINANCING ACTIVITIES</u>			
Proceeds from stock issuance	220 (6)		
Dividends paid		340 (12)	
Proceeds of short-term bank loan	325 (13)		
Net from financing activities	**545**	**340**	**<u>205</u>**
<u>Increase in cash</u>			**120**
Cash at beginning of year			<u>430</u>
Cash at end of year			<u>550</u>

UWorld
YOUR WORLD OF LEARNING
ROGER
CPA Review

FAR 19 - Partnerships

FAR 19 – Partnerships

Table of Contents

Partnerships

Lecture 19.01 – Partnership Operations

Accounting for Partnerships

Accounting for partnerships **differs from corporations** in two significant ways:

- A partnership isn't a taxable entity (Form 1065), so no provisions are needed for current or deferred income taxes.
- The equity section does not distinguish between contributed capital and retained earnings, but instead simply identifies the capital balances of each partner.

Formation

- Assets are valued at fair value
- Liabilities assumed are recorded at their present value
- If noncash (land or equipment) contributions subject to a mortgage are made, the contributing partner's capital account is credited for the fair value of the noncash asset less the mortgage assumed by the partnership.
- Partner's capital account equals the difference between the fair value of the contributed assets less the present value of liabilities assumed.

The **allocation of equity** (**Operation of P/S**) represents virtually most of the testing on a typical CPA exam. Partners are credited for contributions and debited for distributions directly. Income is allocated in three steps:

1. Partners may be **allocated interest** on the average capital balances they maintained during the year.
2. One or more partners may be allocated a **fixed salary** for services rendered to the partnership.
3. The **remaining income** or loss is allocated based on the partnership agreement or, in the absence of agreement, equally (unless capital is the main income producer, as in the case of an investment partnership, in which case income is normally allocated based on capital balances).

For example, assume that Abe, Bea, and Cy are equal partners in the ABC Partnership, and maintained average capital balances during 20X1 of $50, $80, and $20, respectively. To encourage the partners to leave capital in the business, each partner is paid 10% on the capital balances they maintain. Bea runs the store and is provided a $20 salary on top of profits. If partnership income during 20X1 totaled $71, the allocation would be as follows:

Partner	Abe	Bea	Cy	To Allocate
Average capital	50	80	20	
Income				71
10% interest	5	8	2	-15
Subtotal				56
Salary		20		-20
Subtotal				36
Profit sharing	12	12	12	-36
Allocation	17	40	14	--

Lecture 19.02 – Admission of a New Partner

When partners admit a new partner into the partnership, there are *three different methods* that may be applied, depending on the terms under which the partner is being admitted. These are the bonus method, the goodwill method, and the exact method.

- Increase capital by contribution.
- Determine if capital equals agreement as to share. If not, then adjust using one of the following methods:
  - **Bonus method –** When the purchase price is different than the book value of the capital account purchased, bonuses are adjusted between the old and new partners' capital accounts and do not affect partnership assets.
    - Old partners share bonus based on profit and loss ratio prior to admission of new partner (**Bonus Adjust the Right – BAR**).
  - **Goodwill method** – Goodwill is recognized based upon the total value of the partnership implied by the new partner's contribution (**Goodwill Adjust the Left – GAL**).
  - **Exact method –** No goodwill or bonus is recorded. New partner capital account is equal to the assets contributed.

The **admission of a new partner** to a business often requires a reallocation of the capital balances of both the new and old partners. When this occurs, the method of reallocation that is normally used is the **bonus method (adjust the Right)**, in which the new partner transfers sufficient capital to the old partners to leave the new partner with the desired capital allocation (in rare cases, the old partners pay the bonus to the new one).

For example, assume that the DanDee partnership has two partners, Dan and Dee, who share profits on a **3:2 basis** and have capital balances of **$30 and $100**, respectively. Lyon is admitted to a **1/6 interest** in initial capital and profits in exchange for a **$50 contribution** to the partnership. The contribution may be recorded:

Cash	50	
Lyon, capital		50

At this point, however, total capital is $30 + $100 + $50 = $180, and Lyon's share of initial capital of $50 / $180 does **not** equal the 1/6 agreement. Since 1/6 of $180 is $30, not $50, Lyon will have to pay a $20 bonus to Dan and Dee, who share such bonuses as they share profits, 3 to 2. The adjustment is as follows:

Capital	Net assets	Dan	Dee	Lyon
Before admission	130	30	100	
Contribution	50			50
Subtotal	180	30	100	50
Bonus		12	8	-20
After admission	180	42	108	30

Bonus (Adjust the Right)

Cash	50	
Capital – Lyon		30
Capital – Dan		12
Capital – Dee		8

Alternatively, the partnership may use the **goodwill method (adjust the Left)**, in which goodwill is recorded and added to the old partners' capital balances (or in rare cases, that of the new partner), so that total capital is increased to achieve the desired ratio.

In this example, Lyon paid $**50 to own 1/6** of the company, so the implied value of the company is $50 × 6 = $300. Since capital equaled $180 before recording goodwill, implied goodwill is $300 - $180 = $120, and the adjustment is as follows:

Capital	**Net assets**	**Dan**	**Dee**	**Lyon**
Before admission	130	30	100	
Contribution	50			50
Subtotal	180	30	100	50
Goodwill	120	72	48	
After admission	300	102	148	50

Goodwill (Adjust the Left)

Cash	50	
Goodwill	120	
Capital - Lyon		50
Capital – Dan (120 × 60%)		72
Capital – Dee (120 × 40%)		48

Occasionally, a partnership wishes to admit a partner and provide them with a certain fraction of initial capital **without recording either a bonus or goodwill (Exact method)**. In this case, the new partner must pay an amount to the partnership that will result in the desired initial capital allocation.

For Dan and Dee to admit Lyon in this manner with a 1/6 interest in initial capital, Dan and Dee's combined accounts of $130 before admission must represent 5/6 of the new total capital. **$130 × 6 / 5 = $156**, so Lyon must contribute $156 - $130 = $26, as follows:

Capital	**Net Assets**	**Dan**	**Dee**	**Lyon**
Before admission	130	30	100	
Contribution	26			26
After admission	156	30	100	26

Notice that $26 / $156 = 1/6 already, with no need for an adjustment.

Exact method

Cash	26	
Capital - Lyon		26

Retirement & Liquidation

When a **partner retires**, several adjustments usually need to be made:

1. Assets and liabilities are adjusted to fair market value (including goodwill) to determine the value of the retiring partner's interest.
2. The retiring partner's account is reduced by the retirement payment.
3. If the retiring partner's account is reduced below $0, a bonus is paid to adjust it properly, with the other partners paying the cost based on their relative shares of profits and losses (in rare cases, the retiring partner's account is above $0 and the bonus is paid to the surviving partners).

For example, assume that the DanDeeLyon Partnership's three partners, Dan, Dee, and Lyon, share profits and losses on a 3:2:1 basis and have capital accounts of $30, $100, and $50, respectively. Lyon retires: the partnership net assets are appraised at an amount $120 higher than book value, and Lyon is then paid $80 at retirement. The computation of the capital balances of the surviving partners, Dan and Dee, is as follows:

Capital	Net Assets	Dan	Dee	Lyon
Before retirement	180	30	100	50
Appraisal	120	60	40	20
Subtotal	300	90	140	70
Payment	(80)	—	—	(80)
Subtotal	220	90	140	(10)
Bonus		(6)	(4)	10
After retirement	220	84	136	--

When a **partnership liquidates** immediately, all of the assets and liabilities are reduced to cash, with gains and losses reported on sold assets. The resulting capital balances may represent the payments to the partners, but if one partner has been reduced to a deficit (debit) balance in capital, they often do not pay the indicated amount. In such cases, they are credited with a bonus to increase capital to $0, and the amount is taken from the other partners based on their relative sharing of losses.

- Assume all non-cash assets are sold for $0.
- Allocate the loss to all the partners based on their profit/loss percentages.
- If one partner has a deficit balance, allocate the deficit balance to the remaining partners based on their new profit/loss percentages.

For example, assume that the Dan Dee Lyon Partnership, with partners sharing profits and losses **3:2:1 and with capital balances of $30 for Dan, $100 for Dee, and $50 for Lyon, liquidates**. The sale of assets results in a **$120 loss**. The payments to the partners are computed as follows:

Capital	Net assets	Dan	Dee	Lyon
Before liquidation	180	30	100	50
Realized losses	(120)	(60)	(40)	(20)
Subtotal	60	(30)	60	30
Dan's bonus		30	(20)	(10)
Payments	60	0	40	20

In an **installment liquidation**, assets may be sold in stages. In the first stage, all assets not yet sold are written off as a total loss (because of the conservatism principle and since they aren't in cash form and cannot be used to pay partners yet). Any bonus reallocation is made as noted above. The steps involved in later stages appear to be beyond the scope of CPA exam testing.

Joint & Several Liability

Partners in a partnership are said to be jointly and severally liable for the obligations of the partnership. This indicates that a third party with a legitimate claim against the partnership may be successful in an action against any of the partners or all of the partners collectively. As a result, a partner paying a disproportionate amount of the claim will have a claim against the other partners. (ASC 405)

When a reporting entity is involved in an arrangement that creates joint and several liability, that entity, referred to as an obligor, may be required to recognize a liability. A liability will be accrued if the amount of the liability is fixed as of the reporting date and the obligation is not subject to some other authoritative method of accounting.

The amount that will be recognized as a liability will be the total of:

- The amount the obligor is required to pay under the arrangement with co-obligors.
- Additional amounts that the entity expects to pay on behalf of co-obligors.

When a liability is recognized, the offset may be to:

- Cash if the obligation is debt related.
- Expense if the obligation resulted from a loss such as an unfavorable legal settlement.
- A receivable, such as from a co-obligor, subject to evaluation for impairment or collectability.
- An equity account as a result of a transaction with an entity under common control.

UWorld | ROGER CPA Review

YOUR WORLD OF LEARNING

FAR 20 - Governmental Accounting

FAR 20 – Governmental Accounting

Table of Contents

Governmental Accounting

Lecture 20.01 – Overview of Governmental Accounting

The principles of accounting by a governmental unit are different from those of a private business. A private business prepares financial statements (F/S) for use by creditors and investors in making lending and investing decisions. A government's F/S are used to provide accountability for the use of resources and to make **social and political decisions**. As a result, a unique system of financial reporting has been developed, known as **modified accrual** accounting, and is used to account for most of the activities of a typical governmental entity.

Private Business (FASB)	Government (GASB)
Revenues – Voluntary • *Earned &* • *Realizable* • **Accrual accounting** – uses the *Economic* resources measurement focus (all resources available)	**Revenues – Involuntary** • *Measurable* • *Available* • **Modified accrual** – uses the *Financial* resources measurement focus (current resources) Recognize when **Received**: income taxes, business licenses, tolls **Accrue for**: • Property taxes (60 days) • Grants ○ unrestricted – approved ○ restricted – spent
Costs • Selfish / (spend $ to make $) • Expenses, matching, depreciation expense	**Costs** • Unselfish • Expenditures, no matching
Profit motivated Revenue, expenses and Retained Earnings (Net Position)	**Budget compliance** Revenue, expenditures and changes in Fund Balance

Principles

One of the principles that is central to modified accrual accounting is the **interperiod equity concept**. In general, government activity is approved and then carried out on an annual basis.

- At the beginning of the year, the legislative body of the government approves a budget.
- The employees attempt to carry out the directives given to them over the course of that year.
- At the end of the period, the F/S are utilized to evaluate the success of the departments in meeting their directives for that period.

The interperiod equity concept keeps the focus on a single period, with the revenues of the period intended to cover the spending of that period. This is, of course, consistent with the idea of trying to maintain a **balanced budget** so that costs in the current period aren't paid by future taxpayers. At the same time, this focus on evaluating government activity one period at a time means that future periods are essentially ignored.

In modified accrual accounting, a department will usually not account for long-term assets and long-term debt since these represent those future periods. The purchase of an asset is simply treated as a current outflow of financial resources and the proceeds from a long-term borrowing a current inflow. No depreciation is recorded on assets, and interest and principal owed on long-term debt are not recorded until the periods in which they must be paid.

Modified accrual accounting is easiest to understand if the interperiod equity concept focus on one period at a time is kept in mind. In measuring the transactions under **modified accrual accounting**, the following **measurement principles** are used:

- **Revenues** – These are recognized in the period they are **available to spend**, which means collectible in the current period to pay liabilities, or within 60 days after year end. Revenues billed or collected in advance are deferred until the appropriate future period. Revenues that are not measurable are treated as available to spend once they are collected.
- **Costs** – These are recognized using the expenditure principle. Costs are recorded in the period that the obligation to pay them arises, whether this is before or after the period in which the government is actually using the assets or services. Costs are generally recorded when the related fund liability is incurred, except as it relates to unmatured interest on L/T debt, as this is only recorded when it becomes legally due.
- **Reporting** – The F/S that are prepared include a balance sheet to present the financial position and a statement of revenues, expenditures, and changes in fund balance to present the flow of financial resources during the year. There is no equivalent in modified accrual reporting to a statement of cash flows.
- **Accountability** – Budgets are typically developed at the beginning of each year, and the focus of governmental financial reporting is on determination of compliance with budgets and accountability for resources. Any fund utilizing annual budgets must prepare a reconciliation of budget to actual amounts to be presented as supplementary information in the F/S. Elected officials are accountable to their constituents.

GAAP Hierarchy for State and Local Governments

Accounting principles for state and local governments are established by the Governmental Accounting Standards Board (GASB). The codification includes a hierarchy that identifies what constitutes authoritative GAAP for all state and local government entities and the priorities with which they should be applied: that is, Category A first, then Category B. Once the authoritative sources have been exhausted, then appropriate nonauthoritative sources may be considered.

Governmental GAAP Hierarchy	
Category A	▪ GASB Statements ▪ GASB Interpretations
Category B	▪ GASB Technical Bulletins ▪ GASB Implementation Guides ▪ AICPA literature that has been cleared by the GASB
Nonauthoritative Sources	▪ GASB Concepts Statements ▪ Pronouncements and other literature of the FASB, Federal Accounting Standards Advisory Board (FASAB), International Public Sector Accounting Standards Board (IPSASB), and International Accounting Standards Board (IASB) ▪ AICPA literature not cleared by GASB ▪ Practices that are widely recognized and prevalent in state and local government ▪ Literature of other professional associations or regulatory agencies ▪ Accounting textbooks, handbooks, and articles

Annual Budgets

When annual budgets are utilized in the accounting for a government department, *expected sources and uses* may include:

- **Estimated revenues** – Revenues that are expected to be available to spend in the period.
- **Estimated other financing sources** – Expected proceeds from issuance of long-term debt and operating transfers from other government departments.
- **Appropriations** – Expenditures that are expected to occur in the period.
- **Estimated other financing uses** – Expected operating transfers to other government departments.

Budgetary entries are made at the beginning of the year and closed out (reversed) at the end of the year. These estimated accounts are used to control expenditures, account for taxes that are being levied, estimate transfers in and out, and for planning purposes. If a balanced budget has been prepared, the sum of the estimated revenues and estimated other financial sources will equal the sum of the appropriations and estimated other financial uses.

If a budgetary surplus or deficit is expected, it will be reported as an increase or decrease in the equity. The equity section of a government department using modified accrual accounting consists of **fund balances**, and the budgetary account used is **budgetary fund balance – unreserved**. It is identified as unreserved because it represents anticipated activity, but no actual legal commitments.

For example, if the legislative budget for a department using modified accrual accounting includes expected revenues of $700, bond proceeds of $200, expenditures of $500, and operating transfers to assist other departments of $250, the journal entry made at the **beginning of the fiscal year** is:

Estimated revenues	700	
Estimated other financial sources	200	
Budgetary fund balance – unreserved		150
Appropriations		500
Estimated other financial uses		250

Revenues

When using the **modified accrual approach**, revenues are recognized when they satisfy two requirements:

- **Measurable** (quantifiable in monetary terms)
- **Available to Spend** (collectible in the current period or within 60 days of yearend)
  - Uses the **Financial Resources approach,** which measures only the current financial resources available to the Government.
  - The requirement that taxes be available to spend in the current period does not mean the taxes must be collected during the current period. When goods and services are received by the government, it will issue a voucher for payment, but is allowed up to 60 days to pay the voucher. Thus, revenue expected to be collected in the **first 60 days** of the **following** fiscal **year** may be considered **available to spend** in the **current year**.

Revenues and inflows of resources include both exchange and nonexchange transactions:

- **Exchange transactions** – Goods/services/cash of *equal value* are exchanged (GAAP).
  - Purchase electricity, water from enterprise fund.
- **Nonexchange transactions (4 types)** – A transaction in which the government gives/receives without directly receiving/giving equal value in exchange.
  - **"Derived" tax revenues** – Taxes that are self-assessed on exchange transactions (eg, sales tax, income tax, motor fuel tax).
    - The right of the government to receive the taxes arises when the underlying events (income, sales) take place, so revenues are accrued based on the time period of the income or sales that are being taxed.
    - Amounts *collected in advance* of the period to which they apply, such as overpayments of taxes in one period that are being applied to the next, are reported as *deferred revenue.*
  - **"Imposed" nonexchange transactions** – Taxes and fees assessed on assets or rights rather than exchange transactions (eg, property taxes, fines, forfeits, special assessments, licenses, permits).
    - A revenue when use of money is permitted and an asset when entity has a legal claim.
    - With respect to **licenses** and **permits**, the payment is optional, since the citizen may decide not to obtain the license or permit; thus, such amounts cannot be considered available to spend until the citizen pays the bill, so these are **not accrued** in advance.

  - **Property taxes** that have been billed are usually measurable and available and are thus **accrued** in advance of collection. A receivable is recorded, but the amount to be included in revenue is not the same as the amount levied, however. An allowance for uncollectibles must be established. Amounts that are not expected to be collected soon enough to be available to spend in the current period must be deferred.

- **"Government-mandated" nonexchange transactions** – One level of government provides funds to another level of government to be used for a specific purpose (eg, federal grant).
  - Revenue when the eligibility requirements are met.
- **"Voluntary" nonexchange transactions** – Transactions entered willingly by parties (eg, unrestricted grants, voluntary donations).
  - Revenue when the eligibility requirements are met.

For example, assume a calendar-year government levies $2,200 in *property taxes* on 11/1/X1. It expects to collect as follows:

November 20X1	400
December 20X1	900
January 20X2	300
February 20X2	250
March 20X2	225
Estimated uncollectibles	125

The entry to record the **billing** is as follows:

9/1/X1	Property Taxes receivable - current	2,200	
	Revenues		**1,850**
	Deferred revenues		225
	Allowance for uncollectibles		125

The amounts expected during 20X1 and the first two months (approximately 60 days) of 20X2 are considered available to spend in 20X1.

The deferred revenues are **reclassified** at the beginning of 20X2 when they represent the current year:

1/1/X2	Deferred revenues	225	
	Revenues		225

Collections of cash are applied to receivables or reported as revenues, depending on whether or not they were previously accrued. For example, if $2,000 of previously accrued property taxes is collected, the entry is:

Cash	2,000	
Property taxes receivable - current		2,000

If licenses and permits of $500 are **received**, the entry is:

Cash	500	
Revenues		500

Uncollectible accounts could either be written off or reclassified from current to delinquent. If they are **written off**, the accounting is done in the same manner as private businesses, reducing the allowance and the related receivables. If $100 of uncollected property taxes is written off, the entry is:

Allowance for uncollectibles	100	
Property Taxes receivable - current		100

Once the due date for a tax bill has passed, any remaining receivables and allowance accounts may be identified as **delinquent accounts**.

Property Taxes receivable - delinquent	100	
Property Taxes receivable - current		100
Allowance for uncollectibles	100	
Allowance for uncollectibles - delinquent		100

Of course, the allowance account may be adjusted, based on an aging of the remaining receivables. Just as the original entry to the allowance account reduced the net revenues recorded, adjustments are made to the revenues account. For example, if the allowance is reduced by $25 based on an aging, the entry is:

Allowance for uncollectibles	25	
Revenues		25

So far, the only receivable we have discussed is for property taxes. Because of the restriction that revenues must be both measurable and available, the only common source other than property taxes that might be accrued is a **grant** from another government unit.

For example, if our client is a local government, and the state government authorizes a $900 **unrestricted grant** that will be paid to the local government later in the current year, the entry at the time the grant is *approved* is:

Receivable from state grant	900	
Revenues		900

The *collection* of the grant is straightforward:

Cash	900	
Receivable from state grant		900

If the state grant is **restricted**, then it is not considered available until the local government has acted in accordance with the restriction. For example, if the $900 state grant is paid to the local entity immediately, but stipulates that the money must be spent on the purchase of new equipment, the receipt of the money (assuming no prior accrual occurred) is recorded as follows:

Cash	900	
Deferred revenues		900

When $600 of the money is *spent* on appropriate equipment, an expenditure of $600 is reported and a simultaneous entry is made to show that this portion of the grant is now available:

Deferred revenues	600	
Revenues		600

If the remainder of the grant money is not spent, it may have to be returned to the state government:

Deferred revenues	300	
Cash		300

The proceeds from the issuance of Long-term debt is recorded in the governmental fund as an "other financing source," not as a revenue.

Cash	1,000	
Other Financing Source		1,000

Expenditures

Under modified accrual accounting, costs are reported in accordance with the expenditure principle, which means that the focus is on the outflow of financial resources to pay for the good or service rather than on the benefits resulting from the cost. Thus, there is no parallel to the matching principle, and no attempt to amortize costs that benefit multiple periods.

Because of the importance of adhering to budgets in the governmental process, the initial entry in connection with the acquisition of an asset or service is made when the **order is placed** with the vendor. An open order is known as an **encumbrance** and can be considered a form of estimated expenditure. Unlike an appropriation, however, this represents an actual legal commitment, and requires that a portion of the fund balance be reserved.

For example, if an **order to purchase supplies is placed**, and the governmental entity estimates that the invoice for the supplies will be $900 when received, the following entry is made:

Encumbrances	900	
Reserved for Encumbrances		900

When an **order has been filled**, two entries need to be made. The first is to cancel the encumbrance, since it is no longer an open order. This just involves reversing the entry made when the order was placed:

Reserved for Encumbrances	900	
Encumbrances		900

The actual invoice from the vendor is also recorded. Keep in mind that it might not be for the exact same amount as was estimated in the encumbrance. If the supplies ordered earlier are billed to the government department for $890, the entry to record the approval for payment is:

Expenditures	890	
Vouchers payable		890

The actual **payment** of the voucher later on is recorded as follows:

Vouchers payable	890	
Cash		890

Notice that the purchase of the supplies is recorded as an expenditure, even though the supplies may not have been used yet. This is known as the **purchases** method. It contrasts with the approach used by private businesses to record supplies as expenses only once they are used, known as the **consumption** method.

To avoid exceeding budgetary limits placed on the department, the sum of the expenditures recorded to date and the open encumbrances should not exceed the appropriations. For example, if appropriations for supplies were recorded in the initial budgetary entry for $1,500, and expenditures to date are $890, open encumbrances for additional orders should not exceed $610. If it appears the budget for the year will be exceeded, the department should usually request a supplementary appropriation or other modification to the legislative budget.

Keep in mind that purchases of fixed assets are recorded as expenditures at the time of delivery of the assets to the government. Also note that the government may bypass the recording of encumbrances for repetitive expenditures, such as **salaries and wages** of employees. Note: At the end of any reporting period, the remaining balance of funds that are available for use for a city would be = Appropriations – Encumbrances – Expenditures = funds available.

Expenditures may be *categorized* in detail in several different ways:

- **Function or Program** – The category identifies the purpose or objectives of the expenditure. Examples are highways and streets, health and welfare, education, general government, **public safety**, disaster relief, and defense. Program includes drug addiction, education, and elderly. (**WHY - Purpose**)
- **Organizational Unit (department)** – This category groups expenditures based on the government's organizational structure. Examples include **police and fire departments**, city clerk, personnel department, parks, and recreational departments. These can be combined to form a Function category, such as public safety.
- **Activity** – This category classifies expenditures by activity which allows the ability to measure economy and efficiency of operations (eg, **police protection**).
- **Character** – The category identifies the fiscal period that the benefits are expected. Examples are *debt service-past* (matured interest and principal), *current services-present* (salaries and supplies), and *capital outlay-future* (police car and construction expenditures) (**WHEN**).
- **Object** – This category identifies the types of items purchased or services obtained. Examples are personnel services, salaries, rent, utilities, depreciation, and supplies. (**WHAT - Type**)

- The statement of Revenues, Expenditures and changes in Fund balance generally reports expenditures by function within character classifications. Budgets often report expenditures by object class.
- Function must be presented in either statement or footnotes.

Closing Entries

At the end of the fiscal year, several closing entries are required under modified accrual accounting. One is to close the entry that was made at the beginning of the year to record the budget.

For example, if the legislative budget included expected revenues of $700, bond proceeds of $200, expenditures of $500, and operating transfers to assist other departments of $250, the journal entry made at the **beginning of the fiscal year** would have been:

Estimated revenues	700	
Estimated other financial sources	200	
Budgetary fund balance – unreserved		150
Appropriations		500
Estimated other financial uses		250

At the **end of the year**, the closing entry is:

Budgetary fund balance – unreserved	150	
Appropriations	500	
Estimated other financial uses	250	
Estimated revenues		700
Estimated other financial sources		200

This is simply a reversal of the opening entry and is unaffected by the actual revenues and costs during the year.

The **second closing entry** that is needed is comparable to private businesses, and involves the *nominal accounts* created during the year for inflows and outflows related to revenues, other financing sources, expenditures, and other financing uses.

For example, if revenues recorded during the year totaled $710, other financial sources $190, expenditures $490, and other financial uses $230, the **closing entry at the end of the year** is:

Revenues	710	
Other financial sources	190	
Fund balance – unreserved		180
Expenditures		490
Encumbrances (for outstanding purchase orders)		X
Other financial uses		230

Notice that the excess of inflows over outflows of $180 is closed into fund balance – unreserved, which is the modified accrual accounting equivalent to retained earnings (or retained earnings – unappropriated) of a private business.

A third closing entry is needed for **open encumbrances**, that is, orders that were placed during the year but not fulfilled as of the end of the year. Since an encumbrance represents a legal commitment to purchase, it reduces the unreserved fund balance.

For example, assume that, during the year, orders totaling $500 were placed, and $470 of those were fulfilled, with the remaining $30 still open at year-end. As a result, there is a debit balance of $30 in Encumbrances and a credit balance of $30 in Reserved for encumbrances prior to the closing entries. The closing entry needed at year-end is:

Fund Balance – unreserved	30	
Encumbrances		30

The unreserved fund balance is reduced because of the commitment, and a separate fund balance – Reserved for Encumbrances now identifies the outstanding orders on the balance sheet. This can also be accomplished in the previous closing entry as the X above.

The fourth closing entry is needed if the government department elects to **keep track of its inventory** in the General fund. The purchase of inventory is usually recorded as an immediate expenditure (**Purchase method**).

If the **Consumption method** is used, Inventory would be debited as goods are purchased. This is used in government-wide statements. It is useful, however, for the legislative body to be aware of any remaining inventories at yearend, since this may affect the budget for purchases in later years.

For example, assume that the department purchased $300 of supplies during their first year of operations, but didn't use all of them, having an inventory of $80 at the close of the fiscal year.

To account for the outstanding inventory without affecting the unreserved fund balance, the following entry is made:

Inventory of supplies	80	
Reserved for inventories		80

In subsequent years, the inventory and related reserve account are adjusted up or down to account for changes in the inventory level. So, if the inventory of supplies at the end of the **second** year of operations is only $50, the closing entry to account for the decrease from the previous year is:

Reserved for inventories	30	
Inventory of supplies		30

It may be useful to summarize the net effect on fund balances of the various closing entries. Let's repeat all the closing entries discussed in this section (keeping in mind that the numbers used were arbitrarily selected). The starred items representing accounts whose entire balance is being eliminated as a result of the entry.

The closing of the **budgetary accounts**:

Budgetary fund balance – unreserved *	150	
Appropriations *	500	
Estimated other financial uses *	250	
Estimated revenues *		700
Estimated other financial sources *		200

The closing of the **nominal accounts:**

Revenues *	710	
Other financial sources *	190	
Fund balance – unreserved *		180
Expenditures *		490
Encumbrances (for outstanding po's)		X
Other financial uses *		230

The closing of the **encumbrance accounts:**

Fund Balance – unreserved	30	
Encumbrances*		30

The **adjustment to ending inventory:**

Inventory of supplies	80	
Reserved for inventories		80

If this represents the first year of operations for the specific government department, **the equity (fund balance) section** of the balance sheet will report the following amounts:

Fund balance – Unreserved	150
Fund balance – Reserved for encumbrances	30
Fund balance – Reserved for inventories	80

Lecture 20.02 – Fund Types

Government activities are not all accounted for using the modified accrual method. Some activities closely resemble the activities of private businesses, and use accrual accounting. A **self-balancing set of accounts**, known as a **fund**, is established for each category of activity.

Three Categories of Funds

There are 3 broad categories of funds and these contain **11 fund types**:

- **Governmental Funds** – Generally have a budgetary focus and the main emphasis of reporting is the sources, uses and balances of *current financial resources*. These are for activities that are primarily funded by taxation or other mandatory payments and are virtually unique to government. **Modified accrual** accounting is used.
- **Proprietary Funds** – Generally have an operations orientation and the main emphasis of reporting is determining income, financial position, changes in financial position, and cash flows using the economic resources approach. These are for activities that are primarily funded by voluntary payments for goods and services by users, and that resemble businesses. **Accrual accounting** is used, in a virtually identical fashion to private businesses.
- **Fiduciary Funds** – Generally are oriented toward the accounting for assets and the main emphasis of reporting is net position and changes to net position using the economic resources approach. These are for activities that most closely resemble not-for-profit organizations, including trusts and agency activities. The trust and custodial funds use **Accrual accounting**.

Five Governmental Funds

- **General** – This fund accounts for and reports any activity or function by the government unit that is not being accounted for in another fund, such as general operations, public safety, public works, culture and recreation. Revenue sources include income, sales and property taxes, fees, fines, licenses, permits and grants. Unassigned fund balance.
- **Special Revenue** – These funds are used to account for and report specific revenues from *earmarked* sources that are restricted or committed to be used to finance designated activities other than Capital Projects and Debt Service. An example is a gas tax that finances repairs and maintenance of the roads. Revenue sources include fees, grants, specific taxes and other earmarked revenue sources. Restricted or committed fund balance.
- **Capital Projects** – These funds account for major acquisition or construction activities of capital assets, other than those financed by proprietary or trust funds. This fund accounts for and reports the financial resources that are restricted, committed or assigned for these types of capital outlay. An example is the construction of a city hall, convention center or a county courthouse. Revenue sources include special tax revenues, proceeds from bonds, transfers or capital grants.
- **Debt Service** – This fund is responsible for accumulating and making interest and principal payments on the tax-supported debts of the governmental funds. The DSF accounts for and reports the resources that are restricted, committed or assigned for this long-term debt purpose. The expenditures may also Include premiums on issuance of bonds. Revenue sources include portions of property taxes and transfers.

- **Permanent** – These funds account for and report assets whose principal is restricted and may not be spent (nonexpendable fund) but must be invested permanently (the income is, however, spendable/expendable—endowment fund). Investments are reported at their fair values, with a few minor exceptions as per GASB 72. Revenue sources are usually from the investment earnings of the trust.

A government unit must have one general fund, but can establish as many special revenue, capital projects, and permanent funds as needed to account for the various activities that fit these categories. A debt service fund is only needed if the entity issues general obligation debts.

Two Proprietary Funds

- **Internal Service** – These funds render services or provide goods to other funds within the government entity, charging the other funds directly for those services. An example is a maintenance dept, IT dept, janitorial dept or a motor pool. Revenue sources include billings for services, grants and interest earnings.
- **Enterprise** – These funds account for activities financed by voluntary payments for goods and services rendered to the payers. Often a user fee is paid. Examples include city-operated water utilities, airports, transit systems, public hospitals, public universities, public housing, lotteries or post offices. Revenue sources include charges for services, interest and investment income, shared revenues (property or gas tax) and transfers in.

A government will establish as many enterprise and internal service funds as needed to account for activities that fit these descriptions. Although it is acceptable for these funds to receive some tax money, the majority of revenue must be earned from sales of goods or services.

Four Fiduciary Funds

- **Pension trust** (and other employee benefits) – These account for government employee pensions and other post-retirement benefits for which the government is trustee. 2 RSI schedules are required: Funding progress & employer contributions.
- **Investment trust** – These account for pooled resources that are being invested on behalf of multiple government entities for which this specific government entity is trustee.
- **Private purpose trust** – These account for resources that are being held for the benefit of private persons or organizations or other governments. Examples include a fund to hold cash for unclaimed tax refunds or escheat property as well as a scholarship fund. Could be expendable or nonexpendable.
- **Custodial** – These account for collected amounts that must be transferred to other funds or outsiders. An odd characteristic of custodial funds (formerly referred to as *agency funds*) is that all of the assets held belong to others (held in a custodial capacity), so assets always equal liabilities, and the custodial fund has no equity section at all. Examples include special assessments and the property tax assessor.
    - Special assessment (streetlights, sidewalk)
        - Government obligated – capital projects or debt service fund
        - Government NOT obligated –Custodial fund

Fiduciary funds account for resources held by a government in a trustee or custodial capacity for other entities.

- All **trust funds** make use of the **economic resources measurement focus** and the **accrual** basis of accounting in the same way as proprietary funds.
- **Custodial funds**, however, are a bit atypical in that they only report assets and liabilities. Accordingly, custodial funds do not report equity and do not utilize measurement focus but do employ the **accrual** basis of accounting to recognize assets and liabilities.

Summary

The **modified accrual** funds are (**PD**-**C**onsents-to-**S**moking **G**rass):

- **P**ermanent
- **D**ebt service
- **C**apital projects
- **S**pecial revenue
- **G**eneral

The **accrual** funds are (**I-PIPE-C**onstantly):

- **I**nternal service
- **P**ension trust
- **I**nvestment trust
- **P**rivate-purpose trust
- **E**nterprise
- **C**ustodial

Lecture 20.03 – General Purpose Financial Statements

Financial Reporting

A Comprehensive Annual Financial Report (CAFR) of a governmental entity consists of three sections:

- Introductory
- Financial
- Statistical

The introductory section will include a transmittal letter and the statistical section will include financial, economic, and demographic information. The focus of the accounting, however, is the financial section, which consists of five components:

1. Management discussion & analysis (MD&A)
2. Government-wide F/S
3. Fund F/S
4. Notes to the F/S
5. Required supplementary information (RSI) other than MD&A

1 - Management Discussion & Analysis (MD&A)

The first section of the financial report is a discussion by management of the significant activities of the government as a whole during the reporting period and for the future. It also provides an overview of the government's financial activities. MD&A is considered to be Required Supplementary Information (RSI). Items to be included are:

- **Comparison with prior year** – A brief discussion of the F/S with an analysis of amounts that changed considerably from the preceding year.
- **Overall F/S** – Condensed information from the government-wide F/S to follow with discussion of overall results.
- **Individual fund statements** – Key account information from the individual fund statements to follow with analysis of individually significant accounts.
- **Variance analysis** – Discussion of major differences between the original and final budgets for the year and actual results for the year.
- **Long-term activities** – Discussion of significant capital asset and long-term debt activity for the year, and the condition of infrastructure assets.
- **Expected events** – Descriptions of known facts, decisions, and conditions that may have a significant effect on future financial position and results of operations.

2 - Government-Wide Financial Statements

The financial statement presentation in the second section of the financial report consists of two F/S for the overall government entity:

- Statement of Net Position
- Statement of Activities

The government-wide F/S are prepared on the **economic resources measurement focus** and **accrual** basis of accounting. All activities of the primary government are included, except for fiduciary activities, as well as discretely presented component units.

These statements are designed to provide information about **operational accountability**, which shows how effective and efficient the organization has been at using its resources, and the resources available to meet its future obligations.

2a – Statement of Net Position

The Statement of Net Position is a type of balance sheet, except that the form is:

Assets
+ Deferred *outflows* of resources
– Liabilities
– Deferred *Inflows* of resources
= Net Position

- This format is called the **Net Position Format**, which is encouraged, although a *balance sheet format* is also permitted (assets + deferred outflows of resources = liabilities + deferred inflows of resources + net position). Regardless of which format is used, however, the statement of net position will report the residual amount as the **net position**, consisting of **three components:**
  - **Net investment in capital assets** – Computed by taking the value of capital (fixed) assets, less accumulated depreciation, less the debt associated with the acquisition, construction, or improvement of the capital assets.
  - **Restricted net position –** Consists of restricted assets net of liabilities and deferred inflows of resources that are related to restricted assets.
  - **Unrestricted net position** – The residual amount.
- Terms like net assets, fund balance, or equity should not be used.
- It is preferred to present assets and liabilities in order of liquidity.

There are **four columns** on the **Statement of Net Position**:

- **Governmental activities** – Activities that are financed primarily through taxes and other nonexchange transactions.
  - This column reports the consolidated results of all **governmental and internal service** funds.
  - The presentation uses **accrual** accounting, even though the government funds are all modified accrual funds.
  - Capital assets are reported and depreciated in the asset section, and long-term debt is included in the liability section.
  - Interfund transactions within this column are eliminated, so that the internal service fund is often effectively eliminated. Interfund transactions within the enterprise and fiduciary funds are not eliminated, however, so the government as a whole is not actually consolidated.
- **Business-type activities** – Activities that are normally financed through user charges.
  - This reports the consolidated results of all the **enterprise funds**. Note that it does not include internal service funds, which were accounted for in the governmental column.

- **Accrual** accounting is used here as in the individual fund accounting.
- Interfund transactions among the various enterprise funds are eliminated, but not transactions with other fund types.

- **Total** – This column simply adds together the amounts from the two primary government columns for governmental and business-type activities. Note that fiduciary activities were not reported in either of the two previous columns, so this total doesn't actually reflect all of the net assets held by the government.
- **Component units** – Legally separate organizations for which the elected officials of a primary government are financially accountable.
  - This column reports the combined results of all the component units for which separate reporting was selected (those receiving blended treatment were already included in one of the first two columns of this statement).
  - No eliminations are made. (Components will be discussed in further detail later.)

Deferred Outflows and Deferred Inflows of Resources

When the government consumes net assets, it is considered an outflow of resources if it is applicable to the current reporting period. **Deferred outflows** of resources represent the consumption of net assets that are applicable to a future reporting period. Deferred outflows of resources are not assets but are similar in that they have a positive effect on net position.

- Prepaid rent would *not* be an example of a deferred outflow. This is because the outflow of resources, cash, is matched by the inflow of resources, prepaid rent and, as a result, net position has not decreased.
- *Grant expenditures made in advance* of the grantee meeting timing requirements on the other hand, is a deferred outflow. The outflow of resources, cash, is not matched by an inflow of resources and, as a result, net position has decreased.

Similarly, inflows of resources are acquisitions of net assets that are applicable to the current reporting period. **Deferred inflows** of resources are basically the opposite of deferred outflows of resources. They are acquisitions of net assets that are applicable to a future reporting period. Deferred inflows are not liabilities, but they are similar in that they have a negative effect on net position.

- Deferred revenue, for example, would not be an example of a deferred inflow. This is because the inflow of resources, cash, is matched by incurring an obligation to perform, a liability and, as a result, net position has not increased.
- *Grant funds received in advance* of the grantee meeting timing requirements on the other hand, is a deferred inflow. The inflow of resources, cash, is not matched by an obligation as the grant funds would have been received with the passage of time and, as a result, net position has increased.

There is still a lot of confusion as to when an item is an asset or liability and when it is a deferred outflow or deferred inflow of resources, respectively. GASB 65 was issued to provide some clarification.

Many items that result from government activities may be considered deferred outflows of resources or deferred inflows of resources, depending on which side of the transaction the governmental entity is on. Some of the items that are addressed include:

- Current and advanced debt refunding
  - Reacquisition cost in excess of carrying value is a deferred outflow.
  - Carrying value in excess of reacquisition cost is a deferred inflow.

- Nonexchange revenue transactions
  - Imposed nonexchange revenues, such as property taxes, received or accrued in advance are deferred inflows.
  - Government-mandated and voluntary nonexchange transactions paid or received before timing requirements are met are deferred outflows or deferred inflows, respectively.
- Sales of future revenues
  - Amounts paid for the rights are deferred outflows.
  - Proceeds from sale are deferred inflows.
- Sale and leaseback transactions
  - Deferred losses are deferred outflows.
  - Deferred gains are deferred inflows.
- Grants
  - Expenditures paid before timing requirements have been met are deferred outflows.
  - Amounts received before timing requirements have been met are deferred inflows.
- Qualified hedging derivatives
  - A negative fair value is a deferred outflow.
  - A positive fair value is a deferred inflow.

If deferred outflows or deferred inflows are disclosed in the aggregate, the notes to the F/S should describe the details of what is included in the net amounts.

Assets and Liabilities

Examples of items that remain as assets and liabilities include:

- Government-mandated nonexchange revenue transactions
  - Amounts transmitted before eligibility requirements are met, other than timing requirements, are deferred outflows and reported as assets.
  - Amounts received before eligibility requirements are met, other than timing requirements, are deferred inflows and reported as liabilities.
- Prepaid insurance is recognized as an asset
- Commitment fees received for a commitment to originate or purchase a loan are generally recognized as liabilities

Current Outflows and Current Inflows

GASB also describes items that are recognized as current outflows (expenditures), and current inflows (revenues):

- Debt issue costs, other than prepaid insurance costs, are recognized as an expense as incurred.
- Acquisition costs related to insurance activities are recognized as an expense as incurred.
- Loan origination fees other than points that are part of lending activities
  - Are recognized as revenue when received.
  - Are recognized as expense when incurred.
- Purchases of loans
  - Amounts paid to purchase loans are recognized as expense
  - Fees received related to the purchase of loans are recognized as revenues

2b – Statement of Activities

The Statement of Activities reports revenues and expenses similar to an income statement, on the full **accrual** basis.

- This is a consolidated statement except that interfund transactions are not eliminated, when those transactions are between governmental and business-type activities, and between the primary government and discretely presented component units.
- Expenses are reported by function.
- Revenues are also reported on the accrual basis and may be exchange revenues or nonexchange revenues.

Program revenues – Those that are directly associated with the functional expense categories—are deducted to arrive at the net expense or revenue. Program revenues include (but are not limited to):

- Charges for services
- Operating grants and contributions
- Capital grants and contributions

Grants and contributions are reported in the function to which their use is restricted.

The **net (expense) or revenue** is broken out between governmental activities, business-type activities, and component units, the same as in the Statement of Net Position.

General revenues include all taxes levied by the reporting government and other nonexchange revenues not restricted to a particular program.

After that, separate additions or deductions are made for special items, extraordinary items, and transfers (between categories).

If a government had contributions to term and permanent endowments and contributions to permanent fund principal, these would also be shown after general revenues.

Finally, the net position at the beginning and end of the year are reconciled.

Sample City
STATEMENT OF NET POSITION
December 31, 20X1

	Primary government			
	Governmental activities	Business-type activities	Total	Component units
Assets				
Cash and cash equivalents	$ 13,597,899	$ 10,279,143	$ 23,877,042	$ 303,935
Investments	27,365,221	-	27,365,221	7,428,952
Receivables (net)	12,833,132	3,609,615	16,442,747	4,042,290
Internal balances	175,000	(175,000)	-	-
Inventories	322,149	126,674	448,823	83,697
Capital assets, net of acc dep (**Infrastructure**)	170,022,760	151,388,751	321,411,511	37,744,786
Total assets	224,316,161	165,229,183	389,545,344	49,603,660
Deferred outflows				
-Grant Expenditures paid in advance of meeting timing requirements				
-Deferred *Loss* from sale/leaseback				
-Payment to acquire rights to future parking revenue				
Liabilities				
Accounts payable	6,783,310	751,430	7,534,740	1,803,332
Deferred revenue	1,435,599	-	1,435,599	38,911
Noncurrent liabilities:				
Due within one year	9,236,000	4,426,286	113,662,286	1,426,639
Due in more than one year	83,302,378	74,482,273	157,784,651	27,106,151
Total liabilities	100,757,287	79,659,989	180,417,276	30,375,033
Deferred inflows				
-Grant amounts received in advance of meeting timing requirements				
-Deferred *Gain* from Sale/leaseback				
Net Position				
Net Investment in capital assets	103,711,386	73,088,574	176,799,960	15,906,392
Restricted for:				
Capital projects	11,705,864	-	11,705,864	492,445
Debt service	3,020,708	1,451,996	4,472,704	-
Community development projects	4,811,043	-	4,811,043	-
Other purposes	3,214,302	-	3,214,302	-
Unrestricted (deficit)	(2,904,429)	11,028,624	8,124,195	2,829,790
Total net position	**$123,558,874**	**$ 85,569,194**	**$209,128,068**	**$19,228,627**

Sample City
STATEMENT OF ACTIVITIES
For the Year Ended December 31, 20X1

		Program revenues			Net (expense) revenue and changes in net Position			
					Primary government			
Functions/Programs	**Expenses**	**Charges for services**	**Operating grants and Contributions**	**Capital grants and contributions**	**Governmental activities**	**Business-type activities**	**Total**	**Component units**
Primary government								
Governmental activities:								
General government	$ 9,571,410	$ 3,146,915	$ 843,617	$ –	$ (5,580,878)	$ –	$ (5,580,878)	$ –
Public safety	34,844,749	1,198,855	1,307,693	62,300	(32,275,901)	–	(32,275,901)	–
Public works	10,128,538	850,000	–	2,252,615	(7,025,923)	–	(7,025,923)	–
Engineering services	1,299,645	704,793	–	–	(594,852)	–	(594,852)	–
Health and sanitation	6,738,672	5,612,267	575,000	–	(551,405)	–	(551,405)	–
Cemetery	735,866	212,496	–	–	(523,370)	–	(523,370)	–
Culture and recreation	11,532,350	3,995,199	2,450,000	–	(5,087,151)	–	(5,087,151)	–
Community development	2,994,389	–	–	2,580,000	(414,389)	–	(414,389)	–
Education (payment to school district)	21,893,273	–	–	–	(21,893,273)	–	(21,893,273)	–
Interest on long-term debt	6,068,121	–	–	–	(6,068,121)	–	(6,068,121)	–
Total governmental activities	105,807,013	15,720,525	5,176,310	4,894,915	(80,015,263)	–	(80,015,263)	–
Business-type activities:								
Water	3,595,733	4,159,350	–	1,159,909	–	1,723,526	1,723,526	–
Sewer	4,912,853	7,170,533	–	486,010	–	2,743,690	2,743,690	–
Parking facilities	2,796,283	1,344,087	–	–	–	(1,452,196)	(1,452,196)	–
Total business-type activities	11,304,869	12,673,970	–	1,645,919	–	3,015,020	3,015,020	–
Total primary government	$117,111,882	$28,394,495	$5,176,310	$6,540,834	(80,015,263)	3,015,020	(77,000,243)	–
Component units								
Landfill	$ 3,382,157	$ 3,857,858	$ –	$ 11,397	–	–	–	487,098
Public school system	31,186,498	705,765	3,937,083	–	–	–	–	(26,543,650)
Total component units	$ 34,568,655	$ 4,563,623	$3,937,083	$ 11,397	–	–	–	(26,056,552)
General revenues:								
Taxes:								
Property taxes, levied for general purposes					51,693,573	–	51,693,573	–
Property taxes, levied for debt service					4,726,244	–	4,726,244	–
Franchise taxes					4,055,505	–	4,055,505	–
Public service taxes					8,969,887	–	8,969,887	–
Payment from Sample City					–	–	–	21,893,273
Grants and contributions not restricted to specific programs					1,457,820	–	1,457,820	6,461,708
Investment earnings					1,958,144	601,349	2,559,493	881,763
Miscellaneous					884,907	104,925	989,832	22,464
Special item—gain on sale of park land					2,653,488	–	2,653,488	–
Transfers					501,409	(501,409)	–	–
Total general revenues, special items, and transfers					76,900,977	204,865	77,105,842	29,259,208
Change in net Position					(3,114,286)	3,219,885	105,599	3,202,656
Net Position—beginning					126,673,160	82,376,829	209,033,689	16,025,971
Net Position—ending					**$123,558,874**	**$85,596,714**	**$209,139,288**	**$19,228,627**

Lecture 20.04 – Fund Financial Statements & Governmental Funds

Overview

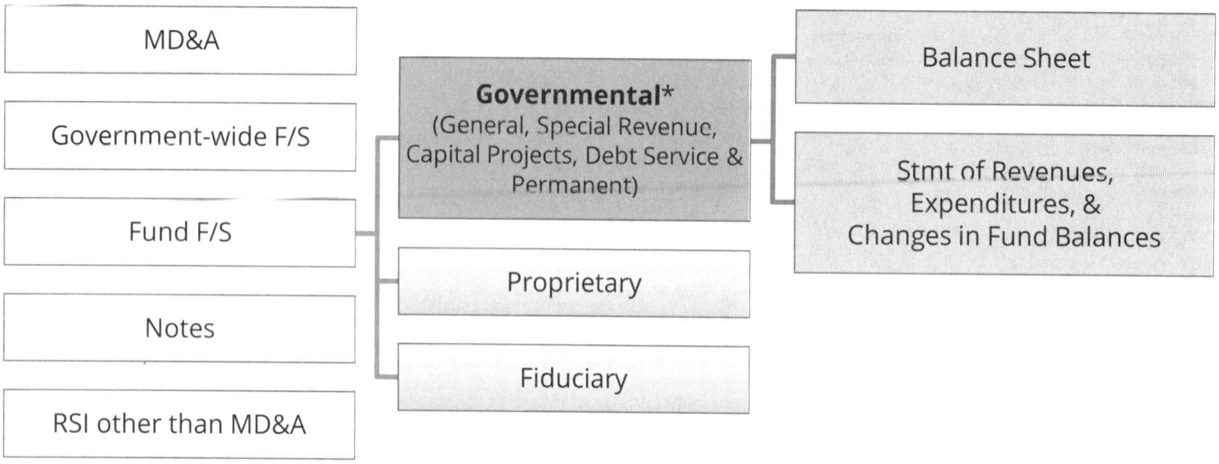

**Modified accrual basis, Current financial resources approach*

3 - Fund Financial Statements

The third section of the report includes information about individual funds and component units. In addition to government-wide statements, GASB 34, as amended by GASB 63, requires several fund F/S. Most governments use fund accounting internally and prepare the government-wide statements with worksheet adjustments from this fund accounting base.

Fund F/S use **fiscal accountability**, which shows the organization's compliance with laws and regulations affecting its spending activities.

Fund F/S are presented separately for the **governmental**, **proprietary**, and **fiduciary fund** categories. Each government has only one general fund; each other fund type may have any number of individual funds, although GASB encourages having as few funds as possible. Fixed assets and long-term debt are not reported in the fund F/S, only in the government-wide F/S.

There will be four complete sets of F/S in most cases.

- **Governmental Funds** – General fund, Special revenue, Capital projects, Debt service & Permanent
    - A **balance sheet** and **statement of revenues, expenditures, and changes in fund balance** will be prepared with columns for each major fund and a total for all minor funds.
    - This time, the reporting will be on a **modified accrual** basis, with a reconciliation of the numbers to the government-wide F/S that were prepared on an accrual basis (and which included the internal service funds).
    - There is no need to identify the specific fund type (special revenue, capital projects, etc.) for the different major funds being reported.
    - The Balance Sheet would also include deferred outflows of resources and deferred inflows of resources, like the government-wide statement of net position.

Governmental Fund F/S – Modified accrual basis, Current financial resources approach, current assets and liabilities only, no fixed assets or L/T debt

- **Balance sheet** (Current Assets + Deferred Outflows = Current Liabilities + Deferred Inflows + fund balance)
  - Fund balance (5 categories)
  - Reconcile fund balance to statement of N/A Government wide (Gov. Activ)
- **Statement of revenues, expenditures, and changes in fund balances**
  - Reconcile revenue and expenditure from modified accrual to accrual

The reconciliation of the governmental fund balance to the government-wide statement of net position includes adjustments for fixed assets, issuance of long-term debt, debt service payments, revenue recognition, accrual of revenue and expenses (modified accrual vs. accrual) and must also include the Internal Service fund. The reconciliation will appear as follows:

Alexes City
Reconciliation of Governmental Fund Balances to
Net Position of Governmental Activities
December 31, 20X1

Total governmental fund balances	$10,000,000
Long-term assets used by governmental funds	61,000,000
Internal service fund balances	1,000,000
Long-term liabilities incurred by governmental funds	(30,000,000)
Net Position of governmental activities	$42,000,000

There may be constraints on how funds can be spent. As a result, there are **five fund balance classifications** that are classified in a hierarchy that is designed to indicate the extent to which government is bound to honor those constraints. The classifications, ranging from the *most restrictive to the least restrictive*, are:

- A **nonspendable fund balance** includes funds that cannot be spent for one of two reasons:
  - They are not in spendable form, such as assets like inventories or prepaid expenses that are not expected to be converted into cash; and long-term loans or notes receivable and property held for resale, unless they are restricted, committed, or assigned.
  - They are legally or contractually required to be maintained, such as the principal balance of a permanent fund.
- A **restricted fund balance** includes funds that are restricted for a specific purpose. Restrictions may be:
  - Imposed externally, such as by creditors, grantors, contributors, or the laws or regulations of others
  - Imposed by law
- A **committed fund balance** includes funds that are required to be used for a specific purpose as a result of constraints imposed by the highest level of decision-making authority.

- An **assigned fund balance** includes funds that the government INTENDS to spend for a specific purpose but are not restricted or committed and do not require assignment by the highest level of decision-making authority.
- The **unassigned fund balance** includes all General funds that do not belong in another classification, such as not being restricted, committed or assigned to a specific purpose.

Sample City
BALANCE SHEET (GASB 54 classifications)
GOVERNMENTAL FUNDS
December 31, 20X1

	General	HUD Programs	Community redevelopment	Route 7 construction	Other governmental funds	Total governmental funds
Assets						
Cash and cash equivalents	3,418,485	$1,236,523	$ –	$ –	$ 5,606,792	$ 10,261,800
Investments	–	–	13,262,695	10,467,037	3,485,252	27,214,984
Receivables, net	3,644,561	2,953,438	353,340	11,000	10,221	6,972,560
Due from other funds	1,370,757	–	–	–	–	1,370,757
Receivables from other governments	–	119,059	–	–	1,596,038	1,715,097
Liens receivable	791,926	3,195,745	–	–	–	3,987,671
Inventories	182,821	–	–	–	–	182,821
Total assets	9,408,550	$7,504,765	$13,616,035	$10,478,037	$10,698,303	$ 51,705,690
Deferred Outflow						
-Deferred loss on sale and leaseback of building						
-Grant expenditures paid in advance of meeting timing requirements						
Liabilities and fund balances						
Liabilities						
Accounts payable	3,408,680	$129,975	$ 190,548	$1,104,632	$ 1,074,831	$ 5,908,666
Due to other funds	–	25,369	–	–	–	25,369
Payable to other governments	94,074	–	–	–	–	94,074
Deferred revenue	4,250,430	6,273,045	250,000	11,000	–	10,784,475
Total liabilities	7,753,184	6,428,389	440,548	1,115,632	1,074,831	16,812,584
Deferred inflows						
-Deferred gain on sale and leaseback of building						
-Grant amounts received in Advance of meeting timing requirements						
Fund balances						
Nonspendable	974,747					974,747
Restricted			100,000			100,000
Committed	40,292	41,034	19,314	5,792,587	1,814,122	7,707,349
Assigned		1,035,342	13,056,173	3,569,818	7,809,350	25,470,683
Unassigned	640,327					640,327
Total fund balances	1,655,366	$1,076,376	$13,175,487	$9,362,405	$9,623,472	**$34,893,106**

Amounts reported for governmental activities in the Statement of Net Position are different because:	
Capital assets used in governmental activities are not financial resources and therefore are not reported in the funds.	161,082,708
Other long-term assets are not available to pay for current-period expenditures and therefore are deferred in the funds.	9,348,876
Internal service funds are used by management to charge the costs of certain activities, such as insurance and telecommunications, to individual funds. The assets and liabilities of the internal service funds are included in governmental activities in the Statement of Net Position.	2,994,691
Long-term liabilities, including bonds payable, are not due and payable in the current period and therefore are not reported in the funds.	(84,760,507)
Net Position of governmental activities	**$123,558,874**

Sample City
STATEMENT OF REVENUES, EXPENDITURES, AND CHANGES IN FUND BALANCES
GOVERNMENTAL FUNDS
For the Year Ended December 31, 20X1

	General	HUD programs	Community redevelopment	Route 7 construction	Other governmental funds	Total governmental funds
Revenues						
Property taxes	$51,173,436	$ –	$ –	$ -	$4,680,192	$55,853,628
Franchise taxes	4,055,505	–	–	–	–	4,055,505
Public service taxes	8,969,887	–	–	–	–	8,969,887
Fees and fines	606,946	–	–	–	–	606,946
Licenses and permits	2,287,794	–	–	–	–	2,287,794
Intergovernmental	6,119,938	2,578,191	–		2,830,916	11,529,045
Charges for services	11,374,460	–	–	–	30,708	11,405,168
Investment earnings	552,325	87,106	549,489	270,161	364,330	1,823,411
Miscellaneous	881,874	66,176	–	2,939	94	951,083
Total Revenues	86,022,165	2,731,473	549,489	273,100	7,906,240	97,482,467
Expenditures						
Current						
General government	8,630,835	–	417,814	16,700	121,052	9,186,401
Public safety	33,729,623	–	–	–	–	33,729,623
Public works	4,975,775	–	–	–	3,721,542	8,697,317
Engineering services	1,299,645	–	–	–	–	1,299,645
Health and sanitation	6,070,032	–	–	–	–	6,070,032
Cemetery	706,305	–	–	–	–	706,305
Culture and recreation	11,411,685	–	–	–	–	11,411,685
Community development	–	2,954,389	–	–	–	2,954,389
Education—payment to school district	21,893,273	–	–	–	–	21,893,273
Debt service						
-Principal	–	–	–	–	3,450,000	3,450,000
-Interest and other charges	–	–	–	–	5,215,151	5,215,151
Capital outlay	–	–	2,246,671	11,281,769	3,190,209	16,718,649
Total expenditures	88,717,173	2,954,389	2,664,485	11,298,469	15,697,954	121,332,470
Excess (deficiency) of revenues over expenditures	(2,695,008)	(222,916)	(2,114,996)	(11,025,369)	(7,791,714)	(23,850,003)
Other Financing Sources (Uses)						
Proceeds of refunding *bonds*	–	–	–	–	38,045,000	38,045,000
Proceeds of long-term capital-related debt	–	–	17,529,560	–	1,300,000	18,829,560
Payment to *bond* refunding escrow agent	–	–	–	–	(37,284,144)	(37,284,144)
Transfers in	129,323	–	–	–	5,551,187	5,680,510
Transfers out	(2,163,759)	(348,046)	(2,273,187)	–	(219,076)	(5,004,068)
Total other financing sources and uses	(2,034,436)	(348,046)	15,256,373	–	7,392,967	20,266,858
Special Item						
Proceeds from sale of park land	3,476,488	–	–	–	–	3,476,488
Net change in fund balances	(1,252,956)	(570,962)	13,141,377	(11,025,369)	(398,747)	(106,657)
Fund balances-beginning	2,908,322	1,647,338	34,110	20,387,774	10,022,219	34,999,763
Fund balances—ending	$ 1,655,366	$1,076,376	$13,175,487	$9,362,405	$9,623,472	**$34,893,106**

Lecture 20.05 – Proprietary Fund Financial Statements

Overview

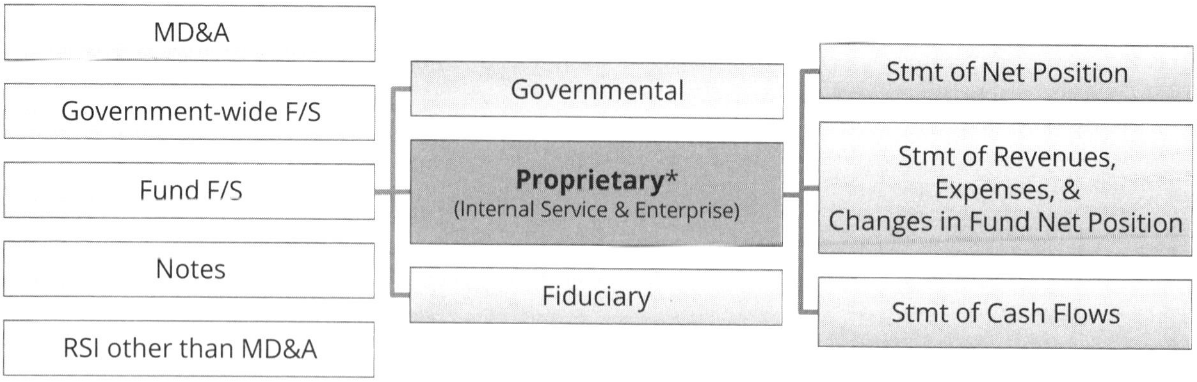

**Accrual basis, Current economic resources approach*

Proprietary Funds—Internal Service & Enterprise Fund

A statement of net position (Balance Sheet), statement of revenues, expenses, and changes in fund net position, and statement of cash flows will be prepared with columns for each major enterprise fund and a total for all minor enterprise funds. The internal service funds are reported in a separate column in these statements (note their inclusion here and *not* with the governmental funds, where they were grouped in the government-wide F/S).

The statement of **cash flows,** with a few adjustments, is similar to that of a private entity, except that there are four sections and a reconciliation (**OINCR**):

- **Operating**
  - Must be prepared under the **direct method** with a reconciliation (indirect) also presented
  - Does not include interest or dividends
- **Investing**
  - Includes interest/dividend income
  - No capital asset acquisition/disposal
  - Loans made
- **Noncapital Financing**
  - Includes interest expense on unsecured loans
  - Transfers, grants, subsidies, and property taxes received
- **Capital & Related Financing**
  - Includes interest expense on secured loans for capital assets
  - Includes financed purchases and sales of capital assets (normally investing)

Some governmental entities are involved in loan programs (eg, low-income mortgage loans or student loans). Making/collecting loans is the primary activity of such entities; thus, their loans, including interest, are reported as operating activities.

A **Reconciliation** of operating income to net cash from operating activities must be provided.

Sample City
STATEMENT OF NET POSITION
PROPRIETARY FUNDS
December 31, 20X1

	Business-type activities Enterprise funds			Governmental Activities
	Water and sewer	Parking facilities	Totals	internal service fund
Assets				
Current assets:				
Cash and cash equivalents	$8,416,653	$369,168	$8,785,821	$3,336,099
Investments	–	–	–	150,237
Receivables, net	3,564,586	3,535	3,568,121	157,804
Due from other governments	41,494	–	41,494	–
Inventories	126,674	–	126,674	139,328
Total current assets	12,149,407	372,703	12,522,110	3,783,468
Noncurrent assets:				
Restricted cash and cash equivalents	–	1,493,322	1,493,322	–
Capital assets:				
Land	813,513	3,021,637	3,835,150	–
Distribution and collection systems	39,504,183	–	39,504,183	–
Buildings and equipment	106,135,666	23,029,166	129,164,832	14,721,786
Less accumulated depreciation	-15,328,911	-5,786,503	-21,115,414	-5,781,734
Total noncurrent assets	131,124,451	21,757,622	152,882,073	8,940,052
Total assets	143,273,858	22,130,325	165,404,183	12,723,520
Deferred Outflows				
Payment to receive rights to future parking Revenue				
Liabilities				
Current liabilities:				
Accounts payable	447,427	304,003	751,430	780,570
Due to other funds	175,000	–	175,000	1,170,388
Compensated absences	112,850	8,827	121,677	237,690
Claims and judgments	–	–	–	1,687,975
Bonds, notes, and loans payable	3,944,609	360,000	4,304,609	249,306
Total current liabilities	4,679,886	672,830	5,352,716	4,125,929
Noncurrent liabilities:				
Compensated absences	451,399	35,306	486,705	–
Claims and judgments	–	–	–	5,602,900
Bonds, notes, and loans payable	54,451,549	19,544,019	73,995,568	–
Total noncurrent liabilities	54,902,948	19,579,325	74,482,273	5,602,900
Total liabilities	59,582,834	20,252,155	79,834,989	9,728,829
Deferred Inflows				
Net Position				
-Net Investment in capital assets	72,728,293	360,281	73,088,574	8,690,746
-Restricted for debt service	–	1,451,996	1,451,996	–
-Unrestricted	10,962,731	65,893	11,028,624	-5,696,055
Total Net Position	**$83,691,024**	**$1,878,170**	**$85,569,194**	**$2,994,691**

Sample City
STATEMENT OF REVENUES, EXPENSES, AND CHANGES IN FUND NET POSITION
PROPRIETARY FUNDS
For the Year Ended December 31, 20X1

	Business-type Activities—Enterprise Funds			Governmental Activities—Internal Service Funds
	Water and sewer	Parking facilities	Total	Total
Operating revenues:				
Charges for service	$11,329,883	$1,340,261	$12,670,144	$15,256,164
Miscellaneous	–	3,826	3,826	1,066,761
Total operating revenues	11,329,883	1,344,087	12,673,970	16,322,925
Operating expenses:				
Personal services	3,400,559	762,348	4,162,907	4,157,156
Contractual services	344,422	96,032	440,454	584,396
Utilities	754,107	100,726	854,833	214,812
Repairs and maintenance	747,315	64,617	811,932	1,960,490
Other supplies and expenses	498,213	17,119	515,332	234,445
Insurance claims and expenses	–	–	–	8,004,286
Depreciation	1,163,140	542,049	1,705,189	1,707,872
Total operating expenses	6,907,756	1,582,891	8,490,647	16,863,457
Operating income (loss)	4,422,127	(238,804)	4,183,323	(540,532)
Nonoperating revenues (expenses):				
Interest and investment revenue	454,793	146,556	601,349	134,733
Gain on disposal of capital assets	–	104,925	104,925	20,855
Interest expense	(1,600,830)	(1,166,546)	(2,767,376)	(41,616)
Miscellaneous expense	–	(46,846)	(46,846)	(176,003)
Total nonoperating revenues (expenses)	(1,146,037)	(961,911)	(2,107,948)	(62,031)
Income (loss) before contributions and transfers	3,276,090	(1,200,715)	2,075,375	(602,563)
Capital contributions	1,645,919	–	1,645,919	18,788
Transfers out	(290,000)	(211,409)	(501,409)	(175,033)
Change in net position	4,632,009	(1,412,124)	3,219,885	(758,808)
Total net position—beginning	79,059,015	3,290,294	82,349,309	3,753,499
Total Net Position—ending	**$83,691,024**	**$1,878,170**	**$85,569,194**	**$ 2,994,691**

Sample City
STATEMENT OF CASH FLOWS
PROPRIETARY FUNDS
For the Year Ended December 31, 20X1

	Business-type activities—Enterprise funds			Governmental activities—
	Water and sewer	Parking facilities	Total	Internal service funds
Cash flows from Operating activities				
Receipts from customers	$11,400,200	$ 1,345,292	$12,745,492	$15,326,343
Payments to suppliers	(2,725,349)	(365,137)	(3,090,486)	(2,812,238)
Payments to employees	(3,360,055)	(750,828)	(4,110,883)	(4,209,688)
Internal activity—payments to other funds	(1,296,768)	-	(1,296,768)	-
Claims paid	-	-	-	(8,482,451)
Other receipts (payments)	(2,325,483)	-	(2,325,483)	1,061,118
Net cash provided by operating activities	1,692,545	229,327	1,921,872	**883,084**
Cash flows from Noncapital Financing activities				
Operating subsidies and transfers to other funds	(290,000)	(211,409)	(501,409)	(175,033)
Cash flows from Capital and related Financing activities				
Proceeds from capital debt	4,041,322	8,660,778	12,702,100	-
Capital contributions	1,645,919	-	1,645,919	-
Purchases of capital assets	(4,194,035)	(144,716)	(4,338,751)	(400,086)
Principal paid on capital debt	(2,178,491)	(8,895,000)	(11,073,491)	(954,137)
Interest paid on capital debt	(1,479,708)	(1,166,546)	(2,646,254)	41,616
Other receipts (payments)	-	19,174	19,174	131,416
Net cash (used) by capital and related financing activities	(2,164,993)	(1,526,310)	(3,691,303)	(1,264,423)
Cash flows from Investing activities				
Proceeds from sales and maturities of investments	-	-	-	15,684
Interest and dividends	454,793	143,747	598,540	129,550
Net cash provided by investing activities	454,793	143,747	598,540	145,234
Net (decrease) in cash and cash equivalents	(307,655)	(1,364,645)	(1,672,300)	(411,138)
Balances—beginning of the year	8,724,308	3,227,135	11,951,443	3,747,237
Balances—end of the year	**$ 8,416,653**	**$ 1,862,490**	**$10,279,143**	**$ 3,336,099**
Reconciliation of operating income (loss) to net cash provided (used) by operating activities				
Operating income (loss)	$ 4,422,127	$ (238,804)	$ 4,183,323	$ (540,532)
Adjustments to reconcile operating income to net cash provided (used) by operating activities:				
Depreciation expense	1,163,140	542,049	1,705,189	1,707,872
Change in assets and liabilities:				
Receivables, net	653,264	1,205	654,469	31,941
Inventories	2,829	-	2,829	39,790
Accounts and other payables	(297,446)	(86,643)	(384,089)	475,212
Accrued expenses	(4,251,369)	(11,520)	(4,239,849)	(831,199)
Net cash provided by Operating activities	$ 1,692,545	$ 229,327	$ 1,921,872	$ **883,084**

Lecture 20.06 – Fiduciary Funds & Notes & RSI

Overview

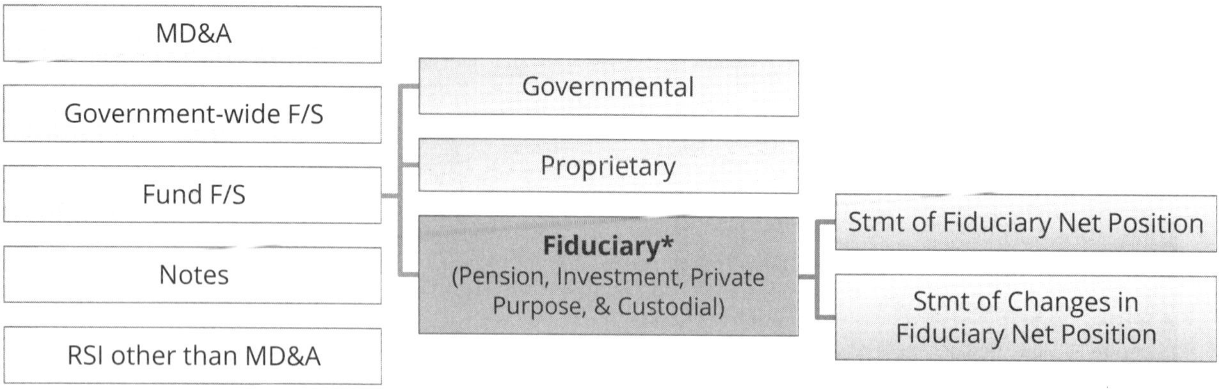

*Accrual basis, Current economic resources approach

Fiduciary Funds

There are four types of fiduciary funds:

- Pension trust
- Investment trust
- Private purpose trust
- Custodial

A **Statement of Fiduciary Net Position** and **Statement of Changes in Fiduciary Net Position** will be prepared with columns for each major fiduciary fund and a total for all minor fiduciary funds. (Major funds will be discussed later.)

Since custodial funds always have a net asset balance of zero (all assets are owed to outsiders and, therefore, have equal liabilities), they will not be included in the statement of changes in fiduciary net position, only on the Statement of Fiduciary Net Position.

The trust and custodial funds use the **accrual basis** and the **economic resources approach**.

Remember that none of these funds were included in the government-wide F/S.

Sample City
STATEMENT OF FIDUCIARY NET POSITION
FIDUCIARY FUNDS
December 31, 20X1

	Employee retirement plan	Private-purpose trusts	Custodial funds
Assets			
Cash and cash equivalents	$ 1,973	$ 1,250	$ 44,889
Receivables:			
Interest and dividends	508,475	760	–
Other receivables	6,826	–	183,161
Total receivables	515,301	760	183,161
Investments, at fair value:			
U.S. government obligations	13,056,037	80,000	–
Municipal bonds	6,528,019	–	–
Corporate bonds	16,320,047	–	–
Corporate stocks	26,112,075	–	–
Other investments	3,264,009	–	–
Total investments	65,280,187	80,000	–
Total assets	65,797,461	82,010	$228,050
Liabilities			
Accounts payable	–	1,234	–
Refunds payable and others	1,358	–	228,050
Total liabilities	1,358	1,234	$228,050
Net Position			
Held in trust for pension benefits and other purposes	$65,796,103	$80,776	

Sample City
STATEMENT OF CHANGES IN FIDUCIARY NET POSITION
FIDUCIARY FUNDS
For the Year Ended December 31, 20X1

	Employee retirement plan	Private-purpose trusts
Additions		
Contributions:		
Employer	$ 2,721,341	$ -
Plan members	1,421,233	-
Total contributions	4,142,574	-
Investment earnings:		
Net (decrease) in fair value of investments	(272,522)	-
Interest	2,460,871	4,560
Dividends	1,445,273	-
Total investment earnings	3,633,622	4,560
Less investment expense	216,428	-
Net investment earnings	3,417,194	4,560
Total additions	7,559,768	4,560
Deductions		
Benefits	2,453,047	3,800
Refunds of contributions	464,691	-
Administrative expenses	87,532	678
Total deductions	3,005,270	4,478
Change in net position	4,554,498	82
Net position—beginning of the year	61,241,605	80,694
Net Position—end of the year	$65,796,103	$80,776

4 – Notes to the Financial Statements

The fourth section of the general purpose F/S is the Notes to the F/S. These are a required part of the basic F/S and should provide information that is not displayed on the face of the F/S and is essential to their fair presentation.

The *Basic F/S* include the government-wide F/S, Fund F/S, and notes (ie, 2, 3, and 4).

Notes should distinguish whether they pertain to the primary government or its discretely presented component units.

The Notes essential to fair presentation include:

- **Summary of accounting policies**, including:
  - A description of the government-wide F/S
  - The basis of accounting applied, such as accrual for government-wide F/S and proprietary and fiduciary fund statements, and modified accrual for government fund F/S
  - Policies regarding cash and cash equivalents; capitalization and determining useful lives; and infrastructure
- **Disclosures** related to:
  - Cash
  - Investments
  - Significant contingent liabilities

- Significant effects of subsequent events
- Pensions and other postemployment benefits
- Significant violations of legal or contractual provisions
- Debt service requirements
- Leases
- Construction and other significant commitments
- Capital assets
- Long-term liabilities
- Deficit in fund balance or net position
- Interfund balances and transfers
- Donor-restricted endowments

- **Related-party transactions**
- A **description** of the **reporting entity**
- **Segment information** for enterprise funds

In addition, GASB 42 requires disclosures about *capital asset impairment* if both (a) the decline in service utility of the asset is large in magnitude, and (b) the event or change in circumstance is outside the normal life cycle of the capital asset (unexpected). If the asset is no longer to be used, it should be reported at the lower of carrying value or fair value.

5 – Required Supplementary Information (RSI) other than MD&A

The fifth and final section of the financial report includes other information required by various GASB pronouncements. The most important is a **Statement of Revenues, Expenditures, and Changes in Fund Balance – Budget & Actual**, called a **Budgetary Comparison Schedule**. This schedule is required for every governmental fund that prepared annual budgets (typically the general fund and special revenue funds, but also sometimes including others).

The **four types of RSI**, other than MD&A, that are **required** under GASB are:

- Budgetary Comparison Schedules
- Information about Infrastructure Assets (for Entities Reported Using the Modified Approach)
  - A schedule reflecting the condition of the government's infrastructure,
  - A comparison of the needed and actual expenditures to maintain the government's infrastructure.
- Claims Development Information When the Government Sponsors a Public Entity Risk Pool
- Two pension schedules:
  - Schedule of Funding Progress (for Entities Reporting Pension Trust Funds)
  - Schedule of Employer Contributions (for Entities Reporting Pension Trust Funds)

A Budgetary Comparison Schedule (BCS) may be presented as RSI or as a separate statement for the general fund and for each major special revenue fund that has a legally adopted annual budget. The BCS presents both the original and final budget as well as actual inflows, outflows, and balances.

The accounting method used for each statement is the basis that was used for the preparation of the fund's budget, even if this differs from the presentation of that fund in the F/S in the second and third sections. Thus, a general fund which was given an annual budget prepared on the cash basis will prepare its Statement of Revenues, Expenditures, and Changes in Fund Balance – Budget & Actual on a cash basis, even though it was reported on an accrual basis in the government-wide F/S and on a modified accrual basis in the fund F/S.

Sample City
STATEMENT OF REVENUES, EXPENDITURES, AND CHANGES IN FUND BALANCES—BUDGET AND ACTUAL (BCS)
GENERAL FUND
For the Year Ended December 31, 20X1

	Budgeted amounts		Actual amounts (budgetary basis)
Revenues	**Original**	**Final**	
Property taxes	$52,017,833	$51,853,018	$51,173,436
Other taxes—franchise and public service	12,841,209	12,836,024	13,025,392
Fees and fines	718,800	718,800	606,946
Licenses and permits	2,126,600	2,126,600	2,287,794
Intergovernmental	6,905,898	6,571,360	6,119,938
Charges for services	12,392,972	11,202,150	11,374,460
Interest	1,501,945	550,000	552,325
Miscellaneous	3,024,292	1,220,991	881,874
Total revenues	91,043,549	87,078,943	86,022,165
Expenditures			
Current			
General government (including contingencies and miscellaneous)	11,837,534	9,468,155	8,621,500
Public safety	33,050,966	33,983,706	33,799,709
Public works	5,215,630	5,025,848	4,993,187
Engineering services	1,296,275	1,296,990	1,296,990
Health and sanitation	5,756,250	6,174,653	6,174,653
Cemetery	724,500	724,500	706,305
Culture and recreation	11,059,140	11,368,070	11,289,146
Education—payment to school district	22,000,000	22,000,000	21,893,273
Total expenditures	90,940,295	90,041,922	88,774,763
Excess (deficiency) of revenues over expenditures	103,254	(2,962,979)	(2,752,598)
Other Financing Sources (Uses)			
Transfers in	939,525	130,000	129,323
Transfers out	(2,970,256)	(2,163,759)	(2,163,759)
Total other financing sources and uses	(2,030,731)	(2,033,759)	(2,034,436)
Special Item			
Proceeds from sale of park land	1,355,250	3,500,000	3,476,488
Net change in fund balance	(572,227)	(1,496,738)	(1,310,546)
Fund balances—beginning	3,528,750	2,742,799	2,742,799
Fund balances—ending	$ 2,956,523	$ 1,246,061	$ 1,432,253

Lecture 20.07 – Component Units, Infrastructure, & Major Funds

Overview

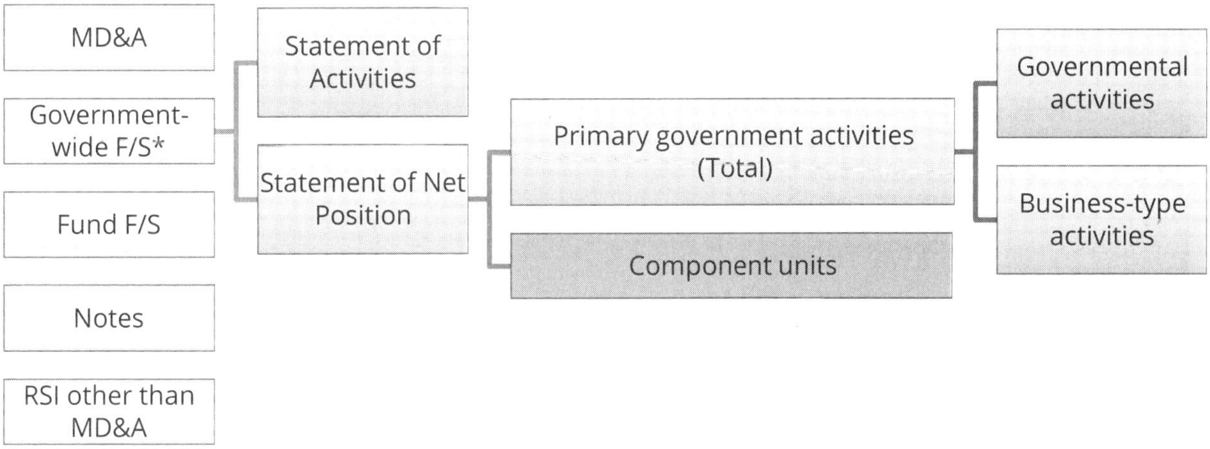

**Accrual basis*

Component Units

Defined

A component unit is an autonomous organization (eg, a school district) that operates with separate budgets and management, but is included in the financial statements of the primary government where:

- The primary government controls a **voting majority** of the autonomous organization's governing board. In the absence of a governing board, this criterion is considered to be met if the primary government performs the duties a governing board would normally perform.
- The autonomous organization is **fiscally dependent** on the primary government. In this context, dependence means the primary government:
    - Establishes and approves the organization's budget
    - Determines the organization's tax rates or amounts charged for services
    - Provides approval before the organization can issue debt
- The autonomous organization is a **financial benefit or burden** to the primary government.

Accounting

The accounting for component units may be either:

- **Discretely presented** (ie, separately stated) – Separate accounting for the activities of the component unit in separate columns is usually appropriate when:
    - Management consists of separately elected officials,
    - Budgets are developed separately from the primary government, and
    - The services provided are *not* primarily to the government itself.
- **Blended** – When the component unit serves other parts of the primary government, or is dependent on the overall government legislative body for funding or budgeting, it may be

more appropriate to account for the activities of the component unit along with the remaining funds of the government.

- Where it serves the other departments and is paid by those departments, an *internal service fund* may be appropriate.
- Where funding is received from services to outsiders, an *enterprise fund* may be appropriate.
- Blending is also required for a component unit that was incorporated as a not-for-profit corporation with the government as the only corporate member.
- Shown in the *Governmental Activities column.*

An entity that raises and holds economic resources for the direct benefit of a government (eg, a library society that raises money, which will go to the government operating the library) is required to be reported as a component unit.

If all three of the following criteria are met, **discretely present** the entity as a component unit in a separate column:

- **Direct benefit** – The funds are nearly totally all for the direct benefit of the primary government, its component units, or its constituents.
- **Majority** – The primary government or its component unit is entitled to a majority of the economic resources received or held by the separate entity.
- **Significance** – The resources are significant to that primary government.

Component Units Presentation Summary

Discrete Presentation in separate column if:
▪ Separate elected governing board
▪ Legally separate
▪ Fiscally independent – ie, authority to:
  o Determine its budget
  o Levy taxes without approval
  o Issue bonded debt without approval

Blend with other funds if:
▪ Activities cannot be separated, and it would be misleading to exclude them.
▪ Governing body is same as primary government.
  o Financial burden/benefit relationship exists, *or*
  o Primary government has operational responsibility for unit.
▪ Unit provides services almost entirely for benefit of primary government.
▪ Unit's debt is expected to be repaid by primary government.

Infrastructure

Accounting for infrastructure assets (streets, sidewalks, highways, etc.) in the governmental activities column has several complications. The **preferred approach** is to account for these assets at historical cost and **recognize depreciation**.

Several governments find the recordkeeping burdensome, however, since the ongoing expenditures for repairs, maintenance, and improvements for such assets can make it difficult to gauge total costs. It also tends to result in lives for these assets which are, in a sense, indefinite in duration.

GASB 34, as amended by GASB 63, permits governments to omit depreciation on infrastructure assets if they can demonstrate that the regular costs incurred to maintain them give them an indefinite life. This is called the **modified approach**. This approach may be used if the government:

- Uses an asset management system to manage the infrastructure and
- Documents how the assets are being preserved at a minimum level established by the government.

If these conditions are met, infrastructure assets are recorded as capital expenditures and are *not* depreciated; however, additions and improvements are still capitalized. Two schedules are included in the required supplementary information:

- A schedule reflecting the condition of the government's infrastructure
- A schedule comparing needed and actual expenditures of maintaining the infrastructure

Intangible assets that are identifiable should be recognized in the statement of net position at historical cost.

Major Funds

On the fund F/S, we report by major fund category as opposed to by fund type. A major fund is:

- General fund
- Other funds representing *both:*
  - **10% or more** of total *category* assets, liabilities, revenues or expenditures/expenses of either Governmental or Enterprise category; **and**
  - **5% or more** of total *entity* (Gov & Enterprise) assets, liabilities, revenues or expenditures/expenses.
- Any other funds that management believes are **useful** to present separately

Lecture 20.08 – Interfund Transactions

There are **four** different **types** of **cash transfers** that may take place between different funds:

- Operating transfers
- Quasi-external transactions
- Reimbursements
- Loans

Operating Transfers

Operating transfers, also called **interfund transfers** are the most common, and represent movements of cash from one fund to finance current period activities in another fund. It also includes establishing or closing out a fund. To distinguish them from ordinary revenues and expenditures/expenses, they are classified as **other changes**.

- The transferee reports the amount received as:
  - **Other financing sources** if using modified accrual accounting
  - **Other revenues** if using accrual accounting
- The transferor reports the amount paid as **other financing uses** if using modified accrual accounting and as **other expenses** if using accrual accounting. These accounts appear on the appropriate operating statements: statement of revenues, expenditures, and other changes or statement of revenues, expenses, and other changes.

If $100 is sent from the general fund to the debt service fund to help finance interest payments that must be made that year, the entry in the **general fund** is:

Other financial uses	100	
Cash		100

The entry in the **debt service fund** is:

Cash	100	
Other financial sources		100

Quasi-External Transactions

Quasi-external transactions are payments from one fund to another for services or goods that are being provided. These are reciprocal transactions, involving an earnings process, unlike the previous examples of operating and residual equity transfers, in which a transfer is made without any benefit received by the transferor.

- The transferee is receiving money that represents earned **revenue**.
- The transferor reports the payment as an:
  - **Expenditure** if it uses modified accrual accounting
  - **Expense** if it uses accrual accounting

Assume the town has a water utility enterprise fund whose customers include, along with the citizens of the town, the other departments of the government. If a bill of $300 is paid by the capital projects fund for water used in the current year, the entry in the **capital projects fund** is:

Expenditures – utilities	300	
Cash		300

The entry in the **enterprise fund** is:

Cash	300	
Revenues		300

Notice that this type of transaction could easily have taken place between unrelated entities in a normal supplier/customer relationship, and that is the reason for identifying these as quasi-external transactions.

Reimbursements

Reimbursements are repayments from one fund to another for costs paid earlier on its behalf.

- The transferee will record the receipt of money as either a settlement of a **receivable** it recorded when making the payment or as a reduction of an earlier **expenditure** or **expense** it recorded.
- The transferor records the payment of money as the settlement of a **payable** it recorded when the other fund paid costs on its behalf or as its own **expenditure** or **expense**.

Assume the general fund paid $900 for 9 government employees to attend a conference, including 4 employees of the general fund itself and 5 employees of the internal service fund. The internal service fund later reimbursed the general fund $500 for its employees.

At the time of payment for the conference, the **general fund,** if it were **not** aware it was going to later be reimbursed, would have recorded:

Expenditures – conference	900	
Cash		900

When the **internal service fund** later reimbursed the general fund, it would then have recorded:

Expenses – conference	500	
Cash		500

This would have reduced the net expenditure of the **general fund**:

Cash	500	
Expenditures – conference		500

On the other hand, if both funds knew at the time of the conference that the general fund would later be reimbursed, the entry in the **general fund** for its payment would have been:

Expenditures - conference	400	
Due from internal service fund	500	
Cash		900

At the same time, the **internal service fund** would have recorded:

Expenses – conference	500	
Due to general fund		500

The later reimbursement would settle the due to/due from accounts.

Loans

Loans are temporary transfers between funds that are to be repaid later. They are handled through interfund **receivable** and **payable** accounts.

For example, if the enterprise fund lends $400 to the special revenue fund, the entry in the **enterprise fund** is:

Due from special revenue fund	400	
Cash		400

The entry in the **special revenue fund** is:

Cash	400	
Due to enterprise fund		400

Of course, the later repayment involves both funds making the exact opposite entries from the original loan entries.

Transfers are reported on the government-wide statement of activities. For transfers to be reported, they must be between governmental activities and business-type activities. Two kinds of transfers that are reported include:

- Permanent transfers
- Recurring transfers from either governmental activities to business-type activities, or vice-versa

Permanent transfers are made once, while the recurring transfers are typically made annually. A reimbursement would not be included, but a quasi-external would.

Lecture 20.09 – GASB Concept Statements

The Governmental Accounting Concepts Statements form the GASB's conceptual framework which provides a foundation to guide the Board's development of accounting and financial reporting standards (much like FASB Concepts).

GASB Concept Statement 1 – Objectives of Financial Reporting

This concept statement **establishes the objectives** of general purpose external financial reporting by state and local governmental entities and applies to both (1) governmental-type and (2) business-type activities.

The characteristics that affect financial reporting of **governmental-type activities** are:

- **Primary** characteristics of government's structure and the services it provides:
    - The representative form of government and the separation of powers
    - The prevalence of intergovernmental revenues
    - The services provided to taxpayers
- **Control** characteristics resulting from government's structure:
    - The *budget* as an expression of public policy and financial intent and as a method of providing control
    - The use of fund accounting for control purposes
- **Other** characteristics:
    - The dissimilarities between similarly designated governments
    - The significant investment in non-revenue-producing capital assets
    - The nature of the political process

The Board has identified three groups as the **primary users** of external state and local governmental financial reports:

- The citizenry
- Legislative and oversight bodies
- Investors and creditors

Financial reports are used primarily to:

- Compare Actual financial results with the legally adopted budget
- To assist in determining Compliance with finance-related laws, rules, and regulations
- To assist in evaluating Efficiency and Effectiveness
- To assess Financial condition and results of operations

The Board believes that financial reporting plays a major role in fulfilling government's duty to:

- Be Publicly **Accountable** in a democratic society (taxpayer has a "right to know").
- Provide information to assist users in assessing **interperiod equity** (are current-year revenues sufficient to pay for current-year services or whether future taxpayers will be required to assume burdens for services previously provided).

State and local governmental financial reports should possess these basic characteristics: **understandability, reliability, relevance, timeliness, consistency, and comparability**.

The financial reporting **objectives set forth in GASB Concept Statement 1** are:

Financial reporting should assist in fulfilling government's duty to be publicly **Accountable** and should enable users to assess that accountability by:

- Providing information to determine whether current-year revenues were sufficient to pay for current-year services
- Demonstrating whether resources were obtained and used in accordance with the entity's legally adopted budget, and demonstrating compliance with other finance-related legal or contractual requirements
- Providing information to assist users in assessing the service efforts, costs, and accomplishments of the governmental entity

Financial reporting should assist users in **evaluating the operating results** of the governmental entity for the year by:

- Providing information about sources and uses of financial resources
- Providing information about how it financed its activities and met its cash requirements
- Providing information necessary to determine whether its financial position improved or deteriorated as a result of the year's operations

Financial reporting should assist users in assessing the level of services that can be provided by the governmental entity and its **ability to meet its obligations** as they become due by:

- Providing information about its financial position and condition
- Providing information about its physical and other nonfinancial resources having useful lives that extend beyond the current year
- Disclosing legal or contractual restrictions on resources and the risk of potential loss of resources

Governmental **business-type activities** (run like a private business) are also subject to the objectives stated above because they are part of the government, so they are therefore publicly **accountable**. Some business type activities are characterized by an exchange relationship involving "user charges," while others involve receiving significant operating subsidies, capital grants, or taxes from the general government.

GASB Concept Statement 2 – SEA Reporting

(amended by Concept Statement 5)

This concept statement further develops the objective, elements and characteristics of **service efforts and accomplishments** (SEA) reporting.

The objective of SEA reporting is to provide more complete information about a governmental entity's performance than can be provided by the traditional F/S and schedules to assist users in assessing the economy, efficiency, and effectiveness of services provided.

This would expand the amount and types of information being gathered and reported externally; The Board believes that including SEA measures as part of General Purpose External Financial Reporting (GPEFR) would represent a significant improvement in financial reporting practices for state and local governmental entities.

Ideally a governmental entity should:

- Establish and communicate clear, relevant goals and objectives
- Set measurable targets for accomplishment
- Develop and report indicators that measure its progress

The elements of SEA reporting include:

- Measures of service effort
- Measures of service accomplishments (output and outcome measures)
- Measures that relate service efforts to service accomplishments (efficiency and cost-outcome measures)
- Narrative or explanatory information

GASB Concept Statement 3 – Communication Methods in GPEFR That Contain Basic F/S

This Concept provides a conceptual basis for selecting communication methods to present items of information within **general purpose external financial reports** (GPEFR) that contain basic F/S.

- These alternative communication methods include recognition in:
  - Basic F/S
  - Disclosure in notes to basic F/S
  - Presentation as required supplementary information
  - Presentation as supplementary information

Each of these communication methods is defined, and criteria are developed to help the GASB or a preparer of a financial report determine the appropriate method to use to communicate an item of information.

GASB Concept Statement 4 – Seven Elements of F/S

This Concepts Statement establishes definitions for the seven elements of historically based F/S of state and local governments. Elements are the fundamental components of F/S.

The elements of a **Statement of Financial Position** are:

- **Assets** – Resources with present service capacity that the government presently controls.
- **Liabilities** – Present obligations to sacrifice resources that the government has little or no discretion to avoid.
- **A deferred outflow of resources** – A consumption of net assets by the government that is applicable to a future reporting period.
- **A deferred inflow of resources** – An acquisition of net assets by the government that is applicable to a future reporting period.
- **Net position** – The residual of all other elements presented in a statement of financial position.

The elements of the **Resource Flows Statements** are:

- An **outflow of resources** – A *consumption* of net assets by the government that is applicable to the reporting period.
- An **inflow of resources** – An *acquisition* of net assets by the government that is applicable to the reporting period.

A **Resource** in the governmental context is an item that can be drawn on to provide services to the citizenry.

GASB Concept Statement 6 – Measurement of Elements of F/S

This statement establishes two approaches for measurement used in F/S.

- **Initial amounts** are more appropriate for assets that are used in the entity's business, enabling it to provide goods and services. Initial amounts are based on transaction prices or amounts assigned to an asset when it was acquired or a liability when it was assumed.
- **Remeasured amounts**, which are more appropriate for assets that will be converted into cash, financial assets, and for liabilities when there is uncertainty regarding the amount or timing of payments, involves remeasuring an asset or liability as of the balance sheet date.

There are four measurement attributes that are used in F/S:

- *Historical Cost* – the price paid to acquire an asset or the amount received when a liability was incurred in an exchange transaction.
- *Fair value* – the price that would be received to sell an asset or paid to be relieved of a liability in an orderly transaction between market participants.
- *Replacement cost* – the amount that would be paid to obtain resources with equivalent service potential in an orderly market transaction.
- *Settlement amount* – the amount that would be realized from disposal of an asset or the amount at which a liability could be liquidated when there is no active market.

UWorld | ROGER CPA Review

YOUR WORLD OF LEARNING

FAR 21 – Not-for-Profit Accounting

FAR 21 – Not-for-Profit Accounting

Table of Contents

Not-for-profit Accounting

Lecture 21.01 – Not-for-Profit Accounting – Financial Statements

Overview

The focus of reporting for a not-for-profit organization (NPO) is on presenting basic information for the *entity as a whole*. (ASC 958) NPOs focus on providing delivery of services funded with public or private resources that generally come from contributions or fees that are not taxable. NPO accounting covers **four different groups:**

- Health care
- Colleges and universities
- Voluntary health and welfare (VHWO) (United Way, Red Cross, Greenpeace, Salvation Army)
- All others not above (fraternities, labor unions, museums, libraries, nonprofit organizations)

Accrual accounting is used and the financial statements (F/S) that must be prepared for all such organizations parallel the **three basic F/S** (balance sheet, income statement, statement of cash flows) used by private businesses. Their reporting emphasis is on disclosing the sources of resources and how they were expended. The three basic statements include:

- Statement of Financial Position
- Statement of Activities
- Statement of Cash Flows

Statement of Financial Position (B/S)

The Statement of Financial Position (B/S) reports assets, liabilities, and net assets (equity) of the NPO. Assets and liabilities may be classified or reported in order of liquidity and payment date. Assets with donor restrictions must be reported separately from those that are not restricted. The net asset section of the statement includes two accounts:

- **Net assets *without* donor restrictions** are those resources of the NPO that are available for the general use of the entity and can include assets set aside by the **board of trustees**, including a board-designated endowment fund, since a true restriction must come from an outside donor. Net assets without donor restrictions are the remainder of the net assets of an NPO after considering those that are subject to donor-imposed restrictions.
- **Net assets *with* donor restrictions** are those resources of the NPO that are subject to donor-imposed restrictions. For example, a donor may stipulate that a sum be earmarked for cancer research or for the improvement of a building, or may only be used after a prescribed period of time or upon the occurrence of an event.
    - This category also includes endowments. An **endowment fund** is an established fund of cash, securities, or other assets to provide income for the maintenance of the NPO. In this case, the

A **donor-imposed restriction** is any stipulation that specifies a use for a contributed asset that is more specific than just broad limits resulting from the nature or purpose of the NPO, or from the environment in which the NPO operates (ie, the restriction will eventually **lapse** due to **time, use** or **purpose**).

donor restriction is to protect the original donated amount (aka, the principal or corpus) from being depleted.

- The *earnings* from the endowment, however, may be either *with* or *without* restriction. That is, a portion of the fund's income/gains may be required to be reinvested and added to the principal, or the fund's income or gains may be available for operational expenditures by the NPO.

Not-for-Profit Organization
STATEMENT OF FINANCIAL POSITION
June 30, 20X1 and 20X0
(in thousands)

	20X1	20X0
Assets		
Cash and cash equivalents	$ 75	$ 460
Accounts and interest receivable	2,130	1,670
Inventories and prepaid expenses	610	1,000
Contributions receivable	3,025	2,700
Short-term investments	1,400	1,000
Assets restricted to investment in land, buildings, and equipment	5,210	4,560
Land, buildings, and equipment	61,700	63,590
Long-term investments	218,070	203,500
Total assets	$292,220	$278,480
Liabilities and net assets		
Accounts payable	$ 2,570	$ 1,900
Refundable advance		650
Grants payable	875	1,300
Notes payable		1,140
Annuity obligations	1,685	1,700
Long-term debt	5,500	6,500
Total liabilities	10,630	13,190
Net assets		
Net assets *without* donor restrictions	115,228	103,648
Net assets *with* donor restrictions	166,362	161,642
Total net assets	281,590	265,290
Total liabilities and net assets	$292,220	$278,480

NPO Statement of Financial Position (B/S) Summary

- Assets = Liabilities + Net Assets
- **Without** donor restriction
  - Unrestricted or restricted by the board of trustees
- **With** donor restriction
  - Temporary restriction that will lapse due to time, use or purpose
  - Endowment funds (permanent)

Lecture 21.02 – Not-for-Profit Accounting – Statement of Activities

The Statement of Activities (I/S & R/E) reports revenues, net assets released from restriction, and expenses. These amounts are separated into two columns on the statement: one for amounts without donor-restrictions and one for those with donor-restrictions.

- **Revenues, gains, and other support** typically include contributions from donors and investment income. They are reported in the appropriate column depending on whether the revenues have donor restrictions.
  - Property is included at FMV at the date of the gift.
  - Services are included only if they are professional services and the NPO would have otherwise paid for them.
  - Investment income reported in the With Donor Restrictions net asset column should represent only net capital gains or other income that will remain part of the permanent donor-restricted endowment.
- **Net assets released from restriction** reports only formerly donor-restricted net assets that became free of donor restrictions during the year, generally due to the *expiration of time restrictions* or the *performance of purpose restrictions*. Such amounts are reclassified from the With Donor Restrictions column to the Without Donor Restrictions column.
- **Expenses** are reported only in the Without Donor Restrictions column. The expenditure of net assets with donor restrictions has the effect of releasing the assets from restriction, and is reported as both a release, as discussed in the preceding paragraph, and an expense from the Without Donor Restrictions category. However, remember, that donor-restricted net assets designated for endowment funds generally cannot be spent. Expenses are categorized as program services, support services, or combined costs. Expenses will be discussed in further detail in another lecture.

Summary of Changes in Net Assets on Statement of Activities

	Without **Donor Restrictions**	***With*** **Donor Restrictions**
Revenues	Increase	Increase
Released assets	Increase	Decrease
Expenses	Decrease	N/A

Not-for-Profit Organization
STATEMENT OF ACTIVITIES
Year Ended June 30, 20X1
(in thousands)

	Without Donor Restrictions	With Donor Restrictions	Total
Revenues, gains, and other support:			
Contributions	$ 8,640	$ 8,390	$ 17,030
Fees	5,400		5,400
Investment return, net	6,650	18,300	24,950
Gain on sale of equipment	850		850
Other	150		150
Net assets released from restrictions:			
Satisfaction of program restrictions	11,990	(11,990)	
Satisfaction of equipment acquisition restrictions	1,500	(1,500)	
Expiration of time restrictions	1,250	(1,250)	
Appropriation from *donor endowment* and subsequent satisfaction of any related donor restrictions	7,200	(7,200)	
Total net assets released from restrictions	21,940	(21,940)	
Total revenues, gains, and other support	43,630	4,750	48,380
Expenses and losses:			
Program A	13,100		13,100
Program B	8,540		8,540
Program C	5,760		5,760
Management and general	2,420		2,420
Fundraising	2,150		2,150
Total expenses	31,970		31,970
Fire loss	80		80
Actuarial loss on annuity obligations		30	30
Total expenses and losses	32,050	30	32,080
Change in net assets	11,580	4,720	16,300
Net assets at beginning of year	103,648	161,642	265,290
Net assets at end of year	**$115,228**	**$166,362**	**$281,590**

Statement of Cash Flows

STATEMENT OF FINANCIAL POSITION

	20X1
Assets	
***	
Liabilities and net assets	
***	
Net assets	
Net assets *without* donor restrictions	115,228
Net assets *with* donor restrictions	166,362
Total net assets	281,590
Total liabilities and net assets	$292,220

Lecture 21.03 – Contribution Revenue

Many contributions received by a not-for-profit organization (NPO) are **unrestricted gifts** of cash, and are reported as revenues in the **without donor restrictions** (no DR) section of the statement of activities (ASC 958):

Cash (operating activity)	100	
Revenues (no DR)		100

It is common, however, for NPOs to **receive gifts** that are **restricted**.

For example, a hospital might receive a donation of $500 with the stipulation that it be spent on the hospital's cancer research program. This causes the donation to be included in **with donor restrictions** (DR), and is recorded as follows:

Cash (operating activity)	500	
Revenues (DR)		500

Later, when the hospital actually **spends the money** on research, that satisfies the restriction.

Two entries are needed. The first is to report the release of the restriction:

Net assets released (DR)	500	
Net assets released (no DR)		500

The second is to report the research costs:

Expenses (no DR)	500	
Cash		500

Note: The net of the increase in "net assets without donor restrictions" (no DR) and the increase in the "Expense" (decreases – no DR) has *no net effect* on net assets without donor restrictions.

Finally, a donation of cash may stipulate that only the income generated from investing the cash may be spent. The donation is reported as **net assets with donor restrictions**.

For example, assume $1,000,000 was donated to **endow** an ongoing cancer research program. The donation itself is reported as follows:

Cash (financing activity)	1,000,000	
Revenues (DR)		1,000,000

If the money earns interest income of $40,000, that money is spendable:

Cash	40,000	
Revenues (no DR)		40,000

Statement of Cash Flows

The Statement of Cash Flows is comparable to the same statement for private businesses, reporting cash flows from operating, investing, and financing activities. Either the direct or indirect method may be used.

- **Operating** activities represent most of the cash flow effects of the items reported in the **statement of activities**.
  - Inflows include revenues collected
  - Outflows include expenses paid.
  - Contributions that can be spent on operations are included as well.
- **Investing** activities represent the cash flow effects of **asset** transactions.
  - Inflows include proceeds from the sale of assets and sales of works of art.
  - Outflows include payments for asset purchases.
- **Financing** activities represent the cash flow effects of **liability** transactions.
  - Inflows include proceeds from loans.
  - Outflows include principal payments on loans.
  - Contributions that are subject to donor restrictions are included as well.
  - Financing activities includes two categories:
    - Proceeds from donor-restricted contributions
    - Other financing activities

Statement of Cash Flows Summary

- **Operating activities** – flow from statement of activities
  - Direct or indirect; if direct, indirect reconciliation **not** required, though may be presented, as shown below
  - Revenues with and without donor restrictions
  - Revenues, expenses, interest income/expense, dividend income
  - Contribution revenue is usually operating
- **Investing activities** – flow from buying and selling assets
  - Investments acquired/sold
  - PP&E acquired/disposed of
- **Financing activities** – flow from borrowings and repayments
  - 2 categories
    - Proceeds from donor-restricted contribution
    - Other financing activities
  - Donor-restricted revenue
  - Eg, money restricted for L/T purpose
    - Payment on bonds, N/P, money restricted for endowment
    - Money restricted for acquisitions of PP&E
  - Contribution for long-term purpose is financing.

Not-for-Profit Organization
STATEMENT OF CASH FLOWS
Year Ended June 30, 20X1
(in thousands)

Cash flows from operating activities:	
Cash received from service recipients	$ 5,220
Cash received from contributors	8,030
Cash collected on contributions receivable (promises to give)	2,615
Interest and dividends received	8,570
Miscellaneous receipts	150
Interest paid	(382)
Cash paid to employees and suppliers	(23,808)
Grants paid	(425)
Net cash used by operating activities	**(30)**
Cash flows from investing activities:	
Insurance proceeds from fire loss on building	250
Purchase of equipment	(1,500)
Proceeds from sale of investments	76,100
Purchase of investments	(74,900)
Net cash used by investing activities	(50)
Cash flows from financing activities:	
Proceeds from contributions restricted for:	
Investment in perpetual endowment	200
Investment in term endowment	70
Investment in land, buildings, and equipment	1,210
Investment subject to annuity trust agreements	200
	1,680
Other financing activities:	
Interest and dividends restricted for reinvestment	300
Payments of annuity obligations	(145)
Payments on notes payable	(1,140)
Payments on long-term debt	(1,000)
	(1,985)
Net cash used by financing activities	(305)
Net decrease in cash and cash equivalents	(385)
Cash and cash equivalents at beginning of year	460
Cash and cash equivalents at end of year	$ 75
Reconciliation of change in net assets to net cash used by operating activities:	
Change in net assets	$ 16,300
Adjustments to reconcile change in net assets to net cash used by operating activities:	
Depreciation	3,200
Fire loss	80
Actuarial loss on annuity obligations	30
Increase in accounts and interest receivable	(460)
Decrease in inventories and prepaid expenses	390
Increase in contributions receivable	(325)
Increase in accounts payable	670
Decrease in refundable advance	(650)
Decrease in grants payable	(425)
Contributions restricted for long-term investment	(2,740)
Interest and dividends restricted for long-term investment	(300)
Net unrealized and realized gains on long-term investments	(15,800)
Net cash used by operating activities	**$ (30)**
Supplemental data for noncash investing and financing activities:	
Gifts of equipment	$140
Gift of paid-up life insurance, cash surrender value	$80

Lecture 21.04 – Functional Expense Analysis & Disclosures

Functional Expense Analysis

In addition to the three F/S required of all NPOs, an analysis of functional expenses is required. The analysis is not an additional financial statement. Instead, it is a detailed schedule of expenses broken down by function such as program expenses and support services. It may be presented on the face of the statement of activities, as a separate statement, or as a note to the NPO's F/S. In such an analysis, the following detail is provided:

	Program Activities				Supporting Activities			
	A	**B**	**C**	**Program Subtotal**	**Mgmt & General**	**Fund-raising**	**Supporting Subtotal**	**Total Expense**
Salaries & benefits	$6,660	$3,510	$1,553	$11,723	$1,017	$ 864	$1,881	$13,604
Grants to other organizations	1,868	675	1,733	4,275				4,275
Travel & supplies	801	912	449	2,162	192	486	678	2,840
Services & prof. fees	144	1,341	540	2,025	180	351	531	2,556
Office & rent	1,044	540	405	1,989	196	90	286	2,275
Depreciation	1,296	720	513	2,529	225	126	351	2,880
Interest	154	86	61	302	24	18	42	344
Total Expenses	$11,966	$7,784	$5,253	$25,004	$1,834	$1,935	$3,769	$28,773

- **Program Activities** – (Further the mission of the organization) These are expenses that are directly related to the program. For example, a relief organization might report categories for emergency relief, community education, training, research, hospice services, etc. In the example above, Programs A, B, and C represent program services of the NPO.
- **Supporting Activities** – (Secondary to the mission) Fund-raising expenses and General and Administrative expenses are reported.
  - Management & General – marketing, tax preparation, printing annual report, business management, budgeting.
  - Fundraising – (Print & mail pledge cards, maintaining donor list, preparing and distributing fund raising materials, merchandise sent to potential contributors, salaries of fundraisers, and conducting other activities designed to solicit contributions)
  - Membership development – Soliciting for potential members and for dues, costs associated with member relations and similar activities

Statement of Activities Summary	
Public support	▪ Donated ▪ Eg, contributions, grants, bequests, pledges, special event revenues
+ **Revenues**	▪ Earned ▪ Eg, membership dues, investment income, client service revenue, fees
– **Program expenses**	▪ Furthers the mission of the organization ▪ Boat depreciation, research, community services, public health, and education
– **Support services**	▪ Secondary to the mission ▪ **Management & General** – Marketing/ tax prep/print annual report ▪ **Fundraising** – Print and mail pledge cards, maintaining donor list, merchandise sent to potential contributors, salaries of fundraisers
Excess of revenue over expenses	

Again, the analysis of functional expenses may be presented on the face of the statement of activities, as a separate statement, or as a note to the NPO's F/S. One specific type of NPO is a **voluntary health and welfare organization (VHWO)**, which provides community services financed by voluntary contributions from the general public, such as the Red Cross or Greenpeace.

Management & general expenses include the **cost of soliciting funds** other than contributions and membership dues. This includes advertising and other costs of promoting goods or services for sale to customers; costs of responding to requests for proposals for customer-sponsored contracts, or of administering such contracts. They are not considered fundraising expenses.

Disclosures

Required disclosures for NPOs include:

- Information on endowment funds – net asset classification, composition, and changes; spending policies; related investment policies.
- The board's interpretation of the laws underlying the NPO's classification of donor-restricted endowment funds, including its interpretation of the ability to spend from **underwater endowment funds**. These are endowment funds whose fair value at the reporting date is less than either:
    - the original gift value, or
    - the amount required to be maintained in the fund, either by law or donor stipulation.
- The NPO's spending policies regarding endowment funds, including underwater endowment funds.
- How the NPO computes its fundraising expenses to amounts raised ratio, if such a ratio is disclosed.

Lecture 21.05 – Contributions

Contributions of Services

Donations of services are normally not recorded. However, when an organization receives donations of **professional services** that it normally would have compensated (**essential services**), the service provider is helping to defray expenses of the NPO and should be reported as a donor.

Essential if:

- Services create or enhance a non-financial asset (inventory, land, building) - OR
- The services require specialized skills (doctor, lawyer, accountant)

For example, if a hospital receives *donated time* from retired nurses that enables them to avoid hiring and paying additional workers, and the estimated amount that time would have cost the hospital is $30,000, the following entry is made:

Expenses (no DR)	30,000	
Contribution Revenue (no DR)		30,000

Notice that the donation increases the nursing expense as well as contribution revenue, and is reported in net assets without donor restrictions, since services that have been provided cannot be withdrawn later.

NPOs also frequently receive donations of services from volunteers providing **unskilled services** that it would **not** have contracted to obtain had they not been donated. These are excluded from the financial reporting since they do not assist the organization in defraying its expenses.

In some cases, services may be provided by the employees of an affiliated NPO. The same basic rule applies as to whether or not to recognize those services in that essential services are recognized and nonessential ones are not. The amount at which they will be recorded will generally be the affiliated NPO's cost. If, however, the cost is significantly higher or lower than the fair value of the services, they may be reported at either the affiliated NPO's cost or the fair value.

For example, if volunteers come regularly to a hospital to visit with lonely patients and read to them, they are certainly performing a service that is valuable and appreciated. Nevertheless, if the hospital does not provide such visitations on a paid contract basis with anyone, then these donated services are not considered relevant in evaluating the NPO itself, and no entry is made.

Contributions of Property

Contributions of property are normally reported as revenues in the same manner as contributions of cash. They may be reported as net assets with or without donor restrictions, depending on the conditions of the contribution.

A special rule may be applied, however, to certain donations of **art, artifacts, or antiques.** If the NPO intends to use these items *for display* or research purposes only, the organizations cares for it themselves and if sold, the proceeds must be reinvested in other collectibles, then it is permitted to exclude the donation from its F/S entirely. This avoids having the organization appear to possess great wealth (and, thus, not need public support) when it is holding assets that cannot be used to finance the operations of the NPO. If they don't meet the above requirements, then they would recognize both an asset and a revenue.

If the NPO reserves the right to sell the asset, however, it will have to include its value on the F/S and report a donation unless the proceeds of any sale are strictly limited to the purchase of replacement art, artifacts, or antiques. They may, however, show it as net assets with donor restrictions.

If they receive **donated materials**, they will also record both an asset and a support revenue. If, however, the materials are "pass through" (donated clothing), then they would debit an expense and credit contribution revenue without donor restrictions.

Gifts in kind are noncash contributions to a not-for-profit organization. They are recorded at FMV.

Marketable Securities

NPO's are required to use fair value accounting for most equity and debt investments and report realized and unrealized gains and losses directly in the statement of activities. (ASC 958-320-35)

- Doesn't cover Equity Method securities

Pledges

Unconditional promises to give to an NPO may be accrued as receivables (net of allowance) by the organization in the period in which they are made. In doing so, however, the NPO should establish an appropriate **allowance for uncollectibles**, and treat pledges that aren't due to be paid until a future period as time-restricted donations. The pledges are *recorded at PV* for annuities or amounts not expected to be collected for over a year. Cash contributions, however, are a revenue or gain when received.

Conditional promise to give (eg, matching) are pledges that contain donor-imposed conditions that represent a barrier that must be overcome as well as a right of release from obligation. Such promises will become payable to the entity when the donor-imposed conditions have been met. As a result, conditional promises to give are not recognized as revenues until they become unconditional. This occurs when the conditions on which the promise depends have been substantially met.

Conditional contribution – Funds received before donor-imposed conditions are substantially met are recognized as liabilities until such time as the promises become unconditional.

Determining Whether a Contribution is Conditional

A contribution is considered **conditional** only if both of the following are true (ie, otherwise, the contribution is considered unconditional):

- There is a barrier that must be overcome (eg, measurable performance-related requirements, such as a specified level of service, a specific output/outcome, matching, or other events outside the control of the recipient, etc.), **and**
- The donor has a right to the return of assets transferred or a right to be released from their obligation to transfer assets.

Determining Whether a Contribution is Restricted

If a contribution is determined to be unconditional, one must then determine if it is restricted or unrestricted. That's right—a donor-imposed condition is not the same as a donor-imposed restriction.

- As alluded to above, a **donor-imposed condition** depends on whether there is *a barrier that must be overcome* before the recipient is entitled to the assets, and whether the contributor has a *right to the return of assets* transferred *or the right to be released* from its obligation to transfer assets. For example, a donor pledges to match donations received if the donee first raises $10,000 from other donors.
- A **donor-imposed restriction**, in contrast, merely *limits the use* of the contribution; it does not affect whether the recipient is entitled to the contribution. An example of a donor-imposed restriction might be that a contribution can only be used to buy shoes for needy children.

Assume that an Independence Day pledge drive by the NPO in 20X1 has netted promises totaling $20,000, with half of the pledge due by the end of the current year and the remainder due by the end of 20X2. Based on experience, the organization expects 10% of pledges not to be honored. The entry to be recorded when pledges are received is:

Pledges receivable (at PV)	20,000	
Allowance for uncollectible pledges		2,000
Revenues (no DR)		9,000
Revenues (DR)		9,000

Assuming collection is as expected, the pledges collected in 20X2 effectively eliminate the time restriction:

12/31/X2	Net assets released (DR)	9,000	
	Net assets released (no DR)		9,000

Agent or Trustee

(like custodial fund – eg, United Way)

If collect money for others, such as a foundation, it can be considered either contribution revenue or a liability at FMV. (ASC 958-605) It is considered a **revenue** if either:

- They have variance power over the donation to redirect the money (OR)
- The beneficiary of the donation is financially related (ongoing economic interest in the net assets of the other).

Cash	x	
Contribution Revenue		x

- If don't meet Either of the two above, record as a **liability.**

Cash	x	
Refundable advance (liability)		x

Example: donor provides funds not just for disaster relief, but to purchase household goods for a specific family affected by the disaster. In this case, the NPO is acting merely as an intermediary and would recognize a liability, not contribution revenue.

Depreciation

ASC 958 requires all not-for-profit organizations to recognize depreciation in general purpose external F/S using the *same criteria* in allocating the depreciable cost of fixed assets over their estimated useful lives as commercial enterprises.

Colleges & Universities

Private colleges and universities are subject to the same guidance as other not-for-profit organizations. Some special issues that relate to colleges and universities include:

- Tuition remissions & scholarships are revenue (if go to school, it's a revenue)
- Refunds – not revenues

Cash	12,000	
Scholarship expense	10,000	
Tuition remission	8,000	
Tuition revenue		30,000

Lecture 21.06 – Hospitals – Private Sector

Overview

The two types of private-sector health care organizations (think hospitals) are*:

- **Investor-owned** health care entities, which provide goods and services for profit, and
- **Not-for-profit** business-oriented health care entities, which have no ownership interests.

**Note that governmental health care organizations constitute a third type of health care entity.*

Not-for-profit health care organizations:

- Charge fees to remain self-sufficient rather than to maximize profits.
- May receive contributions from resource providers in transactions that are either nonreciprocal or are not proportionate.

Accounting and financial reporting for both types of health care organizations is consistent, although each has transactions that would not be appropriate for the other. For example:

- A not-for-profit health care organization will not have any transactions or reporting related to shareholders' equity.
- An investor-owned health care organization will generally not receive contributions.

Financial Statements

Four statements and **notes** to the F/S are presented for a private sector heath care organization, including:

- Balance sheet (Statement of Financial Position)
- Statement of Changes in Net Assets (or Equity)
- Statement of Cash Flows
- Statement of Operations (Activities)

The statements may have other titles that are appropriately descriptive, such as a statement of financial position instead of the balance sheet, or a statement of activities in place of a statement of operations. The statement of cash flows, however, should be entitled as such.

Balance Sheet

The Balance Sheet (Statement of Financial Position) classifies assets and liabilities as current or noncurrent on a similar basis as for-profit entities. Net assets of a **not-for-profit** health care organization are identified as **with or without donor restrictions**, similar to other not-for-profit entities. Net assets *without* donor restrictions, however, include those that are *contractually limited*, such as assets limited as to use by an outside party other than a donor—eg, restrictions imposed by state law on many health maintenance organizations (HMOs).

Statement of Changes in Net Assets

As is true for other NPOs, contributions restricted by the donor, such as for long-term purposes (eg, an endowment), would not be reported in the Statement of Operations. They would instead be reported in the Statement of Changes in Net Assets as a revenue increasing net assets with donor restrictions, as appropriate.

Statement of Cash Flows

The Statement of Cash Flows, like other not-for-profit entities, is prepared similarly to a statement of cash flows for a private business, reporting cash flows from **operating** activities, from **investing** activities, and from **financing** activities.

Statement of Operations

The Statement of Operations (Activities) is required to include a **performance indicator**, which may be described as *operating income, revenues over expenses, revenues and gains over expenses and losses, or performance earnings.* The performance indicator is a measure of operating income or loss. It helps in comparing the performance across health care organizations with different organizational forms. Regardless of what description is used, the performance indicator is to be clearly labeled.

- Not-for-profit, business-oriented health care entities are required to report the performance indicator on the same statement that presents the total changes in net assets without donor restrictions.
  - A description of the nature and composition of the performance indicator is to be included in the notes to the F/S. The performance indicator **includes** items related to investments in debt and equity securities:
    - Dividends, interest, and similar investment income
    - Realized gains and losses
    - Unrealized gains and losses on trading securities
    - Credit losses
    - Unrealized gains and losses and impairments on equity investments
- Other changes in net assets may be presented in the same statement or separately.
- Additional classifications may be used for components within the performance indicator, such as operating and nonoperating, expendable and nonexpendable, recognized and unrecognized, or recurring and nonrecurring.
- Certain items are **excluded** from the performance indicator and are reported separately as changes in net assets (see illustration below).

Patient service revenue includes revenues for medical services such as doctors, surgery, and most hospital stay costs, etc. and is accounted for in accordance with the new ASC 606 revenue recognition rules.

- Patient service revenue **excludes charity care,** which isn't billed but is disclosed in the F/S. Charity care is also *not* considered uncollectible account expense (ie, credit loss expense).
- **Net patient service revenue** is patient service revenue after reductions for*:
  - **Implicit price concessions** (ie, a reduction in the price based on the amount the entity does not expect to collect) and
  - **Contractual adjustments** for third-party payments.

  **Note that credit loss expense is claimed separately as an operating expense.*
- Sometimes, the amount collectible cannot be determined at the time the services are provided, such as when a health care facility is required by law to provide emergency services, regardless of the patient's ability to pay. In this case, a contract is likely to have been bypassed, which would require postponing revenue recognition until it can be determined that the patient has the ability and intention to pay or that the service should be classified as charity care.

Donated supplies are recognized as a revenue at FMV in the period received and as either an asset or an expense.

Supplies or Expense	100	
Unrestricted contribution – other operating Revenue (no DR)		100

Statement of Operations (Activities) – Hospital (PP-NO-ONE)

Patient service revenue

(**P**rovisions for implicit price concessions and contractual adjustments)

Net patient service revenues

\+ **O**ther operating revenues, gains/losses

- Nonmedical – Parking, gift shop, cafeteria, tuition (auxiliary activities)
- Donated supplies & equipment
- Restricted grants
- Net assets released from restriction used for *operations*

(**O**perating expenses)

- Credit losses (ie, bad debts), drugs, doctor salaries, G&A, depreciation, interest

Results from operations

\+ **N**onoperating revenues (Other Income)

- Unrestricted donations, gifts, bequests
- Unrestricted interest & dividend income
- Unrestricted grants
- Donated services

Excess of Revenues/Gains over Expenses/Losses **(Performance indicator)**

Items reported separately from performance indicator:

- Donor-restricted contributions
- Contributions of long-lived assets without donor restrictions
- Equity transfers
- Discontinued operations
- Transactions with owners acting in the capacity as an owner
- Items reported in, or reclassified from, other comprehensive income
- Unrealized gains/losses on investments other than trading securities

Increase in Net Assets Without Restrictions

Governmental Health Care Organizations

Governmental health care organizations are generally considered governmental entities that are engaged only in business-type activities, similar to utilities. As such, a governmental health care organization will present F/S prepared in accordance with the same requirements applied to enterprise funds.

Summary

<table>
<tr><th>Type of
Health Care Organization</th><th>Authoritative Guidance</th><th>Required F/S</th></tr>
<tr><td>Investor-owned (for-profit) health care entities</td><td>FASB</td><td rowspan="2">▪ Balance sheet (Statement of Financial Position)
▪ Statement of Changes in Net Assets (or Equity)
▪ Statement of Cash Flows
▪ Statement of Operations (Activities)</td></tr>
<tr><td>Not-for-profit business-oriented health care entities</td><td>FASB</td></tr>
<tr><td>Governmental health care organizations</td><td>GASB</td><td>▪ Statement of Net Position
▪ Statement of Revenues, Expenses, & Changes in Fund Net Position
▪ Statement of Cash Flows</td></tr>
</table>

Sample Business Oriented Not-for-Profit Hospital
STATEMENTS OF OPERATIONS (ACTIVITIES)
Years Ended December 31, 20X7 and 20X6
(in thousands)

	20X7	20X6
Changes in net assets without donor restrictions:		
Revenue, gains, and other support:		
Net patient service revenue	$85,156	$78,942
Premium revenue	11,150	10,950
Other revenue	2,601	5,212
Net assets released from restrictions used for operations	300	-
Total revenues, gains and other support	99,207	95,104
Expenses:		
Operating expenses	88,521	80,585
Depreciation and amortization	4,782	4,280
Interest	1,752	1,825
Provision for *credit losses*	1,000	1,300
Other	2,000	1,300
Total expenses	98,055	89,290
Operating income	1,152	5,814
Other income:		
Investment income	3,900	3,025
Excess of revenues over expenses (Performance Indicator)	5,052	8,839
Change in net unrealized gains and losses on other than trading securities	300	375
Net assets released from restrictions used for purchase of property and equipment	200	
Change in interest in net assets of Sample Hospital Foundation	283	536
Transfers to parent	(688)	(3,051)
Increase in net assets without donor restrictions	$ 5,147	$ 6,699

See accompanying notes to financial statements.

Sample Business Oriented Not-for-Profit Hospital
STATEMENT OF CHANGES IN NET ASSETS
Years Ended December 31, 20X7 and 20X6
(in thousands)

	20X7	20X6
Net assets without donor restrictions:		
Excess of revenues over expenses	$ 5,052	$ 8,839
Net unrealized gains on investments, other than trading securities	300	375
Change in interest in net assets of Sample Hospital Foundation	283	536
Transfers to parent	(688)	(3,051)
Net assets released from restrictions used for purchase of property and equipment	200	-
Increase in net assets without donor restrictions	5,147	6,699
Net assets with donor restrictions:		
Contributions for charity care	140	996
Contributions for endowment funds	50	411
Net realized and unrealized gains on investments	10	10
Net assets released from restrictions	(500)	-
Increase (decrease) in net assets with donor restrictions	(300)	1,417
Increase in net assets	4,847	8,116
Net assets, beginning of year	72,202	64,086
Net assets, end of year	$77,049	$72,202

UWorld | ROGER CPA Review

YOUR WORLD OF LEARNING

FAR 22 - Business Combinations & Consolidations

FAR 22 – Business Combinations & Consolidations

Table of Contents

Business Combinations & Consolidations

Lecture 22.01 – Business Combinations & Consolidations

Overview

ASC 805 represents a conceptually more consistent method of consolidation and improves financial reporting by reflecting the **economic entity concept**. Under the economic entity concept, the consolidated statements are prepared as if the group of legal entities were one economic entity. The method will

- Better reflect the investment made by the Acquirer,
- Enhance financial statement comparability between companies, and
- Provide more complete and relevant financial information.

When one corporation, the **Acquirer** (*the Parent*) acquires **control** (a controlling financial interest) in another entity, the **Acquiree** (*the Subsidiary*), this creates a relationship requiring the preparation of consolidated financial statements (F/S) at each balance sheet date. The Acquisition date is the date on which the acquirer obtains a controlling financial interest in the Acquiree.

- A controlling financial interest is most commonly obtained when one entity obtains a majority of the voting equity of another.
    - Note, however, that there are circumstances where an entity can own more than 50% of the voting equity of another entity and not have a controlling financial interest. This would typically be when control is only temporary or when majority ownership does not provide the holder with control over the entity.
- A controlling financial interest may also be obtained due to the relationship between the entities. The controlled entity would be considered a variable interest entity (VIE) under ASC 810. The entity with control is considered the primary beneficiary of the VIE and, having a controlling financial interest, will be required to prepare consolidated F/S.

Investor / Investee	0 – 20%	**Adjusted cost method**
	20% – 50%	**Equity method** (One-line consolidation)
Acquirer / Acquiree	50% +	**Consolidations** (During year adjusted cost or equity – gets eliminated at year end)

Lecture 22.02 – Steps in Applying the Acquisition Method

Overview

All consolidations must be performed using the **acquisition method**. (ASC 805) An acquisition is considered to be a financial transaction executed by the Acquirer, and the resulting entity is considered to be a continuation of the Acquirer. As a result, the assets and liabilities of the Acquiree are acquired at **fair values** (ASC 820) at the **acquisition date,** and **income** of the Acquiree is only included from the **date of acquisition on.**

There are **four steps** in applying the acquisition method.

1. Identify the Acquirer

In a stock-for-assets transaction, the acquirer is the one giving the assets and acquiring the stock. In stock-for-stock transactions, however, various factors will be considered in determining which entity is the acquirer and which is the acquiree. Factors to consider may include:

- The entity that initiated the transaction
- Representation in management and governance
- Relative voting rights

Identifying the acquirer can be very significant since the assets and liabilities of the acquirer remain at book value and those of the acquiree are reported at fair value.

2. Determine the Acquisition Date

The acquisition date is the date on which the acquirer obtains a **controlling** financial interest over the acquiree. In the case of an equity acquisition, it is the date on which the acquirer's holdings became a majority. In the case of a VIE, it may be the date on which a lease, a sale or purchase contract, or some other relationship was entered. The acquisition date is also referred to as the **measurement date**. It is the date as of which:

- Identifiable assets acquired and liabilities assumed are measured at fair value by the acquirer.
- The acquirer begins to recognize the revenues and expenses of the acquiree in the acquirer's consolidated F/S.

3. Recognize and Measure Identifiable Assets Acquired, Liabilities Assumed, & Noncontrolling Interest

Identifiable assets, including those that are and are not included on the F/S of the acquiree, and liabilities assumed are generally measured at **fair value**. Other measurements are based on prescribed standards.

In some cases, the acquirer will **not recognize** assets or liabilities that are included in the F/S of the acquiree. Examples include:

- Any goodwill recognized on the F/S of the acquiree.
- Prepaid rent or accrued rent resulting from recognizing operating lease payments on a straight-line basis.

- Deferred tax assets or liabilities, which will be measured by the acquirer on the basis of the differences between the newly recorded amounts and the tax bases of assets acquired and liabilities assumed.

Identifiable Intangible Assets

The acquirer recognizes all identifiable intangible assets at fair value at the date of acquisition. An intangible is considered identifiable if either:

- It represents a legal or contractual right; or
- It can be sold, transferred, licensed, or otherwise disposed of by itself.

Examples of newly created identifiable intangibles include:

- **Marketing-related intangibles** – Trademarks, trade names, noncompetition agreements
- **Customer-related intangibles** – Customer lists, customer contracts
- **Artistic-related intangibles** – Plays, operas, books, magazines, pictures, videos, films, music
- **Contract-based intangibles** – Licensing, royalty, advertising, lease and franchise agreements, construction permits
- **Technology-based intangibles** – Computer software, mask works, trade secrets, recipes

Private Company Alternative

Nonpublic entities may elect to **not recognize noncompetition agreements and customer-related intangibles** that cannot be sold or licensed separately. This effectively increases the amount recognized as goodwill or decreases the amount reported as a gain on bargain purchase. An electing entity must amortize goodwill.

Noncontrolling Interest

The acquirer also recognizes any noncontrolling interest in the acquiree at fair value. **Fair value** is considered to be market price of a single share multiplied by the number of shares on the acquisition date. A **noncontrolling interest** results from the acquirer having a controlling financial interest that is not 100% of the voting equity of the acquiree.

- In the case of a stock acquisition, the noncontrolling interest would be the portion not owned by the acquirer (ie, the minority interest).
- In the case of a VIE, it may be 100% of the ownership of the entity.

The noncontrolling interest is a component of stockholders' equity and is required to be reported in the **stockholders' equity section** of the balance sheet. (ASC 810) The amount reported as the noncontrolling interest is periodically adjusted for its share of net income and other comprehensive income:

- Net income will include all revenues, expenses, gains, and losses of the parent and all subsidiaries, after adjusting for intercompany items.
    - An appropriate amount will be allocated to the noncontrolling interest on the income statement (I/S) and will be closed to the noncontrolling interest account.
    - The remainder will be allocated to the parent and will be closed to retained earnings.
- Other comprehensive income will include all amounts recognized by the parent and all subsidiaries, after eliminating intercompany items.
    - An appropriate amount will be allocated to the noncontrolling interest on the statement of comprehensive income and will be closed to the noncontrolling interest account.

- The remainder will be allocated to the parent and will be closed to accumulated other comprehensive income.

4. Recognize and Measure Goodwill/Gain From Bargain Purchase

The acquirer will recognize consideration given, if any, at its fair value.

- Any assets transferred are included at fair value with any difference between fair value and book value treated as a gain or loss on disposal.
- Stock issued is recognized at fair value with a credit to common stock for any par or stated value and additional paid-in capital for the difference.

Most **costs incurred** in relation to the transaction will be **recognized as expense** when incurred. This includes:

- Any general expenses incurred
- Costs directly related to the acquisition, such as attorney or appraiser fees
- Indirect costs, such as the costs of printing new stationery or developing new training manuals, finder fees

One **exception** is the cost of issuing and registering debt and equity securities issued in the combination.

- Costs of issuing equity securities reduce additional paid-in capital.
- Costs of issuing debt securities are capitalized and amortized as debt issue costs.

Considering all the factors involved in recognizing a business combination, and all the different measurements, it would be very unusual for the entry recognizing the combination to balance.

- If the amount necessary to balance the entry is a debit, it will be recognized as **goodwill**.
    - Goodwill is measured as the excess of the consideration given over the fair value of the underlying net assets acquired.
    - The fact that the consideration is greater indicates that the company as a whole is worth more than the fair value of its net assets.
- If the amount necessary to balance the entry is a credit, it will be recognized as **gain on bargain purchase**.
    - The gain is measured as the excess of the fair value of the underlying net assets acquired over the consideration given.
    - The fact that the consideration is less indicates that the company may not have been a going concern and may not have had the ability to dispose of assets and settle liabilities at their fair values.

The acquisition is recorded in one of two ways:

- The acquirer can record the individual assets acquired and liabilities assumed (ie, a merger), or
- Record the transaction as an investment.

The acquirer will often record the individual assets acquired and liabilities assumed when there is no need to maintain separate records for the acquiree, either for internal purposes or for external reporting purposes. When this is the case, the process is as follows:

- Assets acquired and liabilities assumed are recognized at their fair values.

- Consideration is measured as follows:
  - Cash paid is recognized as a reduction to cash
  - Stock issued is recognized at its fair value with the par value credited to common stock and the remainder to additional paid-in capital.
  - If other assets are transferred, consideration will be the fair value and a gain/loss is recognized as if they were sold for their fair values.
  - Any previous investment, if accounted for at adjusted cost or under the equity method, is also included at fair value with a gain/loss recognized as if sold for that amount.
- Noncontrolling interest, if any, is recognized as a component of stockholders' equity at its fair value.
- Any remaining **debit** necessary to balance the entry is recorded as **goodwill**.
- If a **credit** is necessary (paid less than net fair value for acquiree), the bargain is recorded as a **gain** on the I/S.

Once the initial entry has been recorded, the acquirer will apply GAAP going forward, and there is no special accounting required after the period of acquisition.

Lecture 22.03 – Examples #1 & #2 at Date of Acquisition

Recording the Acquisition

When the acquirer records the transaction as an investment, recording the acquisition is quite straightforward. The Investment in acquiree is debited for the purchase price, meaning the total fair value of the consideration paid by the acquirer. Essentially, this is the balancing entry to offset the accounts being credited in the remainder of this entry. The book values of the acquiree accounts are ignored.

- Cash is credited for any amounts paid.
- Common stock is credited for the par value of any shares being issued by the acquirer.
- Additional paid-in capital is credited for the excess of the fair value of any shares being issued over their par value.

There is no entry to retained earnings since the acquirer does not retroactively combine the income of the acquirer in a purchase. The Acquiree's income is included from the date of acquisition (prospective, not retroactive).

Measurement Period & Measurement Period Adjustments

In some circumstances, the acquirer may believe that the measurement of the fair value of an acquiree, which is used to determine an appropriate acquisition price, is reliable, while the fair values of some of the individual identifiable assets acquired and liabilities assumed could not be reliably determined on a timely basis.

If the acquirer is required to prepare consolidated F/S *prior to* being able to obtain a more accurate measurement, the following procedures will be applied:

- The asset or liability for which a reliable fair value has not been determined will be recorded at management's *best estimate* based on information that is available with that amount referred to as a *"provisional" value*.
- As a result of using the provisional values, the amount reported as goodwill may be over- or understated, depending on the overstatement or understatement of the assets and liabilities recorded at their provisional amounts.
- Depreciation, amortization, interest income or expense, and other revenue and expense items that are affected by those values are recognized as if the provisional amounts are the actual fair values and the consolidated F/S are prepared accordingly.

The entity then has one year from the date of acquisition, referred to as the *measurement period*, to obtain a more reliable measurement. If management is unable to do so, the provisional amounts are accepted as the actual amounts and the items are accounted for as comparable items would be. Neither the items nor their I/S effects will be adjusted.

If, on the other hand, management can obtain a more reliable measurement, the following procedures will be followed:

- The assets or liabilities will be adjusted to the amounts that would have been their carrying values as of the balance sheet date if they had originally been recorded at their more reliable amounts.

- The I/S effects, including such items as depreciation and amortization expense, interest net of amortization of discount or premium, and other items that would have been affected by the change in carrying value will be recalculated as if the appropriate amount had been used on the date of acquisition.
  - Current period amounts are adjusted to reflect the correct amounts that would have been reported if the assets and liabilities had been originally recorded at the appropriate amount
  - Amounts related to prior periods were originally required to be accounted for as prior period adjustments, correcting items for the previous period, if comparative F/S are presented, and recording the net change as an adjustment to beginning retained earnings if only single period F/S are presented.
  - The adjustments to prior period I/S items are reported in the current period's I/S on a "catch up" basis.
    - They may be included with the current period's amounts with the amounts for the prior period disclosed in the notes to the F/S; or
    - They may be reported separately from the current period's amounts on the face of the I/S.

Preparing Consolidated Financial Statements

When the acquirer records the initial transaction as an investment, it will prepare consolidated F/S each reporting period. Preparing consolidated F/S involves a process under which:

- The investment is eliminated, as are the acquiree's (subsidiary's) equity accounts.
- Those assets and liabilities that were part of the original acquisition and are still on the books will be adjusted for differences between their book values and fair values on the acquisition date.
- The I/S effects of differences between book and fair values will be recognized in income to the extent that they apply to the current period and to retained earnings to the extent that they apply to prior periods.
- The effects of interentity transactions are eliminated.
- The noncontrolling interest will be recorded in equity based on the fair value on the date of acquisition adjusted for changes due to income or distribution since that date.

Pushdown Accounting

One of the more cumbersome aspects of preparing consolidated F/S is keeping track of the differences between the fair values and the carrying values of the acquiree's assets and liabilities at the acquisition date. Each period, until all of those items have been disposed of or settled, an adjustment will be required to recognize that difference as well as any depreciation, amortization, impairment, or other adjustment that would have been made to it since the date of acquisition.

GAAP provides an alternative in the form of pushdown accounting. When an acquiree decides to adopt pushdown accounting, it adjusts its assets and liabilities to the same amounts at which they will be reported by the acquirer (parent) and account for those assets and liabilities going forward on a basis similar to that which would be applied by the acquirer (parent). As a result, the consolidation process is simplified and the acquirer (parent) will only be required to eliminate interentity transactions, recognize the noncontrolling interest, and eliminate the investment account.

An acquiree is not required to adopt the pushdown basis of accounting but may decide to do so in any period in which there is a change in control event. If, for example, an investor with the ability to exercise significant influence over an investee acquires additional equity resulting in a controlling financial interest, the acquiree could adopt pushdown accounting in that period.

- An election to adopt pushdown accounting is irrevocable.
- If an entity does not elect to adopt pushdown accounting in the period of a change of control event, it may do so in a subsequent period and will account for the change as a change in accounting principle.

Examples of Consolidations on Date of Acquisition

Class Example #1

Assume the following balance sheets are available for P Co. and S Co. at 12/31/X1:

Accounts	P Co.	S Co.
Cash	1,000	100
A/R		
Inventory		
Equipment (PP&E)	8,000	500
A/P		
Bonds Payable		
$1 CS	(1,000)	(100)
APIC	(3,000)	(100)
RE	(5,000)	(400)

If P issues 150 shares of stock to acquire all of S, and the stock being issued has a market value of $6 per share, the entry to record the acquisition is:

Investment in S	900	
Common stock		150
Additional paid-in capital		750

If the purchase were for an equivalent amount of cash instead, the entry would be:

Investment in S	900	
Cash		900

Notice that none of the information about the acquiree is needed, since an acquisition is recorded at the purchase price, not at the underlying equity of the acquiree. Also note that the entry is not affected by the percentage acquired.

Combining Equity

When consolidated F/S are prepared, the separate trial balances of the acquirer and acquiree are combined on a **worksheet** into a single set of numbers for presentation purposes. In the process, certain account balances must be eliminated or adjusted. This includes all accounts that treat the two companies as separate entities, since the presentation is designed to report them as a single entity. The consolidation process eliminates reciprocal items that are shown on both the acquirer's and acquiree's books. These eliminations are necessary to avoid double counting the same items which would misstate the F/S of the combined economic entity.

The concept of consolidated statements is that the resources of two or more companies are under the control of the acquirer. Consolidated statements are prepared as if the group of legal entities were one economic entity, based on the **economic entity concept.**

After an acquisition, the preparation of a consolidated financial statement requires substantial adjustments, since the investment has been recorded at the purchase price, not the underlying equity of the subsidiary.

The **entry to combine equity** includes all of the following elements:

- All of the equity accounts are debited to remove 100% of the acquiree account balances.
- Investment in acquiree is credited to remove the account.
- Investment is credited (for investments held prior to acquisition - Fair value of previously held equity interests in acquiree)
- Noncontrolling interest is credited (multiply the active market price on the acquisition date × the number of shares held by the noncontrolling parties)

If the fair value of net identifiable assets of the acquiree is *less than* the aggregate of the consideration transferred, plus the acquisition date fair value of previously held interests, plus the fair value of noncontrolling interest, **goodwill** is recognized.

If the fair value of net identifiable assets of the acquiree *exceeds* the aggregate of the consideration transferred, plus the acquisition date fair value of previously held interests, plus the fair value of the noncontrolling interest, then a bargain purchase occurs. A **gain** is recognized by the acquirer in the current period's I/S for the bargain purchase.

The calculation of Goodwill and Gain is as follows:

Fair value of consideration transferred (cost to the acquirer)
\+ Fair value of previously held equity interests in acquiree
\+ Fair value of noncontrolling interest
<u>(-) Fair value of net identifiable assets of acquiree</u>
Goodwill or Gain from bargain purchase

Goodwill is defined as "an asset representing the future economic benefits that arises from other assets acquired in a business combination that are not individually identified and separately recognized."

In addition, the entry will usually require adjustments to Identifiable asset accounts whose fair value differed from book value on the date of the original acquisition, and an entry for goodwill for the remaining difference in the entry. The following approach is needed:

- Assets that were sold prior to the balance sheet date are ignored.

- Identifiable Assets still being held at the balance sheet date are adjusted for the difference between the fair value and book value **at the date of Acquisition**.
- The other identifiable assets acquired, liabilities assumed, and any noncontrolling interest are measured at fair value. Any **newly identified intangible assets** of the acquiree must also be recognized.
- Any remaining **debit** necessary to balance the entry is recorded as **Goodwill**.
- If a **credit** is necessary (paid less than net Fair Value for Acquiree) the bargain purchase is recorded as a **gain** on the I/S.
  - Acquired assets and liabilities at **fair market value** (FMV). (Goodwill and FMV write-up)
    - Excess of FMV over BV considered FMV Increment (write up)
      - Land
      - PP&E
      - Inventory
      - Other Identifiable Assets (ID assets)

C/S	X		100% of acquiree (C/S, APIC, R/E)
APIC	X		
R/E	X		
ID Assets (to FMV)	X		
Goodwill	X		
Investment in acquiree		X	
Investments held prior to acquisition in Acquiree		X	
Noncontrolling interest (@FMV)		X	

If an adjustment occurs to an asset which is **depreciable or amortizable**, an additional entry must be made to account for the depreciation or amortization between the purchase date and financial statement date. Intangible assets that do not have definite lives, such as **goodwill, will be tested for impairment** on an annual basis pursuant to ASC 350.

Class Example #2

Assume that P Co. acquired all (100%) of the stock of S Co. in an acquisition on 12/31/X1 for a payment of $900 cash. At the time, the book value of S was $600, and all of the assets and liabilities had fair values equal to their book values, with the exception of equipment with a remaining life of 5 years and a fair value $100 higher than book value. The accounts of the two companies at 12/31/X1 are presented in a worksheet, along with the combining entry:

Everything acquired @ **FMV** of stock given or cash paid:

Purchase price		**$ 900**	
FMV	FMV increment	**$ 700**	FMV Appreciation **equipment $100**
BV		**$ 600**	

Accounts	P Co	S Co	Debits	Credits	Consol
Cash	100	100			200
Equipment	8,000	500	100		8,600
Inv in S	900			900	--
Goodwill			200		200
$1 CS	(1,000)	(100)	100		(1,000)
APIC	(3,000)	(100)	100		(3,000)
RE	(5,000)	(400)	400		(5,000)

To acquire Investment: (In books)

Investment	900	
Cash		900

To consolidate: (On worksheet)

C/S	100	
APIC	100	→ (100%)
R/E	400	
Equipment	**100**	
Goodwill	**200**	
Investment		900

Goodwill is the balancing entry in the above: it represents the excess of the $900 investment over the $700 fair value of the net identifiable assets ($600 book value + $100 excess of fair value over book value of equipment = $700).

Lecture 22.04 – Example #3 at Year End

Consolidations After the Date of Acquisition

Class Example #3—Acquire 100%, consolidate at year end

The following example assumes the acquirer used the equity method to account for the majority investment during the year.

Let's look at a consolidation performed after the date of acquisition. Again, assume that P acquired all (100%) of S on 12/31/X1 for $900 cash, that equipment with a 5-year life had a fair value exceeding book value by $100 on 12/31/X1, and that goodwill, which came to $200 on 12/31/X1, is believed to be impaired as of 12/31/X2 and, as a result, only worth $195. Income during the year for P was $3,000 and S was $150. The investment is accounted for under the Equity method. Let's look at the consolidating worksheet that might appear one year later, on 12/31/X2:

Summary: Acquire 100% for $900 on 12/31/X1, and consolidate on 12/31/X2

- Income during the year:
  - P - $3,000
  - S - $150
- Equipment useful life = 5 years
- Goodwill Impaired by $5
- Investment accounted for under the **equity method**.

To account for S's income under the equity method:

Investment	150	
Equity in earnings (I/S)		150

To Depreciate the Equipment (100/5 = $20):

Equity in earnings (I/S)	20	
Investment		20

To record Impairment of Goodwill:

Equity in earnings	5	
Investment		5

Investment

900	
150	20
	5
1025	

To consolidate at year end:

C/S	100	
APIC	100	
R/E	550	
Equipment (100 – 20)	80	
Goodwill (200 – 5)	195	
Investment		**1,025**

Accounts	**P Co**	**S Co**	**Debits**	**Credits**	**Consol**
Cash	3,100	250			3,350
Equipment	8,000	500	80		8,580
Inv in S	1,025			1,025	--
Goodwill			195		195
$1 CS	(1,000)	(100)	100		(1,000)
APIC	(3,000)	(100)	100		(3,000)
RE	(8,125)	(550)	550		(8,125)

In the earlier example, the retained earnings of P and S were $5,000 and $400, respectively. The retained earnings of both companies have changed, of course: P earned $3,000 from its separate operations, and S earned $150. P's bookkeeper has used the equity method of accounting, and has reported $125 equity in earnings of S. This is because the $150 income is reduced by depreciation on the $100 equipment excess over 5 years, for $20, and impairment of goodwill resulted in a $5 reduction in its carrying value from $200 to $195.

Similarly, the net adjustments to the equipment and goodwill accounts are reduced by accumulated depreciation and impairment adjustments, respectively. In the above example, no separate accounts were presented for accumulated depreciation and impairment adjustments, so adjustments were made to the asset accounts directly.

Lecture 22.05 – Example #4 – Noncontrolling Interest

When one entity obtains a controlling financial interest in another entity, it may or may not entail the acquisition of the acquiree's equity securities, such as when a primary beneficiary has a controlling financial interest in a VIE. In addition, even when it does, the acquirer often acquires less than 100% of the acquiree's outstanding stock. The portion of the acquiree's equity that is held by parties or entities other than the acquirer is referred to as the **noncontrolling interest**.

The noncontrolling interest is considered a portion of shareholders; equity and is required to be reported in the shareholders' equity section of the balance sheet. It is originally recognized at fair value as of the date of acquisition:

- If the shares are traded in an active market, the per share market value will be multiplied by the number of shares owned by others.
- If the shares are not traded in an active market, an alternative method will be applied in determining fair value.

The noncontrolling interest is adjusted for:

- The noncontrolling interest's share of the acquiree's net income; and
- The noncontrolling interest's portion of distributions by the acquiree.

The consolidated I/S will include the revenues, expenses, gains, and losses of both the acquirer and the acquiree.

- The I/S effects of interentity transactions, including sales of merchandise, the performance of services, loans, leases, and the sale of other assets, are eliminated.
- The result is considered consolidated net income.
  - A portion, equal to the acquiree's unadjusted net income multiplied by the noncontrolling interest's percentage ownership in the acquiree, is allocated to, and recognized as an adjustment to the noncontrolling interest.
  - The remainder is allocated to the acquirer and recognized as an adjustment to retained earnings.

A similar approach is used in allocating other comprehensive income. The consolidated statement of other comprehensive income, or combined statement if the one-statement approach is used, will reflect all items of other comprehensive income for the period for both the acquirer and the acquiree, after eliminating interentity items, if any.

- A proportionate amount of those attributable to the noncontrolling interest's share is allocated to, and recognized as an adjustment to, the noncontrolling interest.
- The remainder is allocated to the acquirer and recognized as an adjustment to accumulated other comprehensive income.

Class Example #4

Assume that P Co. acquired 90% (10% noncontrolling interest) of the stock of S Co. in an acquisition on 12/31/X1 for a payment of $900 cash. At the date of acquisition, S Co. had 100,000 shares of stock outstanding with an FMV of $8 per share. The book value of S was $600, and all of the assets and liabilities had fair values equal to their book values, with the exception of equipment with a remaining life of 5 years and a fair value $100 higher than book value. The accounts of the two companies at 12/31/X1 are presented in a worksheet, along with the combining entry.

The consolidating worksheet would appear as follows:

Purchase price		**$ 900**
FMV	**FMV increment**	**$ 700**
BV		**$ 600**

The FMV of the noncontrolling interest at the date of acquisition is 100,000 × $8 = $800,000 × 10% = $80,000.

The calculation of Goodwill or Gain is as follows:

Fair value of consideration transferred (cost to the acquirer)	$900,000
+ Fair value of previously held equity interests in acquiree	0
+ Fair value of noncontrolling interest	$ 80,000
(-) Fair value of net identifiable assets of acquiree	($700,000)
Goodwill or Gain from bargain purchase	**$280,000**

Accounts	P Co	S Co	Debits	Credits	Consol
Cash	100	100			200
Equipment	8,000	500	100		8,600
Inv in S	900			900	--
Goodwill			280		280
$1 CS	(1,000)	(100)	100		(1,000)
APIC	(3,000)	(100)	100		(3,000)
Noncontrol Int.				80	(80)
RE	(5,000)	(400)	400		(5,000)

Keep in mind that the income reported for 20X1 will be the **Acquirer's income only**, since purchases are accounted for prospectively, not retroactively. The acquiree's income (or 90% of it, in the case of a 90% purchase) is included from the date of purchase onward.

To acquire 90% of Investment: (Noncontrolling interest) (In books)

Investment	900	
Cash		900

To consolidate: (On worksheet)

C/S	100		(100%)
APIC	100		(100%)
R/E	400		(100%)
Equipment	**100**		
Goodwill	**280**		
Investment		900	
Noncontrolling int. (minority int.)		**80 ($800 FMV × 10%)**	

Lecture 22.06 – Example #5 – Noncontrolling Interest at Year End

Acquire 90%, consolidate at year end

When consolidated F/S are prepared at year end or in subsequent years, the working paper eliminations are similar. The entries for intercompany transactions are the same as for a 100% acquisition. However, an important difference in the worksheet for the less than 100% acquisition is that the worksheet must reflect the noncontrolling interest in the acquiree. In the I/S, consolidated net income is adjusted to disclose the net income or loss attributed to the noncontrolling interest. Comprehensive Income is also adjusted to include the comprehensive income attributed to the noncontrolling interest.

Class Example #5

Let's assume P Co. **Acquired 90% of S Co**. stock for $900 on 12/31/X1, at which time the acquiree's total stockholders' equity was $600 and the fair value of net identifiable assets was $700. Equipment with a 5-year life had a fair value exceeding book value by $100 on 12/31/X1, and goodwill is believed to be impaired by $8 as of 12/31/X2. Income during the year for P was $3,000 and S was $150. S declared and paid dividends of $10 during the year. The investment is accounted for under the Equity method. At the date of acquisition, S Co. had 100,000 shares of stock outstanding with an FMV of $8 per share.

Summary: Acquire 90% for $900 on 12/31/X1, and consolidate on 12/31/X2

- Income during the year:
  - P - $3,000
  - S - $150
- Dividends paid by S = $10
- Equipment useful life = 5 years
- Goodwill Impaired by $8
- Noncontrolling interest $80,000
- Investment accounted for under the **equity method**.

At 12/31/X2, the separate balances of P and S and the consolidating adjustments might appear as follows:

Accounts	P Co	S Co	Debits	Credits	Consol
Cash	3,109	240			3,349
Equipment	8,000	500	80		8,580
Inv in S	998			998	--
Goodwill			272		272
$1 CS	(1,000)	(100)	100		(1,000)
APIC	(3,000)	(100)	100		(3,000)
Noncontrol Int.				94	(94)
RE	(8,107)	(540)	540		(8,107)

Purchase price		**$ 900**
FMV	**FMV increment**	**$ 700**
BV		**$ 600**

To account for S's income under the equity method:

Investment (150 × 90%)	135	
Equity in earnings (I/S)		135

To account for S's Dividend paid under the equity method:

Cash (10 × 90%)	9	
Investment		9

To Depreciate the Equipment (100/5 = $20):

Equity in earnings (I/S)	20	
Investment		20

To record Impairment of Goodwill:

Equity in earnings	8	
Investment		8

Investment

Debit	Credit
900	
135	9
	20
	8
998	

To consolidate at year end:

C/S	100	
APIC	100	
R/E (400 + 150 -10)	540	
PP&E (100 – 20 dep)	80	
Goodwill (280 – 8 impairment)	272	
Investment		**998**
Noncontrolling int. [80 + (10% × $150 income) – (10% × $10 div)]		**94**

Notice that the investment account was initially recorded at a cost of $900. It was then increased by 90% of the $150 of income ($135) and was reduced by the $9 dividend, the $20 ($100 / 5yrs) of depreciation and the $8 impairment loss on goodwill, resulting in an ending balance of $998.

The change in the noncontrolling interest was attributed to a portion of net income ($15) and dividends ($1) of the acquiree being allocated to the noncontrolling interest (80 + 15-1 = 94)

Required disclosures on the **income statement** include the total consolidated Income and the income broken out between the Acquirer and Acquiree. For example:

Net Income	$ 3,150
Net income attributable to noncontrolling interest in acquiree	(15)
Net income attributable to acquirer	$ 3,135

Statement of Retained Earnings

- **Combine Income**

Statement of Retained Earnings	
	Beginning RE
+/–	Prior Period adjustment
	Adjusted beginning RE — Acquirer only
+	**Net Income** ▪ Acquirer (whole year) ▪ Acquiree (acquisition date)
	(Dividends — Acquirer only)
	Ending retained earnings

Lecture 22.07 – Intercompany Transactions

The process of consolidation results in the presentation of a single set of F/S, which treats the Acquirer and Acquiree as a single entity. Since an entity cannot engage in business transactions with itself, adjustments will have to be made on the consolidating worksheet in order to eliminate the effects of **intercompany transactions**. There are four types of such transactions that commonly appear on the CPA exam:

- **Dividends paid** from the Acquiree to the Acquirer.
- **Sales of inventory** from one of the companies to the other.
- Sales of **property, plant, and equipment** from one to the other.
- Purchases by one of the **bonds** issued by the other.

In principle, an eliminating entry has a simple objective: to remove any evidence from the consolidated F/S that the event occurred. If a transaction produced a receivable and payable, the elimination would involve debiting the payable and crediting the receivable. If a transaction produced a revenue and expense account, the elimination would involve debiting the revenue and crediting the expense.

There are, however, special complications associated with each of the 4 transactions cited above, since their effects often involve income on one side of the transaction but not on the other. These can be exceptionally complicated when the income is being reported by the acquiree in cases where the acquirer owns less than 100% of the acquiree. For the CPA exam, though, questions about intercompany transactions have consistently directed the candidate to ignore the noncontrolling interest (minority interest). As a result, there is no need to make distinctions between **upstream** (acquiree-to-acquirer) and **downstream** (acquirer-to-acquiree) transactions.

Dividends paid by the acquiree to the acquirer must be completely eliminated in a consolidation, since an entity cannot pay dividends to itself. The manner in which the elimination entry is made depends on the accounts presented in the exam problem. Actually, there is no effect on the balance sheet to remove, since the equity accounts of the acquiree and the investment of the acquirer are eliminated in the combining of equity. The only exception is if a dividend has been declared but not yet paid, in which case an elimination of the receivable and payable may be needed:

Dividends payable	100	
Dividends receivable		100

When there is a noncontrolling interest, dividends payable to the noncontrolling shareholders are not eliminated, since they are actual amounts owed to outside creditors. Additionally, since they represent the portion of the acquiree not owned by the acquirer, they won't be included in the combined equity of the consolidated entity anyway.

On rare exams, a consolidating worksheet will include the statement of retained earnings and I/S. When this has occurred, the acquirer has always used the cost method to account for the investment, reporting dividend income from the acquiree.

The eliminating entry is as follows:

Dividend income (I/S)	100	
Dividends paid (R/E)		100

When only a balance sheet is presented, this entry isn't needed, since both accounts are closed to retained earnings at year-end.

Dividends paid by the acquirer are not eliminated (except in the rare cases that the acquiree owns some stock in the acquirer, in which case that part is eliminated). As a result, once an acquisition has taken place, the consolidated statement of retained earnings will only report dividends paid by the acquirer. This is consistent with the fact that the equity accounts of the acquiree are eliminated in a consolidation.

Intercompany sales of inventory are the most common intercompany transactions. They have as many as three effects on the F/S that may need to be eliminated:

- Sale vs. Purchase
- Receivable vs. Payable
- Profit in Ending Inventory

Let's assume that P Company has an item in inventory that was purchased from an outside suppler for $4, and that it is sold to S Company late in the year for $5. It remains in the ending inventory of the subsidiary at year-end, and the invoice has not yet been paid to the parent.

The elimination of the intercompany sale-purchase is as follows:

Sales	5	
Cost of sales		5

Remember that purchases are included in the computation of cost of sales, explaining the credit side of the entry. Keep in mind the above entry need not be made in an exam problem asking only for balance sheet effects, since both of the above accounts are closed into retained earnings at year-end.

The elimination of the intercompany receivable-payable is as follows:

Accounts payable	5	
Accounts receivable		5

The elimination of the intercompany profit in ending inventory ($5 - $4 = $1) is as follows:

Cost of sales	1	
Inventory		1

Remember that ending inventory is included in the computation of cost of sales, explaining the debit side of the entry. If the problem only requires preparation of a balance sheet, the debit is made to retained earnings instead of cost of sales.

Of course, in most cases, the intercompany buyer will have paid for some or all of the goods purchased during the year, so the intercompany receivable-payable entry will be less than the intercompany sale-purchase entry. Also, some or all of the purchased goods will have been resold to outsiders before year-end, so the profit to be eliminated will not be the profit on all sales, only that on the purchased items still remaining at year-end.

When one of the companies in a consolidated group **sells a depreciable or amortizable asset to the other**, two eliminations will probably be needed:

1. Elimination of the gain on sale.
2. Elimination on the additional depreciation or amortization resulting from the markup of the asset.

Let's say P has equipment with a $50 cost and $20 accumulated depreciation on 1/1/X1, and sells it to S for $45. On the date of sale, the asset has an estimated remaining life of 3 years. In order to see the effects of the sale, look at the following comparison:

Account	Acquirer P	Acquiree S	Change
Equipment	50	45	(5)
Accumulated depreciation	(20)	(0)	20
Book value	30	45	15
20X1 depreciation	10	15	5

To eliminate the changes that resulted from the sale itself, the following entry is made:

Gain on sale of equipment	15	
Equipment	5	
Accumulated depreciation		20

Notice that this entry returns the equipment to its $50 cost and $20 accumulated depreciation. If only a balance sheet is presented in the problem, the gain is debited to retained earnings instead.

Although not theoretically preferred, the following entry will correct the book value, and is permissible as an alternative:

Gain on sale of equipment	15	
Equipment		15

After reducing the book value of the asset from $45 to $30, the depreciation over the subsequent year must be reduced in preparing financial statements for the year ended 12/31/X1:

Accumulated depreciation	5	
Depreciation expense		5

This reduces the depreciation from $15 to $10 for the year. In a balance sheet problem, the credit to depreciation expense is made to retained earnings instead.

Finally, **bonds issued** by one of the companies may be purchased by the other, and there are as many as three eliminations that may be needed:

- Investment in bonds vs. bonds payable
- Interest revenue vs. interest expense
- Accrued interest receivable vs. accrued interest payable

Let's assume that the acquiree issued an 8% bond at its $1,000 face value several years ago, and that the acquirer purchased the bond on the open market for $900 plus accrued interest on 12/31/X1. Also assume the bond pays interest annually on January 1.

To eliminate the bond itself, the following entry is made:

Bond payable	1,000	
Investment in bond		900
Gain on retirement		100

Notice that the purchase of the bond of one company by the other is treated as an early retirement, as it would have been had a single entity bought its own bond on the open market.

Since annual interest of $1,000 × 8% = $80 is due tomorrow, the acquirer must have paid $80 accrued interest on the purchase date, and this must be eliminated as well:

Accrued interest payable	80	
Accrued interest receivable		80

Since the bond was purchased at the end of the year, no intercompany interest income has resulted, so there is no elimination. Had the bonds been held throughout the year, not merely acquired at year-end, interest revenue and interest expense would have been eliminated, though the different carrying values of the bond would have created complications that the exam has avoided testing.

Intercompany Transactions – Summary

- **Intercompany PP&E**
    - Seller of PP&E:

Cash or A/R	100	
Accumulated Depreciation	60	
PP&E		120
Gain		40

    - Purchaser of PP&E:

PP&E	100	
Cash or A/P		100

    - To Fix on Worksheet at year end:

Gain	40	
PP&E	20	
Accumulated Depreciation		60

- To fix over depreciation (40/10 = $4):

Accumulated Depreciation	4	
Depreciation Expense		4

- **Intercompany Bonds**
  - Issuer of bonds at face/par value

Cash	1,000	
B/P		1,000

  - My subsidiary purchases the bonds from the outside investor for $980 (1,000 – 20 discount = 980 CV):

Investment	1,000	
Cash		980
Discount		20

  - To eliminate on the worksheet at year end:

Bonds payable	1,000	
Investment in Bonds		980
Gain on retirement		20

- **Intercompany inventory sales**
  - Seller of Inventory:

Cash	100	
Sales Revenue		100
COGS	80	
Inventory		80

(note that intercompany profit is $20 or 20% of 100)

  - Purchaser of Inventory:

Inventory	100	
Cash		100

  - Assume the purchaser sells 90% of the inventory purchased for $200:

Cash	200	
Sales Revenue		200
COGS	90	
Inventory		90

- To eliminate on the worksheet at year end:

Sales Revenue	100	
Inventory (20% profit in ending)		2
COGS		98

If given a Worksheet, eliminate the following Entries (Panic approach):

- Investment account = always zero at the end
- Eliminate 100% of acquiree's – C/S, APIC, R/E
- Set up noncontrolling interest (adjust for % of income and dividends)
- Dividend Income if cost method or investment income if equity method
- Dividends paid by Acquiree
- Intercompany transactions (sales, COGS, unrealized inventory profits)
- Intercompany gains/losses on sale of PP&E
- Intercompany receivables/payables
- Bond investments
- Set up excess FMV of PP&E over BV
- Record goodwill
- Record depreciation on excess FMV of PP&E
- Record Impairments of goodwill

Some problems on the CPA exam involve the use of a **three-part worksheet**, consisting of an I/S section, a section for the statement of retained earnings, and a balance sheet section. When provided a three-part worksheet, the best approach is to:

1. Post all of the adjusting journal entries to the worksheet.
2. Complete the I/S section by:
   - Calculating the net balance for each I/S line item.
   - Total each column for the I/S section. The net amount in the final column will be net income.
3. Complete the statement of retained earnings section by:
   - Copying the totals from the I/S section on the net income line of the statement of retained earnings section.
   - Calculating the net balance for each line item in the section.
   - Total each column for the section. The net amount in the final column will be ending retained earnings.
4. Complete the balance sheet section by:
   - Copying the totals from the statement of retained earnings section on the retained earnings line of the balance sheet section.
   - Calculating the net balance for each line item in the section.
   - Total each column for the section.

The following **additional disclosures** are also required:

- The portion of consolidated net income and comprehensive income attributable to both the acquirer and the noncontrolling interest.
- The amounts attributable to the noncontrolling interest for each of the following:

  - income from continuing operations;
  - Discontinued operations; and
  - Components of other comprehensive income.
- A reconciliation of the annual change in reported amounts of noncontrolling interest, including separate disclosure of the following:
  - Consolidated net income attributable to noncontrolling interest;
  - Investments by and distributions to noncontrolling interest; and
  - Each component of comprehensive income.
- A footnote schedule showing the effects of transactions with the noncontrolling interest on the equity attributable to the noncontrolling interest.

Combined Financial Statements

Combining the financial positions and results of operations of related entities may be useful to financial statement users even though the requirements for the preparation of consolidated F/S have not been met. Although consolidated F/S may not be prepared when one entity does not have a controlling financial interest in another, it may be appropriate to prepare **combined F/S**. Combined F/S are often prepared, for example, for two or more entities that have common ownership, such as the unconsolidated subsidiaries of a parent. Combined F/S may also be prepared for two or more entities under common management.

Combined F/S are very similar to consolidated F/S in that the effects of interentity transactions are eliminated. They are different, however, in that:

- Amounts are not adjusted to fair values.
- The equity accounts are combined rather than being eliminated.

Variable Interest Entities (VIE)

Under ASC 810, a reporting entity is required to include another entity in its consolidated F/S when the reporting entity has a controlling financial interest in it. An entity can have a controlling financial interest in another entity without owning any equity in the other entity, in which case the controlled entity is referred to as a **variable interest entity (VIE)**. The reporting entity with a controlling financial interest is referred to as the **primary beneficiary** and is required to prepare consolidated F/S that include the VIE.

A VIE relationship often occurs as a result of one of two common circumstances:

- An entity forms a separate entity for the purpose of holding certain assets or incurring liabilities. This may be done to keep items off of the balance sheet, referred to as *"off balance sheet financing."* It also may be done for legitimate business reasons, such as setting up a separate entity to acquire assets to be leased to the reporting entity while passing tax benefits to the owners.

- An entity enters a relationship with another that occupies so many of the other entity's resources and becomes the focus of its operations, making the other entity essentially a division of the reporting entity.

The reporting entity will evaluate significant relationships with other entities to determine if it is the primary beneficiary of a VIE. The evaluation consists of 4 steps:

1. The natures of the entities and their relationship are evaluated to determine if there is a potential for a VIE, considering certain *exempt relationships* identified in ASC 810 (eg, a for-profit entity will generally not consolidate with a not-for-profit entity).
   - If the other entity qualifies as a business, it is not subject to the VIE rules. This exemption does not apply, however, when the business, by its design, operates primarily for the benefit of the reporting entity.
2. The potential VIE is evaluated to determine if it is self-sufficient or if there are indications that it is dependent on some form of additional subordinated financial support. Does the other entity have *one or more characteristics of a VIE*?
   - There may not be sufficient equity to sustain normal operations.
   - The equity holders may not have the normal characteristics of equity holders.
3. The reporting entity determines if it has a *variable interest in the potential VIE*, meaning that it will be affected if the value of the other entity's assets increase or decrease.
4. The reporting entity determines if it is the *primary beneficiary*, which is an entity with a variable interest in the potential VIE that both:
   - Has the *power* and authority to *direct* the *operations* and activities of the potential VIE that are most significant to its economic performance.
   - Participates in the VIE's *profits and losses* to an extent that is potentially *significant* to the VIE.

When a reporting entity determines it is the primary beneficiary of a VIE, it is required to prepare consolidated F/S, treating the VIE as a subsidiary.

- If the entities are **not related**, the creation of the relationship will be treated as comparable to an acquisition and the same principles for recognizing the combination and for preparing consolidated F/S will be followed.
  - Assets and liabilities of the VIE are reported at their **fair values**.
  - The VIE's equity accounts are eliminated.
  - The noncontrolling interest may represent 100% of the equity of the VIE.
- If the entities are **related**, the combination and subsequent consolidated F/S will be prepared using **book values**.

Alternative VIE Accounting Approach for Nonpublic Entities

The Private Company Council (PCC) has established an alternative accounting approach for nonpublic entities. A private reporting entity does not need to evaluate a legal entity under the VIE GAAP guidance if *all* of the following conditions apply:

- The reporting and legal entities are under common control.
- Neither of the entities are under the common control of a public company.
- The legal entity is not a public company.
- The reporting entity does not have a controlling financial interest in the legal entity.

If the alternative accounting approach is elected, it must me be applied to all legal entities that fit the criteria above.

A reporting entity that elects this approach should disclose the following:

- The nature and risks of being involved with the legal entity.
- How involvement with the legal entity affects the reporting entity's financial position.
- Carrying amounts and classification of assets/liabilities on the balance sheet resulting from such involvement.
- The maximum exposure to loss resulting from such involvement, or if it can't be quantified, a disclosure that says so.

  If the exposure to loss exceeds the carrying amounts of assets/liabilities, information that explains the excess exposure, such as terms of arrangements that may require the reporting entity to provide financial support.

UWorld
YOUR WORLD OF LEARNING
ROGER
CPA Review

FAR 23 – Research Appendix

FAR 23 – Research Appendix

Table of Contents

Research Appendix

Lecture 23.01 – Research Task Format

Research is tested in its own independent task-based simulation problem. Each FAR exam will include at least one Research type TBS. The Candidate will be asked to search through the database to find an appropriate reference that addresses the issue presented in the research problem. A scenario is presented in which the candidate must find the answer in the authoritative literature using a pre-determined list of codes. You will be provided with a searchable database containing the FASB Accounting Standards Codification™ (ASC) for this purpose. The candidate will choose the appropriate code title from the drop-down list and then enter a specific reference number applicable to their given scenario.

Using the Authoritative Literature tab, the candidate will search for keywords associated with the question using the search box, which will pull up all references within the literature to those keywords. From there, the candidate should use the "search within" function to find specific instances of keywords within each subsection. Keywords will be highlighted in the text and the candidate can go through them to find the relevant text that answers the research problem.

Research questions will also alert the candidate if they have correctly formatted their answer by displaying "Your response is correctly formatted" in a box below the candidate response if the candidate has entered reference numbers correctly. For example, single-digit reference numbers (such as "paragraph 3") may be formatted as a two-digit response (such as "paragraph "03"). A good tool is to also use the "Research" tab to look up answers to other TBS in the exam; for example, if a TBS asks you about a particular Financial Statement, use the Research tab to assist you in solving this TBS.

The FASB Accounting Standards Codification™ (FASB ASC) is a complete reorganization of all of the separate U.S. Generally Accepted Accounting Principles (GAAP) standards into one topically structured body of authoritative guidance.

FASB ASC is the sole source of authoritative U.S. accounting and reporting standards for all nongovernmental entities, superseding all existing non-SEC accounting and reporting standards. The FASB ASC did not materially change any existing principles, but it will require financial professionals to familiarize themselves with the new organization and numbering system of the new codified standards.

Suggested Approach

When performing a research question on FAR, the first step will be to determine the area from the FASB Codification in which the item is most likely covered. The areas to choose from are:

100s - General Principles – It is very unlikely that this area will be selected. There is only one topic in this area, Generally Accepted Accounting Principles, which designates the ASC as the only authoritative source of GAAP.

200s – Presentation – This area will be selected if the question relates to the actual presentation of information on one of the F/S. It does not address how items are to be accounted for or how amounts are to be determined. Within the area, a specific topic will be selected.

Within that topic, a subtopic is also to be chosen. For some topics, the only subtopic will be subtopic 10, "Overall". Other topics will have two or more subtopics, the first of which will be subtopic 10, "Overall". Determine if one of the subtopics other than "Overall" appears to more directly relate to the question being asked or the issue being raised. If not, select subtopic 10, "Overall".

Topics and subtopics, excluding "Overall" within the Presentation area include the following:

- 205 Presentation of Financial Statements
  205-20 Discontinued Operations
  205 30 Liquidation Basis of Accounting
  205-40 Going Concern
- 210 Balance Sheet
  210-20 Offsetting
- 215 Statement of Shareholder Equity
- 220 Comprehensive Income
- 225 Income Statement
  225-20 Unusual Items
  225-30 Business Interruption Insurance
- 230 Statement of Cash Flows
- 235 Notes to Financial Statements
- 250 Accounting Changes and Error Corrections
- 255 Changing Prices
- 260 Earnings per Share
- 270 Interim Reporting
- 272 Limited Liability Entities
- 274 Personal Financial Statements
- 275 Risks and Uncertainties
- 280 Segment Reporting

300s – Assets – This area will be selected if the question relates to the reporting of an asset. It may involve determining whether or not it will be reported on the financial statements, the amount at which it will be reported, the accounting for the asset while it is being held or for its disposal, or related disclosures. Within the area, a specific topic will be selected.

Within that topic, a subtopic is also to be chosen. For some topics, the only subtopic will be subtopic 10, "Overall". Other topics will have two or more subtopics, the first of which will be subtopic 10, "Overall". Determine if one of the subtopics, other than "Overall" appears to more directly relate to the question being asked or the issue being raised. If not, select subtopic 10, "Overall".

Topics and subtopics, excluding "Overall" within the Assets area include the following:

- 305 Cash and Cash Equivalents
- 310 Receivables
  310-20 Nonrefundable Fees and Other Costs
  310-30 Loans and Debt Securities Acquired with Deteriorated Credit Quality
  310-40 Troubled Debt Restructurings by Creditors
- 320 Investments – Debt and Equity Securities
- 321 Investments – Equity Securities
- 323 Investments – Equity Method and Joint Ventures
  323-30 Partnerships, Joint Ventures, and Limited Liability Entities

- 325 Investments – Other
  325-20 Cost Method Investments
  325-30 Investments in Insurance Contracts
  325-40 Beneficial Interests in Securitized Financial Assets
  326 Financial Instrument – Credit Losses
- 330 Inventories
- 340 Other Assets and Deferred Costs
  340-20 Capitalized Advertising Costs
  340-30 Insurance Contracts That Do Not Transfer Insurance Risk
  340-40 Contracts with Customers
- 350 Intangibles – Goodwill and Other
  350-20 Goodwill
  350-30 General Intangibles Other Than Goodwill
  350-40 Internal Use Software
  350-50 Website Development Costs
- 360 Property, Plant, and Equipment
  360-20 Real Estate Sales

400s – Liabilities – This area will be selected if the question relates to the reporting of a liability. It may involve determining whether or not it will be reported on the financial statements, the amount at which it will be reported, the accounting for it while it is owed, its settlement, or related disclosures. Within the area, a specific topic will be selected.

Within that topic, a subtopic is also to be chosen. For some topics, the only subtopic will be subtopic 10, "Overall". Other topics will have two or more subtopics, the first of which will be subtopic 10, "Overall". Determine if one of the subtopics, other than "Overall" appears to more directly relate to the question being asked or the issue being raised. If not, select subtopic 10, "Overall".

Topics and subtopics, excluding "Overall" within the Liabilities area include the following:

- 405 Liabilities
  405-20 Extinguishment of Liabilities
  405-30 Insurance Related Assessments
  405-40 Obligations Resulting from Joint and Several Liability Arrangements
- 410 Asset Retirement and Environmental Obligations
  410-20 Asset Retirement Obligations
  410-30 Environmental Obligations
- 420 Exit or Disposal Cost Obligations
- 430 Deferred Revenue
- 440 Commitments
- 450 Contingencies
  450-20 Loss Contingencies
  450-30 Gain Contingencies
- 460 Guarantees
- 470 Debt
  470-20 Debt with Conversion and Other Options
  470-30 Participating Mortgage Loans
  470-40 Product Financing Arrangements
  470-50 Modifications and Extinguishments
  470-60 Troubled Debt Restructurings by Debtors
- 480 Distinguishing Liabilities from Equity

500s – Equity – This area will be selected if the question relates to the reporting of equity. It may involve determining whether or not it will be reported on the F/S, the amount at which it will be reported, the accounting for equity transactions, distributions, or related disclosures. Within the area, a specific topic will be selected.

Within that topic, a subtopic is also to be chosen. For some topics, the only subtopic will be subtopic 10, "Overall". Other topics will have two or more subtopics, the first of which will be subtopic 10, "Overall". Determine if one of the subtopics, other than "Overall" appears to more directly relate to the question being asked or the issue being raised. If not, select subtopic 10, "Overall".

Topics and subtopics, excluding "Overall" within the Equity area include the following:

- 505 Equity
  505-20 Stock Dividends and Stock Splits
  505-30 Treasury Stock
  505-50 Equity-Based Payments to Non-Employees
  505-60 Spinoffs and Reverse Spinoffs

600s – Revenue – This area will be selected if the question relates to the recognition of revenue. It may involve determining whether or not it will be reported on the F/S in a given period, the amount that will be recognized, the accounting for deferred revenue, accounting for revenue recognized over time, or related disclosures. Within the area, a specific topic will be selected.

Within that topic, a subtopic is also to be chosen. For some topics, the only subtopic will be subtopic 10, "Overall". Other topics will have two or more subtopics, the first of which will be subtopic 10, "Overall". Determine if one of the subtopics, other than "Overall" appears to more directly relate to the question being asked or the issue being raised. If not, select subtopic 10, "Overall".

Topics and subtopics, excluding "Overall" within the Revenue area include the following:

- 606 Revenue from Contracts with Customers
- 610 Other Income
  610-20 Gains and Losses from the Derecognition of Nonfinancial Assets
  610-30 Gains and Losses on Involuntary Conversions

700s – Expenses – This area will be selected if the question relates to the reporting of expenses. It may involve determining whether or not an expense will be recognized, the period in which it will be recognized, the amount that will be reported, the classification of the expense, or related disclosures. Within the area, a specific topic will be selected.

Within that topic, a subtopic is also to be chosen. For some topics, the only subtopic will be subtopic 10, "Overall". Other topics will have two or more subtopics, the first of which will be subtopic 10, "Overall". Determine if one of the subtopics, other than "Overall" appears to more directly relate to the question being asked or the issue being raised. If not, select subtopic 10, "Overall".

Topics and subtopics, excluding "Overall" within the Expenses area include the following:

- 705 Cost of Sales and Services
  705-20 Accounting for Consideration
- 710 Compensation - General
- 712 Compensation – Nonretirement Postemployment Benefits
- 715 Compensation – Retirement Benefits
  715-20 Defined Benefit Plans – General

715-30 Defined Benefit Plans Pension
715-60 Defined Benefit Plans – Other Postretirement
715-70 Defined Contribution Plans
715-80 Multiemployer Plans

- 718 Compensation – Stock Compensation
  718-20 Awards Classified as Equity
  718-30 Awards Classified as Liabilities
  718-40 Employee Stock Ownership Plans
  718-50 Employer Share Purchase Plans
- 720 Other Expenses
  720-15 Start-up Costs
  720-20 Insurance Costs
  720-25 Contributions Made
  720-30 Real and Personal Property Taxes
  720-35 Advertising Costs
  720-40 Electronic Equipment Waste Obligations
  720-50 Fees Paid to the Federal Government by Pharmaceutical Manufacturers and Health Insurers
- 730 Research and Development
  730-20 Research and Development Arrangements
- 740 Income Taxes
  740-20 Intraperiod Tax Allocation
  740-30 Other Considerations or Special Areas

800s – Broad Transactions – This area will be selected if the question relates to an area that affects more than one financial statement, more than one asset, liability, equity, revenue, or expense account, or some combination. When transactions affect more than one area, such as leases, business combinations, or nonmonetary transactions, it is treated as a separate topic with its effects on other topics referenced. Within the area, a specific topic will be selected.

Within that topic, a subtopic is also to be chosen. For some topics, the only subtopic will be subtopic 10, "Overall". Other topics will have two or more subtopics, the first of which will be subtopic 10, "Overall". Determine if one of the subtopics, other than "Overall" appears to more directly relate to the question being asked or the issue being raised. If not, select subtopic 10, "Overall".

Topics and subtopics, excluding "Overall" within the Broad Transactions area include the following:

- 805 Business Combinations
  805-20 Identifiable Assets and Liabilities, and Any Noncontrolling Interest
  805-30 Goodwill or Gain from Bargain Purchase, Including Consideration Transferred
  805-40 Reverse Acquisitions
  805-50 Related Issues
- 808 Collaborative Arrangements
- 810 Consolidation
  810-20 Control of Partnerships and Similar Entities
  810-30 Research and Development Arrangements
- 815 Derivatives and Hedging
  815-15 Embedded Derivatives
  815-20 Hedging – General

815-25 Fair Value Hedges
815-30 Cash Flow Hedges
815-35 New Investment Hedges
815-40 Contracts in entity's Own Equity
815-45 Weather Derivatives

- 820 Fair Value Measurement
- 825 Financial Instruments
  825-20 Registration Payment Arrangements
- 830 Foreign Currency Matters
  830-20 Foreign Currency Transactions
  830-30 Translation of Financial Statements
- 835 Interest
  835-20 Capitalization of Interest
  835-30 Imputation of Interest
- 842 Leases
  842-20 Lessee
  842-30 Lessor
  842-40 Sale and Leaseback Transactions
- 845 Nonmonetary Transactions
- 850 Related Party Disclosures
- 852 Reorganizations
  852-20 Quasi-Reorganizations
- 853 Service Concession Arrangements
- 855 Subsequent Events
- 860 Transfers and Servicing
  860-20 Sales of Financial Assets
  860-30 Secured Borrowing and Collateral
  860-40 Transfers to Qualifying Special Purpose Entities
  860-50 Servicing Assets and Liabilities

900s – Industry – This area will be selected if the question relates how an accounting area is treated in a particular industry. When an industry has special principles for the presentation of its F/S, the accounting for an asset, liability, equity, revenue, or expense, the accounting for a broad transaction, or special disclosures, the topic will be selected from within that industry. Within the industry, a specific topic will be selected.

Within that topic, a subtopic is also to be chosen. For some topics, the only subtopic will be subtopic 10, "Overall". Other topics will have two or more subtopics, the first of which will be subtopic 10, "Overall". Determine if one of the subtopics, other than "Overall" appears to more directly relate to the question being asked or the issue being raised. If not, select subtopic 10, "Overall".

Topics and subtopics, excluding "Overall" within the Industry area include the following:

- 905 Agriculture
- 908 Airlines
- 910 Contractors – Construction
  910-20 Contract costs
- 912 Contractors – Federal Government
  912-20 Contract Costs
- 915 Development Stage Entities
- 920 Entertainment – Broadcasters

- 922 Entertainment – Cable Television
- 924 Entertainment – Casinos
- 926 Entertainment – Films
  926-20 Other Assets – Film Costs
- 928 Entertainment – Music
- 930 Extractive Industries – Mining
- 932 Extractive Industries – Oil and Gas
- 940 Financial Services – Brokers and Dealers
  940-20 Broker-Dealer Activities
- 942 Financial Services – Depository and Lending
- 944 Financial Services –Insurance
  944-20 Insurance Activities
  944-30 Acquisition Costs
  944-40 Claim Costs and Liabilities for Future Policy Benefits
  944-50 Policyholder Dividends
  944-60 Premium Deficiency and Loss Recognition
  944-80 Separate Accounts
- 946 Financial Services – Investment Companies
  946-20 Investment Company Activities
- 948 Financial Services – Mortgage Banking
- 950 Financial Services – Plant Title
- 952 Franchisors
- 954 HealthCare Entities
- 958 Not-for-Profit Entities
  958-20 Financially Interrelated entities
  958-30 Split-Interest Agreements
- 960 Plan Accounting – Defined Benefit Pension Plans
  960-20 Accumulated Plan Benefits
  960-30 Net Assets Available for Plan Benefits
  960-40 Terminating Plans
- 962 Plan Accounting – Defined Contribution Pension Plans
  962-40 Terminating Plans
- 965 Plan Accounting – Health and Welfare Benefit Plans
  965-20 Net Assets Available for Plan Benefits
  965-30 Plan Benefit Obligations
  965-40 Terminating Plans
- 970 Real Estate – General
- 972 Real Estate – Common Interest Realty Associations
- 974 Real Estate – Real Estate Investment Trusts
- 976 Real Estate – Retail Land
- 978 Real Estate – Time-Sharing Activities
- 980 Regulated Operations
  980-20 Discontinuation of Rate Regulated Accounting
- 985 Software
  985-20 Costs of Software to Be Sold, Leased, or Marketed
- 994 U.S. Steamship Entities

Once the specific topic and subtopic have been selected, the appropriate section should be determined. The sections, which are uniformly numbered within each subtopic, including the "Overall" subtopic, each address a specific aspect to the accounting for the topic, when the subtopic is "Overall" or the subtopic for any other. A section will only appear within a subtopic when it is relevant and, as a result, all sections will not be listed under every subtopic.

The sections are:

00 Status – This section provides information about the changes that were made to the subtopic, which paragraphs were affected, the source of the change, and the date on which the change was put into the Codification.

05 Overview and Background – This section provides a general overview and background of the subtopic without summarizing the requirements. It often contains material to enable a user to understand the situations that are typically covered by the standard.

10 Objectives – This section indicates the high-level objective of the standard, although it does not provide guidance as to the main principle of the standard.

15 Scope and Scope Exceptions – This section indicates when the guidance does or does not apply including, perhaps, a description of the entities that must or are not required to apply the principles, or the transactions to which it does or does not apply.

20 Glossary – This section includes definitions of terms that are unique to the principle.

25 Recognition – This section indicates the circumstances under which an item will appear on the F/S, including the criteria for an item to be recognized, the time at which or period in which it will be recognized, and the location within the F/S where it will appear.

30 Initial Measurement – This section indicates the amount at which the item will appear on the F/S when it is first recognized.

35 Subsequent Measurement – This section indicates how a balance sheet item will be accounted for once it is recognized on the F/S. It may indicate, for example, that an item should be amortized or depreciated, adjusted to fair value, adjusted to amortized cost, or tested for impairment.

40 Derecognition – This section indicates how a balance sheet item will be removed from the F/S once it has been recognized and provides a basis for gain or loss recognition.

45 Other Presentation Matters – This section provides information about the specific placement or handling of an item on the F/S. Examples may include whether an item is required to be reported as current or noncurrent, the section of the income statement or the statement of cash flows in which it will appear, requirements for a specific description to be used to identify the item on the F/S, or where an item may not appear on the F/S.

50 Disclosure – This section describes the disclosure requirements for the topic other than those that would be included due to the general disclosure requirements indicated in ASC Topic 235, Notes to F/S.

55 Implementation Guidance and Illustrations – This section provides guidance as to how to apply the standard in simple and general situations and, when appropriate, provides illustrations. Illustrations may be of F/S or sections thereof, schedules, footnotes, or a description of the methodology for applying the standard.

60 Relationships – This section provides references to other subtopics that are related to this subtopic and may provide more information that is relevant to it.

65 Transition and Open Effective Date Information – This section indicates when changes in principles go into effect and how an entity makes the transition from the outdated standard to the new one.

70 Grandfathered Guidance – This section includes principles that do not apply to current transactions but may still apply to the preparation of F/S due to historical transactions, such as the pooling-of-interests method for preparing consolidated F/S.

75 XBRL Elements – This section provides coding information required by XBRL, which stands for the Extensible Business Related Language, so that financial information can be appropriately tagged to facilitate financial analysis.

Once the appropriate section has been identified, scroll through that section to find the particular paragraph that provides the information sought.

Sample Research Question

Identify the section of professional standards that specifies where cash received from selling available-for-sale debt securities should be disclosed on the statement of cash flows.

FASB ASC	320	10	45	11

Explanation: The question applies to the sale of investment securities, indicating that the topic will be Topic 320, Investments – Debt and Equity Securities. The question does not specify a particular industry and the only subtopic under topic 320 is subtopic 10, Overall. The question specifically asks where, on the statement of cash flows, the proceeds from the sale of the securities will appear, which relates to the presentation on the financial statements, indicating section 45, Other Presentation Matters.

Upon scrolling through that section, there is a heading before paragraphs 11-13 indicating "Cash Flow Presentation". Scanning those paragraphs will reveal that in paragraph 11 it states in the first sentence "Cash flows from purchases, sales, and maturities of available-for-sale securities and held-to-maturity securities shall be classified as cash flows from investing activities and reported gross for each security classification in the statement of cash flows."

UWorld
YOUR WORLD OF LEARNING
ROGER
CPA Review

FAR 24 - Final Review

FAR 24 – Final Review

Table of Contents

Lecture 24.01 – FAR Final Review

You finished your FAR Course...now what?

A quick guide to the final days leading up to, and following, the exam

I. FINAL REVIEW

Now is the time to make connections and solidify your understanding of the topics you found most challenging, and to review the most heavily tested topics on the exam.

- ❑ Review your SmartPath data to ensure you have hit all targets. Revisit any areas marked "Needs Improvement."
- ❑ Reread your course notes and review your digital flash cards.
- ❑ If it is included in your program package, use the Cram Course to do a final review of the most heavily tested topics.
- ❑ Take at least one Full CPA Practice Exam in your QBank to hone your test-taking skills in an environment that follows the same 5-testlet, 4-hour structure of the exam.
- ❑ Checkout an AICPA Sample Test at www.cpa-exam.org to familiarize yourself with the exam format and welcome (instruction) screens.

II. DAY OF THE EXAM

- ❑ Get a good night's rest before heading into your exam.
- ❑ Arrive to the Prometric testing center at least 60 minutes before your appointment so you have time to park, check-in, and use the restroom before your exam begins.
- ❑ Bring your Notice to Schedule (NTS) and two forms of acceptable identification (see Intro for more details).
- ❑ Proceed through check-in: store belongings, get fingerprinted, have photo taken, sign log book, get seated, write your Launch Code (from your NTS) on your noteboard.
- ❑ Don't stress. You've prepared for this; now, just breathe and power through!

III. DURING THE EXAM

- ❑ Remember your FAR Exam time strategy, and jot down the times at which you want to be at your benchmarks:
    - FAR includes calculations
    - Allocate 80 seconds per multiple choice question as a benchmark
    - Allocate 15-25 minutes per task-based simulation, depending on complexity
    - Plan to use no more than 10 minutes per research question
    - Take the standard 15-minute break after the 3rd testlet – it does not count against your time
    - (Remember that any other break will count against your time)

FAR: 4 Hour Exam					
Testlet 1	**Testlet 2**	**Testlet 3**	**Break**	**Testlet 4**	**Testlet 5**
33 MCQs	**33 MCQs**	**2 TBSs**		**3 TBSs**	**3 TBSs**
45 min	**45 min**	**30 min**		**60 min**	**60 min**

- ❑ You will be given 10 minutes to review the welcome screens and exam instructions. You should already be familiar with these screens after taking the AICPA Sample Test, and can bypass them during your exam.
- ❑ Once you begin testing, make sure to read each question carefully, paying close attention to the keywords that dictate the question's intention (eg, *except, is greater than, must, never*).
- ❑ Take note if your questions are getting more difficult. That's a good sign! A progressively harder exam indicates that you are performing well.

IV. AFTER THE EXAM

- ❑ Remember, it is normal to not feel great afterwards. It's a tough exam and designed to challenge your confidence and competencies.
- ❑ Relax and celebrate! You've earned it.
- ❑ Your scores will be released within a couple of weeks.
- ❑ GOOD LUCK!!!